The Greenwood Encyclopedia of Clothing through World History

The Greenwood Encyclopedia of Clothing through World History

Volume 2
1501–1800

Edited by Jill Condra

GREENWOOD PRESS
Westport, Connecticut • London

Library of Congress Cataloging-in-Publication Data

The Greenwood encyclopedia of clothing through world history / edited by Jill Condra.
    p. cm.
  Includes bibliographical references and index.
    ISBN 978-0-313-33662-1 ((set) : alk. paper) — ISBN 978-0-313-33663-8
((vol 1) : alk. paper) — ISBN 978-0-313-33664-5 ((vol 2) : alk. paper) — ISBN
978-0-313-33665-2 ((vol 3) : alk. paper)
    1. Clothing and dress—History—Encyclopedias. I. Condra, Jill, 1968-
GT507.G74 2008
391.009—dc22   2007030705

British Library Cataloguing in Publication Data is available.

Library of Congress Catalog Card Number: 2007030705
ISBN: 978-0-313-33662-1 (set)
        978-0-313-33663-8 (vol. 1)
        978-0-313-33664-5 (vol. 2)
        978-0-313-33665-2 (vol. 3)

First published in 2008

Greenwood Press, 88 Post Road West, Westport, CT 06881
An imprint of Greenwood Publishing Group, Inc.
www.greenwood.com

Printed in the United States of America

∞™

The paper used in this book complies with the
Permanent Paper Standard issued by the National
Information Standards Organization (Z39.48–1984).

10   9   8   7   6   5   4   3   2   1

Contents

Preface

The history of clothing and world history go closely in hand, and to trace the evolution of clothing is to trace events that occurred in times and places long ago. Within the context of world events, clothing is a vital piece of material culture that can help to understand what has happened in the past and how it has affected our present. The way in which people dressed throughout time has always indicated, to a great extent, who they are. It also has been an indicator of where they come from, their lot in life, their wealth or poverty, or their occupation. Starting at the cradle of civilization, the following chapters and those in the other volumes trace the evolution of dress from prehistoric times through the classical eras of Rome and Greece to the Middle Ages and onward to the most recent times.

The study of clothing was once solely the provenance of the art historian, interested from the perspective of the paintings and sculptures they studied to understand what the subjects of the art were wearing. This process helped to authenticate and date the art but was not a study unto itself. It wasn't until the last half of the twentieth century that costume/clothing/dress history has become a subject of interest for its own sake. Still closely related to the study of art history, those who study costume have evolved in their own discipline from producing "hemline histories" to developing material culture models, based on anthropology, and other methods to put the clothing they find and study into context.

While a hemline history might look solely at the costumes and their minute details, tracing the evolution of a feature, such as the length of a hemline, to its most recent incarnation, little else about history is included. These original studies of dress were often seen by self-described "serious" historians as elitist and merely the domain of the connoisseurs, implying that, although it may be interesting to look at fashion, it was not exactly important in the face of more rigorous study of military, political, or religious histories, for example. Clothing, and especially fashion, is often seen as frivolous and not the domain of the serious academic, and the original costume historians faced this criticism continually.

In light of this criticism, and as interest in tracing the evolution of clothing became more popular, things began to change. It became obvious that neither costume nor the other aspects of history can be studied in isolation and still provide a full picture and true understanding of history. Tracing the roots of clothing styles by looking at the geography, social setting, political situation, religious affiliation, technological development, pop culture (especially from the 1920s onward), and so forth gives the context from which to look at what people wore and perhaps sheds better light on the reasons they chose to wear the clothes they did. It can also do the reverse and shed light on why certain other social, political, or economic events occurred. Trade, for example, has always been heavily influenced by fashion demands around the world, and many a country has its roots in the trade of textiles used for fashion purposes (e.g., demand in Europe for the fashionable beaver hat allowed for exploration, trade, and development in the newly established colonies of Canada and the establishment of the Hudson Bay Company).

The original clothing histories that concentrated specifically on the clothes themselves remain a gold mine for modern costume and clothing historians and provide a wealth of detailed information about the garments, showing how they were worn and how they were constructed, often showing patterns and details of the textiles that allow students of costume to see every aspect of the garments. Much in the way of general social history can be gleaned from these sources, and taken together with the kind of studies such as the one in this series, a very thorough picture of clothing and world history can be achieved.

PROBLEMS WITH COSTUME EVIDENCE

As many of the authors in these volumes suggest, depending on the era, the sources of evidence to study dress are sometime difficult to interpret and trust as absolute. Unless there is an actual garment, or set of garments, other kinds of evidence must be used to look at the costumes people wore. These sources might include cave drawings, sculptures of the early Greeks and Romans, wall paintings in tombs, hieroglyphics from ancient Egypt, literature, journals, legends, oral histories, paintings of the seventeenth century, or photographs of the twentieth century.

The problem with any of these sources is that the are inherently biased, taken only from the perspective of the painter, photographer, or writer, who is free to embellish or gloss over aspects of the actual situation as he or she feels is fit. Painting a portrait in the eighteenth century, an artist may have been asked to omit a certain less-than-flattering feature of the subject, thus altering the evidence for future study, while presumably pleasing the person who was paying him. It is impossible to know for sure what is true in a depiction of a costume and what is idealized, but nevertheless the evidence is crucial, and the process of gathering as much detail as possible will allow the student of history to piece together a fairly accurate picture of the real thing.

Taking the evidence and backing it up with other sources of historical record only adds to the relative certainty of the claims made about the clothing people wore. Tracing the influences from one set of evidence to the next gives a clearer picture of the whole. The best source of evidence, of course, is the actual garment itself. But, unfortunately, given the organic nature of textiles used until relatively recent times, there are few very early garments surviving intact. As one progresses through time from the early prehistoric period, more and more pieces survive, and these account for the increased amount of information available for the past four centuries or so. Before that, there is little actual material culture left to study. We are fortunate enough to occasionally find the odd textile piece that has been preserved by luck in the dry deserts of Egypt, and there have been the chance discoveries of perfectly preserved "bog people" whose entire person is still intact, clothes and all (even the food they ate just before they died can be determined!). The problem, though, is that as soon as the textiles are exposed to oxygen and humidity, the process of decay begins immediately.

In later time periods, the luscious garments were used and reused, then sold secondhand to poorer people, who wore the garments until they were threadbare and then used them for other purposes. As a result, very few extant pieces survive from before the late sixteenth and seventeenth centuries. For the student of these and later centuries, there are many surviving garments. Yet even these only tell part of the story. This is due to the fact that the extant pieces are usually only the most important garments worn by the wealthiest and most privileged in a society. It is very rare indeed to find a museum well stocked with peasant tunics and aprons. What does survive, and what is so alluring for those of us who adore textiles of any kind, are the beautiful and luxurious gowns, sumptuous skirts, and coats with over-the-top decorations. Often these garments were worn by royalty or courtiers in the great courts of Versailles or Florence in the romantic and exquisite Renaissance. These garments do not, however, represent what everyday people wore in their jobs and occupations. To embark on a study of peasant dress would be a short journey with so little available.

The existing gowns and men's suits, though not showing all facets of society, do represent the most fashionable of the time and are a good representation of the affluence that was shown on the backs of the aristocracy. Their garments were worn as symbols of who they were, where they were stationed in life and society, and to what class of people they belonged. Competition was blatant, and both men and women tried their best, in many eras, to outdo each other in their show of status through their clothing.

It is with all this in mind that costume historians undertake the study of clothing and fashion changes over time. As with any kind of history, the evidence provides only partial information, and so it is even more important to combine all aspects of history, in an interdisciplinary manner, to provide the context for the most accurate picture to be analyzed. Looking at social history alongside the clothing evidence, imperfect as it may seem, gives an excellent taste of the past.

GETTING DRESSED

What people wear on their bodies depends not only on the physical conditions in which they live but also on the availability of resources, the amount of money they have, and their associations within their communities. Clothing is the most personal of effects and can tell more about a person and the life they lead than any other kind of material history. The clothing artifact is precious for historians and anthropologists who study materials of the past. While an ancient piece of pottery or an eighteenth-century chair is valuable to the archaeologist, it indicates only a certain amount about the people who used it. It may inform about the materials available and the technology and design sense of the maker, but not about his size, habits, or personal preferences. On the other hand, clothing can tell a great deal about the individuals who wore the clothes and as such are very valuable to study.

People wear clothes for a number of reasons, including protection from the environment, identification, status, comfort, sexual allurement, beauty, and a myriad of others. It is a recurring theme from chapter to chapter in these volumes that, in all the times and places throughout history, people appear to have dressed for the same reasons as we still do today. How those ideals manifested themselves is what differs from period to period and place to place. For example, what is now considered attractive or a symbol of great status would certainly not have been read the same way in the Renaissance or ancient Egypt—though there are similarities. Precious stones were and remain valuable and show a certain something about the wearer, namely, that they can afford such items. However, the extremely casual nature of clothing in today's society would have been unheard of in times gone by and would have seemed not only unflattering to the human form but also immoral.

Dress has been indelibly linked to manner and morals for centuries, and this is just some of the information clothes can communicate. The functions of dress have varied in detail over the centuries but have remained clear identifiers of the people, place, and time of its wearing.

SCOPE OF THE VOLUMES

There are many terms used in the study of clothing, and they are often used interchangeably to mean what people wore. However, there are some very subtle differences, and it is worth identifying these differences at the outset of this study of clothing in world history. To talk about *clothing* means to talk about the garments people wore, to be sure, but it also encompasses other parts of the decoration and covering of the human form. In this set of volumes, the textiles used for clothing is a great focus, as are the changes seen over time, but there are also frequent glimpses of the other elements that went into personal adornment. Jewelry, headwear, shoes, bags or purses, and other accessories that are held, draped, tied, and attached to the body all affect the clothing of the wearer and the look it achieves. This study undertakes to look at all these things within the parameters of both high fashion, and where possible, peasant clothing.

Dress is a term applied, like *clothing*, more generally to the entire outfit or trend in styles worn by people through the ages. *Costume* implies, increasingly it seems recently, theatrical and special-occasion or fancy dress—things not worn as a norm—but the term is also still used to identify the garments and accessories generally. *Adornment* is another term that identifies objects worn to enhance and dress the body.

These terms are all used as a way of talking about the same or similar things, but depending on the country or culture in question, different terms seem to be more common than others. For example, museums in the United Kingdom tend be called "costume collections," but "dress" is often used in discussion about the garments themselves. For the purposes of this book, all these terms are used purposefully to denote the wearing of garments, both of the wealthy and not-so-wealthy, as well as accessories, cosmetics, hairstyles, and anything to do with how people looked in history.

To make the study as complete and true to the title as possible, historical divisions have been identified into chapters grouped together in the three volumes. All three attempt to cover the important political, social, economic, technological, and cultural history of the times. Introductions to each chapter deal with the major events of the time and place. Each chapter then delves into the clothing people wore and ties the events to the choices people made in their dress.

Early history is covered in volume 1, looking at clothing from prehistoric times to the end of the Middle Ages and Byzantine eras, roughly to 1500. In this volume, discussions focus on several cultures from around the Western world, including Egypt, Greece, Rome, Persia, and the northern portions of continental Europe. Volume 2 follows clothing history from the sixteenth century through the 1800s and looks at clothing in Europe, North America, Latin America, Japan, Korea, India, and China. Volume 3 opens with the postrevolutionary period in Europe at the start of the nineteenth century and covers the history and dress of people throughout the increasingly small world, examining aspects of dress from most regions of the world where there is historical record.

This set of volumes, however, does not claim to cover all of history in all of the world throughout time. This would be an impossible undertaking, so it is with care that the geographical and time divisions have been chosen, as they represent a good sample of the events that were occurring around the world and how these events affected the ways people clothed themselves. Commonalities are evident if close attention is paid to the details within each chapter. For example, rituals surrounding moving from childhood to adulthood are roughly similar in all places and times and usually involve a change in dress style, often accompanied by a ceremony to mark the occasion. Dressing for status and identification is another common theme, as is the idea that children through time and to the present, with few exceptions, have dressed in a strikingly similar manner to their parents after babyhood.

Clothing in every culture and time period is used for ceremonial purposes and carries great meaning and symbolism. Coronation gowns and liturgical attire are painstakingly designed and made, and each element might represent some important idea associated with the monarchy or priesthood. In some eras where religion is of utmost importance to the development of culture, religious garb is studied, but this is not necessarily an important part of clothing in all places or in all time periods and so is not discussed in other chapters at all. It is thus impractical in a work of this huge scope to look at the same aspects of dress throughout. Instead, the time, events, and place dictate the differences in subheadings to most appropriately fit the subject matter. So, during the Byzantine era, religious garb is studied, but once the late twentieth century is covered, religious clothing is no longer emphasized.

Military dress can be a study unto itself, and there are many books and websites devoted to the evolution of armor and military uniforms. In this book, armor is described, for example, in terms of the Renaissance, when it was commonly worn by people; it is also noteworthy as a useful piece of durable material culture, because much has survived where many contemporaneous textile

artifacts have long decayed. Military uniforms are revisited in the twentieth century in the context of the two world wars and the effect this look had on regular
clothing of nonmilitary men, women, and children.

Looking at different places during the same time period will reveal a certain
sameness in the clothing people wore. There was often one prevailing style,
with deviations in detail from place to place. When explorers were off discover-
ing new places in the name of their European homelands, they often brought
their own distinct styles and textiles, which were traded with the locals, hence
creating a merging of styles all over the world. The interchange of goods, especially textile goods, helped to shape the shared fashion choices among many
people far away from each other, resulting in features that were often the same
or very similar. People in Latin America, for example, in many time periods
wore styles very similar to—and with certain aspects exactly the same as—those
in France; in the middle of the twentieth century, women in Buenos Aires were
seen in the highest of high fashions from the French runways. Cultural high-
lights might distinguish certain aspects and interpretations of the *haute couture*
fashions, but they were also decidedly the same in many respects.

What this book is not is a look at the folk costumes of the countries and
times within the scope. While there is the occasional mention of folk dress—
the Scottish kilt, for example—there is little discussion of folk attire. That facet
of study needs its own series of books with a concrete plan to study all the costumes in cultures, historical and more recent throughout time.

HOW TO USE THIS BOOK

These volumes have been written by some of the best writers in the area of costume studies, who are often specialists in one area or era in clothing history
and have spent a good deal of their lives dedicated to the study of clothing
history.

In this look at history and clothing, the abbreviations BC (Before Christ) and
AD (Anno Domini) have been replaced with the newer parlance of BCE (Before
the Common Era) and CE (Common Era).

At the beginning of each chapter, a timeline allows a quick reference to what
occurred, both in terms of general history and developments in the areas of
clothing and textiles, in the relevant geographical areas. Some of the timelines
are more complicated and indicate a greater amount of available information,
while others simply outline some of the key world and textile-related events.

Following the timeline are the introductions to the general histories of time
and place. These vary according to what happened in the specific period and
location and are reflections of economics, political structure and events, monarchies, exploration, technological developments, governments, social pressures
and concerns, religion, military history, and international affairs. All of these are
meant to provide the reader with the context needed to understand the clothing
section that follows.

The portion of each chapter on clothing begins with a general introduction
to the themes in dress of the age and place. Then dress is looked at in terms of
gender, with men's and women's clothing separately discussed. The important
items of clothing are mostly defined within the text, but words that are specific

to clothing history and may not be commonly known are also contained in a glossary at the end of each volume. Each chapter is illustrated with images that reflect what is described—paintings, decorations, or photographs of the actual clothing, depending on the time period. While some images are placed within the text, many more are contained in the color inserts in the center of the volume. Children's clothing is covered in a necessarily smaller section at the end of each chapter, owing to the fact that there is often little information pertaining to the children, especially in very early times, and also that children often dressed in the same or similar styles to their parents. Most chapters also contain a number of highlighted boxes with curious or intriguing information about a certain aspect of the history.

At the end of each chapter, there is a list of recommended books for further study, along with a few websites that will help with further research on the topic and time period. These resources are followed by a list of suggestions (by no means exhaustive) of films, documentaries, or television shows that do a good job of depicting the costume history of the time and place in question. There are markedly more such films available for more recent or modern history, of course. The lists vary in terms of the dates they were made and the countries, but all are English-language movies or programs.

TEXTILE TERMS FROM FIBERS TO FABRIC AND CLOTHING

In order to understand some of what is contained in these books it is important to start this process with some of the basic textile and clothing terms needed to read and comprehend the information. Following is a list of the key terms:

Textile: A general term applied to fibers, yarns, and fabrics; anything to do with the production of these things is part of the textile complex.

Fabric: The piece of cloth used to construct garments and other soft goods. It can be a knit, woven, or nonwoven fabric.

Knit fabric: A fabric produced by one continuous yarn interlooping with one or more yarns. It is stretchy and was not commonly used before the seventeenth century.

Woven fabric: A fabric made through the process of weaving on a loom. Looms have been used in different forms since the beginning of time. Weaving is a process whereby a *warp* thread—the lengthwise thread running vertically on the loom—is alternately interwoven with the *weft* threads that run horizontally, creating a pattern. These threads sit at 90° angles to one another and can be made into all kinds of patterns and designs. Woven fabrics were made as early as the discovery of fibers.

Yarns: Threads that are spun (twisted) from loose fibers cultivated in a range of ways. The spun yarn can be further twisted with other yarns to create *plied yarns* of greater bulk and strength. Yarns can be made from natural fiber or manufactured fibers, or a combination of these.

Fibers: The base substance of yarn. These can be *staple length* (shorter) or *filament length* (longer) and are generally twisted to make the yarn used to make fabric. Fibers can be either natural or manufactured.

Natural fibers: Fibers that are either *cellulosic* and come from plants, such as cotton or linen, or *protein*-based and come from animals or insects, such as wool and silk. Except for silk fiber, natural fibers are *staple* (short) length and are twisted into yarns. Silk, a natural filament yarn, is extruded from the silkworm in one continuous strand.

Manufactured fibers: Fibers made from chemicals extruded through a spinerette into long continuous filaments, which can be cut into staple lengths if desired. These include nylon, polyester, and spandex, to name just a few.

Dyes: Textiles are dyed in many different colors and have been for hundreds of years. They can be dyed with natural or synthetic dyes now, but historically dyes were found in nature and applied to natural fibers. Often maintaining color on textiles was a problem, and *mordants* became a necessary part of the dyeing process. Dyes are generally from an organic source, that is, plant or animal matter. Historical sources of natural dyes include berries, insects, flowers, and other naturally occurring substances. Dyes, which are much smaller molecules than pigments, do not adhere to the surface of a fiber or textile material but rather bond with the fiber chemically and color the fibers throughout. Dyes allow fibers, yarns, or whole textiles to be colored at any time during the textile production process. Since their application is so versatile, different effects can be created.

Pigments: When prints were introduced, a different kind of coloring agent than dye was needed. Pastes or pigments are applied to textiles for printing patterns. The color sits on top of the fibers rather than being absorbed into the core of the fiber. Inorganic pigments must be applied, much as paint would be applied, to the textile or fabric as a whole piece, while fibers or yarns are not generally colored with pigments. A modern example of a pigment application would be stamping (direct) or stenciling (indirect), but the principle remains the same.

The Italian Renaissance

Isabella Campagnol Fabretti

TIMELINE

1401	In Florence, competition proclaimed by the Arte di Calimala to choose an artist to paint the north portal of the baptistery of the Santa Maria del Fiore church
1414	Poggio Bracciolini finds the lost manuscript of the *De architectura* by Vitruvio
1453	Fall of Constantinople
1454	Peace of Lodi between Venice and Milan creates a political balance between the Italian city-states
1455	Johannes Gutenberg publishes the first printed Bible
1469	Lorenzo de' Medici becomes *signore* of Florence
1492	Lorenzo de' Medici dies in Florence; Christopher Columbus arrives in the Americas
1494	Milan captured by the king of France, Charles VIII
1495–97	Leonardo da Vinci paints the "Last Supper" in the refectory of the convent of Santa Maria delle Grazie, Milan
1498	Vasco da Gama reaches the East Indies
1501–04	Michelangelo sculpts "David" in Florence
1503–05	Leonardo paints the "Mona Lisa"
1508–12	Michelangelo paints the frescoes on the vault of the Sistine Chapel
1509	Venice defeated by Cambrai League forces at the battle of Agnadello
1519	Leonardo da Vinci dies
1527	Sack of Rome
1528	Baldassarre Castiglione publishes the *Libro del Cortegiano*
1545–63	Council of Trent
1551	Monsignor Della Casa begins to write the *Galateo*
1590	Galileo writes *De motu*

CULTURE

During the fourteenth century, the literary and philosophical movement known as the Renaissance began in Italy, slowly changing the conception of the individual and involving every aspect of social life. The term *rinascità* was used by Giorgio Vasari (1511–1574) around the midpoint of the sixteenth century to indicate the rebirth of Greek and Roman culture that had been believed lost during the Middle Ages—although the concept had been anticipated, as early as 1345, by the poet Petrarch (Francesco Petrarca, 1304–1374). Many intellectuals soon began to search for ancient manuscripts forgotten in monastic libraries for centuries. They set about copying and studying them and spreading their ideas. Fundamental works by Cicero, Tito Livio, Vitruvio, and others were retrieved, and the culture of antiquity began to be widely known and appreciated. Furthermore, following the fall of Constantinople to the Turks in 1453, many of the Greek intellectuals that escaped came to Italy, where they translated the Greek classics and enriched the cultural panorama with these previously largely unknown works.

The recovery of Classical literature, culture, and philosophy opened the way for the appreciation for the values of the human sciences—in contrast to the divine sciences, the study of religion and theology, which had constituted the main cultural focus during the Middle Ages. The individual human being became the key of the new universe. The intellectuals that cultivated this kind of study were called *humanists*, and they believed in the intellectual power of Man—that he can understand the universe created by God because he himself has been created "in His likeness." Man could, as philosopher Pico della Mirandola (1463–1494) wrote in his *De hominis dignitate*, "achieve what he desires, be what he wishes to be."

Humanists such as Lorenzo Valla (1405–1457), Poggio Bracciolini (1380–1459), Marsilio Ficino (1433–1499), Erasmus of Rotterdam (1466–1536), and Enea Silvio Piccolomini (1405–1464, elected pope in 1458 as Pius II) dedicated their studies to "new" sciences such as natural science, history, and geography. These subjects were approached with a completely different attitude: the world and its phenomena were not read through the Bible but were experienced empirically, through mathematical reasoning and actual experiments. This attitude was considered by most of the Catholic Church as suspicious, even dangerous, and harsh contrasts developed between humanists and the Catholic hierarchy. Literary works by Boccaccio and Erasmus, for instance, were banned, and the works of the classics were censored of any delicate or controversial matter. Nevertheless, scientific advancements progressed at an astounding pace, with new discoveries made in human anatomy by Andrea Vesalio (1514–1564) and Leonardo da Vinci (1452–1519), in astronomy by Nicolaus Copernicus (1473–1543) and Galileo Galilei (1564–1642), and in geography by Christopher Columbus (1451–1506) and Amerigo Vespucci (1454–1512).

These groundbreaking ideas mark the breaking point with the Middle Ages and began to spread widely in Europe thanks to Johannes Gutenberg's (c. 1400–1468) invention of the printing press. The humanist concepts contrasted with the medieval conception of religion and prepared the scene for the traumatic Lutheran schism, inspired by the exposition of Martin Luther's (1483–1546) ninety-five theses at the door of the cathedral of Wittenberg.

POLITICS AND ECONOMY

If Italian cultural life was becoming an inspiration in Europe, the same could not be said of its political situation; at the dawn of the fifteenth century, in fact, Italy was still a medieval patchwork of regional states. Some of them were independent, such as Rome and the Papal States, Florence, and the Republic of Venice with its dominions stretching along the Adriatic coasts and into the Mediterranean Sea. Milan was ruled by the Visconti and, later, Sforza families; the south of Italy was shifting toward the crown of Spain. Mantua, Ferrara, Urbino, and numerous smaller *signorie* and *ducati* dotted the peninsula, their political strength based on the wealth of their rulers, which made it possible to hire mercenary troops to defend them.

A difficult and precarious balance between the Italian states was reached in 1454 with the peace treaty signed at Lodi. Forty years later, however, in 1494, the capture of Milan by French king Charles VIII overturned the balance, opening the new century to a long and tumultuous period of wars fought over Italian soil between Charles V and Francis I. These wars were made even more gruesome by the massive use of the innovation of gunpowder. In 1509 Venetian ambitions on Lombardy and Milan were quashed in the battle of Agnadello, but the darkest moment of the Renaissance era was reached on May 6, 1527, the day on which imperial troops sacked and burned Rome, forcing the pope to hide in Castel Sant'Angelo.

Crucial in the relationships between the states was the role played by diplomats, with ambassadors of the many Italian states residing in foreign countries for the first time. As a result of long negotiations, the 1559 Peace of Cateau-Cambrésis between France and Spain tried once again to stabilize the political situation in Italy: Naples, Sicily, Sardinia, and Milan became Spanish dominions, thus confirming Spanish supremacy in the peninsula; Venice remained independent, but Florence and the kingdom of Savoy owed to France their titles and dominions, while Genoa was very strictly tied to Madrid, as was Rome, necessarily faithful to the Catholic king of Spain.

The economy of the Italian Renaissance was focused around the main merchant cities; while agricultural activities were still essential, the Renaissance was achieved—and funded—by the riches brought into cities such as Florence, Rome, Venice, Milan, and Naples by merchants and bankers who dominated the economic life not only in Italy but, through their foreign connections, all over Europe. New commercial practices were adopted, such as the double-entry bookkeeping system, invented by mathematician Fra' Luca Pacioli (1455–1510) in 1494, and the adoption of January 1 as the closing day for commercial balances and for the payment of interest. Merchant activities were no longer regulated by the seasonal and rural calendar of the Middle Ages; the new time was artificial and yet as real as the numerous clocks that began to appear on most cities' towers.

Despite the persistence in the fifteenth century of pestilence, famine, and social disorder, it is possible to document a steady increase in the Italian population. This is attributed to the increased standard of living conditions, in particular for the lower classes. The vitality in commerce of the fifteenth century is mainly focused on textile trading and the commerce of textile-related raw materials. In Italy, silk fabrics were produced in Lucca, Como, Genoa, Venice, Bologna, and Florence, while wool-weaving mills were mostly located in Tuscany, Lombardy, Mantua, Cremona, and Piacenza. Some linen fabrics were made around Milan (but the vast majority of the aristocracy preferred the linen fabrics coming from the Flanders). Milan, Brescia, and Bergamo were also famous for the production of all kind of military gear. In the South of Italy, where the economy was mostly centered on agricultural products, there were a few areas in which there was some silk-weaving activity, such as in Naples, Catania, and Palermo. Around Naples, there were also hemp fields, the fibers being used both for clothing and to make cordage.

During the fifteenth century, alum mines were discovered in Tolfa, in the Papal States. Alum was a very important chemical used in the textile production, and this discovery was essential because, at the same time, the alum mines of Focea had been occupied by Turks.

Fresh impetus toward the renovation of the society also came from the great geographical discoveries of the last decade of the fifteenth century, made easier by the improvements in nautical tools such as the compass and by more detailed maps and *portolani*. The discovery of the New World in 1492—as well as of new commercial routes to the East, thanks to the journeys of Vasco da Gama in 1498—brought new life to cities such as Lisbon, at the expense of merchant traffic especially to Venice. This shift, though, did not cause immediate damage to the city, and its devastating effects became apparent only in the following centuries.

THE ARTS

The Italian Renaissance can be properly described as an era of unprecedented artistic and cultural splendor. An intellectual fever pervaded every artistic field, and painters, architects, sculptors, and musicians made use of anatomical, mathematical, and scientific research and of the ever-present Classical references. They created masterpieces that still embody the very identity of Western culture.

The first phase of the Renaissance, at the beginning of the fifteenth century, developed in Florence, but a century later it was Rome that became the center of artistic innovation, thanks to the amazing works of art created by Raphael (1483–1520) and Michelangelo (1475–1564) at the papal court. Their art, including the sculpture "David" (1501–1504, Florence, Galleria dell'Accademia) and frescoes at the Sistine Chapel, contributed to the creation of a new figurative language. The Maecenas, or patrons of these artists, were the rulers of the numerous courts in northern Italy and encouraged a similarly rich and innovative artistic production, especially in Lombardy, Emilia-Romagna, and the Veneto.

In Florence in 1401, a competition was announced by the Arte di Calimala, the corporation of the merchants, to choose the artist that would paint the north portal of the baptistery of the church of Santa Maria del Fiore. Two artists were chosen: Lorenzo Ghiberti (1378–1455) divided the space diagonally into two separate areas, creating a perfectly balanced, but rather inexpressive, scene, while Filippo Brunelleschi (1377–1446), using the lessons of the classics, built his representation following a pyramidal structure and focused the attention on the main point in the drama, the hands of the Angel and Abraham. The contest was won by Ghiberti, but Brunelleschi further pursued his researches about the principles of Classical art.

In 1409, Brunelleschi traveled to Rome with fellow artist Donatello (1386–1466). Their purpose was not simply to imitate the style of the ancient Romans but to try to duplicate their creative process. Brunelleschi invented a method that, through the use of specific geometrical rules, allowed the artist to produce the illusion of three-dimensional space and to create a clever balance in the arrangements of objects in the works of art. The perspective was technically already known in the Middle Ages, but the linear-centric perspective was singularly suitable to the humanistic and Renaissance vision of the world—a geometrically measurable world.

The first occasions in which the new theories were used were the sculptures of Orsanmichele and of Santa Maria del Fiore by Donatello, Verrocchio (1435–1488), and Ghiberti himself. In architecture, Brunelleschi put his theories to the test when, in 1436, he began to build the cupola of Santa Maria del Fiore. On a Gothic structure, without any scaffolding, he was able to superimpose an innovative dome that was considered the definitive proof of the brilliance of Man's mind.

Mathematical studies also led to the written theories of perspective in a foolproof method that allowed reality to be described, correlating every part of the artistic composition inside mutual proportions. The concept was strictly connected with the philosophical thinking of the time, which framed the individual inside a measurable environment. Both mathematician Fra' Luca Pacioli (c. 1455–1510) in his *De divina proportione* and painter della Francesca (c. 1410–1492) followed this idea. Della Francesca expressed his ideas in the treatise *De prospectiva pingendi* and conceived his "Flagellation of the Christ" (1444, Urbino, Galleria Nazionale delle Marche) almost as a practical demonstration of the figurative possibilities of perspective. The architecture represented in the paintings is Roman, and the human figures within it are also architectural. There is an absolute immobility that is functional to the balance of the painting. Every figure seems frozen into a geometrical frame, while at the same time all of the people are connected by a cogent perspective grid.

About two decades before, the application of the mathematical rules of perspective had been used for the first time by a young artist, Tommaso di Giovanni Cassai, called Masaccio (1401–1428), in a public commission in his fresco "The Holy Trinity" (c. 1425, Florence, Santa Maria Novella). In this work, Masaccio created a convincing spatial illusion in which all the various elements and figures of the composition, although set in different spatial areas, related to a single vanishing point. Painters such as Fra' Giovanni da Fiesole, also known as Fra Angelico (1396–1455) Paolo Uccello (1397–1475) Benozzo Gozzoli (1420–1497) Pollaiolo (1431–1498) and Ghirlandaio (1449–1494) each represented one aspect of the artistic revolution that was developing from Gothic roots. The spirituality, the study of the role of illumination in paintings, the study of the figures in motion, the relationship between the drawing and the color, the intense work and planning that took place inside the Renaissance *botteghe* (art studio) took the artists from artisans' workshops into real *Accademie* and centers of artistic research.

Among the characteristically Renaissance figurative themes were the personal portraits—no longer idealized representations as had been created in the Middle

Ages, but instead reflections once again of the intellectual focus on the individual. They aimed to express the true essence of the person, who is carefully placed in his or her own identity and reality. Other themes, reflecting the contemporary studies on the classics, were taken from Classical mythology and from the Judeo-Christian tradition, both in sculpture and painting, but historical themes were also common.

The classics were not studied exclusively in Tuscany; another center of research was Padua, in Veneto. In this city where there had been a university in which the classics had been studied since 1222, the new Florentine ideas were appreciated and further researched, particularly in the *bottega* of Francesco Squarcione (1397–1468). Squarcione was an authentic and eclectic Renaissance artist who was at the same time an embroiderer, tailor, painter, and collector of archaeological antiquities that one of his pupils, Andrea Mantegna (1430–1506), passionately studied. From the classics, Mantegna learned the careful balance of figures and the use of perspective to create illusory spaces—a lesson he put in practice in a masterly *trompe l'oeil* fresco in the Camera degli Sposi (Bridal Chamber) in the Ducal Palace in Mantua.

In Venice, artistic research followed a very specific itinerary. In consideration of the exceptional geographical position that allowed for intense and open cultural exchanges, close commercial relationships with the Middle East, and the fluid environment of the lagoon, there was not much space for a rigid mathematical figurative method. Venetian painters and architects focused on color and the relationships between the different shades in order to create a new figurative style that created shapes through the juxtaposition of the colors.

Music was also particularly relevant in this period, and its mathematical rules were more easily understood. After the invention of the printing press, not only written books but also music books were more widely available and very popular in every wealthy household. Music played an essential part in everyday life: the larger spaces available in Renaissance houses offered the possibility of having music rooms, where young sons were often taught to play an instrument; some degree of musical education was also given to daughters—though with caution, as it was feared that too much knowledge, in any cultural field, would interfere with their ability to run the household.

Musical instruments are often represented in paintings and, according to the records in Renaissance inventories, even the middle classes could afford some basic instruments, such as lutes and harpsichords, that were carefully preserved in their own protective cases. During family and social events, professional singers and players were often hired, and music and theater began to merge to create new styles of performance. For instance, at the end of the sixteenth century, a group of well-read men and musicians, the Camerata de' Bardi, founded by Count Giovanni Bardi (one of the best-known members was Vincenzo Galilei, father of Galileo), created a new vocal style—a cross between recitation and singing, appropriately called *recitarcantando*. From these roots later developed the melodrama. The first important example of this new genre was Jacopo Peri's (1561–1633) *Euridice*, presented in Florence on the occasion of the marriage between Maria de' Medici and Henry IV of France. However, it would be Claudio Monteverdi's (1567–1643) *Orpheus*, performed for the first time in 1607, that became the progenitor of the opera. The mutual relationship between the lyrics and music became more important, the recitation faded into singing, and the music illustrated the meaning of the text through the so-called *madrigals*.

ARCHITECTURE AND INTERIOR DESIGN

At the dawn of the Renaissance, the architectural language of the Middle Ages changed because of a concurrent influence of factors. First, the relative peace inside major Italian cities made it unnecessary for private residences inside the city walls to be built as fortresses, with exceedingly thick walls and few narrow windows. Second, following the theories and philosophies expressed by humanist and Renaissance thinkers, it was considered proper to build a house appropriate to the social status of a family, in the same way it was considered proper to dress in a neither too modest nor too grandiose style. A booklet dedicated to new brides instructed them to show guests their homes and "some of their possessions, either new or beautiful, but in such a way that it will be received as a sign of politeness and domesticity, and not as arrogance."

As a result, many Italian cities experienced an intense period of urban renewal, and many new residential buildings were designed and built following the new ideas of etiquette and decorum, among them the theories outlined by Leon Battista Alberti (1404–1472). Alberti was a humanist who wrote influential books about painting (*De pictura*, 1436), architecture (*De re aedificatoria*, 1452), and sculpture (*De statua*, 1464). Deeply influenced by the Classical heritage he was rediscovering in his studies, Alberti defined the architect as the person who "with perfect method can rationally plan and actually realize ... buildings perfectly suitable to fulfill the most important needs of man," because Man was the center of the Renaissance universe. Among these needs were *utilitas* (practicality), *dignitas* (dignity), and comfort. The house had to be imagined as a little state inside which every person was to have the most opportune space and position.

In the *Trattato della economica* (1560) by Giacomo Lanteri, a connection is clearly established between the structure of the house and the business activity and social status of the family who lived in it. The new buildings were characterized by the use of the ancient orders and the proportions of Classical architecture, especially that of Rome. There was a deep dislike of more recent architectural and artistic styles such as Gothic. The Spedale degli Innocenti was the first building since the fall of the Roman Empire to be consciously built following a Classical architectural vocabulary, while the San Lorenzo Basilica and the Church of Santo Spirito document the Renaissance research toward the harmonization of the Classical style with the early Christian tradition.

Following these theories, the exterior of a Renaissance house appeared larger in size, inspired by the solemn style of the Classical antiquity, and was lightened by numerous wide glass-covered windows because, as Pope Pius II wrote about his newly built palace in Pienza at the end of the fifteenth century, "the main quality of a house is the light." The problem was then to protect the large openings of the windows to avoid drafts and inclement weather, both during the winter and in the summer. The best solution was to cover the windows with glass "eyes," small roundels of Venetian-made glass bound together by lead strips and fastened inside a wooden frame. Glass windows appeared in Italy in the fourteenth century: they are mentioned in 1335 in an inventory of a house in Bologna and appear again in a Florentine inventory dated 1391 in which is described twenty-four "white glass eyes" used to cover the windows. Glass windows—or any windows—were, however, usually avoided in the most private rooms of the house, for instance in the *studioli*. In these secluded rooms, the presence of windows was not recommended.

The layout of the new houses was carefully planned; domestic life became the subject of thorough study that redistributed spaces and rooms, providing for specialized areas, each of them dedicated to the numerous events that took place inside the walls—from business meetings to social occasions to concerts or cultural events, eventually recognizing the essential need for privacy, a real luxury in times when most families still slept together with servants and animals.

Typically, middle-class and aristocratic Renaissance houses were designed with more than one level and were generally two or three stories high. On the ground floor was the warehouse and storage rooms, the kitchen, a small office for basic business needs and transactions, and other service areas. Some street-front lots could be rented out as shops. The most important rooms were located on the *piano nobile*, the first floor above ground level, where there was a large rectangular hall (called *sala* in Tuscany, *portego* in Venice) and a number of smaller, square bedrooms (*camere*).

This main hall brought together two separate worlds; in it, political events could be discussed, weddings could be celebrated, or music and theatrical plays could be performed. Also, in simple hospitality, banquets could be offered on behalf of the government. It could be decorated with frescoes, tapestries, or family paintings and usually had built-in benches all around the walls, sometimes with high backrests. Long tables could easily be brought in, assembled, and disassembled, which would leave room for dancing or other entertainment after the meal. Since the function of the hall was essentially that of display, in Venetian *porteghi*, there were almost always military trophies, such as *restelliera* (swords), lances, arrows, and other military paraphernalia. Classical-style busts were displayed over cornices and doorways. Lighting was provided by glass lamps and lanterns. Characteristically Florentine was the presence in the main hall of the *acquaio*, a built-in basin with an elaborate frame, traditionally made with blue-gray *pietra serena* and decorated with coats of arms.

The most important palaces in the late fifteenth and sixteenth centuries had smaller, more private dining rooms for which new styles of furniture were needed. These new styles included smaller *credenze*, used to keep such implements as dishes, forks, and spoons, which were usually owned in sets of twelve.

Domestic life and objects played an active role in the creation of art and culture. Since the modern distinction between fine and decorative art was not yet established, prestigious artists produced domestic and utilitarian objects that no longer just served their specific purpose. They also had to be pleasant to the eyes and, possibly, convey additional messages about the social status and wealth of the family. In Venice, Middle Eastern objects such as perfume burners, ewers, and candlesticks were popular. Turkish carpets were used on the floors or on tables, as is widely documented in the paintings of the time. Also common were practical furnishings such as folding tables, folding stools, and chairs, sometimes decorated by inlaid materials.

In the bedroom, the fireplace and the bed were usually the main features, but, reading the accurate descriptions given in the inventories or observing some contemporary paintings, it clearly appears that beds and other furnishings were lavishly decorated pieces of furniture. An impressive description of a Venetian *camera d'oro* (golden bedroom) is offered by Friar Pietro Casola, who visited the city from Milan at the end of the fifteenth century: "The ceiling was so richly decorated with gold and ultramarine and the wall was so well adorned, that my pen is not equal to describing them....There were so many beautiful figures and so much gold everywhere."

The fireplaces, as defined by Sebastiano Serlio in his architectural treatise posthumously published in 1575, were "essential ornaments of the house" and reached monumental proportions. They were often designed by famous architects and decorated with elaborate sculptures, coat of arms, and inscriptions. A revolutionary heating system was introduced in a house built in Padua in 1524 and is remembered in Serlio's treatise: in a large octagonal music room, the heat came from a furnace located directly underneath the room's floor.

Since bedrooms were usually renovated and redecorated on the occasions of marriages, the main feature of the room was a large, highly symbolic, wooden bed, called *lettiera* in Tuscany, sometimes enriched by paintings set in the headboard and often accompanied by a smaller daybed or *lettuccio*. Other decorative yet utilitarian elements were the *cassoni*, storage chests, usually exhibited in the procession that accompanied the bride from the paternal to the marital home. They could vary greatly in shape and dimensions and were traditionally gilded and elaborately carved or painted with allegorical or biblical stories. A small table, a couple of chairs, paintings, *deschi da nozze* or *da parto* (round paintings celebrating a wedding or a birth), cradles, and musical instruments could also be found in the bedroom. An area of the room was reserved for private devotion: no matter how modest, every *camera* was protected by a painting of the Madonna and Child, and there were religious images made with different materials and techniques. *Acquasantiere* (holy-water fonts), portable altars, and kneelers have also been found in domestic inventories since the fifteenth century and became more and more elaborate in the next century.

An anonymous poem, dated 1459, describes the study inside the Medici palace in Florence and offers an idea of the balanced and educated luxury that characterized the furnishings of these small rooms:

> Then we go into the triumphal and luxurious study
> covered with intarsia and paintings
> . . .
> There are many ornately decorated books
> and vases of alabaster
> . . .
> And everything there is beautiful and fine,
> brought to complete perfection by nature and by human intellect

If a simple *scrittoio*, a desk in the bedroom, sufficed to take care of the family's affairs in smaller houses, in larger palaces the *studiolo* was a multipurpose room that served not only as a room in which to deal with economic transactions, as is repeatedly remembered in the *Libro dell' arte di mercatura* written by Benedetto Cotrugli in 1458, but also as a place to study and keep business and family papers. The family's treasures were kept in this room in a locked safe, which was often the focal point of the room. Among the characteristic curiosities that could appear in a Renaissance studiolo are some of the early scientific instruments, such as spheres used to trace the orbits of the planets, different kinds of sundials, and astrolabes, which were used to cast horoscopes or by doctors for predicting the course of diseases and to decide on the most suitable time for administering medicines or treatments.

HOUSEHOLD TEXTILES

Fabrics could be used in different ways in Renaissance households. Simple linen cloths were used as mosquito nets, while waxed or oiled linen cloths were used as waterproof window coverings in place of glass panes. In a document dated 1576, the belongings of the Odescalchi family of Como are recorded, and the purchase of a large quantity of linen is noted specifically for this practical purpose. Household items commissioned especially on the occasions of nuptials such as bedsheets, pillowcases, towels, and tablecloths were made of linen and were duly embroidered with the family's coat of arms. All the home textiles were accurately listed in inventories, where there was a clear distinction between the *lavorati* (embroidered) linens and those without decorations that were destined to be used by servants. The quantities of household linens are sometimes quite impressive and suggest the idea that families, especially important ones, wanted to be prepared for large-scale entertaining. When not in use, these textile items would be preserved in various types of furniture, such as chests or cassoni, or in drawers under the beds.

The most characteristic use of textiles in the Renaissance house was as wall furnishings. At the time, all the walls were either painted or covered with fabrics. The terms used to define these textile furnishings include *capoletto*, for those initially used to cover the walls behind the beds, and *spalliera*, typically situated behind benches. At the end of the fifteenth century and into the sixteenth, the term used was *paramenti*; these could be made of simple damask or of precious velvets or cloth of gold—a material forbidden by a Venetian sumptuary law in 1476 in the effort to stop the excessive spending in luxury furnishings. Fabrics were also used to make curtains for the windows or canopies for four-poster beds.

Another characteristically Renaissance wall covering was *cuoridoro*, painted and gilded leather. In Venice in the sixteenth century, there were more than seventy cuoridoro workshops, but these leathers slowly became less fashionable and, two centuries later, there were just seven shops left. The technique to make these leather products was quite complex: the leather was first stretched on a wooden frame, then spread with a layer of glue, on top of which was placed the gold or silver leaf. The material was later painted and coated with a transparent varnish.

Tapestries were also considered an appropriate decoration for a Renaissance household, but since they were so expensive, they were used only in the main rooms of the house, where they could be seen and admired by the guests of the family. They came directly from the Low Countries and were greatly appreciated because they were easy to install (they were simply nailed to the walls) and to remove. They were also easy to roll and put in storage and did not fade as quickly as other textiles.

Initially, tapestries were bought piece by piece, but around the second half of the fifteenth century, it became common to order an entire series of tapestries that narrated specific mythological or biblical episodes, creating a sort of frieze all around the perimeter of the room. In 1448, Giovanni de' Medici received a letter from his agent in Antwerp about a series of tapestries he wanted to place in his own dining room: the agent offered him a choice between two different sets of tapestries, one with "stories" or figurative episodes, the other with *verzure*, or vegetable and floral motifs. Sometimes the tapestries were designed by renowned artists, such as the amazing series of tapestries designed by Raphael in which the human figures appeared three-dimensional. These tapestries marked a turning point, after which even in this artistic field the representation of the human figure followed the new realistic Renaissance style. Tapestries were used not only to decorate walls but also to cover chairs and to make bed-covers and pillowcases.

Eastern-designed, geometrically patterned woolen carpets were also use as upholstery and cushion covers, as is seen Renaissance domestic inventories that recorded such things as "carpets for writing desks" or tables, rather than being used on the floors. The carpets offered a touch of exoticism because they mostly came from Anatolia or the Caucasus and were another coveted status symbol in wealthy households, to the point of being represented in almost every painting of domestic interiors in the Renaissance. In fact, one of the best-known groups of carpets were the so-called Lotto carpets, which were actually depicted not only by painter Lorenzo Lotto (1480–1556) but also by many of his fellow artists. Similarly, there are "Bellini" or "Holbein" carpets, indicating types of objects that had been most frequently represented in works created by these painters.

Venetian merchants were the official providers of these kinds of luxury furnishings for almost the entire continent, and they were occasionally even involved in the carpet-making process; for example, Francesco Priuli, a seventeenth-century Venetian merchant who resided in Egypt, sponsored carpet-weaving looms and oversaw their production. Sometimes aristocrats in Italy were not happy to simply buy the carpets brought into stock by merchants and instead ordered customized items.

COSTUME IN THE ITALIAN RENAISSANCE

In this inspiring period of civilization, artistic taste, and advances in science, the privileged role played by dress does not come unexpected. Through carefully constructed costumes, in fact, men and women of the sixteenth century could shape their bodies in order to present themselves as the incarnation of the Renaissance ideal of man and woman, effectively communicating a message of self-confidence and intellectual strength.

Before diving into the description of early Renaissance dress styles, it is important to keep in mind the evolution of new and emerging social classes, such as the wealthy merchants and the skilled craftsmen, who at this historical juncture began to play an increasingly relevant role in fifteenth-century society. The squares and streets of the still medieval cities were the background of a new dress style that, in Italy, is characterized by a long-limbed look. Classical ideas were integrated with the silhouettes of the Gothic period and some Oriental influences. Women depilated or plucked their foreheads in order to highlight the verticality of the figure, made even more evident by the high waistline, the large, almost butterfly-looking sleeves, and the majestically flowing train. To a lesser degree, this gracefulness is also present in men's clothing, characterized by a straight bust, moderately long hair, surcoats often longer in the back, and close-fitting hose.

By the end of the fifteenth century and at the beginning of the sixteenth, Italian clothing was fueling an intense development in the evolution of European fashions. From late Gothic verticalism, the trend moves toward the harmonious exaltation of the human body, the lines and proportions of which were not altered but tastefully emphasized by the imposing flow of the fabrics. The costumes express the atmosphere of refined luxury and elegance of the Italian courts described by etiquette manuals and works such as the *Libro del Cortegiano*, published in 1528 by Baldassarre Castiglione (1478–1529), and the *Galateo* of Monsignor Giovanni della Casa (1503–1556), both of which became best-sellers not only in Italy but also in all the other important European courts.

The superb sumptuousness of the costumes worn by the Italian aristocracy set the standards for all European nobility. Simplicity, although recommended by preachers and scholars, was not an appreciated virtue. Monsignor della Casa strongly advised people to wear dresses that "fit not only the body shape, but also the social rank of the person and the customs of the place she lived in." The lure of luxury, however, was too strong, as indicated by the fact that the numerous sumptuary laws that emanated in every Italian state in the sixteenth century were considered necessary to distinguish the social classes.

Admired and sought after, Italian styles circulated in Europe through the meticulous descriptions given by foreigners or through portraits and collections of woodcuts. These were specifically created in order to gather and document costumes from Italy and, in more ambitious works, from around the world. Enea Vico, in his *Diversarum gentium aetatis*, illustrates with ninety-eight plates the dress in different parts of the globe. Works by Francesco and Pietro Bertelli (respectively, the authors of *Omnium fere gentium nostrae aetatis habitus numquam ante hoc aediti*, Venice, 1563, and *Diversarum nationum habitus*, Padua, 1589) and Cesare Vecellio, just to name the most famous writers, were frequently bought as souvenirs by travelers, thus representing a key element in the diffusion of costumes, long before the first fashion magazines.

Italian princesses such as Isabella d'Este Gonzaga, Lucrezia Borgia, Bianca Cappello, and Catherine de' Medici inspired, in the words of Vecellio, the "new ways in dressing." They became fashion icons, and their costumes were known and copied with the help of doll's dresses in miniature replicas of their outfits that were sent all over Europe. Even the ambitious King Francis I of France in 1515 asked in a letter for a doll "dressed with the same style worn by Isabella d'Este" because he needed to order some new gowns for the ladies of his court.

Given that there were no significant changes in the lower classes' dress style—which, imposed more by need than by fashion, would remain mostly unchanged for centuries—two distinct periods can be identified in aristocratic and middle-class Renaissance dresses. In the first half of the sixteenth century, the garments softly focus on a volumetric effect emphasized by the low junction between the sleeves and the dress and by the generous neckline; the marked waistline of women's *camore* (dresses) and the knee-length *brache* (pants) of the men put an end to the Gothic verticality of the figure, showing instead a clear emphasis on a more mature fullness and imposing breadth. The harmonious feminine beauty of the Renaissance is exemplified by the full hair, tight bodices, and ample skirts, suggesting large and maternal hips.

Such serene ideals were modified in the last decades of the sixteenth century, when the Renaissance faded into the more rigid Mannerism and, in compliance with the rigorous religious strictness recommended by the Council of Trent (1545–63), a shadow of sobriety was cast over the continent—all the more so in Italy, where the Vatican influence was powerful, and in Catholic Spain. The new dresses clearly reflected the growing complexity and artificiality of the political situation, and the female body become almost ''graphic,'' made as it was by two opposing *V*'s, one created by the stiff bodices that encased the woman's torso and the other, upside-down, created by the *faldia* that made the skirts almost conical in shape.

In complete contrast with the almost feminine men's costumes of the fifteenth century, men's fashions of the mature Italian Renaissance highlight their virility, with ample, dark garments, short hair, and carefully trimmed beards. Quite evident is the stiffening of the garments, along with the diffusion of distinctive Spanish fashions, such as the heavy padding of the sleeves, the pointed *farsetti* (doublets), the puffy *brache alla Sivigliana* (Seville-style pants), and the Spanish trademark, the stiff *gorgiera* (ruff). The costumes retained some degree of originality in the still-independent Republic of Venice, the Tuscan grand duchy, and in Papal States, but it was not long before the free men and women of the Renaissance were again prisoners inside their own clothes.

Textiles, Embroidery, and Lace

The fabrics used for clothing in the Italian Renaissance were renowned all over Europe for their quality and beauty of design. They could be made of wool, vegetable fibers, or silk and were often brocaded or embroidered with precious metallic threads. There were many different types of wool cloth, woven in different patterns and weights appropriate for the changing seasons. Extremely valuable were the so-called *panni di Garbo*, woolen fabrics originally imported from the Arabian city of Gerbe and later produced in Florence. Some shops carried *stanforti*, woolen cloth made in the English city of Stanford. The *taleth* was a special woolen fabric produced in Venice exclusively to be sold to Jews.

The importation of cotton from the East brought such wealth to Venice that it was called *herba de oro* (''golden grass''). The most common cotton fabrics were *fustagni*, or fustian (a name that derives from Fostat, a suburb of today's Cairo, Egypt), a mix of wool and cotton fibers that was mainly used to make doublets. *Bombasina* was a cotton fabric used for ordinary underwear. The most luxurious undergarments or shirts, called *camise* or *camicia*, which were often visible peeking through necklines or sleeves (or through slashed overgarments) were made of very fine French linen fabrics such as *tela rensa*, which was imported from Rheims, or the less refined *tela cambrada*, from Cambrai.

Linen fibers were commonly purchased in bulk to be spun and woven by female family members or servants: a notebook showing the expenses of Virginia Orsini in the mid-sixteenth century describes how she paid the gardener's

Adimari wedding procession (Wedding of Bocaccio Adimari and Lisa Ricasoli), Master of the Cassone Adimari, 1440. © Nicolo Orsi Battaglini/Art Resource, NY.

wife's for spinning the linen fibers, a weaver to make the fabric, and others to sew her husband's shirts and some swaddling cloths for the babies. An astonishing quantity of linens could be recorded in wedding trousseaux; just to give an idea, Cassandra Covoni, a Florentine who married in 1526, brought in her trousseau 148 handkerchiefs, 31 aprons, 29 shirts, 25 coifs, 6 pairs of sleeves and 50 *braccia* (about 95 feet/29 m) of linen fabric. The vast majority of these objects would be embroidered, which would usually be done both by the bride and some of her family's relations and by external embroiderers. The kind of embroidery, especially on shirts, is especially visible in a shirt housed at the Prato Textile Museum or in a detail of Sofonisba Anguissola's "Sisters Playing Chess" (1441, Poznan, Muzeum Narodowe).

Silk fabrics dominated the luxury market. They were originally imported from the Ottoman Empire, but the silk industry was later established in several Italian cities, such as Lucca, Florence, Venice, Genoa, and Milan, and was exported all over Italy and Europe. Among the silks produced in these centers were the very light and plain *zendale*, taffeta and satin, often used for linings; damask (with motifs on a satin background); *tabì* (also called *tabin*, *tabinetto*, or *tabinazzo*), similar to damask and favored by Isabella d'Este Gonzaga; *ormesini* (from Ormuz, an island in the Persian Gulf); and the velvet fabrics used for dresses.

Velvets were pile-weave silks on a satin background and were an Italian specialty and the trademark of Italian Renaissance clothing. Appreciated for their three-dimensional effect, these complex fabrics were created by inserting an extra warp yarn in addition to the basic background warp. During the weaving process, small iron tools, called "velvet irons," were inserted between the basic warp threads and the supplementary ones to make a small loop, which was later cut by the weaver, thus creating the pile effect. Velvet irons of different sizes created different heights of the velvet pile, and other decorative effects could be obtained by cutting the loops in some areas, while leaving them in others; the insertions of brocade wefts of gold and silver threads further enhanced the magnificent look of these velvet fabrics.

The complexity of the work involved in creating these textiles was so highly valued that velvet weavers were paid almost three times more than regular weavers, and the fact that they could only make around sixty yards (50–60 m) per year of these amazing fabrics makes it easy to understand why these craftsmen were so admired and appreciated for their work. The different decorative velvets mainly came from Eastern patterns brought to the West through fabrics imported by Venetian merchants. Fabric trading was the business that made many of the important Renaissance families, including the Medici, the Este, the Sforza, and the Gonzaga, very wealthy.

Among the preferred fifteenth- and sixteenth-century fabrics were *zetanini avvellutati*, *altobasso* velvets, and *soprarizzo* or *cesellato* velvets. Zetanini—the name of which derives from the Chinese city of Zayton, where they were originally produced—were silk velvets characterized by what looked like carved motifs in the fabric; the decorative pattern was structured as a sequence of lobed tiles, in the center of which was usually a pomegranate or a vase surrounded by flower or vegetable motifs. Altobasso was characterized by a sculpted effect achieved by the juxtaposition of two (or more) heights of the velvet pile obtained with the skilled use of the velvet irons. Soprarizzo, also called cesellato, owes its textured appearance to the alternation of cut and looped velvet and was often brocaded; in some cases, the details of the pattern could be highlighted with *allucciolature*, very thin gold or silver loops threaded through the fabric and variously twisted in order to achieve the desired decorative effect.

In the most expensive fabrics, the use of precious threads is extensive. A good example is that of the "cloths of gold," a term used for heavily brocaded fabrics using gold yarns. Characteristically Venetian were the *restagni*, fabrics technically reserved only for the *doge*'s clothes but actually worn by many aristocratic ladies. For instance, a bride belonging to the Grimani family in 1517 wore a wedding dress made "half of white silk and half of cloth of gold," which she somehow obtained special permission to wear for just one occasion.

The decorative motifs on fabrics in the fifteenth century can be arranged in two main categories: the *griccia* and the *cammino*. The griccia was a vertical arrangement of vegetable motifs, many of which had their origins in Persian, Chinese, and Indian patterns. The cammino was characterized by a horizontal sequence of lobed motifs framing the Italian artichoke, a pomegranate, or a pinecone, as shown in the detail of the detachable sleeve of Pollaiolo's "Portrait of a Lady" (c. 1470, Milan, Museo Poldi Pezzoli). Both of these patterns were relatively large in scale. Smaller patterns, called *a mazze*—usually small S-shaped branches with the extremities finished by miniature vegetable decorations, little clubs, or occasionally miniature animals such as lions, eagles, or scorpions—appear around the last quarter of the sixteenth century, along with similar but simpler patterns such as stylized slashes.

The high cost of any kind of silk fabric made for the widespread practice for recycling fabrics, which was a common custom even in wealthy households. Many textile collections still preserve items that were made by carefully piecing together smaller fragments of expensive silk fabrics. In the inventory of Livia Tolletina, dated 1580, following the death of her husband, it is carefully specified that the fabrics of many of her dresses as a married woman had been reused as ecclesiastical vestments or as upholstery fabrics for her coach.

In light of this frugal practice, an even more unusual fabric type emerged as characteristic of the Renaissance. Called *stratagliati* or *accoltellati*, these were mostly simple silk satins, but also damask and velvet, and were slashed and cut following specific decorative patterns: the cuts created little flowers, zigzag motifs, crosses, and other decorations and were made even more evident by the use of fabrics with warps and weft dyed in different colors. This rather bizarre fashion seems to have come from northern Europe, apparently inspired by the torn-apart clothes from the battlefields. Soon these "decorations" appeared in both men's and women's clothing, creating a growing concern among sumptuary officials all over Italy. Rules were announced to forbid the use of this new style, because the life and possibility for reuse of these fabrics were diminished significantly by the cuts, and in an era in which a fabric routinely lasted more than ten years, this was considered a shameful waste. On the other hand, the use of these "ruined" fabrics highlighted the economic power and wealth of a family.

The already precious Renaissance fabrics were often decorated with magnificent embroidered pieces. Especially renowned were the fabrics from Milanese or Venetian workshops. Artists of the caliber of Botticelli, Pollaiolo, Raphael, and Perin del Vaga, among others, created embroidery patterns used for both clothing and household furnishings. Among these patterns, many were mottos and heraldic symbols. Castiglione in his *Libro del Cortegiano* advised that the clothes, besides being decent, also had to be decorated with "ingenious inventions" and fitting mottos. In 1493, Beatrice Sforza wore a precious sleeve with the embroidered motto, suggested by Leonardo da Vinci, "*a bon droit*," while Bona di Savoia Sforza had a sleeve embroidered with a phoenix decorated with diamonds and pearls; it was so valuable that it was inventoried with her jewels. Similarly precious is the *frenello* worn on the top of the head of the "Lady in Yellow" portrayed by Alessio Baldovinetti (1465, London, National Gallery). This rather harsh-looking lady is also wearing on her serious forehead a thin black *lenza*, usually a fine black silk cord. Her sleeve is prominently decorated embroidery that probably represents her coat of arms. Embroidery was also used to embellish handkerchiefs, furnishings, gloves, and shirts. Some of the shirts in the wardrobe of Bianca Maria Sforza, embroidered in gold and decorated with pearls, were worth more than 50 ducats; others belonging to Lucrezia Borgia were worth twice as much.

Lace fabrics began to appear in clothing and furnishings toward the end of the fifteenth century. These light and precious trimming fabrics were, according to legend, created by a young Venetian woman trying to imitate with her needle the foamy appearance of a rare algae, *Hlymeda opunzia*, that she had received from her lover. Legends aside, needle lace probably evolved from the complex cutwork embroidery that Venetian ladies used to make as creative pastime; bobbin laces, on the other end, would not be born until the first quarter of the sixteenth century.

Sewing and any other form of needlework were recommended activities that contributed to safeguarding the virtue of women in households. This is confirmed by the titles and dedications of the numerous lace and embroidery pattern books published in the Renaissance. These books were also enriched by engravings representing domestic scenes with women teaching young girls the art of needlework, thus promoting educational relationships among women.

Both needle and bobbin lace were used to decorate the necklines and cuffs of men's and women's camise (undergarments or shirts) or table and bed linens. The lady portrayed by Paolo Veronese (1565, Douai, Musée Municipal) is wearing wide lace cuffs in a typical pattern of the first half of the sixteenth century. An elegant lace trimming is also visible on her camisa through the central opening of the overgown and at the neckline.

The patterns identifiable in early lace fabrics, dated to the second half of the fifteenth century, were essentially geometric, with recognizable influences of the contemporary late Gothic patterns. Sixteenth-century laces have vegetable scrolls, mostly with acanthus, oak, and vine leaves—symbols of virginity, strength, and life, respectively—as their motifs. Among the leaves were pomegranates (symbolizing abundance and fertility) and other flowers, and occasionally animals, such as rabbits, peacocks, or even dolphins.

Scrolls were often mixed with *grottesche*, "grotesques," a composite pattern inspired by the contemporary rediscovery of the frescoed decorations of Nero's Domus Aurea in Rome. In the grottesche, architectural details such as banisters and columns were mixed with medallions, festoons, mermaids, sphinxes, fountains, and many other heterogeneous patterns, such as the two-tailed mermaid that appears in the lace pattern-book authored by Vecellio in 1591. The "Corona delle Nobili et Virtuose Donne" and a bobbin lace border dating to the last decade of the sixteenth century preserved in the collections of the Centro Studi del Tessuto e del Costume di Palazzo Mocenigo, Venice, show lace patterns.

Knitted fabrics appear during the Renaissance. These tighter-fitting fabrics were much needed to make the male hose that were in fashion at the time. They were also occasionally used to make pants or doublets, such as the knitted doublet in green and beige silk dated to the end of the sixteenth century, preserved in Paris in the collections of the Musée de la Mode et du Textile.

Other trademarks of the mature Venetian Renaissance style were the gathered hairstyle, the large jewel pinned in the center of the bodice, the pearl necklace, and the long gold belt.

Color

The colors used in Renaissance clothing were not accidental; they follow a precise and meaningful chromatic code, contributing to the definition of the complex social and political structure of the time. Through the colors of clothing, it was possible to identify ranks, appointments, and positions of the wearers.

Technical improvements in dyeing methods allowed for a wider range of available shades and made the Renaissance a wonderfully bright period. The most precious color was, of course, gold, which was theoretically reserved to royalty but actually worn by almost everybody in the upper classes. Other commonly used colors were green, different shades of blue (*alessandrino*, *biavo*, *pavonazzo*), and black. For more modest or religious dresses, the dyes were gray and brown. Red was very expensive, obtained with *chermes*, a rich red dye extracted from the cochineal insect, and was a coveted status symbol reserved to the aristocracy.

In the first half of the fifteenth century, it was still common to combine two or more colors in one outfit. Stripes were very popular, with checkered patterns far less common, as seen in the hose and codpiece worn by the suitor in the foreground in the painting "Penelope and the Suitors" by Pinturicchio (1509, London, National Gallery). He is also wearing a farsetto with sleeves detachable from the shoulders, and his camisa flows out from both the shoulder and the cuffs. Characteristic of early Renaissance style were the long hair and the velvet hat covering the head. The color combinations were made even more striking thanks to the use of contrasting colored linings and trimmings.

The subtle allegoric meaning of the color code, which could become even more complex with the mixing of different colors, is a medieval heritage. The use of specific colors was recommended by looking at the season, the month, the character of the wearer, and the quality of that person. If crimson was a pre-rogative of royalty, green was appropriate for youngsters, especially in the month of May. It was not by chance, then, that Isabella and Beatrice d' Este dressed their maids in green for a May celebration toward the end of the fifteenth century. Light blue was considered suitable for young women of marriageable age, while red was appropriate for gentlemen and men of justice. A white shirt meant purity for women and chastity for men.

Different colors were used throughout Italy to distinguish social classes or to identify public men of office. In Genoa, black was the color of choice for the doge and the aristocracy, while in Rome, various shades of red (*scarlatto, rosato, rosa secco*) and a light blue were worn. The Medici family in Florence preferred to use purple.

The Republic of Venice came to the point of devising a complex chromatic code to identify different public roles inside the government. For instance, the *procuratori*, the most important public officials, were the only ones allowed to wear crimson *veste* and imposing robes with wide sleeves. The council of the doge wore veste dyed in purple, and red was reserved for the members of the feared Council of Ten, a powerful office that, among other things, took care of important national security issues. Everybody else was theoretically required to wear black, a constraint that was only superficially followed because, if the veste of the majority of Venetians were black, beneath them was hidden a rainbow of colors. Among them, the *pavonazzo* was a color that could lawfully be used by almost everybody in the most diverse circumstances. This precise shade has not been clearly identified: it seems that it could vary from violet to peacock blue to a dark-purplish blue.

Black was also the usual color of mourning. Often people would routinely reuse dark-colored clothing already present in their wardrobe, but these mourning clothes were characterized by simple fabrics and by the absence of any kind of costly decorations. In Venice, though, aristocratic women wore a specific dark *corrotto* (from *cuor rotto*, "broken heart") dress with a long train that, a few days after the funeral, was tied at the waist and eventually, after a decent period of time, was cut off.

Another color-coded system was enforced at the universities. In Padua and Bologna, the various faculties were distinguished by different colors: white was the color used for the humanities, red was symbolic of medicine, and so on.

A color could also be charged with explicit negative meaning. The most common example was yellow, which was the color prostitutes wore in almost every Italian city—it was in fact mandated for prostitutes to wear in order that they be easily identifiable. A yellow circle was also the badge to be worn, sewn onto the clothing, by Jews in Venice.

Sumptuary Laws

All over Italy, the exaggerations in luxurious clothing or the adoption of immoral fashions such as too-generous necklines or too-long trains, as decried by St. Bernardino da Siena, were symbols of vanity. In a society so deeply influenced by Catholic teachings (although economic concerns also played a large part in these laws), it is then understandable that Italian states felt forced to issue severe and meticulously detailed laws and regulations trying to limit, or forbid altogether, the use of extravagant cloths of gold, jewels, silk fabrics, and precious furs. A very large number of sumptuary laws were written in Milan, Bologna, and Florence, and even in the smaller centers of Savona, Cremona, Modena, Messina, and Ascoli. In Venice, the Magistrato alle Pompe created a very thorough set of laws, still preserved in the State Archive, and the minuteness of these rules make them invaluable descriptive evidence of dress history. Interestingly, being written by men, the sumptuary laws mainly sanctioned feminine luxury, granting some latitude only on the occasion of weddings or visits of foreign rulers, because reasons of state compelled most Italian polities to forgo every sumptuary restriction during civic or religious festivities or, particularly, for state visits of foreign dignitaries.

Indeed, many examples of sumptuary legislation contain impassioned pleas against self-indulgence and being immoderate, or partaking in unseemly luxury. The problem was that clothing showed status in society, and in order to get around the laws dictating dress, several strategies were devised to continue showing off elegant attire. One solution was simply to pay the respective fines—a prac-

King Maurus and his daughter Ursula in her room, by Vittore Carpaccio shows examples of clothing details for both men and women. © Cameraphoto Arte, Venice / Art Resource, NY.

tice, *pagare le pompe* or "to pay for luxury," that became a luxury and a status symbol in itself. Another answer was to try to pass new and unlawful clothing off as old and continuing to wear it. Rulers often conceded the use of forbidden fashions or materials on used clothing because of the expense of having to replace them to obey the new laws. So, if something appeared old, even if it was new, the wearer could continue to show his or her status and get away with breaking the sumptuary laws.

Far from discouraging the wealthy from wearing costly attire, sumptuary legislation allowed them to indulge in fine clothing, providing they were willing to pay for that privilege. Eventually, sumptuary watchdogs had to settle for constantly renewing more and more tolerant laws, allowing once-forbidden fabrics or colors to be worn.

The belief that wearing splendid and costly attire was a natural concomitant of high rank and personal merit was ancient. By the fifteenth century it was axiomatic that the superior virtue intrinsic to persons of high rank necessitated the external symbolism of costly clothing. Rulers were expected to wear cloth-of-gold gowns, crimson silk, and scarlet wool, sometimes decorated with silver and gold embroidery, sable, or ermine, because these rare and beautiful materials appropriately embellished high office. They provided a useful way of identify the leader. In a period when the faces of the rulers were not universally familiar, just the sight of these awesome garments inspired reverence among ordinary people.

Construction Techniques

Because in the Middle Ages the structure of garments was simple, they did not require specific skills to be cut and sewn. However, beginning with the early Renaissance, fashions required the calibrated use of padding—for instance, in the farsetti or in the sleeves—and the skilled pleating of cloth. Tailors began to play an essential role in the construction of garments.

The first and most important step in the creation of a dress was the careful measuring of the client, followed by the selection of a suitable pattern from the "secret" collection that every master owned. This was carefully kept and was accessible only to his family and close collaborators. The pattern, cut on paper or leather, was then transferred to the fabric, and to further customize it, any alteration that was needed was traced with chalk markings, much as a suit is tailored today. Finally, following the customized pattern, the fabric was cut—an operation that, because of the expense of the fabric, was strictly reserved to the master tailor. The actual sewing could be done either by the tailor or, needlework being the base of the education of any proper woman of the time, by someone in the household. There is ample evidence that even in the most aristocratic and rich families, although dresses were cut by tailors, they were put together not only by the maids of the house but also by the lady herself. This was particularly likely if the dress was structurally quite simple.

Keeping the Wardrobe

During the Renaissance, feminine work was, essentially, domestic work. Stefano Guazzo, in his treatise *Dell' honor delle donne* (1587), describes the duties of the "honest" housewife:

> This woman would not have reached the peak of virtue, if beyond the preservation of goods she would also not provide to increase them with her own industry, in such a way that all households servants would be kept busy with some useful activity.

Guazzo goes on to describe the various tasks that were mostly related to "the textiles for the use and ornament of the house ... or the needlework, the distaff, the wool winder, the breeding of silkworms ... the keeping count of the laundry."

Laundry itself was not an everyday activity during the Middle Ages and the Renaissance. Usually it was only done two or occasionally three times a year, in the spring and fall, and this custom easily explains the large number of undergarments and household linens mentioned in the inventories. The process was excruciatingly long, and a large number of servants, almost all of them women, were employed in this kind of work. It all began with soaking the laundry. The "soap" of the time was lye, a mix of ash and warm water, that was poured over the laundry and then boiled. Everything had then to be rinsed and spread out on the grass and bushes to dry. Hardly anything was ironed in the early Renaissance, although a tool called *pressa per tessuti* (fabric press) was already known at the time. It would be in the sixteenth century, with the custom to dine over beautiful embroidered tablecloths, that the press became a household item. These were sometimes beautifully engraved and carved and set in a prominent place in the dining room.

The immaculate shirts of the sixteenth century needed to be ironed, too. To this purpose, *lisciatoi* were initially used—round and smooth stones or pieces of glass that gave the fabrics, especially linen, a characteristic sheen and stiffness.

THE WARDROBE OF A RENAISSANCE ARISTOCRATIC WOMAN

The 1400s

Women of the early Renaissance were burdened with the difficult task of representing the embodiment of grace and harmony. Their noble posture was marked by the verticalism of the lingering Gothic style, and their walk was fair and self-assured. Elegant, well-read, refined, yet modest, these women were also expected to be careful administrators of the family possessions and to exhibit the social and economic power of the family by wearing appropriate dresses.

The typical feminine outfit of the fifteenth century was an undergarment or shirt called a *camise* or *camicia*, a gown or *camora*, and an overgown. The woman's forehead was plucked to make it very high, and she would often wear elaborate headdresses in the shape of turbans or beehives. The gown had a myriad of names, including *gonna*, *gonnella*, *sottara*, and in Tuscany *gamurra*, but the most common was *camora*. It was initially a very simple garment, made with dark and unostentatious fabrics, but it became progressively more elaborate and precious, especially in the second half of the fifteenth century and later, when brocaded velvets, sometimes enriched with gold threads, were the main fabrics of choice. The gowns were characterized by very high waistlines and often had long trains, which were opposed all over Italy by conservative clergymen. Bernardino da Siena, for example, compared trains to the tail of the Devil! Legislators and husbands alike opposed the use of trains due to the profligacy of fabrics and sinful ostentation of pride.

The length of trains worn by Venetian noblewomen concerned the patriarch of Venice, Lorenzo Giustinian, so much that he tried to forbid them, threatening excommunication to those who wore them. He was faced by the defiant reaction of Venetian ladies, who appealed to the pope, asking his permission to keep wearing their magnificent dresses "for the honor of their families." The pope granted permission upon the payment of a tax. Ironically, shortly thereafter, following the advent of a style inspired by the Classical world, trains begin to disappear in Italy, although they remained present elsewhere in Europe.

In the Venetian Republic, trains were not the only fashion detail that was causing concern to sumptuary officials; necklines were very generous, too—to the point that Milanese friar Casola, on his visit to Venice in 1494, was astonished and observed that Venetian ladies' necklines were sometimes so wide, he was afraid the dresses would slide off their shoulders. Interestingly, the dress worn by St. Ursula in the detail of the "Arrival of the English Ambassadors" (1494, Venice, Gallerie dell'Accademia) shows, instead, a moderate boat-shaped neckline. St. Ursula's dress is composed of a thin linen camisa that veils the modest neckline. She wears detachable sleeves made in two different parts, the lower one vertically slashed to let the camisa puff out. The waistline is rather high, and the skirt falls straight to her feet. The long, red, draped mantle is a symbol of nobility and at the same time predicts her martyrdom. An elegant hairdo made of hair braided with strings of pearls completes the outfit.

These gowns also document another peculiarity of fifteenth-century clothing: Because the technique of widening the sleeve hole was not yet known, sleeves were either separated from the dress for a more comfortable fit, divided into upper and lower sections and laced at the shoulder and elbow; or slashed with *fenestrelle* ("windows") that let the undergarment peek out through the openings. These sleeves became a very elegant accessory, made with contrasting—and often very precious—fabrics and fastened to the dress with fabric ribbons that could be finished with precious metal caps called *puntali* made in gold or silver. Sleeves themselves were frequently decorated with intricate embroidery, perhaps representing a coat of arms, heraldic symbols, or animals, and even sometimes enriched with pearls and jewels. In the documents of the Visconti family, a sleeve is mentioned that has "413 large beads" worth more than 1,279 *fiorini*. In the portrait of Bianca Maria Sforza painted by Antonio de' Predis (1493, Washington, National Gallery), the soon-to-be bride of Maximilian of Hapsburg is wearing a precious gold filigree bonnet enriched with pearls and precious stones. A lenza crosses her forehead and her hair is gathered in the *coazzone*, a ponytail covered in ribbons.

Petticoats were covered with a rich overgown. Overgowns were tight-fitting on the bust but very wide on the back, where sometimes there was also a moderate train. It was mostly considered a winter garment.

The *pellanda* was a garment characterized by magnificent lines and long, trailing sleeves and was decorated with precious trimmings, such as stripes, braids, fringes, gold and silver embroidery, and very early examples of lace. The term came from the North European *houppelande*, a similar garment worn in the Middle Ages. The confirmation of the importance of the pellande in the Renaissance lies in the fact that these garments ranked among the first items mentioned in wedding inventories as some of the most expensive possessions, thanks to the fur linings clearly visible at the edgings. A beautiful example is seen in the work of the Master of the Adimari cassone (c. 1450, Florence, Galleria dell'Accademia), representing a detail of an elaborate wedding procession, which offers a complete overview of aristocratic early Renaissance clothing, from the sumptuous pellande worn by the two ladies on the left to the fur-lined *giornee* of the men on the right. One of the men wears a red *mazzocchio*, the typical Florentine headgear, worn with the long scarf called *becchetto*.

Frequently, pellande were enriched by the characteristic workmanship of gathering the pleats in a tubular shape, aiming to fashion the human figure to make it look well proportioned and graceful. The elaborate portrait of Ginevra d'Este shows the pleated workmanship of the bodice, the precious embroidered sleeve, and the plucked forehead.

Cotte, similar in shape to camore, were dresses considered more appropriate for summer use, as they were made with lighter-weight fabrics. The dress was closed in the front with buttons or hooks and eyes, through which ribbons were threaded to close the front of the dress. Over the cotta, women wore the *giornea*, an overgown that was open at the sides and often cut low in the back. A giornea is worn, for instance, by one of the ladies-in-waiting of the Queen of Sheba in a painting by Piero della Francesca, "The Queen of Sheba and Her Ladies-in-Waiting" (1452–1466, Arezzo, Church of San Francesco). All the ladies wear dresses that show the typical gathering that shapes the bust, and they wear different overgowns. The white-fringed giornea of the lady in the picture is sleeveless and has a long train, and the openings at the sides reveal the red cotta underneath. The giornea (pink in the painting) is worn with the sleeves left hanging.

The cotta, called *zorneta* in Bologna, was originally a garment that belonged to the male wardrobe and was made of very precious fabrics, such as the gold or silver cloths prohibited by Venetian sumptuary laws in 1455. Lodovica Tornabuoni, in her cameo portrait inside the "Birth of Saint John the Baptist" (1485–1490, Santa Maria Novella, Florence), is wearing a giornea made of a silk fabric characterized by the typical fifteenth-century pomegranate motif and decorated at the openings with leaf-shaped appliqués. The elegant petticoat in clearly visible from the center and side openings, as is the fringed linen handkerchief, an accessory that was just beginning to become a status symbol.

In the second half of the fifteenth century, a more intense circulation of fashion ideas became noticeable all over Italy and Europe. Common methods for the diffusion of the new styles were the fashion dolls called *pupe* or *puve*. These dolls were carefully dressed with miniaturized versions of the latest dress styles and circulated in Renaissance courts, both in Italy and abroad. In a letter dated September 10, 1460, for example, Ludovico Gonzaga writes to his wife Barbara asking her to have "a doll made right away, dressed according to the fashion of Mantua in the gown and in the hair." This was probably a political gift to be sent from one of the most refined of the Renaissance courts.

The 1500s

Gowns

"The dress she wore today was a camora made in black satin decorated with golden leaves and assorted sleeves." With these words, Laura Gonzaga described to Isabella, Marchioness of Mantua, in a letter written on December 18, 1502, the dress worn by the fashionable Lucrezia Borgia in a ceremony. At the beginning of the sixteenth century, the ideal woman was no longer the abstract angel of the late Gothic period; she was more voluptuous and fleshy.

The gown or camora (the most commonly used gown style) was known in Italy under various names according to the different regions—*gamurra* or *camurra* in Florence; *camora*, *socha*, or *zupa* in northern Italy; *gonnella* in the south. It was not a fashion novelty, having been used since the early fifteenth century, but its simple lines significantly evolved during the Renaissance, going from the high-waisted, long-trained style of the early period to a low-pointed waist and almost conical skirt of the late sixteenth century, thus following the evolution of artistic styles from the late Gothic to the mature Renaissance and, finally, Mannerism. The neckline undertook a similar evolution, with a series of dramatic changes from the very generous décolletages of the first decades of the sixteenth century, cleavage only barely veiled by the ruffs of the undergarments, to the severe necklines of the second half of the century that hid the bust, which was also compressed into nonexistence, and suffocated the neck in rigid ruffs.

The colors chosen for the camore were subdued in the early sixteenth century, with preference given to darker shades, particularly in Naples and the

South of Italy, a choice easily explained by the strong Spanish influence and presence in the area. In the following decades, brighter shades such as green, red, and pavonazzo (a color between blue and purple) became popular. In the inventories of Lucrezia Tornabuoni, wife of Piero de' Medici, a magnificent camora made in crimson altobasso velvet with gold brocaded sleeves is described. Lucina Brembati, as portrayed by painter Lorenzo Lotto, wears a rich black velvet camora decorated by cuts and slashes showing a distinct Spanish influence. The rich camisa is trimmed with gold embroidery and is completed by an imposing *capigliara* (elaborate hairstyle) dotted with golden bows. The painting is also interesting for the presence, attached to a gold chain, of a gold toothpick, which at the time was a very elegant accessory. The waistline being placed in its natural position made for a significant change from the early years of the sixteenth century.

Almost invariably, the dresses of the most important noblewomen were made with similarly precious fabrics: Eleonora of Toledo, in the famous portrait by Agnolo Bronzino (1545, Uffizi), demonstrated her sophisticated elegance by wearing a camora made of a luxurious Florence-produced brocaded velvet covered in gold weft loops of different lengths.

The coordinated set of an overgown and *sottana*, which was a garment very similar to the camora, both constructed in colors that complemented or contrasted with each other, constituted the base of feminine Renaissance style and represented the fashion trademark of Eleonora of Toledo. She even reduced the size of the short puffed or padded oversleeves (called *baragoni*), making it possible to comfortably wear other garments over the gown. Similar matching outfits could be found among the gifts offered by a husband to dress his new bride, which was the best clothing he could afford; Marco Parenti at the beginning of the sixteenth century ordered for his wife Caterina Strozzi a "gown of crimson velvet," a matching surcoat with a garland of feathers, which was decorated with pearls, and some crimson velvet fabric to be made into long sleeves lined with marten. One of the very few authentic sixteenth-century gowns still in existence is a sleeved sottana, preserved in the collections of the Museo di Palazzo Reale in Pisa. It is made of crimson velvet, and its large neckline confirms the date as the second half of the sixteenth century.

Another style of overgown that should be mentioned is the elegant cassock-type garment, with short sleeves and pockets to hold handkerchiefs or other small objects, known as a *zimarra*. It could be fastened down the front with rows of buttons and was occasionally completed with a train gathered in the back, while the high standing collar and the loose cut of the bodice echoed the lines of the flowing Turkish caftans. The rich zimarra worn by the lady portrayed by Michele Parrasio (1565, Genoa, Palazzo Rosso) is a good example. The zimarra is partially covering a similarly precious camora with a generous neckline, trimmed by lace. The sleeves of the camora are finished with small ruffles. The outfit is accessorized with the typical pearl necklace worn by Venetian noblewomen, and by yet another necklace from which dangles an important jewel. The woman wears one more long gold chain, which was called a *paternostro*. The woman wears pearl earrings and has the fashionable blonde hair gathered on the back of the head, with just a few curls hanging over her ears.

The Eastern feeling of the zimarre was enriched by other Eastern European influences, such as frogs made with silk braidings. Similarly inspired by Middle

East fashions were the very long *turche*, used even in bed to protect from night chills. In the trousseau of Anna Maria Sforza there is, in fact, mention of a "scarlet lined *turcha* to be used at night."

The *vestito*, also known under the name of *roba*, was an overgown worn over the camora and was consistently made with precious and heavy fabrics. It had a tight bodice that widened from the waist down, allowing the camora underneath to show from the central opening.

Sleeves became one of the main feature of a dress. At the beginning of the sixteenth century, they were very large from the shoulder to the elbow, then tight fitting to the wrist. The fifteenth-century custom of cutting and slashing the sleeves still continued but, around the mid-sixteenth century, the most visible features of the dress were the voluminous oversleeves called *brioni, spallini,* or, in Florence, *baragoni*. These oversleeves enriched the solemn silhouette of the camora and contributed to focusing the attention on the upper part of the body. In the detail of Agnolo Bronzino's portrait of Lucrezia Panciatichi (1540, Florence, Uffizi), the gathered, ruffled baragoni and the elaborate camisa have simple jewels, and the black detachable sleeves have been slashed in decorative cuts. The beads on the belt were probably used to keep aromatic paste. Ruffled, embroidered, or lace-trimmed *maneghetti* or *polsini* finish the cuffs, echoing, in the late sixteenth century, the similarly decorated ruff or circular ruff that encircled the head and closed the neckline.

Over the vestito an overgarment called the *robone* was often worn, the substitute for the fifteenth-century pellanda. Its main features were the imposing look and the large sleeves. It was comfortably lined with furs or heavy silk for warmth. "Spanish-style" roboni are mentioned in the inventory of Lucrezia Borgia's wardrobe: they were completely opened in the front, made with precious fabrics, and characterized by large patterns and standing collars. Among the furs used were ermine, squirrel, marten, and lynx, as in the robone worn by Livia da Porto-Thiene in her portrait painted by Veronese ("Countess Livia da Porto-Thiene and Her Daughter," 1551, The Walters Art Museum, Baltimore). The outer shell of the robone is made with the same fabrics of the camora she is also wearing; over her right arm is draped a hide with gold-covered muzzle. Her daughter, Portia, wears a green camora, and her hair is similarly parted in the middle and gathered on the back of the head.

In Venice, Cesare Vecellio, a relative of the more famous Titian, wrote in his fundamental book *Degli habiti antichi et moderni*—an essential collection of pictures that represents dresses from all over Italy, Europe, and the then-known world—that the *romane* was a sort of robone worn especially by courtesans. It was long and opened at the front to "leave the person free to do anything," writes Vecellio. It was also lined with rich fur, making it more comfortable for the women who spent time at their windows trying to catch clients. Nevertheless, in the same years, even "ambitious women" used to wear them in the privacy of their own homes, usually completed with a silk sash called a *posta*.

The more basic mantles, used in Italy since the end of the fifteenth century, were called *sbernie*, and they leave one arm free. The sbernie could also be lined with fur; in fact, capricious Isabella d'Este, described by the queen of Poland as the "inventor of all the most beautiful Italian fashions," on November 2, 1490, ordered a beautiful fur lining for an *albernia* (a corruption of the term *sbernia*) made of eighty of the best-quality and more beautiful furs. More modestly, in the inventories of Bianca Maria Sforza, wife of Maximilian I of Austria, appear several sbernie lined with cat fur, at the time a rare, although domestic, animal. Even more common were the simple mantles, draped around the body and sometimes also covering the head (in that case, especially in the south, called a *vescapo*). Women also wore very short mantles and short hooded capes.

A great innovation of the sixteenth century was the detachment of the upper bodice and the lower skirts of the dress. In Florence, the skirt, without the bodice, was called *baschigna*, a Spanish name. It was worn with the doublet called a *guibbone*—also known by the names of *investitura casso*, *diploide*, *corpetto*, and *corsetto*—which was another garment derived from the male wardrobe. It covered the bust and could be finished at the waist with little tabs or braiding, particularly in the last decades of the century. The guibbone normally had a standing collar and was generally closed in the front with a row of small buttons.

The portrait of Quintilia Fischeri by Federico Barocci (c. 1580, Washington, National Gallery) illustrates the evolution of late Renaissance fashion. The severity of the Counter-Reformist style is quite evident in the disappearance of the neckline and the presence of the pleated ruff (*gorgiera*) trimmed by the ruffs of the shirt that made it necessary to pin up the hair. The bust is squeezed inside a pointed and stiff corset, and the skirt, draped over the still moderate farthingale or *faldia*, took on a conical shape that exemplifies the transition between the Renaissance and Mannerist fashions with the magniloquent lines of the first half of the sixteenth century that become tightly encased into a geometric frame, thus canceling the natural shapes of the woman herself. This new look was completed by the large and lacy ruff that determined the stiff stances that characterize portraits from this time.

Underwear

Since the early Renaissance, the camisa or camicia played a key role in the composition of the dress of the aristocracy. Immaculate linen shirts, sometimes embroidered or trimmed with lace, discreetly peeked out from the necklines and the cuffs of the sleeves, demonstrating the personal cleanliness of the higher social classes. The number of *camise* mentioned in inventories is really surprising but is justified, as mentioned earlier, by the consideration that laundry was done so infrequently. There was no difference, except for the length, in the shape of men's and women's camise, also called *guardacore*. Both were made from very fine linen. The beauty and fineness of these shirts are clearly visible in many paintings, as is the beautiful embroidery that trims the borders. The needlework can be seen on the elegant embroidered shirts preserved at the Museo del Tessuto in Prato. The camisa was often made of thin, sheer fabric that covered the décolletage, frequently embroidered with blue cotton thread.

Camise were the articles of clothing most often made at home, and seamstresses, usually members of the family, could find inspiration for their embroidery from the many pattern books that began to be printed in the sixteenth century. Works such as *Esemplario di lavori* by Nicolò d' Aristotele detto Zoppino, *La vera perfettione del disegno di varie sorti di ricami* by Giovanni d'Ostaus, or Vavassore's *Corona di racammi* were extensively used both to embroider and to create the very first lace fabrics.

Every piece of clothing, whether silk or linen, was embroidered or decorated to make it beautiful. The smocks were often in plain view because, thanks to the numerous slits and slashes of the dresses *alla thodesca* (German-style) and to the wide necklines, more and more of the transparent linen of these shirts was exposed. Shirts were also the most common garment worn by the rich for sleeping. Aristocratic Venetian women were presented with a *camisa de oro*, a golden shirt, on their wedding day—another garment forbidden by sumptuary laws that were largely ignored.

The variety in the styles of shirts are demonstrated by the differences in their necklines. Some were higher necked with thin fabric decorated with thin gold chains, while others were made of simply gathered translucent linen, as seen in the portrait of Camilla Gonzaga by Parmigianino ("Camilla Gonzaga with Her Sons," 1527, Museo del Prado, Madrid).

In the third quarter of the sixteenth century, the simple ruffs that finished the necklines began to become a focal detail. Catherine de' Medici, when she became queen of France, asked to be joined at the court by a skilled Venetian craftsman charged with the very specific duty of preparing her ruffled collars. To obtain the hard, rigid fabric needed to complete this look, the ruffs were often starched and, to set the thick pleating, were treated with honey. The collars begin to assume the shape of the circular ruff in Spain around the mid-sixteenth century and were soon imported to other European countries, including Italy. They were especially used in the states where Spanish political influence was stronger, such as Genoa, Naples, and the southern regions.

A variation on the theme of the circular ruff is constituted by the collar known as the "Medici collar" after the second Italian queen of France, Maria de' Medici. These collars, which were also very popular in Venice in the late sixteenth century, stood opened as fans, framing the head, with their precious lace fabrics kept in place by a metallic structure.

In the second half of the sixteenth century, in order to obtain the desired sculpted silhouette, women wore over their camisa a corset called a *casso* or *busto*. The corset was often made of wood, or metal. Interestingly, in 1547 Venetian sumptuary legislators warned of the dangers of wearing corsets, calling them a harmful and dangerous fashion that sometimes "caused pregnant women to miscarry, and many others to die and their children to be born weak and crippled." Instrumental in the creation of the ideal silhouette of the late Renaissance was, along with the corset, the farthingale, in Italy called the *faldia*, *faldiglia*, or *verducato*. This garment was originally worn in Spain, where it was the *verdugado*, between 1470 and 1490. The skirt was worn over the farthingale in a conical shape. The Italian version went from the waist down and was made with a cotton fabric, stiffened by tow, wood, or metallic circles in order to support the skirt. Occasionally the faldia was also worn in plain view as a skirt: Paola Gonzaga counts some *faldiglie* in her wardrobe as early as 1500—for instance, a "damask faldia with black velvet hoops."

A more intimate piece of underwear was the panties, although they were very rarely mentioned in documents. One typically sixteenth-century curiosity was the *calzoncini alla galeotta*, a cross between underwear and outerwear that was politely called "invisible pants." Legend says that Lucrezia Borgia introduced them upon her arrival in Ferrara. Outrageous because they were very similar to men's *braghe*, calzoncini were mentioned in a gossipy letter addressed to Isabella d'Este Gonzaga, dated January 23, 1514, from Bernardino Prosperi, her fashion informer. He writes that these scandalous garments were so disliked by the government of the city of Ferrara that it had been decided to allow men to place their hands inside the skirts of women to verify if they were wearing this hated piece of underwear. This act carried significant risks, however, because if a man did try to establish that a woman was wearing the invisible pants and found that she was not, instead, he himself was to be condemned to have his "guilty" hand cut off! A very daring use of these "pants" was made by Venetian courtesans, who would wear them under dresses and flash them by lifting up their skirt. A very rare exemplar of calzoncini alla galeotta, dated to the second half of the sixteenth century and made with raw linen embroidered all over with blue thread with the motto "Voglio il core" ("I want your heart") is in the Textile Museum in Prato.

Other essential underwear items were hose, socks (calcetti), and the related strings (cintoli). Noblewomen sometimes wore hose made of fabrics that were dyed in the colors and with the emblems of their family. Alternatively, the hose could be richly embroidered with the family's coat of arms. In Bergamo in 1540, sumptuary laws forbade embroidered or decorated hose, allowing only the use of simple wool hose. Since they could not be washed very often, they were worn with short needle-made linen socks underneath. To make the hose as tight fitting as possible, they were fastened to the legs with cintoli.

Accessories

Benvenuto Cellini wrote in his autobiography that Duchess Eleonora di Toledo asked him to make "a gold belt decorated with precious stones and numerous beautiful little figures," and such a belt is, in fact, recorded in an inventory dated August 25, 1545. The preciousness of this accessory offers just a hint of the luxury and refinement of the objects that completed the toilette of a Renaissance gentildonna (noblewoman). No Renaissance outfit would be complete without a number of elegant accessories: from immaculate underwear to elegant slippers, from useful flea pelts to elaborate jewels, accessories finished the look of a proper lady.

The most necessary accessories were buttons, especially indispensable in obtaining the tight-fitting look of the time. Buttons could be flat, round, or tear shaped (peroli) and were made from precious materials such as silver, gold, mother-of-pearl, and amber. They could be carefully carved, and it was typical of the late Gothic period to carve heraldic symbols on them. Another accessory that played an essential role in the look of the dresses was the brooch, traditionally round and decorated with a large precious stone.

In the early Renaissance, because of the exquisite elegance of the hairstyles or coiffure, hats were not very popular. Older women covered their heads with severe veils secured with agucchie da pomella (pins), but thinner veils were largely preferred by younger women because they did not cover the elaborate hairstyles that were in fashion at the moment. At the beginning of the sixteenth century, hats began to become more common, although Anna Gonzaga, in her wardrobe's inventory made in 1582, counted just one velvet hat. Lucrezia Borgia in 1504 counted among her accessories ten very rich hats and, according to one of Isabella d' Este's fashion scouts, just one of them could have been worth more than 10,000 ducats. These hats were mostly made with rich velvet fabrics, as in the portrait of Giovanna d'Aragona by Raphael (1518, Paris, Louvre), and decorated with precious brooches with emblematic symbols, medals, or egrets. Less common were straw hats, although Cesare Vecellio remembers the broad-brimmed straw hats covered or lined with light silks worn by Florentine women.

Footwear and Other Accessories

Graceful slippers called *scarpette*—also known as *zibre* or *zibrette* in Milan, *cibre* in other cities in northern Italy, and *tapine* in the south—were used throughout Italy. These shoes had been worn since the late fourteenth century and were originally flat and often made of the same fabrics as the dress or in fine leather, meticulously decorated with carved or stamped motifs.

The early version of the slippers evolved into a new style called *pianelle*. These did not cover the heels and were characterized by a very tall wedge created by overlapping layers of cork covered in leather. They were created for the utilitarian purpose of protecting the feet from the mud and garbage in the unpaved streets, but they soon became an extravagant accessory. They could be covered in velvet, like the pair found in the Victoria and Albert Museum costume collection in London. They were also sometimes decorated with inlaid mother-of-pearl and named *calcagnini* or *calcagnetti*. These shoes eventually had soles as tall as twenty inches (50 cm). Such unsafe "heights" were severely prohibited by sumptuary magistrates, concerned about the dangers caused women falling over—falls that frequently caused miscarriages or other injuries. Nevertheless, with the usual persistence, Venetian women continued to wear these peculiarly styled footwear, prompting Friar Casola to exclaim that the calcagnini transformed "dwarves into giants."

The passion for this fashionable footwear was so widespread that in 1542 a *popolana*, a woman belonging to the lower social classes, included in her trousseau three pairs of leather calcagnini and a more precious pair made of velvet. The price of a pair of calcagnetti was high, but nevertheless Bianca Maria Sforza owned several pairs of slippers covered in velvet, damask, and embroidered satin. The eighty-two pairs of slippers recorded in the wardrobe of Lucrezia Borgia were made of gilded and painted leather. It was, in fact, in Spain that most of these shoes were produced, because of the widespread local availability of cork and leather, two essential materials used in shoemaking. A popular, and much more sensible, type of footwear was the leather ankle boot called *borzacchino*, favored for traveling thanks to its practical design.

Italian Renaissance ladies carried fans and sometimes purses and wore gloves. From rich ostrich fans to the simple duck foot–shaped fans called *ventole*, fans were already a useful and seductively intriguing accessory. They could be embroidered or made of cardboard with decoupaged motifs fixed simply on a stick. The fan itself could also be made in lace and could have ivory, wood, or tortoiseshell handles. In an inventory of the Medici family, there is a record of a fan decorated with diamonds and rubies and set with small figures, masks, wreaths, and other "*a grottesca*" patterns inspired by contemporary frescoed decorations. Popular all over in Italy, fans in Genoa were generally replaced by coquettish flower bouquets.

It was rare, but Renaissance women also carried purses. In the early Renaissance, examples were generally made of leather that were decorated with gold- or silver-embossed patterns. They were worn suspended from a simple leather belt around the woman's arm. In the sixteenth century, they became more elaborate and dangled from heavy gold chains used as belts. Lucrezia

Borgia owned three purses decorated with extensive gold embroidery in gold thread, trimmed with blue silk tassels. Women kept a few essential items in their purses, such as thread and a thimble made in silver or even gold (objects symbolic of women's virtues), along with ivory combs, small boxes for perfume, and needle cases filled with needles. A technological novelty—clocks that were small enough to fit inside a lady's purse, along with even tinier clocks, so small as to fit on a woman's ring—were created by a clockmaker from Vicenza. The new clocks did not take the place of solar clocks, but these too were becoming tiny. The always fashionable Isabella d' Este asked one of her fashion scouts to look for a "small solar clock" light and small enough to fit in her purse.

Gloves were meaningful accessories to Renaissance women and an essential complement of any elegant outfit. They could be made of silk or linen but were most often made of very fine leather (even fish skin). They were usually decorated with intricate embroidery and lined with fur such as squirrel, marten, or sable. The most popular were made in Milan and Padua, and in many Renaissance portraits, they are worn on just one hand and appear to be slashed (*stratagliati*) on the knuckles in order to let the precious stones of rings show. Characteristic of the period were perfumed gloves, scented with flowery or aromatic scents. Eleonora of Toledo received a pair of gloves in crimson silk scented by perfumer Ciano on December 20, 1549. Isabella d'Este Gonzaga was very skilled in preparing scented gloves, which she often gave away as gifts; on one occasion, she sent a pair to the queen of France, who used them only for special events. Made in Italy, scented gloves, writes Vecellio, were also worn by Neapolitan ladies when they chose not to wear Spanish gloves made in Valencia.

Women also wore fur stoles on their shoulders (Isabella d'Este Gonzaga in 1490 writes in one of her letters of requests to her fashion scouts a "sable with the head intact to be worn as a stole"). Alternatively, they might hold these in their hands instead of wearing them on their shoulders as was done by the vast majority of Renaissance ladies. Stoles were often made of squirrel and marten, which was considered emblematic of marital chastity and faithfulness and for this reason was traditionally given by husbands to their wives. The muzzle of the animal was usually covered by a gold mask studded with precious stones replacing the eyes. A good example of a jeweled muzzle, made in Venice around the mid-sixteenth century, is now in the collection of the Walters Art Gallery in Baltimore.

Besides their significance as a prized complement of feminine clothing, these furs also had a far less refined but very practical purpose. In an age in which personal hygiene was often neglected, human parasites were very common. The so-called *zebelini da man* (fur stole) had the unpleasant task of acting as a catalyst, attracting fleas and lice in order to free their owners of the pests. These were called fleapelts and were worn also in Britain and Germany.

Women also wore muffs to keep their hands warm. These were usually made with precious materials such as brocaded velvets, embroidered silks dotted with pearls and jewels, or valuable furs. The muffs were practical and luxurious accessories.

The hands of gentlewomen were also kept busy by handkerchiefs, fine and rather big linen squares decorated with embroidery, small lace trims, or fringes, as shown in the detail of the fresco by Ghirlandaio, "The Birth of the Baptist." In order to be really elegant, the handkerchief had to be immaculate. A large number of these accessories are mentioned in inventories and wedding trousseaux, and they were occasionally very expensive, made of silk and gold. The custom to trim these accessories with needle-made *punto in aria* lace was so common that in Milan in 1584, even sumptuary laws allowed the use of this pricy decoration, so long as it was not wider than a twentieth of a *brazo* (arm, an ancient measure) of silk.

Jewelry

Although Alessandra Macinghi Strozzi in a letter to her son Filippo dated August 31, 1463, advised him to be thrifty in collecting his wife's wardrobe, she recommended he let her decorate the dresses with pearls and other jewels. She explained that jewels were not just decorations but also family investments (it was common to use jewels or expensive clothing to repay debts). The most precious among the luxurious Renaissance accessories were, of course, the jewels themselves, and there was an amazing array of gems to choose from. Some were "practical" jewels, such as the golden *agugelli*, the *puntali* that finished the ribbons used to fasten the sleeves to the bodice of the dress, or the belts decorated with pearls and precious stones or buttons, but most were jewels used decoratively to add solemnity and value to a dress. Women also wore ancient carved stones and cameos.

Among the favorite precious materials were diamonds, mainly used to encircle a large precious colored stone. Typically Italian is the use of coral, particularly in the south. Pearls have special meaning because of their naturally elegant appearance and their symbolic meaning of chastity. A perfect pearl necklace was the gift of choice for Venetian brides, and for the same reason, pearls were absolutely forbidden to courtesans, who replaced them with mother-of-pearl, glass, or silver beads on their necklaces.

A very symbolic piece of jewelry is, of course, the ring. A ring was the customary gift for brides and, peeking from the slashes in gloves, many women wore other rings of precious stones. These were often chosen according to their attributed powers. Emeralds were frequently used in bridal jewelry because they were supposed to incline the wearer toward chastity and increase wealth; rubies were believed to have the power to reconcile discord and combat lust; and sapphires encouraged marital chastity. These rings were offered to the bride during the ceremony of the *anellamento*, an event that took place in the bride's home, where her future husband would place a ring on a finger believed to be directly connected to the heart by a vein. The most typical of these

Elisabetta, one of the main characters in the *Cortegiano* by Baldassarre Castiglione, the "bible" of the Renaissance, is wearing a very peculiar dress embellished by an embroidery in Cufic characters along the neckline. A scorpion dangles from the lenza on the forehead. © Scala / Art Resource, NY.

rings were of two joined hands with a meaningful inscription on the inside, like those preserved in the collections of the Bargello Museum in Florence and the Victoria and Albert Museum in London.

Valuable ornaments highlighted the complexity of early Renaissance hairstyles; jewels such as the *frenello*, a rather big jewel made with a central stone surrounded by pearls or diamonds, stand out on the neatly tied hairstyle, as in Piero della Francesca's "Battista Sforza, Duchess of Urbino" (c. 1465, Uffizi, Florence) in which the lady wears a dark camora with precious detachable sleeves, a jeweled string with pearls decorates her neck, and her hair is elaborately arranged in tresses bound with veils with a frenello towering on the top of the head.

The thin black line of the lenza, from which small pendants and curious symbols dangled, was in stark contrast to the white high forehead. A curious pendant was a scorpion on the forehead of Elisabetta Gonzaga, wife of Guidobaldo da Montefeltro.

Bocchette were jeweled necklaces and were echoed by the *paternostri*, precious belts composed by large gold beads inside which were aromatic pastes. From the paternostri also hung *pomanders*, gold or silver filigree spheres containing sponges imbued with perfumes or scented pastes.

There were many different styles of chain necklaces, both large and small, with various types of links. Brooches could be used to fasten mantles or to be pinned on velvet *barete*; often these jewels were inscribed or carved with a motto or a coat of arms. Cameos were also very popular, either ancient Roman or made with semiprecious stones carved in Classical styles.

Earrings were a novelty never before worn in Italy; in one of his *Diarii*, Marin Sanudo documents that at a party in the Sagredo Palace in Venice in 1525, a lady exhibited for the first time a pair of "small gold rings with a large pearl" as was in the customs of "Moorish women." Large and irregular pearls with elaborate gold frames were, in fact, favored, but sometimes rather curious shapes could allude to different and more practical uses. For instance, little jars or urns were used to keep aromatic pastes and diffuse perfumes in close proximity to the lady's nose. In Naples, earrings called *cercielli* or *cioccaglia* were very popular.

Hairstyles

Describing the evolution of Renaissance feminine hairstyles requires an analysis of the individual personalities and tastes of Renaissance ladies as expressed by their amazing variety of coiffures. Except for girls and unmarried young women, for whom it remained customary to have the hair either very simply arranged in a knot at the nape of the neck or simply left loose, early fifteenth-century women favored the vertical appearance of the late Gothic period. Women plucked or shaved their foreheads and temples, plucked their eyebrows, and drew their long hair back to the nape of the neck and arranged it in nets or tied it with bows or ribbons. Sometimes the hair was tucked under a cap.

More complicated arrangements appeared at the midpoint of the fifteenth century. For example, Battista Sforza has her hair drawn from the high plucked forehead and massed over the ears in tresses bound with a satin ribbon, the ends of which fall loose. A draped veil, with a jeweled pin, falls at the nape of her neck, and a gold and pearl jewel sits on the top of the head, held in place by a white ribbon.

A variation on this style is shown in Pollaiolo's "Portrait of a Woman" (c. 1470, Milan, Poldi Pezzoli Museum). From the plucked brow, her hair is swept back and arranged on a thick coil, twisted into a crown shape and bound with a small cord. Jewels and pearls shine on the top of her head, and the ears appear curiously covered by a translucent silk veil. The presence of pearls is very common, with a hairstyle in which many strings of pearls were twisted together and braided into the hair, called a *vespaio* (vespiary).

Foreign styles such as the *sella* (a saddle-shaped hairstyle) or the French *henin* were seldom worn and then always with moderation and decorum. Beatrice d'Este and Isabella d'Aragona are described taking a short walk in Milan on May 1, 1492, with their heads "arranged in the French style with the horn and long veils." The northern European–style hairstyle looked like horns (two thick, wired tresses) placed on top of the head and was a style vigorously opposed by Italian preachers, who saw in it a clear demonic allusion.

Typically northern Italian is the *coazzone*, a thick ponytail wrapped in the veil and decorated by ribbons or precious pearl strands. It was secured on

The duchess is wearing a dark camora with precious detachable sleeves. A jewelled band with pearls decorates her neck, and the hair is elaborately arranged in tresses bound with veils. A frenello towers on the top of the head. © Scala / Art Resource, NY.

the top of the head with the *girello* and decorated with a lenza, the thin black silk cord that crossed the forehead with hanging pendants. The coazzone was often used together with a bonnet made with luxurious materials such as gold, silver, or gilt copper.

Older women and more austere beauties often covered their heads with veils or, mainly in domestic situations, with the *asciugatoio*, a plain white cloth. In Venice, the white veil was reserved for unmarried girls, while married women preferred a black veil, which, as Vecellio wrote, "makes every woman more beautiful." Another characteristic Venetian style was the so-called *fongo* (mushroom) hairstyle, which had two tresses bound with ribbons and coiled in a donut shape on the top of the head. It was finished with a "fringe" of hair framing the face. This equivocal hairstyle was adopted by noblewomen and courtesans alike, and therefore the only indication of this woman's "profession" was in the beads of her necklace: courtesans did not have the characteristic light of pearls, and in fact pearls were forbidden to dubious women and allowed only for married ladies.

The dawn of the new century brought new hairstyles in which the classic proportions of the mature Renaissance led to more austere looks, ranging from

The imposing capigliara, a hairstyle realized by braiding together hair and fabric, dominates this portrait in which is also visible a zebellino da mane in the hands of the lady. © Erich Lessing / Art Resource, NY.

the very dignified hairstyle of Maddalena Doni portrayed by Raphael, to the neat coiffure of Venetian Paola Querini. A new style was made popular in 1509 by fashion icon Isabella d'Este Gonzaga, who launched the *capigliara*, a voluminous cross between a hairstyle and a headdress, worn with parted hair. It is possible to trace its origins back to the fifteenth-century *balzo*, another typical Italian headdress, customarily worn on the back of the head. The capigliara was made by braiding the hair with *postiches* (in Venice, human hair of different qualities was for sale at several stalls in St. Mark's Square), bows, ribbons, and flowers, and although Isabella tried at first to reserve the privilege to wear the new style to her closest friends, it was not long before the fashion spread all over northern Italy.

In the second half of the sixteenth century, fashion called for less voluminous coiffures, where the hair was kept close to the head. Flattering examples of these modest styles are those worn by Eleonora di Toledo and by Countess Lucia Albani Avogadro. These less flamboyant styles were made even more practical with the emergence of larger circular neck ruffs.

Very different solutions, on the contrary, were becoming quite popular in Venice in the last quarter of the sixteenth century: the whimsical taste of Venetian ladies restyled the two-horn coiffure. Even more curious was the completely unflattering hairdo where curls were piled up in a sort of tall pyramid shape on top of the head, in what can be described as an anticipation of the seventeenth-century *fontange* (fountain) style. The stiffness required to achieve this fountain-look was obtained by soaking the hair with egg whites, gum arabic, and resins.

Beauty Secrets

Despite the beliefs of Federigo Luigini, who in his book *Libro della bella donna* (1554) cursed the inventors of perfumes and cosmetics because, he said, "the work of God does not have to be altered in any way," Renaissance ladies who did not use the numerous beauty secrets circulating at the time were very rare. Outward beauty was thought to reflect inner nobility, and the great emphasis on the beauty of the face can help in explaining the large number of portable mirrors made of steel or glass that are mentioned in inventories of the time.

There were many recipes to help achieve the ideal fair complexion and preserve the bloom of the young body. Some of these beauty secrets were already known in Classical times, as Roman poet Ovid documented in his *Ars amandi*, a poetic compendium of love and seduction tips. In the fifteenth century, the passion for the Classical world helped in spreading the knowledge of Ovid's work, and thanks to the invention of the printing press, many of the formulas, previously orally handed down as women's secrets, were collected and published.

In the book of prescriptions written at the end of the fifteenth century by Caterina Sforza, called the *Experimenti*, her alchemical recipes for medical conditions number in the dozens. Detailed recipes "to make a woman beautiful" included recipes to regenerate the complexion, for example; to do this, women were to boil snakeskin in white wine. To aid hair growth, an infusion of snails and mallow was advised. To make hair blonder, the dye recipe included ingredients such as saffron, sulfur, and cinnabar. Sforza also concocted several different "beauty waters" to brighten the complexion and remove freckles.

Similar books—such as Leon Battista Alberti's *Amiria*; the *Notandissimi secreti dell'arte profumatoria* by Giovanventura Rossetti, published in Venice in 1560; or the *Secreti* by Isabella Cortese, also published in Venice in 1584—offered other useful recipes, using ingredients that nowadays appear mysterious, if not scary. Cortese declared to have discovered these secrets during her journeys in eastern Europe, and she promised to reveal how to remove facial spots and make a beautiful face "of fifteen years of age." To whiten the face, it was recommended that a woman mix rosewater, rock salt, cinnamon, powdered lily bulbs, egg whites, and milk—or, according to another "secret," lemon juice, white wine, breadcrumbs, and nutmeg—and then apply to the face. A more dangerous recipe recommended the use of ceruse, a substance very high in lead content and therefore extremely poisonous.

To remove hair from the forehead, in accordance with the fashion of the first half of the fifteenth century, tweezers were not always enough and depilatory creams made with caustic lime were used. These often led to severe burns to the skin. The dangerous ingredients of many of these "beauty" recipes were sometimes responsible for permanent damage and premature aging. Isabella d'Este, one of the most devout users of these beauty secrets, was described by poet Pietro Aretino (1492–1556) in 1534 as "dishonestly ugly and even more dishonestly made up." Baldassarre Castiglione, author of the previously mentioned *Cortegiano*, pitied Isabella and her "smeared face."

In every book of "secrets," there were numerous formulas to make blonde hair dyes. Blonde was the favored hair color, especially in Venice. Some of Caterina Sforza's recipes were herbally based *lisci* (lotions) that guaranteed amazing results and could, surprisingly enough, last for more than a month. Also, in the *Ornamenti delle donne*, published by Marinello in 1569, there are no less than twenty-six recipes to dye hair different shades, from red to ashblonde. Venetian ladies spent endless hours on their roof terraces dressed in outfits described with utmost precision by Vecellio in his 1598 book *Habiti antichi et moderni di tutte le parti del mondo* (*About dress from all over the world*): They wore a light *schiavonetto*, a sort of thin, embroidered linen tunic, and a straw hat without the crown covering their head, with their hair spread and hanging over the brim. In this way, they could keep their skin pale and make their hair pale as well. They constantly moistened their hair with the blonding formula, a home-made bleaching mixture of lemon juice, ammonia, and urine. The combined effect of the formula and the sun exposure bleached the hair to the signature Venetian blonde.

To keep the hair shiny, it was washed with surprisingly modern frequency; the wedding journey of Lucrezia Borgia from Rome to Ferrara was interrupted numerous times to allow the princess and her ladies-in-waiting to refresh their locks. Isabella d'Este, too, used her hair as an excuse for not having quickly answered a letter received from her husband: "Since I washed my head today, I spent so much time drying it, that the day just went by." To facilitate this long process, it was necessary to possess numerous hair towels, mentioned in large number in wedding trousseaux. If the hair was not very thick, it was enhanced by false hair that was sold at the markets in many different colors.

These beauty potions and tools, jars, and other paraphernalia could be placed in the *camera*, the bedroom, on a typically Renaissance piece of decorative furniture, the *restello*, essentially an elaborate carved, painted, and gilded shelf that could be completed with a glass mirror and pegs to hold clothing and other personal items such as combs. It first appeared in Venetian household inventories dating from the second half of the fifteenth century. The restelli became so luxurious in their decorations and in the materials used that a sumptuary law promulgated in 1488 prohibited them, but, as always, this law was largely ignored.

Even though the ladies of the upper classes took great care of their bodies with aromatic and scented baths with rose, jasmine, and other perfumed oils and the same oils were generously sprinkled on clothing, handkerchiefs, and gloves, generally speaking bathing was not a common practice. On the contrary, bathing was considered dangerous, for example, for pregnant women. Wearing clean linen shirts instead of taking many baths became synonymous with inner and outer cleanliness, decorum, and health. It was one of the duties of the proper woman to provide a large number of them in her wedding trousseaux and to take care of them.

Unpleasant smells were disguised by the use of various fragrant pastes, such as civet, Indian musk, and amber, which were kept in little jars attached to gold belts. Perfumes arrived in the West with the Crusaders; at that time, Venice began to import sandalwood, cloves, aloe, civet, Arabian incense, Egyptian balm, and iris powder—scents also generously used by men. Raw amber was preserved in golden pomanders (from the French *pomme d'ambre*), small globes of Arabic origin, made of gold or gilded silver and decorated with enamels, with a pierced surface that let out the scents of fragrant resins. It could be opened in two hemispherical pieces and had a ring attached, which was worn as pendant. A curiosity of the time was the *uccelletti di Cipro*, or "Cyprus birds," which were solid perfumes kept in small leather cases in the shape of tiny birds. These were used with sachets of lavender flowers, rose petals, and other blooms to scent linen chests and under mattresses.

To finish off the toilette, the whitened complexion was, on occasion, brightened with *pezzuola di Levante*: a small piece of cloth dyed with a decoction of rock alum, caustic lime, and brasil, an Asiatic plant (*Cesalpinia brasiliensis*) that produces a vivid red. It was used not only on the lips or cheeks; Venetian courtesans colored their nipples with it. The health and whiteness of the teeth were preserved, following the advice of poet Aretino, with a vigorous rubbing with a napkin in the morning and after the meals and a rinse with pure water; Isabella d'Este also used a secret recipe from the queen of Aragon to rinse her teeth and leave them fresh. Fingernails were shined with *polissoirs*, such as those sent in 1505 by Emilia Pia di Montefeltro to Isabella d'Este, described as "slivers of wood covered on one side with leather" to buff her nails.

It is interesting to notice that usually in these "books of secrets" also appear recipes, advice, and suggestions for medical treatments. A crucial concept of the time was, in fact, that of the communication between the inside and the outside of the body, explaining why cosmetic and hygiene appeared closely related. For example, it was thought that washing the hair with lye, besides making the hair strong, blond, and beautiful, could also strengthen the brain and the memory.

It is not surprising, then, that domestic medicine had a lot in common with beauty secrets and that medical recipes were mixed with beauty recommendations in books of secrets such as the *Secreti de reverendo donno Alessio Piemontese* (1555), in which more than 350 recipes of medicines were gathered, representing the translation for a wider public of medicines used by professionals. In these "medical" recipes, ingredients were largely the same ingredients used in beauty potions. They were often unusual, and occasionally dangerous: frogs and snakes mixed with herbs, plants, and seeds, some local, some imported, mixed and crushed in a mortar. Ginger, cinnamon, cloves, nutmeg, eggs, and butter cooked with liquids and distilled were all also used. The exoticism of ingredients coming from distant places seemed to suggest the promise of a miracle cure.

These luxuries, indulgences, and treatments were judged with extreme severity by clergymen, who saw them as decadent and conducive to promoting lust. Makeup and beauty practices were considered an alteration of the "image of God"; Alberti, in the third book of *Della famiglia*, blamed the use of ceruse, brasil, and rosewater for prematurely wrinkling the skin. Unfortunately, the disapproval of preachers and husbands alike did not have much effect on the women who used the books of secrets. These volumes were reprinted and published for decades.

RENAISSANCE MEN

The 1400s

Man or woman, the clothing worn by men of the fifteenth century shared numerous traits with feminine costume; analogous features include the slightly unbalanced gait, the extreme tightness of the clothing, and coats that were slightly longer at the back. Furthermore, the effeminate look of men was completed by the clean-shaven face, the rather long flowing hair to the shoulders, and the generous use of perfumes. These affectations outraged clergymen, who addressed these fops as *vanerelli sfacciati* (brazen faces).

A typical man's outfit in the early Renaissance was composed by pretty much the same articles of clothing as were worn in the fourteenth century. Although not often mentioned, very basic underwear made with linen fabric was worn, such as briefs (in a Milanese inventory, there are no less than ten pairs of them recorded) and shirts. The briefs, called either *sarabula* or *intercula*, were essentially short, while the camisa or shirt was significantly longer, sometimes reaching halfway down the thigh, and was cut very simply following a tunic or "T" pattern with a wide boat-neckline and a full sleeve. The immaculate linen of the shirts was frequently, though not always, elegantly trimmed with embroidery in black or dark blue thread, usually placed at the neckline and cuffs in the same way as on women's shirts. Around the end of the century, the basic pattern of the shirt evolved to a style with ruffle at the neck, along with small lace edgings or *pontine*, an anticipation of the late-sixteenth-century ruff.

Over their underwear, men wore a doublet or farsetto (also called *giubbetto* or *zuparello*) that, everywhere in Italy, was characteristically short. In Venice, the excessively short *gavardine* worn by the young noblemen were barely tolerated. In Florence, sumptuary officials proscribed the *farsettino al bellico*, a doublet that was just long enough to barely cover the belly button. And in Milan, this peculiar fashion almost caused a diplomatic incident when the ambassador of Maximilian of Hapsburg, who was charged with the duty of escorting Bianca Maria Sforza to marry the emperor, tactfully suggested that the Milanese gentlemen sent to accompany her would wear longer farsetti in order not to arouse any scandal in that country. The farsetto often had a V-neck in the front and was laced loosely with strings across the linen camisa. The sleeves could be very large at the elbows and much tighter at the wrist.

To cover the legs, men wore *calze solate*, or *calzebraghe*, which were tight-fitting footed hose made of wool with a central seam in the back. They could be very brightly colored, and it is a characteristic Italian Renaissance costume—but also of costume in northern Europe—to wear parti-colored hose. These were hose made with longitudinal stripes in two or more different colors, often taken from the family's coat of arms, or *scaccate*, or decorated with a checkered pattern: they could be called *divisate* or *strisciate*, meaning that they were made with pattern. It was fashionable to wear the hose as casually as possible, perhaps leaving them partially rolled down as in Antonio Pisanello's "Studies of Men Hanging" (c. 1435, New York, Frick Collection) or untied. In order for these hose to remain tight fitting, they needed to be tied with strings to the lower edge of the farsetto, where a half-moon shaped piece of linen was sewn to avoid tearing the fabric of the farsetto itself.

Because the farsetto style was so short and the hose could not completely cover the briefs or the tails of the shirt, a new fashion piece was developed called the codpiece or *braghetta*. This was destined to play a controversial role in Renaissance male fashion. This fabric triangle, originally designed with the simple and decent role of covering the groin area, over the years became a highly decorated piece of clothing with attributes of virility, in ways that, in the following century, became rather distasteful.

Over the farsetto or doublet, men wore an overgown or *giornea*. There were many different styles of giornee, but they were very similar to the women's style of cloaks, open at the sides with a scooped neck in the back. It had a bad reputation with churchmen because it was considered pretentious—quite often it was made of expensive fabrics and lined with precious furs, preferably in contrasting colors. Still, contemporary inventories show that not all giornee were flamboyant designs, and some were, in fact, simple linen garments. Often it was decorated with fringes and patterns cut into the fabric and usually the colors were inspired by the family's coat of arms.

The typical decoration of the giornea, also used in women's clothing, was the *incannucciata*, the skilled gathering of fabrics in a thickly pleated pattern, used especially to shape and emphasize the chest area, creating the ideal silhouette of the time. The gathered giornea was long enough to partially cover the hose. The silhouette was typically wide at the chest with a curved abdomen in the fifteen century. Some giornee were also embroidered, such as the three magnificent giornee ordered by Ludovico il Moro for himself and two of his courtiers, made with crimson-dyed satin and embroidered with pearls and jewels.

Other types of overgowns were the *mongino*, a sort of mantle made with simple wool cloth, and the *turca*, an Eastern-style overgown that was characteristically rich, such as that received by Galeazzo Visconti in 1489. This was a magnificent garment made with cloth of gold and lined with lynx fur.

A simple mantle was, however, the most common choice for most men, and it was used both by the aristocracy and the middle classes, and even by members of the clergy. It could be made in anything from simple wool cloth to the most luxurious fabrics, such as the one worn by the doge of Venice that was entirely in cloth of gold.

Among the legacy of Gothic fashions was the *guarnacca*, an overgown with characteristic hanging sleeves. A wonderful example is worn by the central figure of the "Journey of the Magi," painted by Benozzo Gozzoli in the Palazzo Medici-Riccardi in Florence (1459–1461). The *pellanda*, also known under the northern European name of *houppelande*, was worn by men as well as women. The male version was much shorter, reaching to the knees. It could sport all manners of sleeve shapes, including wide, funnel-shaped sleeves, open hanging sleeves, or slit "bagpipe" sleeves. The guarnacca and pellanda were often made of extremely expensive fabrics; Alberto d'Este wore a garment made with gold cloth and Niccolò III had a similar houppelande of the same fabric.

Older men in Florence wore the *lucco*, a wide, sleeveless, usually black mantle with open side seams made in silk for the summer and wool, lined with fur, for winter use. In winter, it was closed and ruffled at the neck. As the century progressed, the lucco was replaced by the *roba* or *robone*. This was a much more

"The Adoration of the Magi," Benozzo Gozzoli, 1459. The central figure wears a rich guarnacca lined with fur with long hanging sleeves. © Erich Lessing / Art Resource, NY.

imposing coat lined with furs that became widely popular in the sixteenth century. Despite this, Cosimo I stated in 1562 that the traditional lucco would be mandatory for public officials, doctors, and humanists who appreciated its traditional look.

The Venetian equivalent of the lucco was the *vesta*, a black overgown that, in the Republic of Venice, was mandatory clothing, worn by almost every man over the age of twenty-five. The vesta was long, made with wool for the winter or light silks for the summer, and was closed at the neck with metallic hooks and eyes. It could easily become a real overgown with a fur lining; as documented by contemporary paintings, favorite furs were lynx and marten.

It was quite easy to identify not only the social status of the man from his clothing but also his profession. In Pistoia, the *pretori* (judicial officials) wore a black velvet mantle, while in Pavia, jurists wore crimson-colored clothes. At the University of Bologna, as in Padua and in other similar institutions, different colors were used to identify the diverse courses of studies: a pavonazzo tunic was worn by the students of canonical law, crimson by the lawyers, black by the artists. A similar, and utopian, color code was in use in Venice, as has already been mentioned, but Venetians largely disregarded it.

The 1500s

In striking contrast with the ethereal and rather feminine appearance of the fifteenth-century man, masculine fashions of the early sixteenth century tended to build and emphasize a broad and horizontal figure, a trend imported from northern Europe and Spain. This style, which increasingly characterizes Italian costume, was an immediate consequence of the loss of autonomy and political independence of the Italian states, which were at the time losing their international status and political significance to emerging new nations such as France, Spain, and Germany. The battle of Pavia in 1525, at the end of which the king of France himself, Francis I, was taken prisoner and had to negotiate his freedom with emperor Charles V of Hapsburg, determined Spanish dominance in Italy, a dominance that bore a direct relationship with the emergence of pumpkin-shaped breeches and with the growing importance of wearing dark colors, especially black.

Many people were very much opposed to this fashion "invasion." Andrea Calmo (1510–1571), for example, in one of his letters published in Venice in 1543, complained about these styles as being so expensive that they could almost "ruin a family," while Castiglione repeatedly advised men to be moderate and to adapt and modify these foreign manners, making them more suitable to the Italian tastes. Castiglione recommended that the clothing of a proper courtier needed to be a way "to reveal how they want to appear, and how they want to be considered, dressing accordingly and acting in such a way that clothes can help him to be highly considered." In other words, costumes really contributed to create the image of the person wearing them. Although masculine elegance was as luxurious as that of women, the always moderate Castiglione suggested that the proper man needed to wear clothing "always suitable to his own condition," abstaining from expensive excesses.

The general trend of the mature Renaissance was toward the horizontal division of the clothes, with distinct garments for the upper and the lower parts of the body. Especially meaningful is the evolution that separated the late medieval and early Renaissance long hose into two different parts. The socks and the *cosciali* used to cover the thighs were ancestors of modern trousers or pants.

The main masculine garments were the camisa (shirt), the socks or pants, the overgowns, the *zimarra*, the *gabbano*, the *cappa*, the *tabarro*, and finally the *manto*.

The camisa was ruffled at the neck and cuffs, with the ruffles gathered by a short collar decorated with embroidery. The whiteness of the linen shirt was, more than ever, an essential Renaissance status symbol, and this immaculate background highlighted the embroidery that gradually became more and more elaborate. It was sometimes made of red or black silk and gold thread and was usually visible at the opening on the neck. The ruffles became denser and dramatically contrasted with the black doublet or giubbone, highlighting the white *stratagliate* sleeves *en pendant*, the breeches, and the outrageous codpiece peeking out from under the flaps of the doublet.

The circular ruff, or *gorgera*, which would not appear until the last quarter of the sixteenth century, soon became so relevant that it was a separate accessory fastened to the giubbone through strings or hooks. Occasionally it had to be supported by a hidden metallic structure.

The black doublet or giubbone eventually replaced the earlier farsetto. It was made of different materials, from the plain *fustagno* or wool cloth to various types of silk fabrics that could be decorated with the cuts and slashes seen on women's dresses (called *stratagliati* or *accoltellati*). These slashed patterns sometimes seemed to appear random, as in the portrait of Ottaviano Grimani, Procuratore di San Marco (1541, Kunsthistorisches Museum, Vienna). Alternately, the cuts were carefully arranged to create complex figures such as crosses, flowers, or zigzags. The quality of the materials and dyes revealed precious information about the wearer, pointing to his social status. The dress of Grimani reflected the masculine ideal of the time: His hair is parted in the middle and paired with an immaculate beard and moustache. His doublet reaches the waist, where it joins the puffed *braghe*. His codpiece is made in two different colors, and the outfit is completed by the black vesta worn open on the front.

The giubbone style of doublet often had a pointed waist and could be lined (*soppannato*). It kept its original stomach padding, maintaining the same silhouette as before. At the beginning of the sixteenth century, it had a very wide neckline, and in the second half of the century, the neck was covered with the camisa peeking out from underneath. The line of the collar had a long, thin slit closed by a high standing collar.

The *saio* or *saione* was a sixteenth-century sleeved garment with a marked waist and a longish skirt the went at least to midthigh and often reached the knees. It was buttoned or laced at the front. The saio was worn over the giubbone, and around 1520, it had short sleeves that let the giubbone sleeve show. It was sometimes made of two or more different colored or patterned fabrics.

Soled hose made way for breeches (*braghe* or *braghesse*), but regular hose were still used and were often brightly colored. Knitted hose that appeared around the end of the sixteenth century completely superseded woven hose because of their elasticity, which allowed for a tighter and more comfortable fit. Men continued to wear the scandalous *braghetta* or codpiece, which still had the practical purpose of connecting the two parts of the braghe. The codpiece's original triangular shape became more and more indecent when the design became more phallic with horn shapes and excessive padding added. The practicality of the fifteenth-century codpiece, that pocket of sometimes questionable taste, disappeared, and the accessory evolved into an icon of virility, to the point that the braghetta was even worn under armor. This is evident in the portrait of Guidobaldo della Rovere (1532, Galleria Palatina, Palazzo Pitti, Florence), where the noble warrior exhibits a rather short haircut and the characteristic Renaissance beard and is wearing body armor rounded at the chest, paired with a rather narrow waistline. The armor is embellished with a striped decoration, and on his head he wears a helmet. The lower part of the armor, however, is missing and his underclothes are clearly visible. He wears the usual breeches with the coordinated braghetta, the scandalous object of severe criticism by ladies and preachers alike.

The overgowns and robes really show off the fashions of the typical Renaissance man. These garments were large and ever-broadening garments called *robone* or *zimarra*. The robone was usually made of velvet or wool cloth and stopped at the knees. It was completely open at the front and had wide lapels (*revers*) that showed off the precious furs or silk lining. The similar, only slightly less grand, zimarra was usually made with very expensive and showy fabrics and was especially suitable to be used inside the house, because it was much more comfortable. It was inspired, as was the feminine version, by the loose Turkish caftan. It was much different from the tailored male dresses used outside the home and was also completely open at the front and could be lined with furs. The sleeves of the zimarra were short, reaching only the elbow and letting the sleeves of the giubbone underneath show through. These were carefully made in contrasting colors and fabrics. A further variation on the theme of the robone is the *pretina*, which was long and buttoned up to the waist, similar to the dress of contemporary priests.

The mantle was the overgown of choice of the aristocracy. It was made of velvet or wool cloth and was an indispensable garment, along with the traditional lucco. In Florence, for example, in order to participate in the political life of the city, men had to wear either a lucco or a mantle to enter the city council. A shorter jacket called a *cappe* was like a cloak but barely reached the hips. This garment was commonly worn almost everywhere in Europe and in the north of Italy was called *bohemio* or *tudesco*. It could be completed with fake ornamental sleeves. In Italy, the cappe was considered proper dress for men-at-arms and was characteristically decorated with braid trimmings that were positioned to define the essential lines of the body. These expensive decorations were forbidden by sumptuary laws everywhere in Italy but were nevertheless used and are mentioned in numerous inventories.

In the second half of the century, clothes began to become more "specialized," especially regarding traveling clothes, such as the felted wool mantles called *feltri* that were useful for protecting people from the wind and cold. Another example, the *sanrocchini*, was a waterproof mantle made with waxed cloth.

Furs were a typical Renaissance status symbol. These were generally not worn as garments in themselves but were rather used as a lining of most winter clothes, such as the guarnacca, which was characterized by long hanging sleeves. Children also wore lynx-lined clothing for warmth. Among the favorite furs were lynx, which was appreciated for its fullness, sable, or squirrel. More modest linings were made of lamb hides.

The more flamboyant styles seen at the beginning of the century progressively became more moderate and austere, which reflected the political, economic, and religious events of the time rather than strictly personal tastes. The influence of Mannerism and especially the sobering effects of the Council of Trent were manifested by the predominance of less showy colors in the last two decades of the century. The men became much more masculine as the century progressed, with a more rigid silhouette. The giubbone became more padded than ever, especially on the stomach because of the influence of the French *panseron*, which was closed by a long row of buttons. The standing collar became very high and was almost covered by the rigid neck ruff. Men's breeches became longer and were less puffy, although they were padded in the thighs still to produce larger looking "muscles." The *braghesse alla Sivigliana* were worn, filled with tow (fiber dust) or sawdust in order to obtain the fashionable roundness.

Accessories

The accessories used by men to complement their outfits in the early Renaissance were not very different from those used in the fourteenth century. Heads were mainly covered by hoods, often draped and arranged with such creativity as to draw harsh criticism from the always present moral scourge, Bernardino da Siena: he reproved the capricious styles devised by youngsters to wear them, some so whimsical that they bore a strong resemblance with the Eastern turbans worn by merchants coming to such Italian cities as Venice, Florence, and Milan for commercial exchange. Hoods could be separate accessories or part of an overgown, such as a houppelande or pellanda. A good example of the evolution of the late medieval hood is the *mazzocchio* or *cappuccio alla Fiorentina* (Florentine hood). According to historian Benedetto Varchi, this hood was, in 1527, made from a stuffed cloth circle that encircled the head and a double band of the same cloth that was draped over the right shoulder and could also serve as a scarf to wind around the neck.

The *berretta* is another characteristic headwear style the fifteenth century. Its most common shape was that of a plain crown without a brim, a typical Italian fashion that was highly criticized elsewhere in Europe, especially in France. It was most often made of velvet, and among the fashionable colors were first of all red, followed by black, then white or blue. A variation on the berretta was the *berretta civile*, which was used by almost every man at the time. This was a trapezoidal hat that was considered suitable for military men and public officials and was used to advertise the man's leading and ruling role. It became wider as it got taller. A slightly shorter version of this berretta was the characteristic headwear worn by medical doctors, lawyers, and merchants. It had a band under which these busy men kept their notes, in a custom that continued until the twentieth century. The use of berretta to complement the clothing continued in the sixteenth century when, in keeping with the humanistic climate, the hats were often decorated with expensive brooches, antique cameos, or carved semiprecious stones representing Classical mythological episodes or characters.

Less common, but still occasionally worn, was the *cappello* hat. It had a pointed or rounded crown and was made either of silk or the fashionable beaver felt imported from the New World (in this case, Canada). Straw hats were also rarely worn by wealthy men, though they were popular with those in the lower social classes. When richer people did wear straw hats, they were made with extra fine, almost translucent, straw, mostly coming from Cremona and, later, from Tuscany, where Cosimo I encouraged the production of such hats.

In the late Renaissance, hats continued to be worn, but they were more made of plain or patterned velvets, sometimes decorated with jewels. Masculine bonnets or *cuffie*, very much used in the Middle Ages, were still worn for ceremonial dress, for example, by the doge of Venice. Older men favored the new knitted cuffie because they were much more elastic. Nightcaps were also popular and were mentioned in almost every personal inventory. These, of course, were worn only indoors.

Men also carried handkerchiefs. These were originally designed for use when cleaning or blowing noses, but as with the feminine version, handkerchiefs—initially very simple and plain, white linen squares—became much more elaborately embroidered and decorated over time. They were eventually made of expensive silk fabrics and often intricately embroidered with silk threads. In the sixteenth century, in fact, embroidered handkerchiefs, decorated by four small tassels at the corners, were the common gift from a wife to her husband.

Gloves represented a meaningful detail in Renaissance fashion. They were usually made of soft suede, but they could also be made of silk or other cloth. Gloves were sometimes embroidered in silk thread, but gold or silver threads were sometimes used for the most elaborate ones. Typical Renaissance decorations were the cuts and slashes that echoed those on the clothes. For ceremonial occasions, and especially balls, it was customary to wear extra-fine gloves. Those made in Milan were especially popular and desirable.

This accessory often carried special meaning or was the focus of peculiar traditions. For example, in Naples, students, on the day of their graduation, offered the archbishop of Naples two pairs of gloves. A more specialized and

The detail of the glove documents the custom to slash and cut not only fabrics, but also leather. © Erich Lessing / Art Resource, NY.

practical type of glove was the falconer glove, used since the early Middle Ages to hunt with the help of the falcon. It was made of particularly strong and thick leather for one hand only, had a very wide embroidered cuff, and was often decorated with braid and trim. To walk with a falcon on one's hand protected with this accessory was highly fashionable.

Belts were not considered an especially important or showy accessory. They were most often simple leather bands or plain silk strings from which dangled the *scarsella*, a small pouch that substituted for the pockets that were missing in the garments themselves. In the sixteenth century, *poste,* or silk sashes, were more popular than belts.

Footwear in the early Renaissance was basically nonexistent, as there was no real need for proper shoes because soled hose were still widely used. However, with the decline of soled hose and the appearance of brache, shoes became important accessories. In the late fifteenth century, fashionable shoes had a rather pointed toe, but they became wider at the toe by the beginning of the sixteenth century. Shoes in Italy were generally made of velvet or silk fabrics, or of leather, which was preferred by youngsters. They particularly liked the shoes made of red leather from Spain that were sometimes decorated by the same slashes that were all the rage on clothes. Tall leather boots appeared in the second half of the sixteenth century and seem to have had Spanish origins.

Renaissance men were not ashamed to wear jewelry and bought it often, justifying their purchases with the fact that it could be readily converted into cash if necessary. The majority of these expensive items were, in one way or other, connected with the ancient Classical world. Cameos, medals, rings, and brooches were usually decorated with figures of Greek or Roman gods and goddesses or other similar themes. They were often even authentic Roman relics. Chains for the neck were very much in fashion at the height of Renaissance fashion splendor midway through the sixteenth century. These were often large, heavy necklaces; if one chain was considered an appropriate masculine adornment, the custom of wearing more than one neck chain was considered reprehensible. The medieval beliefs that precious stones had magic powers were still popular, and espe-

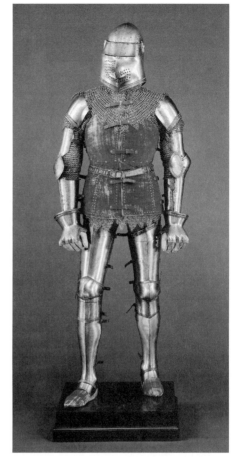

A suit of armor, ca. 1400. © The Metropolitan Museum of Art / Art Resource, NY.

cially beautiful or unusually large jewels were even given names. The ruby was called ''the sign of the Caduceus,'' and the large diamonds with three dangling pearls were called ''the Wolf.''

In both the fifteenth and sixteenth centuries, men often indulged in wearing perfumes and partook in beauty treatments. Galeazzo Maria Sforza, one of the vainest men of his time, was known to appear with blonde wavy hair one day and black straight hair the next; he greatly appreciated precious oriental perfumes and scented baths and even had manicures. Men's hairstyles in the late fifteenth century were rather long, and they were clean shaven. In the following century, men became much more masculine and consequently their hair was cut short, and they grew beards and moustaches that were well groomed.

Given the deficiencies in personal hygiene, perfume continued to be very much appreciated (and necessary) in the late Renaissance. Accessories containing perfumed pastes were popular, such as the Cyprus birds, which were bird-shaped leather bags that could be kept in the *scarselle*.

Some men wore eyeglasses during the Renaissance, as is in evidence in a fresco painted by Tomaso da Modena in 1352 in the chapter room of the episcopal seminary of Treviso. From this time, glasses for both near- and far-sighted men were quite common. Renaissance spectacle frames were recovered in 1982 in the excavations in Via de' Castellani and are now in the Archaeological Museum in Florence.

Finally, men started to carry pocket watches with them everywhere. These little clocks were new to men of the Renaissance. They, as did women, also wore watches attached to rings they wore on their fingers.

Knights and Armor

After the thirteenth century, military gear underwent considerable technical and form transformations that were the obvious consequences of the evolution in the art of war. New weaponry, at first, increased the need for armor in order to efficiently protect the knights, but within a few decades, the same armaments caused a decline in the demand for armor for much the same reason. At that point, cannons and harquebus were so powerful that the old-style armor was powerless to stop their shots.

The Renaissance knight rode in the saddle of a harnessed and armored horse, completely covered by his iron armor, decorated by his insignias and creating an

The clean lines of this armor are partially covered by the red giornea opened at the sides. © Erich Lessing / Art Resource, NY.

imposing figure. There were great differences between the armor of regular soldiers and that of noblemen, but some elements were essential gear of all military men, such as the *cuoietto*, the *corsaletto* or body armor, the helmet, the round shield called a *rotella*, and the sword.

The cuoietto was the typical garment of men of arms, used for hunting or during military campaigns. It was much appreciated for its practicality and for the protection it offered to the wearer from sword thrusts and even from bullets—although for that purpose, the corsaletto was much more appropriate. The cuoietto was made of leather, hence the Italian name (from *cuoio*, leather), but whereas simple soldiers or mercenaries could afford only rough goat leather, noblemen wore refined cuoietti made with the finest materials, such as suede. These were decorated with elaborate embroidery. A cuoietto preserved in the collections of the Centro Studi del Tessuto e del Costume di Palazzo Mocenigo in Venice from the end of the sixteenth century is made of beige suede, embroidered in green silk and silver thread. It is open at the sides but could be closed by threading a leather string through eyelets. A white leather band prevented the shirt from coming out the side openings. It was closed down the front with wooden buttons and was lined with beige taffeta.

Another marvelous leather cuoietto example was worn by the Duke of Savoy returning from his military expedition to Hungary. It was buttoned down the front with gold buttons and worn over a satin giubbone with sleeves decorated with ornamental slashes. Much rarer were fabric-made cuoietti, but these were mainly used for ceremonial occasions and not meant to protect the wearer. The heavily padded garment had a pointed waist, with small flaps on the shoulders.

The corsaletto was armor made of steel plates that covered the upper part of the body. For simple soldiers, these were their only protection, while wealthier men had accessories such as the *bracciali*, jointed with pivots, to cover the arms. From the lower edge of the corsaletto, there was a thick *sottana*, made of knitted fabric that covered the junctions with the cosciali, worn to guard the upper legs. These were jointed to the *schinieri* for the protection of the lower part of the legs.

Early Renaissance examples of armor are easily distinguishable by their sleek and clean lines, interrupted only by the stylized joints of the elbows and knees. Great efforts were, in fact, made to produce armor that could be at the same time both functional and aesthetically pleasing, and examples are still preserved in numerous Italian museums and collections. For the most important, wealthy clients, specialized craftsmen created customized armor, much like a tailor would create custom-fitted suits. There was also the option, though, of simply choosing a set of armor from ready-made pieces, usually produced in a semi-industrial fashion. These came in three sizes. All the pieces could be marked with the maker's logo and custom decorated with the wearer's mottos or insignias.

Renaissance knights also, of course, wore helmets. The typical helmet of the late fifteenth and sixteenth centuries was shaped like a sparrow's beak, pointed at the mouth and nose. It had a protective visor that was usually creatively enriched with symbolic decorations, such as a fox, the classic symbol of cunning; a bear, synonymous with strength; or a wolf, to indicate courage. From the lower border of the helmet hung the *goletta* made of knit metallic fabric that protected the neck. The top of the helmet was often decorated with a plumed crest with chiseled or gilded insignia.

Through the fifteenth and sixteenth centuries, Milan boasted an absolute supremacy in the production technology of armor, both in terms of protection and beauty. Workshops such as the Modroni, Merate, and Missaglia were all held in very high esteem by the Duke of Milan. The superiority and above-average standards of the Milanese armor were proudly shown off on the occasion of the wedding of Lodovico il Moro to Beatrice, when along the via degli Armorari, the artisans exhibited their works by putting fully armored knight models outside their shops. When the ceremonial procession passed along that street, it seemed that a long line of warriors with closed helmets was waiting to pay homage to the sovereign on his wedding day, but these were really early advertising models.

Sixteenth-century armor does not show any peculiar technical advancements in comparison to that of the previous century. The attention was instead focused on the embellishment of the armor, characterized by a strong rounded chest and decorated with intricate *niello* and chiseled patterns, often at least partially gilded, that were produced by skilled craftsmen who were different from those who actually made the armor. The armor was especially elaborate for tournaments, where braiding or colored motifs were painted in black, blue, or dark red. The contrast between the shiny and matte iron created beautiful decorative patterns. While the original use of armor was becoming less and less important, it became fashionable to wear at least one element of armor even in civilian life. Men wore swords, for example, in daily life and even at balls, where they were more of a hindrance.

CHILDREN OF THE RENAISSANCE

Being a child in the Renaissance must have been exceedingly uncomfortable. Beginning at birth, newborns were tightly and completely wrapped in swaddling clothes, leaving just the head and occasionally the tips of the fingers free. Their feet were covered, but they could move inside the fabric. The custom of swaddling newborns continued up to one year of age and was justified by the theory that the body of the newborn was too soft and needed protection and a strong structure (the tight swaddling clothes) to support it. Moreover, it was believed that the wrapping practice helped the legs to grow strong and straight.

There are several examples given paintings of the time, mostly representing the Nativity, in which both the patterns used in the swaddling and how fancy the swaddling clothes themselves were are plainly visible. If the poor could not afford much more than plain cotton swaddling clothes, for the higher social classes these fabrics were intricately embroidered or made with fabrics decorated in woven patterns, such as *diamantine*, a fabric characterized by a diamond pattern, or alternatively with a checkered pattern like those portrayed in the detail of the "Birth of the Virgin" painted by Bartolomeo Vivarini in the *Misericordia Triptych* (1473, Venice, Church of Santa Maria Formosa). In the painting, both the geometric patterned swaddling clothes and the small pouch that let the child's feet move a little are clearly identifiable. Authentic swaddling clothes displayed at the Victoria and Albert Museum of Childhood in London are trimmed with cutwork, needle lace, and embroidery.

In other cases, the thin linen swaddling clothes were covered by embroidered stripes in which gold, silver, and silk threads created intricate patterns, highlighted with pearls and other jewels. In 1493, a damsel of the court of Ludovico il Moro in Milan recalled that his son was "covered in cloth of gold, in a very elegant gilded cradle with four columns and a canopy in blue silk and gold braiding." Among all these luxuries, however, it does not seem that babies were any happier. Just a glance at their expressions tells the truth about the discomfort they felt inside these golden traps!

After the swaddling clothes were removed, they were replaced for both boys and girls by the same kinds of clothing. The inventories suggest that children wore giornee or *giorneuzze* (small giornee), cloaks that opened at the sides, with a scooped neck in the back. They were made of brightly colored fabrics. It seems, in fact, that the simpler *guarnelli*, made of a darker and rougher fabric, were instead reserved for domestic situations.

A sort of transition dress was the *ungarina*, usually worn by boys between age two and four; the name refers to the heavy braiding decorations, very common in clothing of eastern European countries. This was a bell-shaped dress that reached the ankles, closed in the front with frogs, and was made with luxurious fabrics. It allowed for some much needed freedom of movement.

Even in the Renaissance, parents prided themselves on elegantly dressing their children for ceremonial occasions. The always watchful clerics complained about

> how much time parents do spend in combing their hair, and, in the case of girls, even dyeing them blond or curling them. How much money is spent embroidering little hats, sewing silver braiding on small capes and on painted leather shoes. (R. Levi Pisetzky, in *Costume e la moda nella societá Italiana*, 1978)

At about age 5, children began to wear mainly miniaturized versions of their parents' style of dress. Little boys wore farsetti and giubboni and soled hose, while girls wore corsets and skirts like their mothers. Boys' breeches were open at the back to help them in their toilet training and help avoid accidents.

Adult-style clothing was worn by young Lunardo Pesaro in the "Pala Pesaro" painted by Titian between 1519 and 1526. He is represented wearing a doublet called a *saion*, with large sleeves that were very wide at the elbow. The doublet is finished with a short embroidered stand collar.

A remarkably comprehensive selection of children's clothing is offered in the portrait painted by Bernardino Licinio (1535, Rome, Galleria Borghese). His brother's family is shown, with each of the five children represented in the painting offering an example of the traditional dress considered suitable for their specific age. The baby wears elegantly gathered swaddling clothes, the oldest son wears the giubbone, and the little girl wears the petite camora, while another of the boys wears the velvet berretta trimmed with a feather. The last of the boys wears a simpler dress and natural loose hairstyle; every possibility in dress is represented. A white *gamurrino* is worn by little Bia de' Medici in what appears a perfect replica of a lady's outfit, complete with a pearl necklace, gold chain, and gold belt; the only detail hinting at her age is the hairstyle, which is cut short, parted in the middle, and combed behind the ears.

Girls were always dressed to imitate their mothers, wearing exact replicas of dresses worn by their mothers and accessorized in the exact same ways. Often the only difference was in the hairstyles, which differed depending on the age of the girl but were often shorter than their mother's. Girls would be adorned in precious jewelry or garlands of gold and wore pearls or, especially appropriate for girls, coral accessories. Coral is often seen in Renaissance art on the children in a painting. The shape of the coral tree was considered to be similar to a child's hand and therefore was thought to protect the child from evil forces and immunize them from poisons.

The evolution of fashion toward the end of the sixteenth century is shown by the children of the Cuccina family in Veronese's "Presentation of the Cuccina Family to the Virgin" (c. 1572, Dresden, Gemaldegalerie). The stiff style worn by adults is also worn by the children, who all wear smaller replicas of the adults' outfits. The boys wear pointed giubboni and puffy breeches made with slashed fabrics. These garments give away the provincial origin of the family as coming from Bergamo, a city that was under the Venetian domination. The oldest daughter's dress matches in every detail that of her mother, down to the corset that she had to wear underneath the camora and the standing fanlike collar made with precious needle lace.

B. Licinio, Portrait of a family shows typical clothing of women, men, and children of the Renaissance. © Scala / Art Resource, NY.

COMMON CLOTHING FOR COMMON PEOPLE

Men and women of the lower classes did not share the fashion concerns of the rich. Their priorities were mainly practical: clothing had to actually cover and protect the body—and sometimes even these basic needs were not fulfilled. The really poor people quite often could not afford to wear a real dress and wore nothing more than a covering made of sackcloth and a pair of tattered brache, as shown in the detail of the "Miraculous Healing of the Daughter of Benvegnudo da S. Polo" by Giovanni Mansueti (c. 1505, Venice, Gallerie dell'Accademia). The number of these poor people was very high in Italy, as a document dated 1505 shows: In the Venetian Republic, there was a growing concern about the rising population of "beggars, men and women ... dressed with sackcloth that wander about the city." In an effort to halt the growth of this phenomenon, it was ordered that every "approved" poor person needed to exhibit a license sewn in plain view on their clothing. Paintings by Caravaggio (c. 1571–1610) often show common people in less than flattering situations, wearing common clothes—certainly not in the ideal of the other Renaissance painters.

Male farmworkers and peasants did not wear much, either. They just barely covered and protected themselves from the elements, usually weating only pants and shirts (brache and camise) that were essentially articles of underwear for the rich. These were primary garments, often tied at the waist with a simple leather belt in order to have freedom of movement during the hard work in the fields.

The peasants' very few articles of clothing were used for months at a time and discarded only when torn into pieces. During holidays and market days, men dressed up their outfits with small ruffs called *lattughe* placed at the neck of the camisa, a doublet, and a straw hat. Similarly, the women wore a long dress that reached the feet and was made of simple wool cloth. These dresses were trimmed at the lower hem with an embroidered velvet band. Over this dress women may have worn a black overgown, with a silk sash. They wore white shoes, multicolored ribbons in the hair, and a necklace made with coral or silver beads. Country folk coming to Venice from other areas of the mainland were easily recognizable by their straw hats that were decorated with colored feathers.

Although real luxuries were exceedingly rare among country people, they were not unheard of, and in 1525 in Bologna, authorities felt the need to create a sumptuary law to forbid peasants from using gold cloth or expensive dyes such as the red *grana*, even if used only in minor dress details. Jewels were restricted, too: farmer's brides could not "wear any sort of gold ornament worth more than three *bolognini* or silver buttons weighing more than eight ounces." In 1574, rural women were allowed to wear coral necklaces, while gold necklaces and other gold accessories (e.g., buttons) or pieces of jewelry were still forbidden.

Craftsmen who lived in the cities followed the trends in upper-class clothing styles, but their clothing styles did not evolve with the same velocity. The fabrics used were also much simpler, rough even, and dyed in dark and sober shades. Commoners and craftsmen dressed not very differently from peasants: a smock, a pair of brache, and a doublet or, during the winter season, the warmer *gonnella*. Rough-soled hose completed their outfits. Porters wore a *gabbana* that reached to the knees and was tied with a rope, tattered hose, and coarse shoes; when they had to carry heavy loads, they would cover their head and shoulders with a rough sackcloth worn as a hood.

Common women wore dresses similar to those of their rich counterparts, but they too had to use strong and hard-wearing fabrics, usually dyed in dark colors. The use of bright colors was very rare in the lower classes because of the high cost of the dyes. Women, over the camisa, wore a simple dress that had two belts, one placed under the breasts and the other around the waist. The *cioppetta* was the overgown and had detachable sleeves fastened to the dress with fabric ribbons. An ample mantle protected both men and women from bad weather.

Despite the sumptuary laws applied to the lower classes, which often dictated the colors they could wear and were intended to curb the lavish spending on decorated fabrics, women still strove to embellish their clothes, and appreciable results were achieved with imitation jewelry such as mother-of-pearl bead necklaces. In some cities, Brescia, for example, chroniclers of the time observed that, despite sumptuary laws, blacksmiths, shoemakers, and grocers

> did cover their wives in crimson velvets, silks and damasks ... the sleeves of their dresses were very large and lined with the same furs used by the aristocracy; the heads of those commoners did shine with pearls and rich crowns.... [Even] shoemaker's wives were wearing dresses in cloth of gold and embroidered with pearls. (R. Levi Pisetzky, in *Costume e la moda nella societá Italiana*, 1978)

The situation was the same in Florence, where, despite laws of 1546 and 1570 forbidding the use of all sorts of embroidery or decorations in clothing, women still wore these extravagant clothes.

Crimson, though banned by law for commoners and peasants, was found in another kind of clothing worn by the lower classes: uniforms. Servants in noble

ORPHANS

Other members of the lower and less fortunate social classes that could be easily identified from their clothing were the orphans: In Venice during the Renaissance, numerous were the institutions created especially to take care of these unlucky children, and guests of the different orphanages were recognizable from the colors of their clothes. Both girls and boys wore a long tunic with a *grembiale* over it, the color of which indicated the institution where they lived: white for the Ospedale di Santi Giovanni e Paolo, red for the Pietà, blue for the Incurabili. Girls covered their hair with a traditional white *fazzuolo*, while boys had a small cap (*berretta*).

or rich households were considered in a very lucky position indeed, because they were usually very well dressed. For example, in the palace of the rich merchant Datini in Florence, several servants were hired for a ceremonial occasion, and each was given a brand-new uniform composed of a scarlet tunic and trousers. They could also quite often benefit from the donations of secondhand clothing from their masters. The Marchioness of Ferrara customarily gave her used (*mezzo frusto*) clothing to her maids, who were very happy about the gifts. Another tradition was to provide a few articles of clothing to young girls working in the household as servants in order to help them to enrich their modest dowries; in the family of an ancestor of Galileo, according to a document dated 1480, the master of the house was mandated "by the terms of the contract" to provide each of his young maids with a *cioppa monachina* (a brownish-colored dress) and a green *gamura* to go in their dowries.

A mixture between religious clothing and the clothing used by commoners was, in Venice, the dress of the *pizzocchere*, derelict widows or indigent women. They wore dark nunlike dresses with the train tucked under the belt, with a *nizioletto*, a sort of half-shawl, covering their heads.

Prostitutes or courtesans were an embarrassing presence in many Italian cities of the time and played an unclear social role. Although their activities usually afforded them more than decent means, sumptuary laws worked against them, forbidding—with the usual mixed results—status symbols such as luxurious clothing and valuable jewels. Clothing and accessories were used to identify these women. In Milan in 1515, courtesans had to wear a white cape on the head and a red sash. In other cities, such as Lucca and Florence, they wore black capes. In Florence in 1546, Cosimo I de' Medici ordered that all prostitutes wear a yellow ribbon in plain view on their clothes. In Venice, courtesans and prostitutes had to wear a yellow headscarf, and jewels—especially pearl necklaces, the symbol of the Venetian noblewoman—were forbidden to them.

RELIGIOUS CLOTHING

The progressive codification and institutionalization of ecclesiastical powers, both in the strictly religious and in the political and economic senses, had a direct consequence on the types of religious clothing, thus reflecting the rather limited willingness of the Roman Catholic Church when faced with innovations. Clothing worn by the regular clergy was set by the guidelines of the provincial synod of Milan in 1311. It was decreed that every ecclesiastic had to wear the costume of the religious order to which he belonged, without any decoration, and the tonsure, thus clearly revealing his position.

This rule was not always strictly followed, and in fact there were numerous infractions recorded in many documents showing how these men disregarded the rules. One of the most revealing—because it sheds a different light on the lives of some of these religious men—is found among the documents of the trial against a certain Suor Deodata, a nun in the monastery of San Iseppo in Venice. In 1571, this nun was accused of having a less-than-proper relationship with some friars, her confessor being among them, and she was accused of giving them gifts such as embroidered surplices, handkerchiefs, shirts, and collars and especially magnificent hats embroidered in silk and gold!

The clothing details in the bills of sale for the wardrobes of the inquisitors were also very intriguing. There is mention of garments such as the *surpellicium* and the *scapularius*. The first was a silk or linen mantle that in the Middle Ages was always lined with some kind of fur; during the course of the Renaissance, the fur disappeared, leaving just the very fine fabric of the mantle itself. This lighter garment became the French *surplis* and the English *surplice*. The scapularius, much like the *almucio,* was a short mantle with a hood that was intended more as an decoration than a practical detail. Around the end of the sixteenth century, it was a prerogative of canons to wear these garments, which marked hierarchical differences inside the church.

The luxury and power of the papal court deeply influenced the clothing styles of almost every member of the clergy outside the Orders. They were granted much more freedom than the regular clergy since they were usually allowed to wear civil clothing, with the exception, of course, of the vestments used during religious ceremonies.

On these occasions, the liturgical vestments, which included several articles of clothing to be used following a specific protocol, showed few substantial variations in comparison with more ancient styles. The most imposing among the liturgical vestments was the *piviale* or cope, a large mantle that in the Middle Ages had a hood. The tendency to reduce the fluctuating fourteenth-century dress appears also in liturgical vestments of the early Renaissance; the chasubles and tunics were significantly smaller, and the shape of the cope changed, the original hood becoming more a decorative triangular piece of fabric that, at the end of the sixteenth century, further evolved into a shield-shaped piece of fabric (the *clipeus*) fastened through buttons to the back of the cope itself.

Cotte, *rocchetti*, and *camici* constituted the white "underwear" to be worn under the vestments. They were made with the thinnest linen fabric and decorated with white embroidery work or, following a characteristic Renaissance trend, precious lace.

Dalmatiche (dalmatics), *tunicelle* (tunics worn by deacons), and *pianete* or *casule* (chasubles) were the most-used vestments. The *pianeta* especially evolved during the sixteenth century, from the former circular cut to a rectangular vestment opened and shaped at the sides, allowing more freedom of movement.

All the vestments were made with the most precious fabrics, but seldom were these fabrics brand new; usually aristocratic families donated to the church the dresses they no longer used or needed, and the garments were carefully unstitched and disassembled to be later refashioned as liturgical vestments. In fact, upon closer inspection, the vestments often appear as patchworks of fabrics, occasionally rather different one from the other. Any new vestment would be properly blessed before being worn for the first time to celebrate Mass.

The liturgical calendar provided for the alternation of different colors for different days or occasions throughout the year. White (or its equivalents gold and silver) was, for instance, used in the most solemn occasions, such as Easter, Christmas, and the celebration of weddings or christenings; it was occasionally also worn for children's funerals. Red was the color used for Palm Sunday, Pentecost, Good Friday, and the celebrations in honor of saints, martyrs, and the apostles; it could also be used for the celebration of the sacrament of Confirmation as an alternative to the color of the day. Green was prescribed for the *tempo ordinario*, that is, for most of the days of the year. Black was for funerary rites, *rosaceo* (a pinkish color) for the fourth Sunday of Lent and the third Sunday of Advent, and purple for Advent and Lent generally. Blue was never a proper liturgical color, but since the Church often needed to recuperate donated fabrics, blue shades could be worn during celebrations in honor of the Virgin Mary.

The colors of the background served to set off the intricate embroidery that, quite often, decorated religious vestments and their smaller coordinated "accessories." Stoles, orfreys, maniples, and calyx veils were the frames for needle-made decorations, such as narrations of episodes of the lives of Christ, the Virgin Mary, and the saints (in the treasury of St. Peter's in Rome is a stole *"de opera anglicano ad figures sanctorum de serico et auro diversorum colorum,"* embroidered *ad opus anglicanum*, a dense pictorial embroidery technique, with gold and many shades of silk). However, not infrequently liturgical clothing is decorated by purely ornamental motifs, such as peacocks or other birds, animals, geometric patterns, or coats of arms of an important family or of a city.

An article of liturgical clothing reserved to the high church hierarchy is the *rocchetto*, or rochet, a short, densely pleated tunic. On top of this, the bishops could wear the *mozzetta*, a garment that appeared around the middle of the sixteenth century and consisted of a short *cappa*, probably derived from the *cappa magna*, a very ample, circular mantle completed by a hood and train, worn by bishops (in purple) and archbishops (in red) inside their own jurisdictions. The cappa was made in plain silk fabrics, occasionally enriched by moiré effect. The rocchetto of the end of the sixteenth century and the beginning of the seventeenth was shorter and enriched by a wide lace border at the bottom and cuffs.

In order to regulate and standardize the use of liturgical vestments, St. Charles Borromeo in 1572 produced *Instructiones Fabricae et Suppellectilis Ecclesiasticae*. This was followed by *Cerimoniale dei Vescovi* in 1600 and *Rituale* in 1614. One recommendation by St. Charles was the consistent use of the small round *zucchetto*, or skullcap; it was made of simple wool cloth, white for the pope and black for everyone else. He suggested it also be worn under the bishop's miter. In addition, he mentioned another element of ecclesiastic clothing that, after an initial appearance at the end of the sixteenth century, would begin to be more clearly identifiable in the next century: the clerical berretta hat, red for cardinals and black for all the other priests. It was divided into three segments that stood rigid because the silk was lined with cardboard.

The task of regulating and controlling feminine religious clothing was, from the very beginning, far more complicated. Despite the astonishing number of convents and monasteries, real vocation toward a cloistered life of poverty and prayer was not so common. Everywhere in Italy, women who were denied by their families the option to marry, as a way of helping to preserve the family's wealth, had only two options. The first was to keep living in their families' homes, unmarried, leading a modest and secluded life; the second, much less desirable but more common possibility led toward the irrevocable doors of a convent or monastery.

> **CHILD CLERGY**
>
> One curiosity of the Renaissance was the numerous baby nuns and priests, as portrayed in paintings, both in Italy and elsewhere in Europe. The destiny of these children was, in fact, sealed by their order of birth, because younger children were usually destined for the convent or priesthood in order to protect the family's wealth. To get this idea into their heads early on, these children were dressed for the part as soon as they could walk. It was common to see many of these miniature nuns and priests strolling around the palaces of the aristocracy. Even the dolls of these little girls were dressed like nuns!

To the "domestic" nuns, the advice was to "give up luxuries" and abandon any vanity, but the sacrifices requested of the "involuntary" nuns were much bigger. After having celebrated their mystical marriage with Christ much like secular brides did, clothed with a sumptuous white silk dress and an immaculate veil and with a ring placed on their finger, they were soon invited by the bishop—for it was he who usually officiated at these rites—to cast off their lay garments for the modest dress of the Order they were entering. They cut their hair short, suppressing any feminine vanity under the veil and *soggolo*.

Despite these recommendations, all the evidence shows that modesty in the dress of these forced nuns was really not a primary issue: since nuns coming from the most important families could count on a conspicuous allowance paid by their relatives for their needs, many indulged in "painting their hands and décolletages," accepting improper gifts such as jewels, or flaunting magnificent and immodest secular dresses. In 1426, Patriarch Querini was reportedly received by the nuns at the Celestia monastery in Venice with long braided hair and in secular dress. And during the Christmas Mass of 1497, Fra Timoteo from Lucca during the homily cried the shame of the Venetian monasteries that he felt were populated with charming and lascivious nuns, much to the disdain of the clergy (G. Bistort, *Il magistrato alle Pompe della Republica di Veneza*, 63).

If in other Italian cities the problem of the forced vocations created numerous disciplinary problems inside the convents, in Venice the situation was so serious that a special public office was created, the *proveditori sopra i monasteri*, charged with the responsibility of avoiding potential embarrassments—such as the discovery that the noble nuns of the Miracoli during Carnival used to "dress up as men in order to put on plays." The actions of the *proveditori*, who resolutely proclaimed that nuns should not wear secular clothing for their plays, were resolutely ignored. Nuns continued to do as they pleased, like the Benedictine nun of the aristocratic monastery of San Lorenzo in Venice who was described around the end of the sixteenth century as looking less like a nun, dedicated to God dressed in her fine white linens. Nor did this reprehensible behavior change with the end of the Renaissance; in 1664, as they welcomed the visit of Cosimo III, Duke of Tuscany, the nuns of the same monastery were fashionably dressed in the French style with breasts half showing, expensive lace in both black and white decorating their bodies. Definitely not a very proper clothing style for a bride of Christ!

THE END OF THE RENAISSANCE STYLE

The dramatic variations undergone by dress styles in the seventeenth century were strictly related to the changing European social and political context. Spanish decadence as the European political leader led to the emerging power of Holland, France, and England and prepared the ground for a long period of wars on the continent. As usual, dress styles developed under the influence of new lifestyles and ideas. The fashionable style, reflecting the contemporary artistic inclination toward free, sometimes capricious forms, characteristic of the early and late Baroque style, abandoned the Renaissance composure in favor of a more relaxed style that did not aim to achieve symmetry or balance anymore.

In the first half of the seventeenth century, the rich Dutch middle class played a leading role in the evolution of European dress styles, while in the second half of the century its place was taken by the refined French court aristocracy, whose elegance, characteristic of the time of Louis XIV, set the example for all the neighboring nations.

If the Spanish fashion that dominated the second half of the sixteenth century had distorted the natural shape of the body, rigidly framing it inside a completely artificial, almost geometrical shape, the new Dutch style gave great importance to comfort and freedom of movement, two leading themes of dress in this period. In Italy, the more popular fashions reflected the current political situation of the Italian Peninsula: Venice continued to be rather independent and original in her dress styles, adapting Dutch ideas to the local taste, while a lingering Spanish influence still dominated in Lombardy, the South of Italy, and, to a lesser degree, Genoa and Rome.

Men's dress, both for the upper and middle classes, followed a severe and moderate style of clothing, exemplified by the preference for very dark colors. The doublet, now called *giubba* and without any of the late Renaissance padding, continued to be the main item in the masculine wardrobe for most of the century. It sported a longer cut and had an almost trapezoidal shape, with long tails sometimes stiffened with cardboard placed between the inner lining and the external fabric. The waistline was a little above the natural position. The giubba was closed in the front by a long series of small buttons. Braiding and other trimmings made with metallic threads often enriched its front, continuing along and covering the seam lines. The breeches, which were at were first still heavily padded, soon became much longer and closer fitting, fastened at the knees with ribbons or laces. Characteristic masculine accessories of the time were long boots tied with ribbons and completed by precious spurs. The hair was initially cut short and paired with a well-cared-for beard, but, as the century advanced, it became more fashionable to wear the monumental wigs that constitute the typical trait of the Baroque era. Unusually, lace was an ornament as common in men's outfits as in women's, and the most appreciated kinds were the sculpted needle laces made in Venice and Flanders; it was used at the cuffs, as collars, and even as decorations on footwear and hairdos.

The seventeenth century was also the time in which the first military uniforms appeared. With the birth of the first nation-states, the armies were reorganized, and in 1635 the French cavalry first begin to wear the *mandille*, a mantle with a large, recognizable cross on the front and back. This was followed in 1664 by the Monferrato regiment in the Piedmont region of Italy, which wore a yellow "modern" uniform.

The dress of the ladies seemed much less structured than in the past, but rigid corsets were still worn under the dresses to achieve the ideal conical shape, albeit "modernized" and made slightly more comfortable and flexible by using bones and pillows as padding. To grace the line of the body, the waist was constricted. The wide ruffs continued to be used at least until the second decade of the century, but they were later replaced by generous and square necklines, only partially veiled by the same lace fabrics that trimmed the clothes.

A dress characterized by a very high and rather cumbersome waistline appeared in the northeast of Italy in the second quarter of the seventeenth century, with the skirt of the dress beginning directly under the breasts. The most common outfit was the *giuppone* (for the upper part of the body) paired with the *sottanino*, a matching skirt. Other garments included the already popular zimarra; the *bombasina*, a sleeved dress made from cotton (*bombaso*); and the *polaco*, a fashion apparently imported from Poland. Numerous other names of dresses appear in the inventories because of the different denominations given to same garments in the various Italian regions.

The dresses were completed by needle-lace aprons and the richly decorated handkerchiefs that fashionable ladies always kept in their hands. The shoes were rounded pianelle, with the eccentric vogue of the Renaissance platform calcagnini being completely abandoned.

There were no significant changes in the costume of the masses. The cut of dresses tried to follow that of the upper classes, but the updating of the garments was slowed by the fact that dresses were used to the point of disintegration and were made with whatever materials were available at the moment. Characteristic features include the absence of any kind of undergarment and the presence of coifs and veils on the heads of women, who, around the middle of the seventeenth century, begin to differentiate by following typical regional customs.

CONCLUSION

The Renaissance was a historical period extremely rich in human achievements and discoveries. The idea of the centrality of Man in the universe brought an unexpected series of consequences in philosophical thinking and in the arts, but also in everyday activities and customs. The history and studies of Renaissance dress cannot leave out of consideration these groundbreaking events. The centrality of the human being in Renaissance philosophical thinking was mirrored by the careful construction of the clothing of the time, which was extremely significant because in this historical period the costumes worn by a specific person represented that individual's social and personal status, both inside the family and in the general society, and they need to be studied in this context to be fully understood and evaluated. This concept was expressed by Baldassarre Castiglione when he affirmed that "the dress represents not a small clue about the personality of the wearer."

FURTHER READING

Italian Renaissance Art, History, and Culture

Amjar-Wollheim, Marta, and Flora Dennis, eds. *At Home in Renaissance Italy*. New York: H. N. Abrams, 2006.

Brown, Patricia Fortini. *Private Lives in Renaissance Venice: Art, Architecture and the Family*. New Haven, CT: Yale University Press, 2003.

Burckhardt, Jacob. *The Architecture of the Italian Renaissance*. Rev. and ed. Peter Murray; trans. James Palmes. Chicago: University of Chicago Press, 1985.

Burke, Peter. *Eyewitnessing: The Use of Images as Historical Evidence*. Ithaca, NY: Cornell University Press, 2001.

Castiglione, Baldassarre. *Il libro del Cortegiano*. Ed. G. Carnazzi. Milan, Italy: BUR, 2000.

Cole, Alison. *Virtue and Magnificence: Art of the Italian Renaissance Courts*. New York: H. N. Abrams, 1995.

Hartt, Frederick, and David G. Wilkins. *History of Italian Renaissance Art*. 6th ed. Upper Saddle River, NJ: Prentice Hall, 2006.

Panizza, L., ed. *Women in Italian Renaissance Culture and Society*. Oxford, UK: European Humanities Research Center, 2000.

Paoletti, John T., and Gary M. Radke. *Art in Renaissance Italy*. 3rd ed. Upper Saddle River, NJ: Prentice Hall, 2006.

Renaissance Dress

Arnold, Janet. *Patterns of Fashion: The Cut and Construction of Clothes for Men and Women, c. 1560–1620*. New York: Drama Book, 1985.

Birbari, Elizabeth. *Dress in Italian Painting, 1460–1500*. London: J. Murray, 1975.

Bridgeman, J. "Dress in Moroni's Portraits." In *Giovanni Battista Moroni, Renaissance Portraits* [exhibition catalogue]. Forth Worth, TX: Kimbell Art Museum, 2000.

Burrosi, M., ed. *L'abito della Granduchessa, vesti di corte e Madonne nel Palazzo Reale di Pisa*. Pisa, Bandecchi e Vivaldi, 2000.

Con gli occhi di Piero: Abiti e gioielli nelle opere di Piero della Francesca [exhibition catalogue], ed. M. G. Ciardi Duprè dal Poggetto and G. Chesne Dauphinè Griffo. Venice: Marsilio, 1992.

Cox-Rearick, J. *Splendours of the Renaissance Princely Attire in Italy* [exhibition catalogue]. New York: King Studio, 2004.

Davanzo Poli, Doretta. *Abiti antichi e moderni dei veneziani*. Vicenza: N. Pozza, 2001.

Frick, Carole Collier. *Dressing Renaissance Florence: Families, Fortunes, and Fine Clothing*. Baltimore: Johns Hopkins University Press, 2002.

Herald, Jacqueline. *Renaissance Dress in Italy, 1400–1500*. London, Bell & Hyman; Atlantic Highlands, NJ: Humanities Press, 1981.

Il libro del Sarto. Reprint, Venice: Fondazione Querini Stampalia, 1987.

Levi Pisetzky, R. *Il costume e la moda nella società italiana*. Torino, Einandi, 1978.

Mayo, Janet. *History of Ecclesiastical Dress*. New York: Holmes & Meier, 1984.

Newton, Stella Mary. *The Dress of the Venetians, 1495–1525*. Aldershot, UK: Scolar Press, 1988.

Orsi Landini, Roberta, and Bruna Niccoli. *Moda a Firenze, 1540–1580: Lo stile di Eleonora di Toledo e la sua influenza*. Florence, Italy: Pagliai Polistampa, 2005.

Orsi Landini, Roberta, S. Ricci, and M. Westerman Bulgarella, eds. *Moda alla corte dei Medici: Gli abiti restaurati di Cosimo, Eleonora e don Garzia*. Florence, Centro Di, 1993.

Pyhrr, Stuart W., and José-A. Godoy. *Heroic Armor of the Italian Renaissance: Filippo Negroli and His Contemporaries*. New York: Metropolitan Museum of Art, 1998.

Tinagli, Paola. *Women in Italian Renaissance Art: Gender, Representation and Identity*. Manchester, UK: Manchester University Press, 1997.

Vecellio, Cesare. *Vecellio's Renaissance Costume Book: All 500 Woodcut Illustrations from the Famous Sixteenth-Century Compendium of World Costume*. New York: Dover, 1977.

Renaissance Lace and Textiles

Bunt, Cyril. *Venetian Fabrics*. Leigh-on-Sea: F. Lewis, 1959.

Davanzo Poli, Doretta. *Il merletto veneziano*. Novara: Istituto geografico De Agostini, 1998.

Podreider, F. *Storia dei tessuti d'arte in Italia*. Bergamo, Instituto Italiano d'Arti Grafiche, 1928.

Tessuti italiani del Rinascimento: Collezioni Franchetti, Carrand. Prato: Museo Nazionale del Bargello, Palazzo Pretorio, 1981.

Woven Splendour: Italian Textiles from the Medici to the Modern Age. London: Middlesex University Press, 2004.

WEB RESOURCES

http://www.bridgemanartondemand.com/index.cfm?event=catalogue.product&product ID=10506

http://www.nationalgallery.org.uk/cgi-bin/WebObjects.dll/CollectionPublisher.woa/wa/ largeImage?workNumber=NG758&collectionPublisherSection=work

http://www.ville-douai.fr/culture/musee/italien.htm#

http://www.museopalazzorosso.it/template1.asp?itemID=60102020&level=4&label=Sala _3_Parrasio-Micheli&sito=6

http://www.utexas.edu/courses/introtogreece/lect7/img13penelsuitrs.html

http://www.thewalters.org/works_of_art/itemdetails.aspx?aid=54

http://www.nga.gov/cgi-bin/pimage?309+0+0

http://www.paliodellecontrade.com/index.php?option=com_content&task=view&id=9& Itemid=65 Madrid, Prado

http://www.museopoldipezzoli.it/PP_inglese/museo/collezioni/pittura/scheda.php?sk_id= 174

http://collections.frick.org/Obj2450$21454

http://www.wga.hu/support/viewer/z.html

MOVIES

The Agony and the Ecstasy (1965)
The Merchant of Venice (2004)
Romeo and Juliet (1968)

The Northern Renaissance

Sara M. Harvey

TIMELINE

1453	Fall of Constantinople
1455	Johannes Gutenberg publishes the first printed Bible
1491	Henry VIII born
1492	Christopher Columbus arrives in the Americas
1494	Milan captured by the king of France, Charles VIII; future King Francis I of France born, considered to be the first Renaissance monarch
1498	Vasco da Gama reaches the East Indies
1509	Henry VIII becomes the second Tudor monarch of England and marries Catherine of Aragon
1515	Francis I becomes king of France
1516	Mary I, daughter of Catherine of Aragon, born in England
1517	Martin Luther posts his Ninety-Five Theses on the portal of the church of Wittenberg
1519	Ferdinand Magellan embarks on the first voyage around the world; Magellan dies in 1521 in what is now the Philippines, leaving his crew to make their way back to Spain in 1522
1527	Sack of Rome; Philip II born in Spain
1531	Church of England breaks from the Roman Catholic Church and recognizes King Henry VIII as its leader
1533	Henry VIII divorces Catherine of Aragon and marries Anne Boleyn; Elizabeth I, daughter of Anne Boleyn, is born
1536	Anne Boleyn executed for treason, adultery, and witchcraft; Henry VIII marries Jane Seymour
1537	Jane Seymour gives birth to Edward VI but dies of complications from childbirth; Lady Jane Grey born in England
1540	Henry VIII marries Anne of Cleves, but the marriage is annulled that same year and Henry marries Katherine Howard
1542	Katherine Howard executed for treason and adultery
1543	Henry VIII marries Catherine Parr
1545–63	Council of Trent

1547   Francis I of France dies; Henry VIII dies, survived by
            Catherine Parr
1553   Edward VI of England dies without heir; Lady Jane Grey
            rules as queen of England for nine days before being
            executed for treason; Mary I, half-sister to Edward VI,
            becomes queen of England and marries Phillip II of
            Spain
1556   Philip II becomes king of Spain
1558   Mary I of England, "Bloody Mary," dies childless and her
            half-sister Elizabeth I becomes queen of England;
            England loses control of the French port city of Calais
            after having held it for more than 200 years
1559   Peace of Cateau-Cambrésis between England, France, and
            Spain
1562   Brutal and bloody battles between Catholics and
            Protestant Huguenots begin in France
1564   William Shakespeare born in Stratford-on-Avon, England;
            Christopher Marlowe born near Canterbury, England
1566   Eighty Years' War between Spain and the Netherlands
            begins
1577–80   English captain Sir Francis Drake circumnavigates the
            world
1588   Spanish Armada, the "Invincible Fleet," defeated by
            England in the English Channel, ending an era of
            Spanish domination and beginning England's rise as a
            world power
1593   Marlowe killed in a bar brawl in London
1598   Edict of Nantes ends the bloody religious wars in France;
            Philip II of Spain dies

The Renaissance began in Italy, but its influences reverberated
throughout Europe. From the lavish salons of France to the
Tudor decadence of England and the artistic richness of the
Netherlands and Germany, Europe was drenched in a new and
rich culture spurred on by great learning. These advances were
tempered, however, by religious tensions between the Roman
Catholic Church and the newly established Protestant Reformation. The vast Hapsburg territories were gathered under the
rule of a single man, Holy Roman Emperor Charles V.

Clothing became indicative of class and status. Wealth, as well
as political and religious affiliation, were flaunted on the backs of
the residents of Europe and painted on a grand scale by some of
the world's most talented artists. Fashion news traveled easily
between countries as intermarriages were arranged between powerful nations. Eastern influences brought in through trade added an
exotic flavor both in textiles and in garment styling. There was, for
the first time, a truly international exchange of ideas.

HISTORY

At the outset of the sixteenth century, Germany was still laboring under the heavy influence of the Gothic medieval age. Slowly, scholarly interest turned toward art, science, philosophy, and fashion. Dissatisfaction with the decadent Catholic Church, so far away from them in Rome, led the austere-minded Germans into the Reformation. Corruption, religious indulgences, and an increasingly strong sense of nationalism culminated on October 31, 1517, with Martin Luther nailing his Ninety-Five Theses to the door of the Wittenberg Church. Luther had the support of the German government, which was looking to get free of the iron grip of the Catholic emperor, Charles V.

Charles V ruled as emperor from 1519 to 1556 and held control over Germany, Austria, the Low Countries,[1] Italy, Spain, and the Spanish territories of North America.[2] At age 19, Charles V ruled one of the largest territories any single monarch had ever tried to govern. In Spain, Charles relied on the wealth of gold, silver, and jewels that poured in from the American conquests. Spain had so much gold that inflation rose to obscene levels. Expensive wars and costly exploration taxed Spanish coffers, and when the money was spent, there was nothing left. Much of the gold went into the Spanish Catholic Church, helping to cement Spain's devout reputation. Spain was known as so orthodox a Catholic nation that the Reformation did not affect it in the least.

The Reformation did, however, put a great deal of strain on the Holy Roman Empire, pitting the Catholic nations against the Reformed ones in a struggle that often brought both sides to bloody battle. This strain was far too much for one man, and Charles found that he did not have the mettle to rule such a disastrously disparate realm. He finally gave up the struggle to maintain peace in his enormous territory and abdicated the throne in 1556, dividing his large empire between his brother Ferdinand (1503–1564) and his son Philip (1527–1598). Ferdinand was granted Austria and the Holy Roman Empire. Philip was given Spain, the Low Countries, and the Spanish settlements in America.

Philip ruled Spain and the Low Countries as the Most Catholic King, Philip II. The Low Countries was home to many prosperous merchants as well as Reformers. Philip sought to bring them under his control and exploit their riches by levying high taxes on the area and garrisoning Spanish troops in the major cities. After a revolt in 1568, Philip fought to keep the Low Countries intact, but by the end of the century, he had relinquished the seven northernmost provinces of the Netherlands, and they formed the Dutch Republic of Holland. Philip was also briefly allied with England by his marriage to Queen Mary Tudor, daughter of Henry VIII.

Henry VIII (1491–1547) ruled England from 1509 until his death in 1547. He became first in line for succession to the throne after the sudden and unexpected death of his older brother, Arthur, in 1502. As heir apparent, young Henry apparently fell in love with his brother's widow, Catherine of Aragon, but was prohibited from marrying her by his father, Henry VII. Catherine and Arthur had been married for only four months, and she claimed the marriage was never consummated. Upon his father's death in 1509, Henry succeeded to the throne of England as Henry VIII and acquired a papal dispensation from

Rome allowing Catherine and Henry to marry. They wed immediately and were jointly crowned king and queen of England.

In the following years, Catherine suffered through several miscarriages and stillbirths. Her first son lived fewer than two months, and her second died even sooner. The only child she had that lived was a daughter, Mary, born in 1516. Frustrated, Henry VIII turned to his mistresses and with them fathered two sons and a daughter. When it was clear that Catherine at age 42 was no longer able to conceive, Henry VIII divorced her after eighteen years of marriage in favor of her lady-in-waiting Anne Boleyn. This was the first of Henry's many whimsical love affairs that spelled disaster for his wives.

This divorce from Catherine took six years to complete and called the very faith of the realm into question. Henry sought a divorce based on the impropriety of having married his sister-in-law, but Catherine was adamant that her marriage to Arthur had never been consummated and held onto the papal dispensation as proof. Meanwhile, Anne insisted that he marry her before she would give in to his sexual advances. She was also a Protestant and urged Henry to convert. They were married in secret in January 1533, and Henry's marriage to Catherine was officially dissolved in May 1533. Catherine was exiled from court and separated from her daughter. She died in 1536, never having seen Mary again.

Anne Boleyn was crowned queen of England on June 1, 1533, and by that August preparations were already being made for the birth of her first child. The kingdom was very disappointed that the child, Elizabeth, was a girl. Anne conceived several more times, but each pregnancy ended in miscarriage. During this period, Henry and England broke with the Catholic Church and Rome, establishing the independent Church of England with Henry at its head.

By 1535, Henry's love for Anne was waning and his attentions were fixed on her lady-in-waiting, Jane Seymour. Anne was given a mockery of a trial on charges of adultery, incest with her brother George, and witchcraft. She was beheaded by an expert swordsman from Calais at eight o'clock in the morning on May 19, 1536.

Within a day of Anne's execution, Henry VIII was formally betrothed to Jane Seymour. The two were married on May 30, 1536, but Jane was never given a formal coronation. With his marriage to Jane, Henry again regarded the Catholic Church more fondly, although he did not seek to reestablish the churches or monasteries that he had all but plundered throughout England. Jane finally gave the king a much-longed-for legitimate son, Edward, on October 15, 1537. Mary Tudor, Catherine of Aragon's daughter, was named the prince's godmother. Unfortunately, Jane did not live to see her son grow up; she died about two weeks after his birth. She was laid in the royal tomb in St. George's Chapel at Windsor Castle, the only one of Henry VIII's six wives to be buried with him.

It was more than two years before Henry took another wife. It is unknown whether he was mourning Jane Seymour or if it only took that long for his advisers to find him a suitable bride. Henry was looking for a foreign allegiance and chose Anne of Cleves as his fourth wife on the basis of her portrait by Hans Holbein. This gave Henry an edge over the rumored alliance between France and Spain, bringing the leverage of the Lutheran princes of the German States. But when Henry and Anne finally met, he was displeased with her. He called her his "Flanders Mare" and sought to get out of the marriage before the wedding was even celebrated. Despite this, they were wed in January 1540, but the marriage lasted only seven months. Not only was Henry displeased with her, but he was also madly in love with her maid-in-waiting, Catherine Howard, a cousin of Anne Boleyn. Anne of Cleves agreed to have the marriage annulled and took the title of "King's Sister." She was given property and a generous stipend and lived on the fringes of the court until her death in 1557.

Sixteen days after Henry's latest marriage was annulled, he was wed to Catherine Howard on July 28, 1540; he was forty-nine and Kathryn was nineteen. By this time, Henry was very overweight and had a wound in his leg, suffered during a jousting accident years before, that had never healed. He called Catherine his "rose without a thorn" and doted on her. But she was young and flirtatious, and her promiscuity earned her a walk to the Tower Green, just like her cousin, Anne Boleyn. Catherine Howard was executed on February 13, 1542, and buried near her cousin in the Chapel of St. Peter ad Vincula at the Tower of London.

Catherine Parr was to be Henry VIII's last wife, married to him on July 12, 1543, eighteen months after Catherine Howard's execution. She was the daughter of a modest noble and was more of a caregiver to the aging king than a bride. Catherine Parr was a steadfast mother figure who reconciled Henry with his two daughters. She was also a dedicated Protestant and in the end helped Henry to more firmly establish the Anglican Church and enable it to become a viable faith that would last for centuries. Catherine was also the only one of Henry's many wives that outlived him. He died on January 28, 1547. Upon the king's death, Catherine was free to marry the man she loved, Thomas Seymour, the late Jane Seymour's brother. She had a child with him but died soon after the birth of her daughter in September 1548.

Edward VI came to power upon the death of Henry VIII in 1547. He was interested in keeping the country a Protestant nation and had Thomas Cranmer, the archbishop of Canterbury, implement the Book of Common Prayer that is still used by Anglicans the world over. However, Edward contracted tuberculosis in May 1553 and died of it in July.

Henry VIII's will had called for Mary, Catherine of Aragon's daughter, to succeed Edward VI, but she was Catholic and Edward's advisers and supporters were fearful of losing their power. They therefore concocted a plot to put Lady Jane Grey on the throne. She reigned for nine days in July before being executed along with her husband, Guilford Dudley, on February 12, 1554.

Mary I then became the queen of England and married Philip II of Spain, solidifying a Catholic allegiance between the two countries. She then persecuted the heretic Protestants of England. Mary thought she was pregnant twice, but the first was a phantom pregnancy, and the second was most likely a tumor that ended her life in November 1558. As stipulated in Henry VIII's will, Elizabeth was to take the throne if both Edward and Mary were to die without an heir.

Elizabeth I ruled from 1558 until her death in 1603. It was known as the golden age in England. She was a Protestant and believed in a unified Church of England but did not engage in the persecution of Catholics. She was a learned woman who surrounded her court with artists and writers. The Elizabethan Age was an era of great creativity and learning. Playwrights such as William Shakespeare, Christopher Marlowe, and Ben Jonson created comedies, dramas, tragedies, and histories that continue to be performed around the world.

Elizabeth never married, although suitors from every major country in the world sought her hand.

Elizabeth's embrace of Protestantism alienated the Catholic nations of Spain and France. Spain moved against England, seeking to forge another alliance by force, but the impressive English navy defeated the Spanish Armada in 1588. This victory destroyed the threat posed by Spain and was a great boon to English morale. France was still an issue, though, especially in light of the French alliance with Scotland and the claim that the Catholic Queen Mary of Scotland made on the English throne.

France played a major role in the Renaissance as a patron of the arts. The Catholic King Francis I ruled the country from 1515 until 1547 and was an admirer of Italian art. Famous and influential artists such as Leonardo da Vinci came to the French court to paint and work. Francis's son Henry married Catherine de' Medici, a daughter of the most influential family in Italy's history, and she brought even more Italian influence to the French court with her Italian courtiers, dressmakers, milliners, maids, cooks, and perfumers.

Francis was close to the crown of Holy Roman emperor, but he lost it to Charles V. In 1520, he sought to ally himself with England against the Holy Roman Empire and Spain. But these early difficulties were to set the stage for his massive military failures. Francis was captured at the battle of La Biocca in the war he waged against the Empire, and to gain his freedom he relinquished his claims on Italy and Burgundy under the Treaty of Madrid. In addition to giving up titles and territorial claims, Francis also had to forfeit his two sons as ransom, giving them up as hostages to Spain, where they spent three years. Feeling that the treaty was invalid, Francis went to war again, with the backing of Henry VIII and Pope Clement VII. But once again, he was defeated. Burgundy was returned to French control, but otherwise this second treaty all but duplicated the Treaty of Madrid.

But Francis had much better luck with domestic matters. Despite the military failures abroad, France was flush with the wonders of the Renaissance at home. The economy was sound, and France was a leader of fashion, art, dance, music, and poetry. He also funded explorations to North America and settled regions in what is now Canada. His one domestic failing was in religion. While France was a Catholic country, it was not so staunch and orthodox as the Spanish and tolerated the Reformed Church in the country. Francis saw this as a valuable political tool that could further ally himself to the Protestant nations against Spain and the Holy Roman Empire. Unfortunately, not all of the French people shared his magnanimity and tolerance and civil war flared between the Catholics and Protestants across France.

Francis I's son, Francis the Dauphin, died under suspicious circumstances at age 17 without having married. The crown thus passed to Francis's second son, Henry, who succeeded as Henry II. Henry ruled from his father's death in 1547 until his own death in 1559. He did not have his father's lenient view of Protestants and was known for his severe persecution and torture of them. Henry also took up his father's cause against the Holy Roman Empire, striving to remove the Hapsburgs from power and replace them with a French lineage. He was more successful than his father but was ultimately defeated.

Henry II was politically savvy and had a plan for solidifying alliances. He fostered the young Mary, Queen of Scots, who was the daughter of the French

Mary of Guise and the Scottish king James V. When the girl was only nine months old, she was crowned queen of Scotland and became a pawn in the very dangerous political games between France and England. Henry II had her married to his heir Francis when both were very young. This gave France a claim to the English throne through Mary's heritage. Henry was a formidable man, but he was killed in a jousting accident when he took a lance splinter to the face; the large piece of sharp wood shot through the closed visor of his helm and pierced his eye and brain.

Francis II took the throne in July 1559 with Mary as his queen. Sadly, he was a sickly child and lived little over a year into his reign. He died from an abscessed ear infection in December 1560. Upon his death, Mary was sent back to Scotland and Catherine de' Medici became the regent of France. Catherine was just as cruel as her husband when it came to persecuting the Protestants.

The next son in line, Charles IX, became the next king of France ruling from 1560 to 1574. Charles married Elizabeth of Austria, forming a tenuous allegiance with the Hapsburgs. But he was a fragile child, much like his brother had been, and not long after the brutal and violent St. Bartholomew's Day Massacre in Paris in 1572, where thousands of Protestants were killed, Charles took to his bed and later died, age 24. He died with no sons and the French crown therefore passed to his younger brother, who became Henry III.

Henry III ruled from 1574 until his death in 1589. He was the favorite child of his mother, Catherine de' Medici. He was lively and artistic and engaged in all the court follies and was rumored to be homosexual. He was elected king of the Polish-Lithuanian Commonwealth shortly before becoming king of France. Henry's reign was rocky, as he was consistently faced with internal warfare between Catholics and Protestants. His brother, the last of his siblings, died in 1584, and Henry produced no heir with his wife, Louise de Lorraine-Vaudémont. The next in line of succession to the French throne was Henri de Navarre, a Protestant. This began the "War of the Three Henrys."

At the urging of Henri I, Duke of Guise, King Henry III wrote an edict outlawing Protestantism and banning Henri of Navarre from succession. However, Navarre defeated the king's troops, and the Duke of Guise allied with the Catholic League and continued to put political pressure on Henry III. In response, Henry III had the duke and his brother assassinated to try and quell the building rebellion. It was all in vain, though, as Henry III was himself assassinated by agents of the Catholic League in 1589.

The Protestant Henri of Navarre, from the House of Bourbon, became the next king of France as Henry IV and ruled until 1610. He was a good ruler who settled the religious strife with the Edict of Nantes, which gave full political and religious rights to the Protestants, but he also converted to Catholicism. He encouraged the French economy with subsidies to the cloth industry. Soon French linen was known as the finest in the world, and France also boasted a healthy silk industry, breaking Italy's monopoly on silk in Europe.

Mary, Queen of Scots, was also facing Protestant and Catholic factions that threatened to tear her country apart. While she had been living in France, Protestantism had come to Scotland and taken a very firm foothold there. She was also forced to acknowledge Elizabeth I was queen of England, even though she felt that her claim was stronger and she had been the choice of Mary I to succeed her as a Catholic monarch.

Mary returned to Scotland in 1561 and found it a nation divided by religion and politics. She was not equipped to cope with such issues. There were bad feelings between her and Elizabeth stemming from both their religious differences and their differing opinions on succession. Both make poor attempts to make peace with the other. Elizabeth offered her favorite courtier, Robert Dudley, Earl of Leicester, to Mary as a suitor. Mary refused and married her cousin Henry Stuart, Lord Darnley, instead. This infuriated Elizabeth, as Darnley was her subject and she had not even been consulted about the marriage. It also put pressure on Elizabeth's hold on the English throne because both Mary and Darnley were considered claimants.

Mary's relationship with her husband soured, however. Darnley was demanding the title of king, not just king consort, and it was rumored that he attempted to injure Mary and cause her to miscarry their child. Nevertheless, Mary's son James was born hale and healthy in 1566. A plot was then hatched to be rid of Darnley, who was growing increasingly violent and problematic. When Darnley was found strangled in 1567, suspicion was cast upon Mary, who had made no pretence that she hated her husband. James Hepburn, Earl of Bothwell, was thought to be behind the plot not only for political gain, but as leverage to force Mary to marry him. Bothwell staged an abduction of Mary in April 1567 wherein he raped her and forced her into marriage. The Scottish lords rebelled and gathered an army against Mary and Bothwell. She was imprisoned in July and miscarried Bothwell's twins.

On July 24, 1567, Mary, Queen of Scots, was forced to abdicate her throne in favor of her one-year-old son, who then became King James IV of Scotland. She escaped her imprisonment in 1568 and tried to raise a small army to retake her throne, but this attempt failed. She then fled to England to seek asylum, only to be imprisoned there by her cousin Elizabeth. Mary was confined in England for eighteen years, during which time there were many inquiries into her role in the death of Lord Darnley and her intentions as a claimant to the English throne. Mary was implicated in many supposed plots to assassinate Elizabeth, but surprisingly, Elizabeth refused to sign any bills that would have legally barred Mary from ever taking the throne of England.

Mary, Queen of Scots, was finally executed on the Tower Green on February 8, 1587. She had been only twenty-four when she was imprisoned and forty-four when she was beheaded. Eventually, her son James was the only heir left available to the English throne and united the kingdoms of Scotland and England as King James I of England.

TEXTILES

Advances in textiles were few in during this time period. A treadle spinning wheel was developed by Leonardo da Vinci, but it was not until 1530 that Johann Jurgin actually built one. This spinning wheel wound the yarn as it was spun, speeding up the process considerably.

The other significant technological advancement in the sixteenth century was that of a knitting machine. Knit stockings were very popular across Europe and had been primarily made by hand throughout the century. William Lee, an English inventor, came to Queen Elizabeth to request a patent for a spring-beard needle knitting machine. However, she thought it would negatively impact the small but growing hand-knitting industry that was supplying the silk stockings for the court, the nobility, and the wealthy. Undeterred, Lee brought his invention to France to be patented.

In addition to the fashion for snug-fitting knit stockings, embroidery was very popular in the sixteenth century. Gowns, bodices, and sleeves, as well as doublets and breeches, were richly embroidered in colorful threads. Chemises and shirts were also embroidered on the visible areas of the cuffs, sleeves, and necklines. This embroidery, called "Spanish work" or "blackwork," was a style of delicate, repeating abstract figures worked in black silk on white linen. The fashion was said to have originated in Spain and was supposed to mimic lace.

Cutwork and drawnwork was also very popular across Europe. An Italian style of cutwork filled the open spaces with delicate embroidery. When this was done on a fine piece of netting, it was called *filet* or *lacis*.[3] While these techniques produced a textile similar in appearance to lace, actual lace making was an entirely different process. Begin in the fifteenth century, lace making spread throughout Europe from France, Italy, and the Low Countries. Various techniques of needle and bobbin laces were being produced for the wealthy and powerful across the continent. By the middle of the sixteenth century, the shirts of the wealthy were decorated with a mix of exquisite embroidery and finely wrought lace.

MEN'S CLOTHING

Early in the sixteenth century, medieval styles were still influencing the dress of the people of Europe. Men wore full shirts of white linen that were gathered to a round or square neckline, which was usually decorated with embroidery. The raglan sleeves were long and full and gathered to a wristband that could also be decorated with embroidery.

Doublets were waist length and laced to the hose, which were made in one piece with a codpiece at the center front. Sleeves were also laced into the armholes of the doublet. In the early decades of the century, the white shirt sleeves were pulled and puffed through openings in the doublet sleeves in the Italian style. Additionally, a sleeved jerkin was sometimes worn over the doublet, primarily in England.

A base was a piece of skirting worn with the doublet brought in from Germany. It originated as a part of military costume and added length to the doublet and fell into deep pleats into a skirt that was worn knee length or shorter. Some men early in the century also persisted in wearing long gowns with wide, bell-shaped sleeves. These wide sleeves were often lined with a contrasting fabric or fur and worn turned back to show off this lining. Some of these gowns were worn open over the doublet and hose, and young men wore their sleeves fashionably turned back very far.

The early years of the century focused on a slim silhouette, but soon it filled out into a series of bulky areas that were padded and puffed and slashed to reveal the colorful lining beneath. This style was referred to as slashings or panes. The story behind the origin of this fashion is attributed to the Swiss army, whose soldiers supposedly stuffed the colorful banners and garments of the enemy into their own clothing for warmth, the swatches of fabric showing in the tears in their own clothes.[4] Both the Swiss and the Germans were both known for wearing uniforms of multicolored fabric, decorated with slashings and panes showing contrasting colors beneath. While the colors were rich jewel tones in Germany, when this style migrated to England it was adopted in more subdued colors.

Shirts, doublets, and jerkins did not change very much through the middle of the century. Instead of a separate base, doublets were being cut with the skirting attached. This was less full than the separate base. Bases were still worn with armor and by military men. Doublets were often cut with a wide U- or V-shaped neckline to show the shirt beneath. Sleeves were made very wide to the elbow and then more form fitting to the wrist. Some sleeves were short and puffed or slashed, others were long sleeves that could hang loose or be worn closed with the sleeves pulled through the decorative openings.

Hose were still laced into the doublets. In this period, the hose was beginning to be divided into upper stocks and nether stocks. The codpiece was still used as a center front closure of the hose. Codpieces could be made padded and shaped into interesting forms. Upper stocks grew more bulky and came to be a distinct piece separate from the nether hose. The upper stocks were also called *breeches*, a name that would become the principal term for these pants. Breeches were constructed in various forms. The basic breeches were moderately full and could be worn just above or just below the knee, but some were very full and rounded and barely reached past the hips. The breeches could be slashed or paned and almost always matched the doublet. Overall, the look was very thickly padded through the shoulders and the hips. Men in England fashioned their clothes after their larger-than-life monarch Henry VIII, who prided himself on his appearance. Nationals allied with or friendly toward England, such as the Low Countries and Germany, also followed these bombastic styles.

Although they were falling out of fashion for young men, gowns were still worn, mainly by older gentleman such as nobles, clerics, merchants, bankers, and tutors. The sleeves of these gowns remained very wide and full, often still worn turned back to show off the lining.

In the second half of the sixteenth century, the width of the male silhouette narrowed. While some padding was still used, it was nowhere near as unrealistically proportioned as previous decades. Doublets were worn cut closer to the body but often had a protruding belly that was stuffed with padding. This odd shaping was known as the "peascod belly."[5] Doublets in general were far more structured, often stiffened with reed or whalebone. By and large, they closed with a series of many small, round buttons, although some were held together with ties tipped with aglets. The doublet's shoulders were capped in a narrow epaulet or sleeve roll that extended slightly over the sleeve, or the armhole could be ringed with tabs (shaped pieces of fabric) or *picadils* (fabric loops). These additions gave width to the shoulders without the cumbersome padding. Tabs and picadils were also used to trim the bottom of the doublet in place of or even in addition to skirting.

Jerkins, the sleeveless jackets, were still worn over the doublets for many nobles and worn on their own by the lower classes. Jerkins often were made with epaulets, very small rolls, tabs, or picadils at the shoulder, especially if they were the primary garment or worn over a doublet that had no shoulder decoration. Jerkins could also be closed with buttons or ties.

The very full, very short breeches known as pumpkin, kettle, or onion breeches were very fashionable for court dress, often worn over full-length

"The Cheat with the Ace of Diamonds (Cardsharp)," 1635, shows the low neckline of women's dresses and a variety of women's clothing details and headdresses typical of the seventeenth century. © Réunion des Musées Nationaux / Art Resource, NY.

hose. *Canions* were leggings often worn in conjunction with the very shortest of breeches, the *culots*. Culots were hardly more than a set of padding worn around the hips and were usually not even seen below the skirting of the doublet. The canions were laced to these culots and usually came to just below the knee. They were a close fit, but not tight. Instead of hose, stockings were usually worn when canions were used, and sometimes the stockings were worn pulled up over the knee. For everyday wear, Venetian breeches were worn. These were voluminous through the hips and tapered to the knee. Large, outlandish codpieces were no longer worn by men. While codpieces were often still used, they were usually of a small, utilitarian scale and well hidden by the deep gathers at the waist of the popular styles of breeches, all of which were very full though the hips.

Gowns had gone completely out of fashion in the late sixteenth century, save for bankers, priests, scholars, older merchants, and a few others for whom the gown was a mark of station. A *shaube*, a sleeveless robe with a large shawl collar, became a popular garment with mayors, sheriffs, and other men of rank. It was voluminous, but open, and could easily be worn over a doublet and Venetian breeches. Capes remained popular and supplanted the popularity of gowns and robes for younger nobles. From the middle of the century on, capes were circular and worn draped from one shoulder to produce a jaunty flare.

One of the most important fashionable accessories for men was the ruff. At first, the fashion was simply for a ruffled edge to the shirt, but slowly more width was desired. Thin strips of fabric were accordion folded or folded in a figure eight and tacked to a band that closes at the front or the back with a hidden fastening. Ruffs provided a large industry for tailors and launderers. They needed a great deal of care to be kept clean and properly starched. At the height of their fashion and their width, ruffs needed more than starch to stay rigid and were worn with a wire understructure called an "underpropper" or a "supportase."[6]

Headdresses and Hairstyles

Men's hairstyles were largely unchanged throughout the sixteenth century. Most men kept their hair cropped and no longer than the shoulder. Some very fashionable men wore their hair cut into short fringes, or bangs, across their foreheads. Neatly trimmed moustaches and small beards were also popular for men across Europe during the 1500s.

Wealthy men, as well as women, enjoyed the use of lavish jewelry in all aspects of their attire. From hats to neckwear, doublets, breeches, purses, and shoes—jewels were pinned on, hung from, and sewn to every piece of clothing. Even men's gloves could be studded or beaded with jewels or precious metals.

Hats for men did change over the century. Beginning as soft caps that resembled berets in the opening years, men's headwear gradually became more rigid and detailed. By the end of the 1500s, a tall-crowned hat with a small brim was the height of fashion. Throughout the period, feathers of various types and colors were used to trim hats and often held in place with a jeweled brooch. German hats were particularly spectacular. They were very wide and round and shaped like a disk perched on top of the head. Enormous and multicolored plumes were worn on these hats, and decorative charms often were suspended underneath.

Footwear

Men's footwear was also an area for fashionable expression, especially since the styles favored a very visible leg. Shoes were square toed at the opening of the century, but with the German influences, a very wide, more rounded toe began to gain popularity. The toes of the shoes expanded so much that a law had to be passed to keep them less than six inches (15 cm) in width. These widths were usually decorated with cutwork or slashing and sometimes had puffs of contrasting fabric pulled through the slashes. Shoes for the court were made of velvet or brocade, but primarily shoes were made of leather. Shoes were flats until the 1570s, when small heels were introduced; the first heels were only about an inch and a half (4 cm) tall. Boots for riding were of very fine leather and often worn with spurs. These boots could reach the knee or be thigh high, depending on the style of breeches worn with them. Plain boots and clogs were worn by the lower classes. Although England, France, and the northern European countries were in conflict with Spain for most of the century, it was from Spain that most of the fashionable styles originated.

WOMEN'S CLOTHING

At the start of the sixteenth century, women's styles were transitioning from the medieval. The wide, long sleeves and heavy gowns from early in the century reflected this transitional period, but once the dominant silhouette was established by the 1530s, it would remain fashionable through the beginning of seventeenth century with only slight variation.

The chemise was the basic body garment for women. Through the medieval period, these were identical for men and woman, but as time went on, each gender varied this garment to suit their own clothing needs and preferences. Early in the century, chemises were plain linen with full sleeves gathered into a band at the wrist and into a wide neckline. The chemise did not show beneath the gown.

Gowns were plain at the outset of the century and not made with rich colors or sumptuous figuring. Skirts were very full and had a bell shape, often with a train behind. Trains sometimes had decorative linings that could be shown when the skirt was lifted to walk or dance. Bodices were fitted and very snug to the body, often made with stiff fabrics for support, but not boned. Women wore a single gown or sometimes wore one layered over another. If layered, the dresses were usually of contrasting colors, and the top skirts would be looped up to display the one beneath. Necklines were predominantly square, with a small peek of the chemise neckline showing. Gowns could also have a rounded neck or a V-neck. Depending on the depth of the V-neckline, lacings could be used to keep the bodice closed.

Sleeves were varied and often designed to be worn in combination with one another. Sleeves on undergowns, or on the gowns of lower classes, were narrow and close fitting with decorative cuffs. Sleeves designed to be worn with an overgrown were reminiscent of medieval gowns, with very wide, bell- or funnel-shaped sleeves with trailing ends.

In the second quarter of the century, international influence began to be more apparent in women's clothing. Throughout England and France, Spanish fashion began dominate, but in Germany, the styles remained uniquely theirs for a longer time. Wool was the favored textile for outerwear and was woven into plain lengths of solid colors. Chemises were of fine linen, utilizing both local and imported textile resources. Skirts were full and pleated or gathered into a waistband.

In Germany, women wore a close-fitted bodice with a square or round neckline that was decorated with banding or embroidery across the bustline. The décolletage was filled in by the chemise. German chemises were worn high to the neck. Sleeves were also close fitted, but alternated with tight bands and slashed and puffed areas. The cuff had a slight point to it and extended slightly over the back of the hand. Hair was caught up in a netted *caul* and topped with a flat, very wide-brimmed hat. These hats were only slightly smaller than the men's hats and were worn with no fewer plumes and dangling charms. Women wore plain gold chains around their necks, and women of rank wore a thicker gold collar that sat close to the throat and could be plain or jeweled.

Elsewhere in Europe, the dominant silhouette was being created in England and France. The custom of layering dresses changed slightly to include an overdress and a petticoat beneath. Bodices and skirts were cut in separate pieces and sewn or tied together to be worn. Bodices began to focus on producing an hourglass shape of a small waist and generous hips and bosom. They became very rigid to enforce this shape and elongated to a deep V at the waist. The join between the bodice and skirt was often hidden by a jeweled belt.

The square neckline remained popular throughout Europe and, like in Germany, some women of England and France wore their fine linen chemises closed to the throat. The neckbands and cuffs began to be more visible in fashionable dress and therefore became another target of decoration. Spanish-influenced blackwork, using black silk thread on the white linen, was a popular style of embellishment. Frills also began to be worn at the neck and wrists as well. These ruffled edges grew throughout the century, eventually becoming a piece of clothing on its own. Although never as popular for women as they were for men, ruffs still played an important part on dressing for court and other high functions and are seen in many portraits of the time.

It was also at this time that the wide sleeves look on a new look. The oversleeves were still worn in conjunction with a closer fitting undersleeve, but the design of both began to reflect this. The oversleeves became very narrow at the shoulder and upper arm, widening very dramatically into a wide bell. The linings of these large sleeves were made with a contrasting fabric or even fur and were often worn turned back to display it. It was fashionable to match the lining of the sleeve to the petticoat.

The undersleeve, however, changed the most during this time period. No longer the sleeve of the gown worn beneath, the undersleeve became a separate piece sewn or tied into the inside of the wide outer sleeve. These undersleeves could be highly decorated with slashing and paning, embroidery, jewels, and velvet. The showing chemise cuffs were also highly decorated with frills and embroidery. Another sleeve type was a simple narrowly fitted sleeve coming from a shoulder roll. Hanging sleeves, derived from Spanish styles, also began to grow in popularity through the middle of the century. Sleeves like these were tied into the armseye with ribbons tipped with *aiglets*. These joins could also be hidden beneath the shoulder roll, an epaulet, or *picadils*.

Toward the third quarter of the century, the silhouette became very stiff. The bodice got heavier and was stiffened with not only fabrics but also a piece of wood, bone, or metal (called a *busk*) that was inserted down the front of the bodice. Further shaping and stiffening could be gained by supplemental boning made from reeds, wood, or bone inserted along the sides of the bodice as well. This helped with the conical silhouette, which was also influenced by Spain. The skirt met the bodice as an inverted cone, shaped not only by the stiff fabric but also by the *farthingale*, a series of graduated hoops of whalebone, cane, or metal sewn into a skirt worn as an underpetticoat. To give the right dimension and attention to the hips, women would often strap a crescent-shaped pillow to their hips called a "bum-roll."

This silhouette was originally brought to England from Spain by Catherine of Aragon in the very beginning of the 1500s, but it took many decades to catch on with the general populace. The *ropa*, or the Spanish *surcote*, was a long outer gown that fastened up the center front from neck to hem and could be worn open or closed. It had a high neckline and was worn unbelted in an A-line silhouette over a gown. These coats originally were sleeveless but later seem to have adopted sleeves in imitation of the English styles. The ropa was most popular during the early years of the reign of Elizabeth I in England.

Throughout Elizabeth's reign, she remained a style leader across Europe. And slowly the width of the farthingale grew and soon the Spanish farthingale was replaced by the wheel farthingale, also known as the French farthingale. Although called "French," the wheel far-thingale was favored in the northern European countries, especially England. Skirts meant to be worn over the wheel far-thingale were extremely wide and full, often topped with a deep frill across the flat top of the skirt. To keep visual balance, the bodices grew very long and pointed, and the sleeves once more emphasized the shoulders. Hats and hairstyles were also tall, further elongating the body.

By the end of the century, the silhouette still resembled the overall form it had taken throughout, but seemed almost a caricature of itself. Ruffs for women grew to very wide proportions, also needing a sup-

Eva Le Gallienne in costume as Queen Elizabeth wears a reproduction of a farthingale with elaborate jewelled fabric and an open collar held up with a supportasse. New York. Courtesy of the Library of Congress.

portase like the men. Ruffs were also worn open for women, following the neckline of the bodice and standing in frills over the shoulders. These were often worn with a wired veil called a *headrail*, *conch*, or *whisk* that stood from behind the shoulders and created a heart-shaped silhouette behind the head and shoulders. Overall, the look was a high crested appearance of inhuman proportions.

Headdress for women went fairly unchanged through most of the early parts of the sixteenth century. A variety of hoods were popular through the first half of the period. The gabled or English hood with its squared and pointed shape was popular until Anne Boleyn introduced the French hood from France. This was a small, less structured crescent that could be worn farther back on the head and show the hair near the face. Veils and lappets hung from the back of these hoods, and they could hang loose or be pinned upon the hood in a variety of styles.

Women often wore their hair in jeweled nets, or for the lower classes, in plain snoods. Later in the century, these nets were often topped with hats that were made to look like men's hats, with tall crowns and small brims but of a much smaller scale and with a more feminine touch in fabric and trim choices. One of the most popular and iconic styles was the *attifet*, a heart-shaped wired head-dress that sat atop the hair, which was brushed aside into two rolls, and sat with its point just touching the forehead. This style originated in France and traveled quickly to become popular in England and Scotland.

Red hair was highly fashionable throughout the century, especially in the latter half and in England. Elizabeth I was a redhead, as was her father, Henry VIII. Women in England dyed their hair in imitation of their monarch and used wigs and false hairpieces to create the fashionable styling. They also favored a pale complexion. To achieve this, ladies kept their faces masked when outdoors. Ladies also paled their faces with substances that modern women would never touch, such as mercuric salts and white lead. It was said that Elizabeth I painted her face in makeup almost half an inch (13 mm) thick.

Spain had a profound effect on women's dress through most of the century, dictating the silhouette and style much of the time. Although it was adopted and modified by each country to be made its own, Spanish influence would hold sway across Europe into Germany and the Low Countries, much of which was under Spanish control. By the end of the century, however, England and France had emerged as style makers for the women of Europe, a role they would hold onto through the seventeenth century and beyond.

CHILDREN'S CLOTHING

Children in the sixteenth century were dressed as miniature adults. Both girls and boys wore gowns until the age of five or six years, at which time the boys were allowed to put on the doublet and hose in what usually was a large family celebration. Girls continued to be dressed as fashionable replicas of their mothers. Royal and noble children were dressed, as befitting their station, in costly silk, velvet, brocade, jewels, and furs. Children were even subjected to the wearing of large ruffs, padded clothes, and farthingales. It would not be until the eighteenth century that the idea of healthful dress for children would even be considered.

NOTES

1. The Low Countries consisted of Belgium, the Netherlands, Holland, Luxembourg, Flanders, and several smaller duchies and areas.
2. The Spanish had settlements in Florida beginning in 1513.
3. Phyllis G. Tortora and Keith Eubank, *Survey of Historic Costume*, 4th ed. (New York: Fairchild, 2005), 172.
4. Tortora and Eubank, *Survey of Historic Costume*, 175.
5. According to Tortora and Eubank, the term *peascod* is derived from "peacock" (*Survey of Historic Costume*, 175). However, others attribute the term to the shape of plate armor; François Boucher, *20,000 Years of Fashion: The History of Costume and Personal Adornment* (New York: H. N. Abrams, 1987), 228.
6. Tortora and Eubank, *Survey of Historic Costume*, 185; Herbert Norris, *Tudor Costume and Fashion* (Mineola, NY: Dover, 1997), 626.

FURTHER READING

Ashelford, Jane. *The Art of Dress: Clothes and Society, 1500–1914.* New York: H. N. Abrams, 1996.

Boucher, François. *20,000 Years of Fashion: The History of Costume and Personal Adornment.* New York: H. N. Abrams, 1987.

Harris, Jennifer, ed. *Textiles, 5,000 Years: An International History and Illustrated Survey.* New York: H. N. Abrams, 1993.

Norris, Herbet. *Tudor Costume and Fashion.* Mineola, NY: Dover Publications, Inc., 1997.

Tortora, Phyllis G., and Keith Eubank. *Survey of Historic Costume: A History of Western Dress.* 4th ed. New York: Fairchild, 2005.

WEB RESOURCES

TudorHistory.org. http://tudorhistory.org.

MOVIES

Anne of the Thousand Days (1969)
Elizabeth (1998)
Genius Galileo (2001)
If I Were King (1938)
Lady Jane (1985)
Martin Luther (1953)
Shakespeare in Love (1999)

The Seventeenth Century

Sara M. Harvey

TIMELINE

1598	Edict of Nantes grants Huguenots political privilege and allows them their own basically self-governed territories in southern France
1599	Oliver Cromwell, Lord Protector of England during the Commonwealth, born in England
1600	Charles I of England born to James VI of Scotland and Anne of Denmark
1602	Dutch East India Company founded
1603	Queen Elizabeth I of England dies; James VI of Scotland takes the throne, uniting Scotland and England and becoming James I of England
1605	The Gunpowder Plot in England, aimed at blowing up the House of Parliament, foiled
1606	Dutch painter Rembrandt van Rijn born in the Netherlands
1607	Jamestown Colony established in what is now Virginia
1611	King James Bible published
1614	James I dissolves the English Parliament; Cardinal Richelieu dissolves the States-General of France, thereby concentrating power in the hands of Louis XIII
1616	William Shakespeare dies in England
1618	Manchu invasion of China; Thirty Years' War begins in what is now Germany
1620	Puritan pilgrims from England arrive at Plymouth Rock in what is now Massachusetts
1622	Jean-Baptiste Poquelin, known as Molière, a playwright and dramatist, born in France
1624	Cardinal Richelieu becomes chief minister of France and centralizes the power of the country
1625	Dutch colony of New Amsterdam founded in what is now New York; Charles I of England takes the throne
1626	St. Peter's Basilica is completed in the Vatican City in Rome
1630	Charles II of England, the "Merry Monarch," born to Charles I and Henrietta Maria of France
1632	Construction of the Taj Mahal, a mausoleum for Mumtaz Mahal, begun in India; great Dutch painter Johannes Vermeer born in Delft

1638	Dauphin Louis-Dieudonné, the future Louis XIV, born in France to Louis XIII and Anne of Austria
1640	Leopold I becomes Holy Roman emperor and reigns until 1705
1642	Civil War in England; Cardinal Richelieu dies in France, and Cardinal Mazarin takes his place as adviser to Louis XIII; Galileo Galilei dies in Italy
1643	Louis XIII of France dies; Louis XIV, the "Sun King," becomes king at age four and will rule until his death in 1715
1644	Manchu conquer China, ending the Ming dynasty; new Qing dynasty rules until 1912
1648	The Peace of Westfalia ends the Thirty Years' War; Fronde Civil War begins in France
1649	Charles I of England beheaded by Oliver Cromwell; English Civil War ends and the Commonwealth of England begins
1652	Cape Town founded by the Dutch in South Africa; Anglo-Dutch Wars begin
1653	Fronde Civil War in France ends
1660	Commonwealth of England ends as the monarchy is brought back during the English Restoration
1661	The Palace of Versailles, a small royal chateau outside of Paris, begins a massive renovation and reconstruction that will take more than two decades to complete
1662	Future Mary II born in England to James II and his first wife, Lady Anne Hyde
1665	Great Plague of London kills tens of thousands and reduces the city's population by a fifth
1666	Great Fire of London destroys two-thirds of the city
1669	Rembrandt dies in Amsterdam
1672	Peter the Great becomes tsar of Russia and rules until 1725
1675	Vermeer dies in Delft
1682	Peter the Great becomes a joint ruler of Russia; French explorer René-Robert Cavelier, Sieur de La Salle, sails the length of the Mississippi River and claims the Louisiana Territory for France; court of Louis XIV officially installed at Versailles, moving the political capital of France away from Paris
1685	Johann Sebastian Bach born in Germany; Charles II of England dies with no legitimate heirs and his brother becomes king and rules England and Scotland as James II
1688	Glorious Revolution in England forces James II from the throne in favor of his eldest daughter, Mary
1689	Mary II rules with her Dutch husband William of Orange
1692	Salem Witch Trials take place in Salem, Massachusetts
1694	Mary II dies childless; William III continues to rule until 1702
1702	William III of England dies; Mary II's sister Anne crowned and rules until 1714

Seventeenth-century costume is often overlooked as nothing more than a transitional period between the better-known Elizabethan (1558–1602) and Rococo (1725–1775) periods. But the 1600s were a time filled with political and social upheaval as well as rich artistic achievement. These many influences can be seen in the dress of the times, nostalgic in the face of such sundering changes but also far-reaching and innovative like the multilayered music prevalent in this time. Never before had art had such a closely connected and profound influence on fashion. The symmetry and restraint so prevalent in the preceding century were cast aside in favor of eccentricity and excess. The seventeenth century brought male fashion into the spotlight, creating a cult-like atmosphere of men's style that would resonate for centuries to come.

Influences on art and fashion moved away from the traditional European centers of Italy and Spain into France and the Netherlands. With the advent of stable and continuous trade with India, the Netherlands built an empire on cotton and tea. The Dutch people freed themselves from Spanish rule and created a republic that would come to be a major trendsetter in painting, fashion, and decorative arts. Art in France moved beyond the simple expression of an aesthetic or the capturing of everyday life into the interpretation of society itself, revolutionizing the significance of art and revealing a new purpose behind its creation.

Religious strife did much to shape the nature of this century. While always at odds with one another, tensions between Protestants and Catholics reached a boiling point in the early 1600s. The austere and often extreme Puritans were expelled by monarchs across Europe and eventually settled in the New World in what would become, in the century to follow, the United States. The Reformed Church, founded by Martin Luther in 1517, held absolute sway in most countries of northern Europe—Holland, Switzerland, Denmark, Germany, Scotland—while the Roman Catholic Church was still dominant in the Mediterranean and southern regions, especially Italy, Spain, and Portugal. It was the countries in between, primarily England and France, that bore the brunt of this conflict between the two religions. Even within the Protestant faith, battle lines were being drawn between the vastly differing factions: Calvinists, Baptists, Anglicans, Methodists. Friction between the Catholics and Protestants, and even among the Protestants themselves, was reflected even in the manner of dress each group chose to wear.

Numerous monarchies rose and fell throughout Europe, and with each new ruler, the standards of royal opulence were raised to new and astronomical heights. France led this trend with King Louis XIV, the *Roi Soleil* or "Sun King," who built the palace at Versailles and kept his courtiers spinning with new trends, rituals, and fashions on an almost daily basis. In contrast to Louis's long reign, England saw a parade of kings throughout the century. These leaders ranged from brilliant politicians to ineffectual fops as a civil war fueled the dissention within Parliament. Royalists squared off against Parliamentarians, dividing families and the country into factions.

This was the age of the *cavaliers* and the colorful characters of *The Three Musketeers*, with their broad-brimmed hats with trailing plumes, velvet capes, and flashing steel, romantically remembered in modern days for risking all for honor, king, and country.

Overall, the seventeenth century was one of great change, great discovery, and great advancement that often came at great cost. A new understanding of style and fashion emerged from France and soon caught hold across the whole of Europe. It is against this background that one must examine the fashions of this time.

HISTORY

The seventeenth century was a time of great social and political upheaval. Change was the only constant in this century that marked the beginnings of the modern era (encompassing 1650–1850). Many laws and cultural concepts that are deeply ingrained in current society were developed in the seventeenth century. Prior to that time, ideas of individualism were unknown, although laws still permeated the system to ensure that the traditional patterns of life continued. The gulf between the wealthy and the working class widened significantly, setting the stage for the further social upheavals in France and the English colony in America in the following century and in Russia in the centuries after that.

The century was dominated by France. Although the Dutch held sway in the world of art, it was France that set the tone for government, literature, and culture. France fostered the idea of absolute monarchy, that the king held total power over every aspect of his kingdom. This notion was cemented by the Divine Right of Kings, the idea that through the natural male line of succession, God had ordained the royal lineage with the indisputable and unquestionable right to rule.

France

In France, a new era of the reign of the Louis began in 1610 when Henry IV (R. 1553–1610) was assassinated. Louis XIII ascended to the throne at age nine with his mother, Marie de' Medici serving as regent. Louis was said to be "poorly educated, sickly, masochistic, and subject to depression."[1] The unscrupulous and manipulative duc de Richelieu (1585–1642) became his closest companion and most trusted adviser, easily usurping the Queen Mother. In 1624, Richelieu was created a cardinal and named Louis's chief minister. Richelieu held the reins of France for eighteen years and created the idea of *raison d'état*, "reason of state," that would justify all of his actions.

Richelieu's plan to create Europe's first absolute monarchy had three goals. The first was to eliminate the country's Huguenots, the Protestants, from political power. France was a Catholic country, but the 1598 Edict of Nantes had granted the Huguenots political privilege and allowed them their own basically self-governed territories in the south. Richelieu attacked the Huguenot stronghold of La Rochelle, and the city finally fell in 1628. Because he had been "unexpectedly humane"[2] in the siege of La Rochelle, the Huguenots gave up their political and military protections in exchange for continued religious tolerance. How tolerant Richelieu actually was is not certain, but many of them left their homeland in favor of the Protestant countries of England and Holland.

THE BOURBONS

Henry IV was originally a Huguenot but later converted to Catholicism, beginning the dynasty of the Bourbon kings.

The second step in Richelieu's plan was to completely subordinate the nobility to the king. He stripped the least trustworthy of the nobles of their fortresses and gave over the supervision of their local administrations to royal officials. Not only did this render potential troublemakers powerless, it helped to centralize the government.

Last, the Cardinal sought to create a "national consciousness of greatness," uniting all the disparate areas of France under one national banner. This was difficult, because there was not one agreed-upon language. Richelieu deeply believed that the masses were best kept docile with hard work and that leisure and frivolity led to unrest. He fostered an idea that individual hardships were to be endured with pride for the glory of France. Richelieu achieved his goals, but the strong central government and downtrodden peasantry ultimately led to the collapse of the French monarchy in the following century.

Richelieu died in 1642, followed by Louis XIII the following year. The young Louis XIV (R. 1643–1714) became king at age four. Although he was destined to be one of the most influential kings in French history, his early years were fraught with danger and intrigue. His mother, Anne of Austria, was a Spanish Hapsburg and was very unpopular with the people of France. Cardinal Mazarin (1602–1661), trained by Richelieu himself, stepped in as the new king's adviser. Mazarin had a personal fortune, but he was constantly borrowing money from the nobility and neglecting to repay it. He also gave preferential treatment to the nobles who had bought into the ranks of the aristocracy and excluded the ancestral gentry from the regency.

In 1648, the disillusioned nobles staged a small revolution known as *La Fronde*, named after a child's slingshot toy that was often used to pelt noble carriages with stones. This revolution sent Mazarin and the young Louis and his mother into exile. Mazarin left the country twice, and on his eventual return, he was forced to make concessions to the disenfranchised nobility. Royal troops advanced on Paris to quell the riots and set the stage for the triumphant return of the king in October 1652. The nobles even welcomed the Queen Mother. They did not recognize that they had played right into Mazarin's hands and weakened their own powers even more.

When Mazarin died in 1661, Louis began his actual reign. He was a masterful ruler, becoming *Le Roi Soleil* or the Sun King, also known as *Le Grande Monarque*, the Great Monarch. He was shrewd and patient, never losing his temper in public. He was a tall man for the times, standing five feet eight inches (1.7 m) without the high-heeled shoes he favored. Louis XIV was also known for his "conspicuous lack of a sense of humor."[3]

In 1660, Louis married a Spanish princess and had several legitimate children with her, although he was far from faithful and fathered many illegitimate children as well. Queen Maria Theresa died in 1683, and in 1685 Louis married the governess of his illegitimate children, Madame de Maintenon.

The Fronde revolt had made Louis XIV wary of the fawning nobles all around him. He therefore orchestrated intricate court rituals and intrigues to keep them occupied. To further isolate his courtiers from a possible base of power in Paris, he moved his royal residence to Versailles, a dozen miles outside of the city. Originally a hunting estate of his father's, Versailles was built into a palace during 1668–1711. At its completion it was one-third of a mile (half a kilometer) long; held ten thousand courtiers, servants, retainers, and dependents; and had 1,400 fountains that were fed by a complicated and costly pumping process from the Seine River. This court was the most admired and imitated across Europe, although most countries could afford to produce only a shallow copy of its grandeur.

Louis was a firm believer in the Divine Right of Kings, citing the unbroken lineage between him and the tenth-century king, Hugh Capet. France was a country of 16 million inhabitants scattered into different social and cultural groups—Normans, Bretons, Burgundians, Basques, Alsatians, and so on. Louis XIV was the first king to actually attempt Richelieu's never-realized goal of bringing these disparate entities under one banner.

The king formed the National Gallican Church, a Catholic establishment that was controlled by the throne of France. The motto of both the Church and State was *"Un Roi, Une Loi, Une Foi"* (One King, One Law, One Faith). Louis revoked the Edict of Nantes in 1685, and nearly all of the remaining 50,000 Huguenots fled to Protestant countries such as England, Prussia, the Netherlands, the Dutch colonies in Africa, and the English colonies in North America. This religious purging actually weakened France, taking many craftsmen and artisans away from France's workforce. Furthermore, the remaining Catholics actually caused more trouble than the Huguenots ever had, constantly calling into question the authority of the king through God.

Louis XIV had begun to secure a national mercantile identity in France. The country traded richly in sugar, chocolate, and tobacco from its colonies. It also had an emerging sericulture market, but that was significantly impacted when the Huguenots took their silk cultivating and weaving techniques abroad, most notably to England's Spitalfields. The government tightly controlled natural resources such as lumber and coal to be available for the growth of commerce. For most of the seventeenth century, France boasted unrivaled leadership in industry and commerce, but England's emerging industrialization would outstrip France in the eighteenth century.

Another of Louis's mistakes was to overstretch his country's martial abilities. In seeking to control Spain and the Netherlands, he brought the ire of a solid bloc of resistance against him as Spain, England, the Holy Roman Empire, the Netherlands, and Brandenburg Prussia joined forces to fight France. Although France could not be defeated on land, it could never quite achieve victory, either, and the aggression ended with a treaty signed in 1697.

Louis XIV died in 1715, after having ruled for seventy-two years and outliving both his son and grandson. His legacy includes not only the most impressive and lavish court Europe has ever known but also the standardization of the French language and creation of the French dictionary. Furthermore, he established the mode of behavior for polite society through his court at Versailles. But in the process, he nearly bankrupted the country with his supercilious and costly courtly life and expensive wars and further widened the gaping maw between the wealthy and the peasantry. As the Sun King's funeral procession marched through the streets of Paris, it was openly mocked.

Great Britain

When Queen Elizabeth I (*R.* 1558–1603) of England died on March 24, 1603, her cousin, James VI of Scotland, son of Mary Stuart, the beheaded Queen of Scots, took the English throne. He was proclaimed James I (*R.* 1603–1625) of the now united kingdoms of England—which included Wales and Ireland—and Scotland. His ascension to the throne ended the Elizabethan era and began the Jacobean.

Throughout the century, the English nobility retained its powers in local government and in Parliament. Even though James was very assured of his position as a result of Divine Right, it was his Scots heritage that caused the most friction between the monarchy and the lower aristocracy. He was seen as a foreigner that could not be trusted, not only because of his ties to Scotland but also his close kinship with France. In addition, his religion was a cause for concern among the people, and his lavish expenditure of money and short-sighted foreign policy were some of the major political issues in his reign. He was also embroiled in the famous "Gunpowder Plot" of 1605, where a group of Catholic dissenters attempted to destroy Parliament with a stash of gunpowder in the cellar. Although not the leader of the plot, Guy Fawkes is the name associated with it. James declared November 5 to be a national day of celebration, although in modern times it is usually an antipapist event with effigies of the pope burned instead of the conspirators.

James I was married to Anne of Denmark, a woman seen to be frivolous and driven by fashion. Their eldest son and heir apparent, Henry, was created the Prince of Wales and Earl of Chester on June 5, 1610, at age 16. He was the first person to be heir apparent to the crowns of both England and Scotland. He was a well-read, charismatic, and artistic young man with a steady temper and charming manner. Tragically, he died of typhoid fever in 1612 at age 18. His younger brother Charles took his place as heir apparent and tried to hold the salons and literary parties for which his brother had been so famous, but he was never as adept as his brother in these matters.[4]

Anne of Denmark did not long outlive her eldest son and passed away in 1619. After her death, the English court became a scene of male debauchery with hardly any female influence whatsoever.

James arranged an engagement between Charles and a Spanish princess, seeking to ally the two nations by means of their common Catholic religion, but the public outcry against an alliance with England's long-time adversary was immense. James was fierce in his rebuke to the people, and in retaliation Parliament drew up the Great Protestation against the union. James then dissolved Parliament and imprisoned four of its most influential leaders. The Spanish engagement fell through, and James then turned to France. He married his son to Henrietta Maria, sister of the French king Louis XIII.

Throughout James's reign, religious intolerance grew. Early on, the king called a conference between the Anglican Church and the Puritans, a very solemn and severe branch of Protestantism, but they could not come to an agreement.

However, James did set one major religious precedent that would reverberate through the centuries to come: he codified the first complete English translation of the Bible. Forty-seven ministers were authorized to complete and compile the translation. It is "perhaps the most remarkable literary achievement a committee has ever made."[5] The King James Bible was published in 1611 and is still in regular use in some churches in the twenty-first century.

When James I died in 1625, his son Charles took the throne, becoming Charles I of England (*R.* 1625–1642). Even though his queen was French, England was very antagonistic toward both France and Spain. This set the stage for the many battles that were draining the monarchs' resources on both sides of the skirmish. In England, Charles gathered the greatest war mustering since Elizabeth I had faced the Spanish Armada in 1588. He forced loans from the nobility and quartered soldiers in their homes without their consent and at their expense. In 1628, Parliament called a halt to such behavior and passed the Petition of Right, forbidding taxation without the consent of Parliament, the billeting of soldiers in private homes, martial law during peacetime, and imprisonment without a specific charge. The king consented to the Petition of Right, but then in 1629 dissolved Parliament and imprisoned nine of its highest ranking members on charges including refusing to vote and meddling in religious affairs. Some of the nobles died in their Tower of London prison.

From 1629 until 1640, Charles I governed without a Parliament, styling himself an absolute monarch like Louis XIII in France. He spent vast amounts of money, since he no longer had to ask permission from Parliament nor justify its use. He also persecuted the Puritans, and many fled England into the Netherlands and the young colonies of America. He also marched on the Scots because, although he was the son of their king, they were refusing to acknowledge him. A compromise with Scotland was finally made in 1639, but not before bankrupting the treasury and forcing Charles to reconvene Parliament in 1640. Immediately, Parliament refused to authorize any more money to King Charles until he settled his long list of grievances and outstanding debts—so he dissolved Parliament once again. This meeting was known as the Short Parliament.

Skirmishes with the Scots continued and Charles bought them off, promising to pay them but never following through. He called Parliament together once more, and this time they made him complete a series of reforms, including a set schedule of when Parliament would meet, regardless of whether he dissolved it or not. This Parliament would stay the focus of political power for some years to come and would be known as the Long Parliament.

Throughout this, the political situation in Ireland had been greatly mishandled. A revolution for national independence was staged by the Catholics, and 30,000 Protestants were massacred in Ulster in the north of Ireland. The insurgency was put down in 1641 by an Act of Parliament, which did not trust Charles to be able to handle the Irish problem.

Also in 1641, radical Puritans tried to push through a bill that would eradicate the system of bishops in the Anglican Church and revamp its entire structure to suit their religious views. It was defeated, but it was the first time that all the Parliamentary radicals had come together to pursue a common goal. They recognized their strength and began to put it into action.

In June 1642, Parliament submitted the Nineteen Propositions, which gave the governing body complete supremacy over the Church, royal administration, and all matters of the royal court, including the rearing and betrothing of royal children. Charles rejected the Propositions, and later that year, he had five of his Parliamentary opponents arrested without just cause, and they took refuge in London. Charles fled north to Nottingham to try to rally an army, while his wife, Henrietta Maria, fled to France with their children, including the heir apparent, twelve-year-old Charles Stuart. In the absence of the royal family, Parliament took over the central government, and a civil war was begun.

The battle lines of England's civil war were not clearly drawn. The country broke along territorial, socioeconomic, and religious loyalties. In a broad sense, these could be summed up in two groups: the Puritan/Parliamentary faction in the south and east of the country controlling London, and the Royalists, who drew support from the landed gentry of the north and west. In all, the Parliamentary forces controlled the wealth and political power of England, but the Royalists were backed up by the traditional landholders who for generations had been loyal to the Crown and the Church. These divisions by no means were absolute, however, as the king had as many supporters in London as Parliament had in Northampton. The Scots proved to be a volatile wild card, not trusting of or trusted by either side of the conflict.

The Puritans came forward with an early victory. Oliver Cromwell (1599–1658), a Puritan and tactician, put together a special forces unit known as the Ironsides. This strictly disciplined unit won an important victory at the Battle of Marston Moor in 1644. From this small force came the New Model Army headed by Cromwell. It was formed of religious and political radicals who were willing to die for their beliefs. This group was rigorously trained and answered wholly to Cromwell. Its soldiers were known by the nickname of "Roundheads" because of their short-cut hair that ran opposite to the fashion of full, long curls on men. The epithet is anecdotally attributed to Queen Henrietta Maria,[6] and it quickly caught on throughout the country.

The Battle of Naseby in 1645 was a decisive one for the New Model Army. With its victory, it drove Charles I into Scotland, where the Scottish army immediately turned him in to the English forces in exchange for the £400,000 they were promised but never paid by Charles himself several years earlier. The Parliamentary moderates were confronted by the radical backers of the New Model Army and Cromwell, but the moderate majority somehow managed to retain control. By 1648, the New Model Army had also defeated the Presbyterian Scots and eliminated any power base the king had remaining, but still the moderate Parliament refused to dethrone him.

In December 1648, Col. Thomas Pride excluded ninety-six members from the Long Parliament, leaving behind only about sixty of the most radical in what was known as "Pride's Purge."[7] The resulting group was known as the Rump Parliament. These sixty men brought King Charles up on charges of treason and were nearly unanimous in their decision to condemn him to death. Charles, still firmly believing in the Divine Right of Kings, would not acknowledge the subordinate authority of the Parliament in this judgment and went to his execution as a martyr. Charles I was beheaded on January 30, 1649, at Whitehall in London. His final words were: "I go from a corruptible to an incorruptible Crown, where no disturbance can be."[8] The Act of Parliament that sealed his fate is still looked upon by many as a clearly illegal act and a stain on England's history.

The next eleven years, spanning 1649–1660, were known as the Interregnum, an interval between two reigns. The radicals that had taken control of the government did not dare call for an election, knowing that popular opinion had turned against them and they were likely to lose their hard-wrought power. So the Rump Parliament continued to sit, putting England under what basically amounted to a dictatorship dominated by Cromwell. He was a driven man, power hungry and strong minded, but also trapped by his position. He realized that England was still a country divided and that the majority of the people were still royalists at heart, even as they swore allegiance to his new regime. He felt he had no choice but to continue ruling the country with an iron fist and trying to keep the ever-present threat of continued civil war at bay.

Both Scotland and Ireland were very hostile toward England. In 1649, the Irish Catholics rebelled again. Cromwell dealt them a harsh blow with the bloody and violent Cromwellian Settlement (1652–1654). This quelled the rebellion but did little to achieve peace, and Ireland would continue to be problematic. In 1650, Charles Stuart, son of the late king, landed in Scotland and gave his formal approval to Presbyterianism as the official religion of Scotland. Although he was raised Catholic in France, he was hasty in converting to Protestantism upon his arrival in Scotland. Upon his father's death, Charles Stuart had been crowned king of Scotland, but it was a title in name only and he held very little actual power. He raised an army against England, but it was soundly defeated and he fled back to the Continent in disguise.

As if he did not have enough to keep him occupied in the British Isles, Cromwell was also forced into an altercation with Holland from 1651 to 1654. This was brought on by England's Navigation Act of 1651 forbidding the import of goods into England or its colonies except on English ships or ships from the country of the goods' origin. This angered Holland, which had developed a great trade hegemony by carrying exports between various countries. Cromwell was victorious against Holland, winning a naval victory against the Dutch in 1654. He also made war against Spain from 1656 to 1658, acquiring Jamaica in the process and securing a profitable sugar trade for England.

But even with all of his victories abroad, Cromwell was not able to control the Rump Parliament back home in England. In April 1653, he appeared in Parliament with a division of soldiers and forced the Rump Parliament to dissolve. That December, Cromwell declared himself Lord Protector of England, Scotland, and Ireland and created a written constitution for his regime. It was called the Instrument of Government and was the first and only written constitution that England has ever had. It gave Cromwell his post for life but stressed it was not a hereditary position. It also banned Catholics and known Royalists from participating in public office and from voting. Freedom of religion was extended to all Protestants, save for those who were involved in extreme sects of Christianity. It also established that a standing army of 30,000 should be maintained at all times.[9]

The Protectorate Parliament was made up of 460 members that were chosen by Puritan sympathizers, as Royalists and Catholics were disenfranchised. But the Parliament still refused to support all of Cromwell's ambitions. He attempted to maintain order in England by dividing it up into twelve districts, each controlled by a general of Cromwell's choosing who reported directly to the Lord Protector. In 1657, he expanded Parliament to a second chamber and agreed to limits on his own powers with the Humble Petition and Advice.[10] Cromwell did not live long enough to see the ultimate success or failure of his concessions to Parliament; he died in 1658. And although it was explicitly stated that the position of Lord Protector was not a hereditary one, Cromwell's son, Richard, succeeded him.

Throughout the 1650s, strict laws were enacted to enforce Puritan austerity upon the populace. There were prohibitions on vice and pleasure, including horse racing, gambling, drinking, dancing, fancy dress/masquerade, theater, cockfighting, and bear baiting, the latter being banned not because of cruelty to the animals but because it promoted public displays of base pleasures and gambling among the spectators.[11] The people of England grew very tired of this restrictive rule as they also chafed beneath the repressive regime of Cromwell. In 1658, not long after Oliver Cromwell's death, the army marched on London and retook control. All surviving Parliamentary members dismissed by Pride's Purge were reinstated. It was then decided that the only way to calm the rampant political chaos was to restore the monarchy. Charles Stuart was invited to return from France and claim his throne. He was crowned Charles II of England (R. 1660–1685) and began his rule in 1660.

Although there was once again a monarchy in England, Parliament was still very strong. In addition to the restoration of the monarchy, the Anglican Church was also reinstated as the official State Church of England and Ireland. Scotland retained the Presbyterian Church as its official faith as per the agreement with Charles II. Protestants and others who did not accept the Church of England were labeled dissenters. Although there was no more threat of imprisonment or political blackmail, the label was still a strong social stigma. Most dissenters in England were middle-class merchants and artisans. In Ireland, it was most of the country's population south of Ulster.

The pendulum of Reformation had swung widely to the other side of the spectrum and the Restoration was a time of ribald humor and lively public pursuit of pleasure. Charles II's court was wild and reckless and full of lavish parties and bawdy drama. Restoration literature and drama were known for the use of intelligently crafted but licentious humor. In art, there was also a revulsion toward anything that stood to remind the people of Puritan austerity. Even portraiture began to take on a very dramatic and over-the-top flavor.

In 1670, Charles II formed an alliance with Louis XIV. In addition to political maneuverings and trade deals, this agreement also allowed England to fully claim the port city of New Amsterdam, which was first taken from the Dutch in the Anglo-Dutch War of 1664–1667. The port was renamed New York, and its loss to Holland ended the threat of Dutch sea trade, leaving England with a complete trade monopoly to its colonies in America. Even though this was a great boon to the English economy, most of the populace was actually very upset by the arrangement, claiming that it gave too much power to France and made England far too subservient.

Charles II was concerned with making peace between the Presbyterian Scots and the Anglican English, but this was an issue he would never see resolved in his lifetime. He also tended to favor the small Catholic community, and although he was a Protestant in word and deed, many accused him of being a Catholic in secret. Charles issued the original Declaration of Indulgence granting penal amnesty to Catholics and dissenters in 1671. However, he was forced by Parliament to repeal it in 1673 and to instate the Test Act, which required anyone seeking to hold political office to swear an oath to the monarch as head of the Church and accept the Protestant form of communion.[12]

It is said that Charles II's alliance with France was the groundwork to make England a Catholic nation.[13] Charles supported Louis XIV in his war against the Netherlands in 1672–1674. When Charles dissolved Parliament in 1681, France helped to support England financially, which was very upsetting to the citizens of both countries.

Parliament at the time of Charles II was decisively split into two parties: The Whigs, also known as the Oxford Parliament, were most interested in maintaining the status quo, while the Tories were avid supporters of the king. When Parliament was dissolved in 1681, the Whigs were all dismissed from their seats, and new elections were held to replace them.

> There was hardly a murmur of protest when Charles II failed to summon a Parliament in 1684 as he was bound to do by the Triennial Act. He was now fully master of his state—financially independent of Parliament and politically secure, with loyal Tory servants predominating in local and national government.[14]

Two very destructive forces ravaged London during Charles's reign. The first was a dramatic resurgence of bubonic plague in 1665. From April to November of that year, roughly 100,000 lives were lost due to the disease. In the following year, 1666, a small fire in a bakery turned into an all-consuming blaze that destroyed two-thirds of the buildings of London within the original city walls.

Although he fathered many illegitimate children, fourteen of which he acknowledged and titled, Charles II never produced a legitimate heir with his wife Catherine of Braganza, the Portuguese princess who brought England control of Bombay and Tangier as her dowry. Although Charles was not faithful to her, he defended her Catholic faith. The king officially converted back to Catholicism on his deathbed in 1685, and most of the populace of both England and Scotland blamed Catherine. She remained in England for several years under the protection of her Catholic brother-in-law, James II, who took the throne after Charles's death, then returned to Portugal in 1692 when the Protestant William III came into power.

The ascension of James II (*R.* 1685–1688) was dreaded in both England and Scotland because he was a staunch Catholic. There was even an attempt to pass an Exclusion Bill that would keep James from receiving his brother's throne. Yet surprisingly, there was no real opposition to his claiming of the crown. In 1687, James created a new Declaration of Indulgence, which granted freedom of worship to all Christian faiths in England, Scotland, and Ireland, including the previously excluded Catholics.

> We cannot but heartily wish, as it will easily be believed, that all the people of our Dominions were members of the Catholic Church, yet we humbly thank Almighty God that it is ... our opinion that conscience ought not to be constrained nor people forced in matters of mere religion.[15]

This was a great stride toward religious tolerance. England was in fear of the Catholic faith, but the small English Catholic minority was just happy to finally be able to worship in peace and no longer be in danger of persecution. The few Catholics in Scotland went about their worship quietly as well, but in Ireland, where Catholics made up the majority, there were more problems. The Irish Catholics thought the measure was too little too late. At the same time, anger in Parliament was beginning to build over James's heavy-handed manner in making decisions of state concerning religion without first consulting them.

James also had to contend with an uprising led by the Duke of Monmouth, one of the many bastard sons of his late brother, Charles II. Parliament tried again unsuccessfully to pass the Exclusion Bill, which would have given the

right of succession to Monmouth. Nevertheless, James easily quelled his neph-
ew's rebellion and executed him and his 320 supporters. Afterward, he created
a standing army of 30,000 soldiers and garrisoned them in London. But the
Parliament continued working against him, and in 1688 a group of Whig and
Tory peers joined forces to invite William of Orange to "defend the liberties of
England."[16]

James II was twice married. His first wife was the Protestant Lady Anne Hyde,
whom he married when he was the Duke of York, before he became king. By
her he had two daughters, Mary and Anne, both of whom were raised Protestant. After Lady Anne died in 1671, James married Mary of Modena in 1673.
She was a devout Catholic and, to the horror of Parliament, their union produced a son, James Francis Edward, in 1688. Rumors abounded that the child
was not a legitimate prince but had been smuggled into the birthing chamber in
a warming pan to ensure the continuation of a Catholic dynasty. The heir to
the throne was born just two days after the archbishop of Canterbury and six
other Anglican bishops refused to read the Declaration of Indulgence from their
pulpits and actively petitioned against the order. They were arrested and sent to
the Tower of London to await trial but were acquitted by a jury a few days later.
That same day, June 30, 1688, seven prominent members of Parliament sent
the official letter of invitation to William of Orange.

William III, Prince of Orange, was married to Mary Stuart, the eldest daughter of James II and his first wife. James had been hesitant to ally himself with
the Protestant Netherlands, but William was his nephew, the son of his and
Charles's sister Mary Stuart, the Princess Royal. Accepting the Parliamentary
invitation, William arrived in England with 15,000 troops on November 5,
1688, and entered London uncontested on December 19. James was allowed to
escape to France, legally abdicating his throne. This would go down in history
as the Glorious Revolution.

In January 1689, a Parliament was convened and met over the course of the
following month. On February 12, the Convention Parliament issued a Declaration of Rights, condemning the actions of James II, laying out the essentials of
Parliamentary supremacy, specifying the control of the treasury, placing limits
on Royal Prerogative, and setting a timetable for more frequent meetings of the
Parliament. Essentially, it was the same powers that Parliament had been seeking with the Petition of Right in 1628. Also on February 12, Mary arrived in
London, and the very next day the couple was offered and accepted the crown
to rule the United Kingdom jointly as William III (R. 1689–1702) and Mary II
(R. 1689–1694). Later in 1689, a bill was passed by Parliament declaring that
only the heirs of William and Mary or the heirs of Mary's Protestant sister,
Anne, were eligible for succession. This disenfranchised James II's son, who
fought the matter but to no avail.

The Catholics in Ireland, who had strongly supported James II, rebelled
against the rule of William and Mary. Although William wanted to be politically
moderate, especially where the Irish were concerned, he was forced into Cromwellian policies by Parliament, which was desperate to keep the peace at any
cost. Catholic worship in Ireland was not expressly forbidden, but all the Catholic schools were closed. Heavy restrictions were also placed on Irish trade, forcing many of the Irish into poverty and setting the stage for the continued
oppression and devastation in the centuries to come.

Mary II died of smallpox in 1694, and William passed away after a fall from his horse in 1702. The crown then passed to Mary's sister Anne, who ruled from 1702 to 1714. Although she had eighteen pregnancies, none of her children survived past the age of eleven and most of her pregnancies ended tragically in stillbirths or miscarriages. The next in line for the throne was Anne's cousin, Sophia of Hanover, granddaughter of James I. But both Anne and Sophia died within weeks of one another and the crown therefore passed to Sophia's son, George, Elector of Hanover, who became George I of Great Britain (R. 1714–1727).

With Anne's death, the Stuart dynasty begun in 1603 came to a close. By the end of the seventeenth century, the British monarchy had changed dramatically. Scotland and Ireland were officially recognized parts of the kingdom and answered to the English throne. Parliament had shifted the balance of power into its own hands, creating a parliamentary democracy. The crown was soon to become nothing more than a symbolic focus of patriotic loyalty as the United Kingdom moved out of the monarchic past and into the democratic future.

The Netherlands

The seventeenth century was a time of great change in all nations of Europe. The Netherlands, known collectively at this time as the Low Countries, broke away from Spain's control in 1579, although Spain did not officially recognize that independence until 1648. The Low Countries were originally conquered by Rome and later incorporated by Charlemagne as part of the Holy Roman Empire. The area had passed into French control and finally into the hands of the Hapsburgs, who were married into the royal line of Spain. In the mid-sixteenth century, the Low Countries became an official possession of Spain through King Philip II. The sixteenth century also brought the Low Countries to the attention of the rest of Europe with its widespread support of religious reformation.

Though under Spanish rule for the entirety of the sixteenth century, the Low Countries were locally controlled by William I, Prince of Orange, who had gained the favor of the Spanish Court but also was a secret opposition leader among his people. He was forced back into Catholicism after converting to Protestantism but always maintained religious freedom and tolerance in his own household and offices.

In 1566, religious intolerances erupted into violence. Many Catholic churches and other institutions were vandalized and desecrated. The Spanish retribution was swift and William of Orange's secret machinations against the Spanish government were brought out into the open. Clashes between the Spanish and the Low Country Protestants, the Calvinists, forced many of the ranking resistance leaders, including William, to flee the area. A new local government was moved into the area, and the seventeenth century dawned as an era of unrest and brutal retaliation as Spain sought to root out heresy and restore a pro-Spanish social order.

In 1568, William returned to the Low Countries and began an armed resistance against Spain that came to be known as the Eighty Years' War. Although he was fighting for the Calvinist cause, William was still a practicing Catholic and advocated religious tolerance on both sides. He found this difficult to explain to his Protestant allies in the Low Countries and in France, who were forbidding Catholic worship and turning a blind eye to Catholic persecution in areas that they controlled.

William of Orange managed to unite seven northern provinces under a single banner before his death, but the southern provinces remained Catholic and therefore loyal to Spain. After the defeat of the Spanish Armada by the English in 1588, William's son Maurice took the reins of the resistance. The Dutch Republic or United Netherlands, as the seven northern provinces came to call themselves, established the country as a place for liberal thought, education, and learning. The seventeenth century is known as the Dutch Golden Age. It was the age of Rembrandt and Vermeer and a whole host of other painters and writers. Amsterdam became the destination for an entire generation of disaffected artists who felt excluded or persecuted in their own countries.

A shared animosity toward Spain brought the United Netherlands, France, and England into a pact against Spain during the Thirty Years' War. At the conclusion of that war in 1648, as part of the Peace of Westphalia, the Treaty of Münster was signed, forcing Spain and the Holy Roman Empire to recognize the Dutch Republic as a sovereign nation. This also put an end to the Eighty Years' War that the Dutch had been fighting against Spain for their independence.

This was also an era when the Dutch economy soared to astronomic heights due to the skill its merchants had in trade. Even England, an old ally, turned against Dutch interests in the seventeenth century. After banding together during the Thirty Years' War, a change of political power in England put the Dutch on the antagonists' side. Beginning in 1651, England made war on the country by enforcing strict controls on the trade system as stated in the Navigation Act, which prohibited Dutch ships from transporting any non-Dutch goods to England or its colonies. This First Anglo-Dutch War lasted only a few years, with fairly few casualties on either side. Tensions mounted when Charles II of England openly struck out at the republic during the Second Anglo-Dutch War, which again lasted for only a short time, 1665–1667. But relations were soured between England and the Netherlands, especially after England allied strongly with France and continued to work against Dutch interests.

William III, Prince of Orange, claimed the title of stadholder in the United Netherlands in 1672. He rallied an army and turned aside a French invasion on Amsterdam the next year. In 1674, the Dutch Republic made peace with England, and in 1676, with France. Louis XIV had great respect for the Dutch people and their republic, and in 1678, the United Netherlands gained control of the Catholic southern provinces, known as the Spanish Netherlands, which had been wrested from Spain by France.

In 1677, William married the Protestant daughter of the Catholic James II of England, Mary Stuart. However, tensions rose anew when Catholic France and the Catholic ruler of England allied once more to give strength to their doctrine and try to push Catholicism back onto Europe. Protestants had been persecuted in France after the 1685 revocation of the Edict of Nantes, which had guaranteed them religious freedom. France then began to assist England in applying religious pressure and passing pro-Catholic legislation, hoping to undermine the Protestant majority. English Protestants turned to the Dutch Republic for support, and by 1688, the British Parliament was begging William to come and assist them in deposing the king. Known as the Glorious Revolution in England, William of Orange arrived with only a small army but was able to march triumphant into London almost without firing a shot. In 1689, with the permission of both England and the Netherlands, William III of Orange was crowned King William III of England, while still holding his title of stadholder. His wife, Mary, was crowned Queen Regnant, and they ruled together as equals over the United Kingdom of England, Scotland, Wales, and Ireland.

Germany and the Holy Roman Empire

The modern notion of Germany as a single, sovereign nation is relatively recent. In the earliest years of the country, it was a loose affiliation of Germanic-speaking peoples but did not fall under one ruler or banner. Even entering the seventeenth century, Germany was still for the most part a confederation of individual provinces and territories that fell under the auspices of the Holy Roman Empire.

The late sixteenth century saw many movements in religion, both Catholic and Protestant. The Jesuits came into the political picture as a militant group devoted to the pope whose aims were to forcibly halt the Protestant incursion. Germany was the center of a continent-wide Jesuit movement. The Jesuit priests often served as confessors to the highest ranking nobles and policy makers in all of Europe. This movement is known as the Catholic Reformation or Counter-Reformation.

The Calvinist Protestant movement was also very strong in Germany and gained legitimacy after the Palatine electorate converted. The Calvinist church in Germany was seen as a mode of social discipline, and many pressed for Calvinism to be considered the official state church of the German territories—which caused a great deal of friction between the powerful and long-established Catholics and the aggressive and popular Calvinists.

The close of the sixteenth century ushered in many hardships for the people of the land, women in particular. Ancient traditions and prejudices forced many working women out of gainful employment. With the religious undercurrents flowing as they were, the witch hunts in Germany were among the most dreaded in all of Europe.

Catholic Hapsburgs, the traditional rulers in the area, fought to hold onto their power and dynastic lands, but Calvinism was gaining strength and popularity among the ruling classes of some of the other areas of the Empire such as Bohemia and Hungary. Many Protestant areas in the east of the empire were able to make a truce with the Turks, gaining their small but politically wieldy support against the Catholics.

The Protestant Union formed in 1608 and raised an army, allying itself with the foreign powers of France and Bohemia. In retaliation, the Catholic League formed in 1609 and made an alliance with Spain. War was imminent, but the assassination of the French king Henry IV diffused tensions for a few years. Several powerful Hapsburg rulers died without legitimate heirs and the man who came to power was a Counter-Reformer bent on stripping the Calvinists of their lands, powers, and protections. In defiance, the Bohemians threw two important councilors out of a castle window in 1618. This began the Thirty Years' War.[17]

The Thirty Years' War, although begun with a single occurrence that pushed the antagonistic factions over the line, was perpetuated by many other circumstances. The Bohemian revolt was actually swiftly dealt with and put down. Bohemia was incorporated into the Austrian lands and brought under the rule of the Holy Roman Empire, deposing the elected Bohemian king Frederick V. Frederick was exiled and the apparent imperial victory sent shock waves across Europe. The Dutch Republic and France allied against the Hapsburgs, who held the imperial throne. In addition, England, Sweden, Denmark, Savoy, and Venice all joined forces against Spain, Austria, Germany, and the Spanish Netherlands (the southern provinces of the Dutch Republic still held by Spain).

Denmark then got deeply involved, with King Christian IV leading forces against the Hapsburgs and their allies. Unfortunately, after France turned back to domestic affairs and dropped out of the conflict, the Danes were handed a sound defeat. But in 1629, Cardinal Richelieu, the regent of France, brought his country back into the fray and negotiated a peace between Sweden and Poland. Sweden then entered the war as France's ally to fight against the Hapsburgs, until major Swedish defeats in 1634 required that country to pull out of the war. By the end of that year, France took control of the anti-imperial war effort. Even though the French government was persecuting Protestants at home, France fought on the Protestant side during the war. By this time, the Thirty Years' War no longer had much to do with religion and was mainly focused on the animosity between France and Spain. Unfortunately, it was the Germans that bore the brunt of this antagonism as the two countries fought not on their home soil, but on the fields of Germany. The war finally ground to a halt without a clear victor on either side, although the Protestant alliance was favored.

The Peace of Westphalia was signed in 1648, ending the Thirty Years' War. Disputed territories were portioned out to the various combatants, mostly to the Protestant anti-Hapsburg side. The Hapsburgs were forced to give up a great deal of power, including the sovereign rights that had been awarded to the individual German princes. These rights now allowed each province to choose the religion of its people and allowed for a tolerant, if yet still strained, relationship between the Catholics and the Protestants of Germany. Spain finally recognized the Dutch Republic, although it still held some small control over the southern Catholic provinces.

THE INQUISITION

Religion was the driving factor of most seventeenth-century conflict, and as much as the rival Christian sects were fighting with one another, they were also attempting to conquer old enemies: the Jews and Muslims. Spain, for most of the Middle Ages, had been a multiracial and multireligious kingdom. The relatively small Jewish and Muslim communities were by and large left alone to worship. The economic strength in banking and trade that these communities brought Spain seemed to make it acceptable to the Spanish Crown that they be allowed that freedom. But in the late fifteenth century, there was a move to expel the Jews from Spain. Many Jews decided to hold onto their estates by converting to Catholicism. These families produced some of Spain's most notable

SALEM WITCH TRIALS

"Many theories concerning the Salem Witch trials of 1692 have been developed. It has been theorized that the Salem Witch trials occurred due because of ergotism. Some have suggested that the victims of these trials were actually suffering from ergotism. According to historian Mary Matossian in her book *Poisons of the Past*, . . . symptoms of the people [were noted] to be sensations of prickling or ants crawling on the skin, distortions of the face, paralysis, hallucinations, convulsive seizures, and dementia. All these symptoms were consistent with those suffering from ergotism." ("Ergot," http://www.plant.uga.edu/labrat/ergot.htm)

saints, theologians, and founders of religious orders. These *Conversos* considered themselves safe from the papal Inquisition, which lasted officially from 1478 until 1834. By the late sixteenth century, the Inquisition had all but run out of heretics and turned instead on what it saw as the purification of the Spanish bloodlines by removing the taint of the Conversos and the heritage of the Jewish converts of the fifteenth century.

But the Spanish Inquisition was surprisingly not involved with the fanatical witch hunts that ravaged across Europe. Although these purges began in the fifteenth and sixteenth centuries, the most popular detection and interrogation handbook was in its twenty-ninth edition in 1669.[18] From 1580 to 1650, there are thought to have been more than 100,000 trials across Europe. Most of these were instigated by mass hysteria, but many of the mobs were composed of the educated as well as the noneducated. The most executions were performed by the Calvinists.

The most famous of the witch trials occurred in Salem, Massachusetts, in 1692. Novelist Arthur Miller in *The Crucible* (1953), an allegory to McCarthyism in America, looked at the inner workings of the witch trial hysteria as well as dramatizing the actual historical accounts of the incident. All told, nineteen women and one man were executed in Salem. Scholars are still trying to decide whether it was simply mass hysteria or perhaps ergot poisoning from diseased rye.

Pagans, fertility cults, and all remaining vestiges of pre-Christian religions were also targeted as "witchcraft." Any negative social commentary or criticism of the Church was enough to raise accusations. At the time, "magic" was nothing more than herbal remedies, charms for luck, and items to ward against evil. But as medical research and knowledge began to emerge, cases of demonic possession and other "black magic"–related maladies began to be diagnosed as diseases such as epilepsy. This forward thinking fostered literacy and moved the common belief system out of the realm of magic and into the realm of intellect. But the break from the old system of superstitions and ramifications from the Church did not happen early enough to help Galileo.

In 1613, Galileo Galilei (1564–1642) began to write about his discoveries that supported the Copernican theory that the Earth moved in orbit around the sun, not the other way around as indicated in the Bible. He was able to come to this conclusion after he had invented the telescope in order to better see the heavenly bodies. He discovered that the planet Jupiter had four small moons that orbited it and was able to give credence to Copernicus's theories. In response, Galileo was admonished by the Inquisition in 1616, and Copernicus's *De revolutionibus orbium coelestium* was banned. Although he was under the patronage and protection of the powerful Medici family and had his theories proven by the imperial mathematician, Johannes Kepler (1571–1630), Galileo was found guilty of advancing seditious theories and placed under house arrest, but this did not stop him from his research or the publication of his findings. When he went completely blind in 1638, the Inquisition allowed him to go to church if he wished but barred him from speaking to anyone while outside of his home. Even in his state of illness, Galileo still managed to make advances that are still important in the current era, including how to apply the pendulum to a clock, theories on sunspots, and how the moon affects the tides. He died in 1642, still considered a prisoner and an enemy of the church.

SOCIOECONOMIC CLIMATE

The idea of individualism was beginning to take hold during the seventeenth century. People were not content to be just one of the faceless masses. But with that rise of individual thought came more laws to control the new entities. Coupled with the ease of making a considerable fortune in trading, social-grasping upstarts were thinking themselves worthy to marry into privileged households. The rules governing marriage, bastardy, inheritance, and even sexuality itself were instituted to be sure these individuals kept to their predestined place in the social hierarchy.

It was not a good time to be anything but wealthy. Beginning in 1619, the common folk were faced with numerous hardships across Europe. Most of the continent was in an economic depression in the 1620s. The sudden opening of trade markets and influx of luxury goods unbalanced the fragile fiscal system of the lower classes, disenfranchising them totally from the upsurge in wealth and power enjoyed by those of higher station. To add to these difficulties, a cold snap known as the "Little Ice Age" had settled across Europe, and harvests would remain unpredictable until after 1650. Plagues also ravaged Europe, killing hundreds of thousands throughout the era. More than half of Europe's population lived in poverty and were on the brink of starvation. Population growth was stagnant with few regional exceptions.

The gap between rich and poor widened incredibly during this time, and across France peasant revolts were common, a foreshadowing of things to come for that country. The common people did not like paying for France's extravagant aristocracy or petty wars with their taxes. The taxes climbed higher and higher, but the pay wages remained the same. Finally, a tax on salt set off the community. Changes were repeatedly promised but if enacted were

> ### LITTLE ICE AGE
>
> "Throughout most of what is commonly called the Little Ice Age (1500–1850) the mean solar activity was quite low, but positive fluctuations occurred around 1540–1590 and 1770–1800. The main westerly storm belts shifted about 500 kilometres to the south, and for much of the time the northern latitudes came under cool continental conditions." ("Holocene Epoch," *Encyclopedia Britannica Online*, http://www.britannica.com/eb/article?tocId=70038)

temporary at best. Throughout the century, the luxury of the aristocracy would be carried on the backs of the peasants all over the continent.

TRADE

At the dawn of the seventeenth century, the Portuguese had a virtual monopoly on sea trade encompassing Asia, India, and Africa. China and India were the chief sources of imported goods to Europe. In 1600, China's and India's economies were both greater than the whole of Europe's, and Europe had a significant trade deficit importing from Asia but exporting nothing there in return.[19]

The end of the sixteenth century saw an increase in Dutch and English ambition to engage in the highly profitable sea trade with the Asian continent. The Dutch and English found themselves in a quid pro quo agreement to help protect one another from the Portuguese and Spanish, who had allied to maintain their respective monopolies. Pirates and privateers sanctioned by their governments brought an element of war into the fierce competition for trade, and "plunder is an effective, but potentially very dangerous way to acquire wealth."[20] Realizing that something needed to be done to organize the chaos on the high seas, the governments of Europe created designated peace zones in international waters known as the "lines of amity."[21] Within these lines, the vessels of various countries were expected to conduct themselves with professional standards, and fighting was prohibited. But beyond the lines, no country held sway and it was a free-for-all described as "an internationally defined zone of anarchy."[22] This arrangement lasted throughout most of the century but did not put a damper on piracy. The seventeenth century was the age of pirates, greatly romanticized by the modern era. To put it mildly, "unarmed trade was out of the question."[23]

In the nations upon which Europe was focusing, the seventeenth century was a time of great change. In China, the Ming dynasty was just ending in the 1640s, and the Manchu or Qing dynasty was rising to take its place. While politically more maneuverable, the Qing did not have the status and respect of their predecessors. The Muslim lands of the Near and Middle East were in the Age of Three Empires. In Turkey, the Ottoman Empire was just beginning to wane after reaching its peak before 1600. The Safavid dynasty that ruled Persia (modern-day Iran) was enjoying the height of its power through 1629. And although Mughal India's political power started to dissipate after 1605, it continued to flourish culturally. The timing of the decline of power of these strong governments could not have been better for the Europeans. After years of stable infrastructure and solid production of goods, the grip of government was starting to loosen just enough for European nations to come in and take advantage of the situation.

One of the earliest trade hubs was Manila in the Philippines. It was mainly used by the Spanish as a stopover point between China and Europe. Many Chinese workers immigrated to the Philippines, creating an ethnically mixed people who were of Chinese, Spanish, and native blood. The Portuguese exerted control over most central Asian and African ports, but slowly and steadily, the Dutch and English were gaining a foothold.

Knowing that nationally they would never overcome Portuguese dominance at sea, the Dutch and English devised privately held companies that would be financed and driven by private investors. England was among the first to incorporate its trade into a privately held company. Chartered in 1600, the British East India Company initially focused on modern-day Indonesia, knowing that Portugal's control was weak in the Spice Islands. The East India Company was granted a monopoly on ports east of the Cape of Good Hope and had the right to exercise force to protect its interests. All the capital required for each voyage was raised by shareholders and returned profits to them at the end of each trip.

In the Netherlands, the more broadly successful Vereenigde Oostindische Compangie (VOC), also known as the Dutch East India Company, was chartered in 1602. Like the British East India Company, the Dutch company was funded by private investors instead of taxes, although both companies did benefit from a wealth of powerful government protections. At first, the VOC functioned like a sanctioned pirate syndicate, preying on Spanish and Portuguese ships laden with trade goods from the East. But the ever practical Dutch were quick to change tactics, devising ways to cripple the Portuguese power in Asia and become the premier trade power of Europe. The Dutch at first specialized in trade, importing and exporting items between Europe and Asia such as fish, salt, wine, timber, and English and Flemish cloth. They were also skilled bookkeepers and developed the world's first exchange and securities system. Although the Dutch were shrewd businessmen, they could not entirely displace Portugal and the two countries agreed on an almost peaceful parallel trade system that focused in different ports in some of the same countries. The Dutch headquartered their offshore dealings in Jakarta and renamed the town Batavia, but they also expanded operations into Taiwan, Ceylon, and Cape Town in Africa.

The greatest stride made by Dutch tradesmen in the seventeenth century was the discovery of nonseasonal trade winds. Dutch ships could cross the southern Indian Ocean outbound from Europe and then dip below the Equator to catch the southeast trade winds on the way back. Not only did this make Dutch trade available all year long, but it also helped them elude the Portuguese pirates, thus securing Dutch domination of the European sea trade.

The Dutch captured the monopoly on nutmeg and cloves in the 1640s and worked hard to restrict the spice trade to drive up their profits. In the 1620s, spices made up 75 percent of Dutch trade, but the Dutch found it hard to exert continued control over it and spices fell to only 23 percent of Dutch trade by the end of the century. The Dutch were not without their ace in the hole, however, and by 1700, textiles made up more than 55 percent of Dutch trade, supplying popular and expensive cotton cloth to Europe from India.[24] The Dutch also rented out their services as couriers for other countries with smaller and weaker fleets, charging a premium toll to carry trade goods to and from other nations. This was such a lucrative business that when England enacted the Navigation Act of 1651, forbidding the carrying of imports to England or English colonies on any ship that was not English, it pushed Holland into war with England from 1652 to 1654. This was not the first skirmish between these two powerful countries, nor would it be the last.

Tensions had erupted into violence between the English and the Dutch first in 1623 when the Dutch authorities ordered an attack on the English factory town on the island of Amboina, Indonesia. The Dutch believed that the English merchants, with help from their Japanese allies, were plotting to take over the region. While it may not have been far from the truth, the information was extracted by torture, and some twenty people were killed for their supposed conspiracy. After this incident, known in Britain as the Amboina Massacre, the English pulled out of the Spice Islands and focused their attentions and trading through Java instead. England was also influential in helping the Persians take back the port of Hormuz from the Portuguese. This established friendly trade between the English and the Persians, which was a boon to the English trade cartel.

Although late in acquiring a foothold in India, the English enclaves there proved to be the longest lasting. Incursions into India by the English in the seventeenth century were sowing the seeds for the imperial British India of the nineteenth and twentieth centuries. Three major Indian trade ports were under English control by the end of the 1600s: Bombay (Mumbai), Madras (Chennai), and Calcutta (Kolkata). This made the English trade empire as strong as that of the Dutch or the Portuguese, but they ran their system very differently. Instead of a strong centralized system, England spread out the responsibilities to underlings and investors. The British East India Company also loaned money to the Crown at absurdly low interest rates in exchange for the automatic renewal of its trade monopoly license.

"The Dutch and English of the early seventeenth century did come to dominate the spice trade to Europe so efficiently that spice caravans to the Mediterranean virtually disappeared."[25] Overland caravans still ran but carried other goods. Overland trade experienced a boom in development during the seventeenth century due to the demand for fur. Siberia became a major player in the fur trade as Europe, China, and the Ottoman Empire increased their demands. In the 1640s, fur traders were able to navigate an all-water route from the central mainland all the way to the Pacific Ocean by way of Siberia's rivers.

Starting in the late 1550s, an enterprising English trading company had sought to capitalize on this method of trade. Despite knowing that an overland and river route through Russia, known at that time as Muscovy, would take considerably longer than a sea route, the possibility of circumventing other trade monopolies and steering clear of pirates and bandits was too tempting. Teaming up with the local Muscovites, the English entrepreneurs began the Muscovy Trading Company and traded overland down through Russia and into Persia and the Ottoman Empire, gaining access to inland trade cities otherwise not accessible by the sea trade.

MUSCOVY TRADING COMPANY

The Muscovy Trading Company was one of the longest lasting of the original trading companies, operating into the twentieth century. Currently, a small apparel company is attempting to resurrect the memory and name of the original company.

English trade was primarily textile based. Cotton and raw silk were at the top of the list, followed closely by indigo, a plant that produced a deep and colorfast blue dye. The English also imported pepper, coffee, and tea, although neither beverage would become very popular or politically important until the middle of the eighteenth century.

The English also established a direct trade route from Europe to Hudson Bay in North America via New York, which was now a small but bustling city. From there, they could easily and cheaply import furs taken from the local forests. The fur trade in North America was dominated by the French, but England was not far behind. Early on, the fur trade required good relations with the local native tribes. These tribes grew quite savvy about the political competition between the different European factions and used it to their own advantage as much as possible to secure tools and weapons to help settle their own tribal rivalries. They also set up monopolies not unlike the sea traders. The Iroquois would trade only with the Dutch in Albany. The Huron and Algonquin of the St. Lawrence River valley would trade only with the French. Basically, whichever nation approached a tribe first or offered the best trade became the favored trading partner to the exclusion of any other country's representatives.

But the lucrative industry took an immediate toll on the wildlife population. Early in the century, sable used to be found all over Europe but soon could be trapped only in Siberia. In North America, beaver became seriously depleted near the mouth of the St. Lawrence River by the end of the sixteenth century, and by the middle of the seventeenth century, that depletion had spread well into upstate New York. Beaver fur was the primary material needed to create the hats that were fashionable from the mid-sixteenth century on. As the trappers moved ever northward in search of their prey, they found the creatures more elusive, less populous, and more difficult to catch, which drove the price steadily upward and made the trade even more lucrative. The French moved inland to trade and trap, searching out new regions to exploit, whereas the British concentrated their trading posts at the port cities and waited for business to come to them. By 1670, England had formed the Hudson's Bay Company and held a monopoly over all trade in and out of the port. By 1679, England had established enough trading posts to operate year-round.

By the eighteenth century, European fur trappers coming from the east were meeting Muscovite fur trappers coming from the west as they searched for enough animals to supply the ever-increasing demand of their home countries.

The seventeenth century was a time of great trade expansion, bringing the luxuries of the east into the homes of Europe. Pepper, cotton, and silk—all considered common items in modern households—were exotic status symbols. This was the age of the seafaring pirate as well as the rugged trapper. Resources from around the world were pouring into Europe, and Western influence increased. Colonialism brought on by trade in the seventeenth century gave rise to the imperialism in subsequent centuries. But in these early years, the world was still flush with its first experience as a truly multinational entity.

ART

Painting

The Dutch Republic emerged as a dominant force in visual art from the beginning of the seventeenth century. After suffering years of control and persecution, the Dutch were open and tolerant of many groups and accepting of various religions, and "17th-century Holland can be regarded as the first modern capitalist democracy."[26] This movement was centered in Holland, one of the principal provinces. Amsterdam and Delft emerged as artistic centers in painting as well as decorative arts.

The Dutch market for artwork was unlike any other in Europe. Paintings were usually commissioned by wealthy merchants, as there was hardly an aristocracy to speak of. The Calvinists held sway in the northern provinces, and they frowned on ostentatious religious art. The prevailing style in the Netherlands was a blend of the sweeping and rich Italian styles, the sensuality of Rubens, and the Antwerp school of Belgium, with a predilection for small, simple paintings meant to be hung in private homes.

It was also a time of unparalleled wealth and status for painters and artisans. Throughout Europe, a new and radical idea was beginning to circulate that true happiness could be found on Earth, rather than waiting for some enigmatic reward in the afterlife.[27] This newfound joy in life found its way into the brilliant colors and extravagant detail found in the paintings of this age, known as the Baroque (after the Portuguese word for an irregularly shaped pearl, *barroco*).[28]

Although the honors would soon pass from Spain, one of the greatest painters of the age was still leaving his mark. Diego Velázquez (1599–1660) was the premier court painter of Philip IV. He was well known for using his amazing techniques to add charm, beauty, and grace to the faces of his homely Hapsburg models, yet still rendering them recognizably. He painted the Infanta Margarita with such tenderness that one can almost overlook the ridiculous proportions of her elaborate court regalia.

Portrait of the Infanta Maria-Margarita, daughter of Philip IV, King of Spain, in wide panier gown. Children wore miniaturized versions of adult clothing. © Erich Lessing / Art Resource, NY.

Velázquez's most famous work is "Las Meninas" ("The Maids of Honor"), depicting the infanta and her retinue, himself at the canvas, and the royal parents looking on from a reflection or perhaps another portrait. The entire composition is based off of a reflection in a gigantic mirror and incorporates the vastness of the room without taking focus from the subjects clustered in the bottom third of the painting. Even as the infanta is receiving a cup from her lady-in-waiting, she is looking at herself reflected, almost coyly. Velázquez paints the moment as if it were captured by a photograph and not carefully constructed brushstroke by brushstroke for hours. It was this masterful technique that assured

Velázquez a long and profitable career. He was the official court painter of Philip IV for thirty-four years.

But Velázquez was alone in his fame among the formerly great hubs of artistry in Europe. The focus had shifted definitively northward. And although many of the seventeenth century's greatest artists would come into Spain, France, England, and Italy to paint, their roots were firmly planted in places like Flanders and Holland. Peter Paul Rubens (1577–1640) was a Flemish painter who mentored another of the seventeenth century's great talents, Anthony van Dyck (1599–1641). Rubens was a diplomat, a linguist, and an archaeologist, all in addition to being a very skilled painter. His paintings gave him the income that allowed him to pursue his other hobbies. Rubens was knighted by King Charles I of England and bestowed with a noble rank by King Philip IV of Spain. He was known for a very dramatic style and the use of fleshy, voluptuous women. Abundant fat was then a very desirable trait in women, suggesting robust health and a family with enough money to provide a sizable dowry.

Van Dyck, one of Rubens's most noteworthy students, was best known for his high, courtly style. This opulence was not popular nor approved of in Holland, so instead of diluting his style, he took his abilities to the French and English courts where his finesse was appreciated. Van Dyck was able to ride this tide of Dutch artistic domination through the end of his life. His style coined the names of the van Dyke beard, for the sharply pointed and trimmed goatees popular for men in the first half of the century, and the van Dyke collar, a wide collar across the shoulders edged copiously with lace. In addition, van Dyke brown, a mix of asphaltum and lignite, is still used in painting today; it was named after the artist because it was a specific mix of pigment made for him by his colormen.

Thought of as the greatest painter of Dutch history, Rembrandt (1606–1669) was born along the banks of the Rhine River as the eighth child of a miller in 1606. His full given name was Rembrandt Harmenszoon van Rijn. He displayed early artistic prowess and was inspired, along with most of the artists in Europe, by Caravaggio's (1571–1610) works. Rembrandt's paintings were in high demand from an early age in his home city of Leiden, and soon he was receiving recognition from Amsterdam as well. Although he was revered enough to take on pupils, Rembrandt made the decision to move his studio to the capital and pursue his painting career with more focus. Not long after his arrival in Amsterdam, he was discovered by a high-ranking government secretary and began to receive lucrative commissions. Rembrandt was becoming known for his light touches and the use of light and expression in his work. He regularly used his family members as models for his paintings, often casting them as allegorical, religious, mythical, or historical figures.

> ## COLORMEN
>
> "Colormen were the experts who mixed the colors to the artist's specifications, carefully recording the information and methods used to obtain each product. Accordingly, a pigment would be mixed with oil and resin for an artist who worked in oils, and gum arabic (a resin from the acacia tree), glycerin, and sometimes chalk were added to pigments for a watercolorist." (Susan Robinson, "From Minerals to Art," *Rocks & Minerals* 74, no. 5 [1999]: 328)

Although he painted many biblical scenes, Rembrandt's work was not limited to religious themes. For example, he was well known for several almost disturbingly detailed paintings of anatomy lessons. But he was best known for capturing the most subtle and intimate facial expressions and an extraordinary amount of detail in clothing. Rembrandt was also a talented engraver, and whether in richly colored oils or stark black-and-white, his attention to detail was outstanding. In his portraiture and contemporary art, an accurate portrayal of costume history can be seen. But even in his allegorical and more fantastical works, the draping fabrics are rendered with the most realistic of details for an authentic assessment of contemporary textiles. In his nudes, the high, fashionable women's waistline can be construed by the almost unnatural placement of the model's own waist.[29]

But as the Thirty Years' War brought the Dutch Republic its hard-won independence and recognition throughout Europe, it also heralded changes in tastes. Rembrandt was at the height of his career when he suffered some of the most devastating losses of his life. After several children who had died in infancy, his beloved wife Saskia finally gave him a son who would live and thrive. Unfortunately, it would come at the cost of her life. Already weak from tuberculosis, Saskia died only a few months after their son, Titus, was born. Rembrandt never recovered from this and engaged in a series of ill-fated love affairs that ruined him financially and drove away his conservative patrons. It was not until the 1660s that he again began to come into vogue, but by that time, he was destitute. He lived happily for some years with his son and mistress, but soon, they were taken from him by death. Rembrandt was left with no one but his granddaughter, for her mother, Titus's wife, had also passed away suddenly. He clung to his painting, but there was a melancholy and desperation in the work. Over the later years of his career, the sharp detail and fine lines were replaced by a broader, almost "unfinished" quality thought to be inspired by the great Renaissance painter Titian (1485–1576). His death was nearly unnoticed at the time, but it did not take long for his posthumous fame to skyrocket.

While Amsterdam would always be the cultural center of the Dutch Republic, Delft was an emerging hub of artistic significance. Jan Vermeer (1632–1675) was one of the leading artists there. Like Rembrandt, he could never stay ahead of his debts and died destitute. During his lifetime, his work was not nearly as appreciated as it was long after his death. Vermeer revolutionized the use of light and shadow in Dutch artwork. At a time when the prevailing styles were heavy, theatrical, and mythical—in a word, baroque—Vermeer's work was marked by its simplicity. He painted domestic scenes with realistic participants in their daily lives. The costumes worn for his paintings were usually taken from his wife's wardrobe and show some of the most accurate depictions of actual garments of the period.

Born in Delft in 1632, Vermeer registered with the Guild of St. Luke as a master painter in 1653. One of his debut paintings, "Saint Praxedis," was completed in 1655. After his marriage to Catharina Bolnes, the couple moved into her mother's house in the "Papist's Corner," the nickname for the Catholic part of Delft. Vermeer was a prolific man in his life, if not in his art. Upon his death at age forty-three in 1675, he had completed only thirty-six paintings but had fathered fourteen children, eleven of whom lived. Unfortunately, he left his family in dire financial straits and his wife was forced to sell many of his paintings. The next year was an especially difficult one for the family, but Catharina was finally able to close off the debts by a special dispensation of the high court citing the ruinous effect of the war with France. In the centuries since his death, Vermeer has emerged as one of the foremost Dutch painters of all time.

Vermeer's work is especially valuable to costume historians, as the garments portrayed not only were actual articles of clothing but also were often recycled throughout several works, thus giving the scholar various views of several pieces. The yellow jacket trimmed with ermine appears in six paintings, the yellow bodice with blue trimming appears in four, and the yellow jacket with the lace collar appears in two. The large, teardrop-shaped pearl earrings made so famous in "Girl with the Pearl Earring" actually appear in eleven out of his thirty-six paintings. His detailed textiles, including the oriental rug table coverings, are also a valuable tool to those studying the fabrics of the period. This attention to textile detail was probably fostered by Vermeer's father, who had spent several years as a satin weaver.[30]

Decorative Arts

During the seventeenth century, the Dutch people were the wealthiest per capita in all of Europe.[31] The broad trading empire gave them contact with cultures hitherto unknown by Europe. While this did not have an immediate impact on the styles and approaches of painting in the country, it did have influence on the decorative arts. In addition to oil paintings, the Dutch, and Delft in particular, were also well known for their blue-and-white glazework.

The Dutch East Indies Company began to import glazed Chinese porcelain into the country in the 1640s. The intricate blue-and-white designs were very popular in China during the Ming dynasty (1368–1644). The Dutch were growing increasingly enamored with all things Eastern and exotic, and rich collectors were snapping up the porcelain as soon as it entered the country. In light of this tremendous demand, Dutch potters and crafters tried to emulate the Chinese porcelain. Their attempts were unsuccessful, but a style that mimicked the look was possible. Called *faience*,[32] it was a ceramic with a white tin oxide glaze painted with fine line work in blue. At first, the Dutch faience was a direct imitation of Chinese imports, but soon it began to take on a decidedly Dutch appearance, depicting local landscapes, local flora and fauna, and hunting scenes. Not just used on vases and dishware, many of these designs were made into large tile plaques that were framed and hung in the home or painted on smaller tiles that were used to decorate kitchens and fireplaces. Once this type of faience became a specifically Dutch art form, it came to be known as "Delftware" or more simply "Delft," after the city where it was first created. Dutch potters later introduced the art of tin glazing to England along with the name, which now applies to wares manufactured in the Netherlands and England. It is distinguished from faience (made in France, Germany, Spain, and Scandinavia) and majolica (made in Italy).[33]

The Dutch were not alone in their passion for all things Chinese. With the introduction of beverages like coffee, tea, and hot chocolate, specialized forms of service were invented. Pots, cups, dishware, and spoons all reflected the type of beverage that would be served with them. Chinese porcelain was in high

CHINOISERIE

"Fanciful European interpretations of Chinese styles in the design of interiors, furniture, pottery, textiles, and gardens.

"The expansion of trade with East Asia produced a lively vogue for Chinese fashions in the 17th–18th centuries. The most outstanding chinoiserie interior was the Trianon de Porcelaine (1670–71), built for Louis XIV at Versailles. The style featured lavish gilding and lacquering, the use of blue and white (as in delftware), asymmetrical forms, unorthodox perspective, and Asian motifs."
("Chinoiserie," *Encyclopedia Britannica Online*, http://concise.britannica.com/ebc/article-9360629/chinoiserie)

demand for things like tea service, but Chinese lacquerware was also very popular. Table settings that would be familiar to the modern eyes began to take shape in the seventeenth century as dishes, drinking vessels, and flatware were specialized for particular meal courses and for specific foods. With silver being imported from North and South America, silverware and silver teapots, pitchers, and other utensils became popular and a coveted status symbol. The importation of cotton also led to its use in tablecloths and individual napkins, which was a new advance in a proper table setting. At this time, cotton was a versatile, easy-to-clean, and sturdy textile, but it was still a luxury reserved only for those who could afford it. Exotic woods from Asia, India, Africa, and the Spice Islands were incorporated into detailed inlay designs for tabletops, chests, armoires, and even wooden floors. As the century progressed, these designs grew more intricate and fanciful, often incorporating motifs from the country of origin. The generic term for this Chinese influence is *chinoiserie*.

Later in the century, the French began to regain their pride and prestige as a fashion leader in the decorative arts. Even the Dutch began to feel the French influence exuded by Louis XIV's lavish Sun Court. When he repealed the Edict of Nantes in 1685, most of the Huguenots fled France, and many settled in the Protestant lands of the United Netherlands. They brought their French styles, tastes, and fashions with them, further extending the French influence on art and craftwork. The wealthy Dutch burghers surrounded themselves in a mix of traditional Dutch art, Chinese imports, and French styles, creating a look that was "eclectic and international."[34]

France led the rest of Europe in designs modeled after the styles of Versailles. As far away as the colonies in North America, copies of French furnishings were being sold. The emphasis was on ornament. Twining vines, leaves, flowers, and creatures real and imagined graced the legs of tables and chairs, the doors of armoires and cabinets, and the canvases of paintings and were fluidly suspended in stone.

Architecture

France also excelled in architecture and landscaping. The Baroque style of architecture was decorative, opulent, and most of all, flamboyant. Rome took a small sliver of glory from France during this time with its villas, piazzas, churches, and palaces. Pope Urban VIII (*R.* 1623–1644) contracted Gian Lorenzo Bernini (1598–1680) to create a grand altar space in St. Peter's Basilica.

Bernini designed the baldachin (1624–1633), and Pope Urban VIII acquired the bronze needed for the structure by dismantling the roof of the Pantheon and having it melted down.

Bernini's work included sculpture as well as architecture. He was responsible for Rome's breathtaking Trident Fountain of the Piazza Barberini (1642–1643) and the Fountain of the Four Rivers in the Piazza Navona (1648–1651). He strove to blend the artistry of sculpture with architecture. Unfortunately, he had a few near disasters along the way, the foremost being his failed attempt at constructing bell towers onto the facade of St. Peter's in 1637— by 1646, their weight was threatening to destroy the historic structure, and they were removed. But Bernini was successful in nearly everything else he created,

seamlessly merging the scale of architecture with sculpture in his "Ecstasy of St. Teresa" (1645–1652). His name became synonymous with the lush baroque style. At his death at age 81, he had served eight popes and achieved international fame and glory that set the standard for scale, form, and design in sculpture and architecture for years to come.

Bernini was Italian to the core and fiercely proud of it. This became readily apparent when he was invited to France by Louis XIV in 1665. Bernini was unimpressed with the French frivolity of design that lacked the weight and depth of Italian artwork. Although he created an exemplar bust of the Sun King that would continue to set the standard for royal sculptors and portraitures to come, his offensive derision about the French architectural style lost him the opportunity to design the Louvre Museum.

Architecture in England was still firmly rooted in a Classical ideal. After the Great Fire of London in 1666, the citizens of London remained convinced that it was part of a Catholic plot to unbalance the city so that a papal reign would be easier to impose. This was not the case, as the fire began in a bakery in Pudding Lane, but the commemorative monument that blamed the fire on "the treachery and malice of the Popish faction" was not removed until 1831. Most of the parts of the original city within the walls, known as the City of London, had to be rebuilt. Architect Christopher Wren (1632–1723) was appointed the task of rebuilding St. Paul's Cathedral, one of the eighty-four churches destroyed. Old St. Paul's had been one of the largest cathedrals in Europe, but throughout its history, its architecture had been unstable. Still a young man in his early thirties, Wren had suggested that the cathedral be remodeled and

GREAT FIRE OF LONDON

The Great Fire of London began in the early hours of Sunday, September 2, 1666, and burned through 373 acres of the city before it stopped on Thursday September 6, 1666. In its path it destroyed around 13,200 houses, and dozens of churches and offices. The true toll of lives lost in the fire is uncertain but officially stands at only four deaths.

submitted plans for his ideas. While the matter was being debated, the Great Fire broke out and put an end of the argument. Old St. Paul's was burned to the ground, and Wren was commissioned to design and build a replacement.

Wren was interested in a centralized Italian Renaissance–inspired design with a great dome and smaller spaces radiating out to the sides. The Anglican clergy balked at such a revolutionary idea and demanded that the church be set up just the way it had always been, in the traditional Gothic manner with a long central hall and the choir and nave set off to either side to form the shape of a cross. Wren was disappointed but submitted an idea that he felt best capitalized on his desires and the clergy's demands. It was approved by Charles II and work began in 1675. However, it was apparent early in the building process that Wren was deviating from his design. Although the central hall was still present, attention was focused on the central area beneath the dome, which was adorned with a facade of classical columns. In the end, it was not the Gothic cathedral that the clergy insisted upon, but neither was it the domed Italian Renaissance version that Wren had originally conceived—the final product was somewhere in between the two, a compromise that made few contemporaries happy. "But building projects on the scale of St Paul's are seldom straightforward, and the design history of St Paul's reveals the doggedness with which Wren pursued his artistic vision: to crown the London skyline with a great domed church."[35]

Literature

The standardization of language, grammar, and spelling had become a priority in both England and France, but the various social orders gave rise to very different forms of literature. The writing in England was witty and bawdy, as well as bitter and disillusioned. The century was one long and drawn-out war or political upheaval—only the names and faces changed. After the Restoration, spirits rose somewhat and a wave of comedies was performed on stages across the country, but there was an undeniable cynicism to the works.

William Wycherley (c. 1640–1716) and William Cosgreve (1670–1729) were admired playwrights. Wycherley's best-known work was *The Country Wife* (1675), a bawdy comedy about a man who feigns impotence with his own wife in order to seduce the wives of his neighbors, until he is foiled by the arrival of a devilishly innocent young woman from the country who sees right through his machinations and turns the tables on him. Rife with lewd puns, sexual situations, and a tangled plotline, *The Country Wife* was rarely performed after its initial debut for the giddy and bawdy court of Charles II and while Wycherley wrote many more plays and poems, he never quite achieved the degree of fame he had with *The Country Wife*.

Cosgreve's most famous work, *The Way of the World* (1700), has been thought of as the greatest of the Restoration comedies, although it was not actually produced until long after the death of Charles II. The mood in England was far less opulent and licentious than it had been in Charles's time and *The Way of the World* hinges on the more innocent plotlines of matchmaking, disguises, and mistaken identity and the comedy of who is seducing whom. Much more conventionally accepted, *The Way of the World* is still occasionally performed. But Cosgreve's true gifts to the English language come from his earlier play *The Mourning Bride* (1697), in which he declares in act 1, scene 1, that "Musick has Charms to sooth a savage Breast" (not "beast" as has been attributed in modern times) and also in Act II, Scene 8 that "Heaven has no rage like love to hatred turned / Nor hell a fury like a woman scorned."[36]

One of England's hallmark authors was John Milton (c. 1608–1674). Written during the Interregnum and published in 1667, *Paradise Lost* is a poem in blank verse. Originally written in ten chapters, or books, it was revised by Milton in 1674 in a twelve-book format. The work deals with the expulsion of Adam and Eve from the Garden of Eden and deals with heaven, hell, and the origin of original sin. Milton was a Parliamentary supporter during the Interregnum and acted as a secretary in the Cromwellian government. He was a prolific writer, completing several works of verse as well as dozens of treatises and pamphlets, drawing his inspiration from biblical sources, as well as creating propaganda for the government. A fervent advocate of free speech and freedom of the press, he was eventually but briefly forced into hiding at the Restoration, fearing persecution as a backer of Cromwell. He lost his sight in 1652, but that did not hold him back from writing. Instead, he dictated his treatises and poems to his assistants daily. At the time of his death in 1674, he had been married three times, was twice a widower, and had fathered five children, three of whom lived into adulthood. He was buried in the Church of St. Giles, Cripplegate, but a monument to him stands in Poet's Corner in Westminster Abbey.

England saw a whole host of treatises and pamphlets published in the seventeenth century. With the increasingly widespread availability of printing presses and a growing educated population, cheap booklets and pamphlets abounded for nearly every topic imaginable. But politics was the leading inspiration for most writers. Thomas Hobbes's (1588–1679) book *Leviathan* (1651) was a pessimistic view of humanity. He proposed that humans live in a state of war with their own natures. Generally sinful and more apt to be wrong, people need to submit to an absolute ruler in order to have peace and stability. That ruler was called "the Leviathan" in his book and was required to save the unrestrained and selfish people from themselves.

John Locke (1632–1704) was an extraordinarily learned man, being both a doctor and philosopher. He was an antitotalitarian activist, and in his monumental essay *A Second Treatise of Government* (1690), Locke spoke out against omnipotent rulers and disagreed with the idea of the need for a leviathan. He believed that humanity was at the core good and capable of social justice without a harsh taskmaster to force compliance. Locke was optimistic about the human condition and felt that, with protections for life, liberty, and property, all people can coexist happily and harmoniously. This philosophy was the basis for both the American and French revolutions in the following century.

But France was still leading the way in literature with dramatists such as Molière (Jean-Baptiste de Poquelin; 1622–1673) and Jean Racine (1639–1699). Molière's works were for the most part comedies and satires. They were moralizing in tone and often full of social commentary. But oddly enough, although he frequently made a mockery of the lofty manners and affectations of the nobles, he was a favorite of Louis XIV and performed regularly as the official palace troupe. More than just a writer, Molière was a director, a stage manager, and an actor. In fact, when he died, it was nearly on stage, where he collapsed, surviving only a few short hours further into the night. It was said that no priest would come to give him last rites, because his plays and life were too scandalous.

Molière loved to exaggerate the foibles of the people and society around him and wrote such masterpieces as *Tartuffe* (which translates to "Hypocrite," especially when it comes to religion), *Le misanthrope* (a person who hates or distrusts humankind), *L'École des femmes* (*The School for Wives*), *Les précieuses ridicules* (*The Affected Young Ladies*, thought by some to be the first comedy of manners), and *Don Juan*. It was *Tartuffe*, one of the most performed of Molière's works today, that was nearly his undoing. He offended both conservative religious types and the snobby gentry by his clever and cutting look at hypocrisy in the upper echelons of French society.

His friend and rival Jean Racine was nearly the complete opposite, writing complex and very Greek-inspired tragedies. He wrote serious plays on the lives of tragic Greek characters such as Andromache, Iphigenia, and Phaedra. Even though he was a member of an outlawed religious sect, the Jansenites,[37] Racine was a popular playwright who won renown across the country. He was well respected and also patronized by Louis XIV, who provided for his wife and children after his death.

Music

In addition to drama, music was emerging as a very important performing art. The Baroque era was where the foundations of classical music were laid. In music, the Baroque period extends from 1600 to 1760. One of the signature elements of the Baroque musical style is the use of polyphony,[38] which is the presence of two or more separate and distinct musical "voices." This had been a popular mode in music throughout the Renaissance, but it began to take on a very distinct form in the seventeenth century. The other important component to Baroque music is counterpoint.[39] Counterpoint is a kind of polyphony but is usually blended into a more homogenous whole, whereas in true polyphony, the differing musical voices and textures are dynamic and playing off of one another to create a distinct sound that is more than just the two melodies blended. The most famous Baroque composers were born in the seventeenth century but did not begin their artistry until the eighteenth. Johann Sebastian Bach (1685–1750) and Antonio Vivaldi (1678–1741) were just children when some of the early Baroque's great names were creating.

In Venice, Claudio Monteverdi (1567–1643) began setting plays to music. It was simple concept: he merely had the actors sing their lines instead of speaking them. Opera, a new medium, was an instant sensation, and by the early 1600s Venice had sixteen opera houses. Monteverdi's first opera was *Orfeo*, which made its debut in 1607. He had a knack for the dramatic and was able to shape the acts into cohesive wholes, making logical moves between arias. Prior to this, the "opera" popular in Naples was really nothing more than a series of loosely related songs that were designed to highlight the vocal abilities of the singer rather than tell a story. Monteverdi's second opera *L'Arianna* opened in 1608. After a series of setbacks, including the sudden death from smallpox of the sixteen-year-old lead, the opera was a great success and guaranteed Monteverdi a pension and commissions for more works. He wrote much church music and flourished in madrigals, which he loved; altogether, he published nine volumes of madrigals.

While in Venice as the *maestro di cappella* (choirmaster or director of music) of St. Mark's Cathedral, Monteverdi began to develop an interest in displaying true drama comprised of real human emotions on the stage in his operas. He practiced writing melodic conversations that would allow the audience to hear the personality of the character not only in the words but even in the notes of the music themselves. It was a great leap that made modern opera what it is.

In France, Louis XIV was instilling the traditional court masques and dramas with this new style of theater, opera. He was very interested in incorporating contemporary dramatic literature, with all its witty, bawdy, and energetic qualities, with the rich textures of the emerging polyphonic musical styles. Jean-Baptiste Lully (1632–1687) was a gifted composer who became central to Louis's court entertainment. Lully's creations were elegant and lavish, full of humor and drama and interesting musical textures. They were very representative of the culture of the French court under Louis XIV. But the world that these operas were written about and performed for was totally removed from the common people. This was the beginning of the great rift in France between the wealthy and the poor that ultimately led to the end of monarchic rule in France in a sudden and brutal manner during the French Revolution in the coming century.

All across Europe, these arts were being created almost entirely for the rich and influential. Most of Europe's population never heard a note of the new music, never saw a moment of the drama or opera, and never read a word of the literature. The painting world began to move out of the churches and into the private homes of the emerging wealthy merchant class. Riches from all over the world were being channeled into Europe and into the hands of a select few. While the concept was not a new one, the scope of the acquisition of these riches was broader than it had ever been before. Taking cues from the opulence of France, many countries' budgets were bankrupted by the need to outshine their rivals. Seventeenth-century art was the realm of the rich and powerful, so much so that the artists themselves often lived like lords. The plight of the common people would soon come to haunt these frivolous governments as the Age of Enlightenment dawned.

TEXTILES

Cotton is the fiber most associated with the seventeenth century. With the development of stable trade routes to India, higher quality Indian cotton became available to Europe for the first time. Although silk was still the luxury textile of choice, cotton was not only a novelty but also versatile, colorful, and exotic. Silk and cotton both had influential roles in Europe's textile development throughout the century.

Cotton

Cotton belongs to the genus *Gossypium*, along with okra and hibiscus. It grows best in temperate climates with adequate levels of rain. The plant requires four inches (100 mm) of rain per month for the first three months of its growth cycle, followed by a three-month dry spell, at the end of which the cotton bolls are harvested. The best-quality cotton grows in coastal locations with rich soil.

Early cotton was first cultivated in Asia and first spun in India. Cotton is thought to have originated in Africa as a small tree, with the fluffy, light, seed-containing bolls having later floated across the world's oceans to Asia and even South America, where the plants were then cultivated by humans. The Moors brought cotton to Spain in the tenth century, but the cultivation was limited to production of candlewicks, stuffing, and embroidery thread. In Germany, the old word for cotton was *baumwolle*, "tree wool."[40]

In the fifteenth century, the Manchester Company of London advertised "cotton-wool" from Smyrna. England was importing raw cotton but lacked the ability to spin fine cottons, producing only fustians and dimities domestically.[41] The country's first exposure to cotton cloth was from Indian imports. Although England's cotton production expanded greatly during the seventeenth century, it would not be until the eighteenth century that the industry became stable. Even so, Indian imports would still be England's chief source of cotton until the nineteenth century.

In India, cotton was prized for the weave, brilliance of color, rich designs, and amazingly colorfast dyes. Indian cotton was known to the ancient Greeks and was famed across the Mediterranean. Spinning cotton was a cottage industry in India, done primarily in the home. As trade developed in the sixteenth century, demand for cotton grew with unimaginable voracity. Different areas of the country specialized in different weaving and printing techniques. In the seventeenth century, India began to centralize its production. Raw cotton grown all across India was transported to Deccan in southern India, which served as the production hub. The industry managers set up centers within Deccan for all steps in the process: The raw cotton was cleaned, spun, and woven into fabric in one location, and the textile was then transported to another area for dying and painting. The coloring process was very involved and required a large and consistent supply of clean water for it to be conducted successfully. The finished textiles were then sent on to a collection point, where they were inspected, graded, and stamped for export to Southeast Asia, Japan, Thailand, China, and starting in the seventeenth century, Europe.

Dyeing

The Indian dye process was painstaking and very involved. The Indians discovered that different mordants could create a variety of colors from one dyestuff. A mordant is a metallic oxide or salt used to treat a textile and make it suitable to receive the dye's pigment. The word comes from the French *mordre*, "to bite," for the caustic nature of the chemical that "bites" into the fibers to allow the pigment to penetrate and create colorfastness. The earliest decorated fabrics were created by applying pigments onto the fabric surface versus embroidery or woven designs. Alum was one of the most common mordants used in premodern dyeing.

Common colors that were used in Indian dyeing were red, violet, green, and yellow. All of these colors could be created from the extract of the madder plant, which was indigenous to the west of the country. In the south, dyers used chay, which was not quite as versatile in color but yielded a more vibrant red than madder did. The different chemical compositions of the mordants reacted with the dyestuffs to allow the dyers a great range of decoration with only a few ingredients. The only color not able to be achieved with madder or chay was blue; but in India the dyers had access to a native plant known as indigo, which produced a rich and vibrant blue dye that could create a very dark navy blue or be diluted to a pale sky blue. With the amazing ability to create stunning colors on cotton and silk, it is no wonder that Indian textiles were in high demand all over the world.

In addition to such breathtaking colors, the Indian textile designers had amazing skill when it came to the pictorial quality of their work. A *qalam*, from the Persian word for "pen,"[42] could be used to apply mordants or wax. A mordant qalam was a slender piece of bamboo, carved with a sharp nib on one end and wrapped with wool or cotton close to the end. This was soaked with the mordant, which dripped down the nib to create a very detailed line drawn on the fabric. This type of cloth was called *kalamkari*.

Resist dyeing uses a wax or paste or even mud to keep certain areas clean of dye, and it can produce very intricate and detailed designs. For resist dyeing, a similar qalam was used, only this had an iron nib and bulb assembly connected to the bamboo handle. The bulb was heated then wrapped with hair. The wax would run from the smooth hairshafts and dribble down to the iron nib and allow extraordinary control for the application of resist. This technique was also used in Java, a region still renowned for its beautiful resist designs known as *batik*. Batiking a two-yard (2 m) piece of cloth takes thirty to forty days.[43] After the resists are applied, the first dyeing takes place. The resists are then removed by scraping or boiling, and new resist is applied and the fabric is dyed again. This process is repeated for as many colors are planned for the textile design. Resists and mordants could also be stamped into the fabric by use of intricately carved wooden blocks called *chit*. Fabric decorated by use of block printing was known in India as *chitta*, "spotted cloth."[44] This became "chintz" in English, and that word is still used in textile description today for a type of printed fabric.

Indian Textiles

In the seventeenth century, the majority of Indian textiles were created with a combination of mordant dye techniques and resist methods. The cotton was first washed in a buffalo milk mixture. The desired design was drawn out on paper and perforated with tiny holes. The paper was then laid over the dried and burnished fabric and rubbed with powdered charcoal, which transferred to the underlying cloth through the tiny holes in the paper. Black outlines were then drawn in with the qalam, using an iron oxide–based mordant. Any part of the design meant to be blue or green was left blank, while the rest of the design was painstakingly painted in with wax. The first dye bath would be the indigo. Indigo will only bond to fibers and become colorfast when used as a bath; it is not colorfast when painted on.[45] The wax was then removed from the textile, and the colored areas in the design were then filled in with an array of mordants. The fabric was then dipped into a dye bath of madder. Unlike with indigo, areas not treated with mordant will not take any madder dye at all. Because the madder reacts to each mordant differently, the cloth would come out of the one dye bath with a variety of colors—black, brown, crimson, purple, lilac, and pink. After washing, the unmordanted areas would still be clean and white. Finally, the leaves and stems in the design are painted with a yellow dye, probably derived from saffron, over the indigo base. This turns the leaves and stems a rich green.

The most popular type of textile produced by this method was a *palampore*. Palampores, from *palang-posh* ("bedcover"),[46] were large-scale cotton textiles that were exported mainly to Europe. The design was inspired by a "Tree of Life" design that came to India through Persia from China. It features a tree with a sinuous trunk that has branches growing off from it. The tree grows from a rocky base and has exposed roots. The trees branches are filled with fruits, flowers, and leaves of all different botanical associations. After export to England, the motifs began to evolve into a more European style, wherein the tree is growing out of an elaborate pot and bears distinctly European flowers and fruits.

India's largest export before trade opened with Europe was the *patola*. Usually made of silk, the patola used a double-ikat weaving technique. *Ikat* is a weaving technique that uses already dyed yarns to create a design. Ikat is usually done with warp threads only and produces a watery effect. In double-ikat, both the warp and weft yarns are predyed and must be matched perfectly during the weaving process. Indian weavers were renowned for their detailed images and ability to consistently produce fine, complex designs. Patolas were made primarily as an export cloth for trade to neighboring kingdoms in Southeast Asia. They were considered fine enough to be gifts for royalty. Only the highest ranking families in India actually used them in their own costume. The patola had spiritual, ritual, and even magical qualities and functions in Southeast Asia.

India's cotton trade was initially conducted with its near neighbors China and Southeast Asia through both sea and overland trade. Although there were ethnic and religious tensions in the port cities, trade flourished between India and China from the third century on. The periodic bans on textile imports of any kind imposed by the Ming dynasty could not compete with the desire for the highly prized patterned cotton kalamkari and silk patola. These Indian cloths were usually considered tribute to royalty, governors, and military leaders.

Similarly, Japan had quite an appetite for Indian cloth. But unlike China and Southeast Asia, the desire for patterned cotton was not based on tribute or a market for inexpensive textiles, but solely for novelty's sake. By and large, the Japanese market was to satisfy the small wealthy class's hunger for the exotic as well as to import goods for the Buddhist temples. The first sustained demand for Indian textiles came from the country's Buddhist temples. Japan did not trade directly with India, however. It traded Indian goods first through the Portuguese, then through the Dutch, and finally through the English beginning in 1542 and extending through the seventeenth century.

But Europe represented by far the greatest demand for cotton and even silk imports from India. Both the Dutch and British East India trading companies managed lucrative outposts in India. By 1625, the British East India Company was importing 220,000 pieces of cloth from Gujarat.[47] When a famine devastated the region in the 1630s, England quickly moved production to Bengal so as not to break the supply chain. Although the economic depression in the 1620s in England hampered the cotton trade, by the 1660s cotton was booming. By the 1680s, the British East India Company was bringing in more than a million pieces of cotton cloth. In the Godavari Delta, the Dutch were using local households to produce cloth for export to the Netherlands. In 1682, sixteen villages, encompassing about 5,960 households, were weaving cotton for the Dutch East India Company.[48] Demand for cotton across Europe peaked during the latter half of the seventeenth century.

European Textiles

England was so successful in its importation of both silk and cotton cloth that domestic manufacturers were openly complaining. Instead of importing raw materials to be woven and dyed in England, the East India Company was bringing in whole cloth, dyed and ready. England had begun to manufacture cotton domestically in 1641, but this tiny industry struggled for most of the century. Eventually, the textile manufacturers managed to petition Parliament to ban printed cottons and silks. Only white cotton and raw silk was permitted to be imported into England.

All over Europe, cheap imposters of chintz, kalamkari, and palampores were cropping up. These imitations were not mordanted and were therefore not colorfast. But their low price and colorful allure was still tempting to many consumers. In 1648, the Dutch East India Company passed an edict to prohibit the importation and sale of counterfeit kalamkari. The largest struggle in the Indian textile business, however, was maintaining a high level in product consistency. Imposing European industrial production standards onto the handcrafted Indian fabrication business caused a great deal of friction between buyers and suppliers.

By the 1670s, European reliance on India for decorated cottons was beginning to fade. With the various edicts restricting trade, European industries blossomed. In France, the government imposed bans on not only the importation of Indian fabrics but also the printing of cottons domestically, feeling that it was taking away from the French silk-weaving trade. By 1686, the demand for the contraband prints had reached a fever pitch. Similar legislation was passed in England, but loopholes permitted exporting fabrics into the American colonies and back into the country.[49]

The first fabric printing house in England opened in 1676 with Will Sherwin as its proprietor. When his patent ran out in 1690, competitors sprang up all over. Richmond became England's center of print production. English printing copied Indian chintz in all possible methods and designs. Most English printing was done by woodblock and used madder as a dyestuff. Madder grew easily in Europe and was inexpensive. Alum and iron oxide were also mordants that were easy to come by in Europe. However, the other color layers were just painted on later in a process known as "penciling," which although was beautifully done, was not as colorfast as Indian methods of layering pigment.

Cotton, with its lightweight and washable nature as well as bright designs, made a large impact on fashion across the world. Beginning in the seventeenth century, it changed the course of costume history in Europe, making available this soft, absorbent, and versatile textile.

Silk

Although cotton was all the rage across Europe, the number-one luxury fabric across the world in the seventeenth century was silk. Silk comes from the larva of the silk moth. It naturally occurs in a filament produced in a single strand that can be more than 1,000 yards (1.2 km) long.[50] The larva wraps the long filament around itself, forming a cocoon. These cocoons must be boiled to loosen the fibers and then reeled into a usable thread. Cultivated silkworms are fed a steady diet of mulberry leaves and produce a white, uniform silk strand; silkworms also grow in the wild, but their diet may vary, which makes them produce a heavier, less lustrous fiber. This coarseness is counterbalanced by the availability of wild silk in many colors such as various shades of green, orange, and yellow.[51]

China was the capital of silk production worldwide for centuries. The secret of silk was closely guarded, and China was wary of international trade for many years. The Ming dynasty was one of the first to allow Western trade with China. When the Qing took over the country in 1644, they allowed the profitable trade to continue but maintained a strict handle on interaction with Europe.

Chinese textiles were full of symbolism with both color and design. These rich, exotic fabrics piqued the keen interest of the wealthy of Europe. Like Indian cottons, when supply could not keep up with demand, domestic imitations were made. *Chinoiserie* was the name applied to European textiles and decorative objects made in the Chinese style. Although chinoiserie used many of the same colors and motifs, the deeper meaning so apparent in Chinese design was conspicuously lacking in European imitations. Seeing an unparalleled business opportunity, the Chinese also created many textiles made with designs and color schemes based on European ornament such as heraldry and flora.

But the European silk industry did not always lean on the East for its supply or its design. In the Middle Ages, Italy began to emerge as a major textile center in Europe. Across the region, different specialties cropped up, with silk weaving focused in Venice, Genoa, and Lucca and elsewhere in Tuscany. Detailed inventories of silk production date back to 1265, and church archives from 1295 list many exquisite silk textiles woven into a variety of patterns, including ecclesiastical scenes, heavy brocades, small florals, roundels, and images of plants, animals, and people.[52] In the seventeenth century, small-scale florals woven into lightweight silks were fashionable.

In the 1630s, the mode was very natural and sinuous, using peonies and chrysanthemums in the ornate baroque style. This style was characterized by the dynamic interplay of color as well as a strong diagonal orientation. Pairings of yellow and blue, green and red, and purple and gold were very popular, but more somber tones such as brown, olive, gray, and rust were also fashionable.

The 1660s were a major turning point in the Italian silk industry. Prior to that time, Italy was Europe's leading silk supplier not only to the textile industry at large but particularly to the royalty of the continent. In 1664, Louis XIV sent his French designs to Italy to be woven and shipped back to him, just as he and his family had done for generations. But that would be the last time he ordered his silks from Italy. From 1666 on, Louis focused his attention on domestic silk production. Lyons became the center of silk weaving in France and even began to usurp Italy's prominence in silk for certain types of textiles.

On the whole, Italy produced more varieties of silks than did Lyons. The patterns developed in Italy's silk centers were used all over Europe for centuries. Florence created a distinctive flame pattern that was used in silks and silk blends and was incorporated into embroidery design repertoires in later centuries. Italy primarily produced fine, plain silks such as taffetas and gauzes, which the French imitated with a great deal of success. But in addition to lightweight silks, Italy produced a great many other kinds of textiles. From 1670 to 1750, *jardinière* velvets were in high demand. These costly and elaborate velvets were primarily created in Genoa. They were woven with a satin ground and pile flowers and embellishments. These were either monochrome in kermes red or indigo, or with vibrant red flowers and rich green stems in velvet on an ivory satin ground. This type of velvet declined in popularity in the eighteenth century but has never fallen completely out of fashion.

Silk was not the only luxury textile produced in Italy. Rich linen-cotton blend white towels with a woven band of indigo were produced all over Italy for use in fine houses throughout Europe. Tuscany was known for its heavyweight fabrics. Silk-linen and silk-cotton blends with small-scale abstract florals were created for use as bedcovers and draperies called *sciamiti*. These textiles were also made in linen-wool blends at a lower price. The rising demand for furnishing textiles kept Italy's silk mills running at capacity. Although France would come to dominate the market for fine silks, the increasing interest in interior design guaranteed that Italy would remain an important textile center. *Brocatelle*, a heavyweight furnishing fabric that features a richly patterned, brocaded, and sometimes padded border was an Italian specialty. Furnishing textiles were almost always blends, with linen and wool becoming two of the most important components. Tuscany was able to maintain its leadership role in the creation of these very desirable interior textiles.

Although Italy and France were the main producers of silk and other fine textiles in Europe, other countries had sericulture of their own. Silk came to Spain with the Moors. The Moorish presence in Spain lasted from 712 until 1492. Crafts such as weaving and architecture flourished with a Middle Eastern flair. After Granada was taken back by the Spanish in 1492, the Spanish Inquisition began. Although the *Reconquista*, the reconquest of Spain, brought out a very patriotic fervor in the Spanish people, their desire for luxury textiles outweighed their distaste for the Moors. Most of the Moors in Spain were expelled, but a few were allowed to remain early on to continue to ply their trade. For years after the Reconquista, the textile designs remained nearly indistinguishable from fabrics created in the Middle East and North Africa. One of the most prominent textiles created in Spain was *samite*, a weft-faced compound twill that became the staple of the Spanish textile tradition. This type of fabric was most likely brought to Spain from Baghdad or possibly Syria.[53]

In the fifteenth and sixteenth centuries, the Spanish Inquisition expelled the remaining Moors, and the silk industry then relied almost solely on Italian immigrants. By the middle of the seventeenth century, Spanish silks all but

SPITALFIELDS

"'Spitalfields' was named after a Hospital and Priory known as St. Mary's Spital, founded in 1197....Following the edict of Nantes in 1685, the Huguenots fled France, bringing with them the skills of silk weaving and building the once grand houses in the conservation area around Fournier Street. Today's leather and textile trades are a continuation of this earlier tradition of weaving." ("A Brief History," http://www.spitalfields.org.uk)

vanish from history, obscured by the resounding success of Italy and France and the growing influence of England.

At the close of the seventeenth century, Lyons in France and Spitalfields outside of London were the two largest silk-producing sites in Europe. As in Italy, different areas in the region of Lyons specialized in different types of silk textile, whereas Spitalfields prided itself on producing the largest variety of silks in one place. The sericulture guilds in France in the seventeenth century kept careful, copious notes like their predecessors in Italy. These guilds regulated labeling in regard to the type of silk used and its content in each textile. It regulated the widths of woven fabric as well as blend ratios. From each guild, there are entries that list each textile by name, width, and fiber content. Fabrics are also described by the density of the warp and the weft as well as the thread count. From these careful records, a very complete picture of seventeenth century has been preserved.

The Quest for Red

While dyers created the finest textiles, the dyers themselves were often considered unclean or pariahs. In the ancient Greek city-state of Sparta, dyers were not allowed to live within the city walls. The Romans, on the other hand, held their dyers in high esteem and considered them under the protection of the goddess Minerva, patroness of wisdom, craftwork, and medicine.[54] After the fall of Rome, the art of dyeing all but vanished in Europe, with nothing but obscure recipes kept by monks and nuns in monasteries and convents. It was not until the Crusades, when Europeans came into contact with the Middle East, that they became interested in dyeing once again. Medieval dyers were first forced into being second-class citizens in weaving guilds, but they soon formed their own groups, and each specialized in dyeing particular colors or fiber types.

Probably the most sought-after color throughout history has been red. Red cloth has been the prized possession of the wealthy and powerful for thousands of years. "Perhaps this explains why, in language after language, the word for red is an ancient one, older than any other color terms save black and white."[55]

Like in India, the madder plant was important to the dyers of Europe. It was colorfast when used with mordants, easy to grow all across Europe, and relatively inexpensive. Unfortunately, the coloring agent is not precise and changed depending on the water's chemistry and temperature along with the air temperature and humidity. Madder can produce a range of colors, but pinpointing the specific color and bringing it out in fabrics was very difficult. Madder can produce a red, but it is a muddy, brick red or a pink tone. Textiles coming from the Ottoman Empire, India, and China were often deep red, but the species of madder and the techniques of the dyeing were unknown in Europe. The European dyers tried many materials to achieve the sought-after red, including lichens and wood, but although the colors started out bright and vivid, they were not colorfast and faded to a pinkish-brown very quickly.

Insects held the key. Early on, dyers all over the word had access to the *Laccifer lacca* insect, known simply as lac. Lacquer and shellac were both derived from this insect, as were some dyes that worked well on leather but not textiles. But the cousins of the lac insect proved to have the right chemical makeup to produce a dye that worked well on fabrics. Oak-kermes, St. John's Blood, and Armenian Red were common names for the material extracted from the insects of the lac family. *Kermes* became the term for all insect-derived red dyestuffs. The very words to describe the color of red are derived from these insects. *Vermillion* comes from *vermiculum*, the Latin word for "worm." *Kirmiz* is the Arabic term for "worm" and is the basis for the word *crimson*.

But in 1519, Spanish conquistadores discovered an Aztec market selling a vibrant red dyestuff. They called it *grana cochinilla*.[56] The kermes reds and cochineals had an excellent affinity for protein fibers—wool and silk—and worked well with alum, a common mordant the world over. Cochineal red became the world's highest valued dyestuff, but for hundreds of years no one outside of Spain knew whether the dye was animal, mineral, or vegetable. Spain held the secret of this valuable commodity close, even as it became the target of espionage, piracy, and bribery.

Throughout the sixteenth century, all of Europe was struggling to crack the secret of the cochineal red or create a substitute. In Venice, dyers found that adding arsenic to the kermes created a brilliant and very colorfast dye. But even that beautiful red was nothing compared to cochineal. Oaxaca, Mexico, was the center of cochineal production. It is refined from an insect that grows on the prickly pear cactus; the females create a fluid of carminic acid that produces a brilliant red dye which remains colorfast for centuries. The natives of Mexico had bred a subspecies of cochineal that was larger and yielded more dye that was brighter in color. Yet even with these higher producing insects, it still took 70,000 dried cochineal females to produce one pound of dye.[57]

At the dawn of the seventeenth century, cochineal was being used all over Europe, but no one except the Spaniards knew what it was. The debate was fierce between those who believed it was a plant and those who thought it was a worm. This created a myth that cochineal was a "wormberry," a berry that ripens into a worm. Throughout the century, the focus was no longer on finding a source for true red dye, but how to find out what this miracle dye was and how to produce it. Meanwhile an unexpected advancement came from cochineal dye itself. Cornelius Drebbel was experimenting with cochineal—some think to create the Philosopher's Stone through alchemy—when he added tin to the mix and turned the dye even more vividly scarlet.[58] Drebbel opened his dyeworks in 1607, but it was not a successful venture until his sons-in-law took over the business in 1633. The color they produced was known as Bow-dye (named for the location of the dyeworks—Stratford-on-Bow, England), Dutch Scarlet (because Drebbel was Dutch), and Kuffler's Color (the name of the two brothers who married Drebbel's two daughters). By the 1660s, the best dyers in Europe had gleaned the secret of adding tin to their cochineal to create a deep cherry color or even a nearly neon red.[59]

Oliver Cromwell, Lord Protector of England, decided that he would clothe his New Model Army in red coats. The wool for the uniforms was produced, spun, woven, and dyed in Gloucestershire and the region became famous for the production of red wool.

Although cochineal was in regular use throughout Europe in the seventeenth century, there was still no proof outside of Spain of what the dyestuff actually was. In the 1660s, the microscope was developed, and one of its first uses was the investigation of the powdered, red cochineal dye. Unfortunately, the images were not clear and although the illustrations done in 1694 were very provocative, the majority of people thought it was a creative fiction. Again in 1704, detailed illustrations were made of cochineal. In them, the eggs and larvae were clearly drawn. Instead of finally shedding light onto the almost two-century-old mystery, it had just the opposite effect of bringing more confusion and disagreement among Europeans. It would not be until 1725 that Europe would finally come to know the truth about cochineal and one of the most abiding mysteries of the textile world would finally be solved.

Embroidery

By far the most popular method of decorating fabric was not dye, but embroidery. The scrolling, bold, baroque designs popular in weaving were also fashionable in embroidery. Exotic birds and animals were common themes, reflecting the interest in the East—India, China, and beyond. The Tree of Life pattern common in India and brought to England printed on palampore bed coverings became incorporated into embroidery designs.

Crewelwork, characterized by the use of heavier wool threads, was also influenced by Indian motifs. Early in the trade partnership between India and England, the Moghul rulers were very interested in English embroidery. Eventually, the Indian craftspeople began to create their own crewel embroidery to sell back to England that consisted of a blend of European, Chinese, and Indian styles.

Crewelwork was a working-class art form decorating workbags, petticoats, pockets, and everyday items. Although crewelwork has remained a popular form of embroidery into modern times, the seventeenth-century technique is known as "Jacobean work."[60]

"Stumpwork" was the quintessential form of embroidery of the seventeenth century. Contemporarily known as "raised work," stumpwork was the name appended to it almost two hundred years later from "embroidered on the stamp."[61] Stumpwork is a pictorial embroidery technique where the figures are padded and rendered in a three-dimensional way. There was never any formal school of thought or rigid rules in stumpwork. Motifs, designs, colors, and the use of scale were up to the imagination of the embroiderer. Most of these works look very fantastical to modern eyes. All open spaces on the fabric were decorated with flowers, animals, and insects, some realistic and some purely imaginary. Scale was less important that symbolism. Each element was representative of a historical, biblical, or political allegory. For example, the caterpillar or butterfly was connected to Charles I, while oak trees, oak leaves, and acorns were associated with Charles II because of the story of how he hid in an oak tree in order to escape the country during the civil war. Biblical scenes were also very popular. But regardless of the time period depicted in stumpwork, the figures are always dressed in the seventeenth-century court fashions.

These designs came from the imaginations of the stitchers, but many pattern books and prestamped kits were readily available across Europe. The stitching was done on a piece of fine linen that was stamped or drawn with the design. It was stitched using a variety of materials: silk threads, wool yarns, metallics, real pearls, tiny beads, feathers, fabric, leather, and jewels. Slips were clipped out and appliquéd onto a ground of white or cream satin. Many times, these satin grounds were also stamped to indicate the placement of the slips. Fill-in features were then embroidered between the padded slips. Some later examples use carved wood, bone, or wax faces, hands, or feet. Sometimes these are painted directly; other times they are overlaid with a thin sheet of silk and then painted.[62] Hands were also created out of wire armatures and then covered in silk threads. Many scenes depict flowers and butterflies with dimensional petals and wings, tents and pavilions with drapes that open and close, realistic figures with real hair and lace, and fine trimmings all in miniature. During the English Civil War, stumpwork took on a highly political air, and Charles I distributed his own hair for use on stumpwork projects all across the country.

For the most part, stumpwork was used on domestic items in wealthy homes. Mirror frames (called "surrounds") and covered boxes (called "caskets" or "cabinets") were the items almost exclusively created with stumpwork. These caskets were used to hold sewing supplies, perfumes, cosmetics, and letters. The embroidered panels were then sent to a cabinetmaker, who would assemble the casket and cover the sides, top, front, back, and doors with the carefully stitched satin. Although raised work had been popular for ecclesiastical vestments since the fifteenth century, this specific type of raised work was popular only in the seventeenth century, reaching its peak of popularity from 1650 to 1680.

Lace

The hallmark textile art of the century was lace. Lace was an important symbol of wealth and status across Europe and became integral to seventeenth-century fashions. The standing collars of the early part of the century were trimmed with cutwork linen. *Cutwork lace* was created when a design was stitched into the fabric and the fabric was cut away decoratively, with the open areas filled in with stitchwork. *Reticella* lace was similarly created, but the underlying fabric was almost completely cut or pulled away, leaving a geometric design of stitchery.

Entering the 1620s, a softer look was fashionable, and new types of lace making developed to take advantage of a hungry market. Flemish *bobbin lace* became extraordinarily popular, as did Italian *needle lace*. These types of lace could provide the deep scalloped edges and intricate detail demanded by the popular modes of the courts. By the 1660s, France was developing its own lace-making industry, in addition to its budding silkworks, and taking the focus away from Italy. French needle lace was even finer and more delicate than even the finest Venetian point lace. As tastes moved away from the structured and padded Italian styles, the elegant and tiny fleur-de-lys and florals of the French lace makers became in high demand.

Across Europe in the seventeenth century, the traditional textile-producing centers were losing their strengths in favor of new up-and-coming fabric makers both on the Continent and beyond. With new textiles available on the market and advancements of dye and weaving technology, fashion made great strides in this period in both surface design and materials.

CHINESE CLOTHING AND TEXTILES OF THE SEVENTEENTH CENTURY

In the summer of 1644, the once-mighty Ming dynasty finally fell to the war-like Manchu, nomads from Manchuria. The Manchu took China's Dragon Throne and began the Qing dynasty, which lasted until 1911. In those centuries, textile production in China developed into a major industry not just serving the imperial household, but setting the standard for trade silks all across the world.

Throughout the entirety of the Qing reign, the ruling Manchu never accounted for more than 2 percent of China's population. The other 98 percent of the populace considered themselves to be Han Chinese, named in reference to the very first imperial dynasty (206 BCE–220 CE).[63] The Manchu considered themselves to be ethnically and culturally different from the native Han and created Qing court dress to reflect this. Prior to 1644, the dress throughout the country in the high ranks to the peasantry had been loose and flowing, reflecting the sedentary and agrarian Han lifestyle. When the Manchu took power, the courtly styles became more slender and spare, incorporating a tunic or coat-and-trousers combination worn with boots. The coats were made with an overlapping center front that closed with a toggle and loop reflective of the nomadic background of the Manchu people.

The Qing court also created a very elaborate system of customs with regard to costume, colors, and motifs to exert their political power over the Han majority. This language of clothing was legislated by strict sumptuary laws. In the early years of the Qing dynasty, these laws were concerned mostly with the hats and insignia badges worn by courtiers in the imperial Forbidden City in Beijing.

Beyond simply maintaining the Manchu cultural identity, the legislation of clothing also aimed to align the dress of the Qing court with Confucian ideals. These ideals included integrity (*zhu*), righteousness (*i*), conscientiousness toward others (*zhung*), altruism (*shu*), and love (*ren*).[64] The Qing court regularly mixed

CONFUCIANISM

"Confucianism, one of the three major religion traditions in China, is based on the teachings of K'ung-fu-tzu (552–479 BCE), known in the west as Confucius. This secular 'religion' focuses on the conduct and practices of people in daily life—the creation of a society based on virtue. Primary relationships are between parents and children, especially fathers and sons. Cardinal virtues include Benevolence, Duty, Manners, Wisdom, and Faithfulness.

"Centered in China, the coexisting ideas and practices of Confucianism and Taoism influence Asia and to a lesser degree, other world cultures." ("Confucianism," http://www.interfaithcalendar.org/confucianism.htm)

Confucian, Taoist, and Buddhist motifs. These three religions coexisted in China, remaining separate but interacting with and influencing each other. In the seventeenth century, religious motifs and themes began to appear on court dress, in addition to ecclesiastic vestments.

This dynastic change coincided with European trade expansion. While trade was interrupted during the Qing takeover, the new rulers soon realized the value of Western trade and not only stabilized commerce with Europe but sought to expand it. Soon tea, lacquerware, porcelain, and silk were being created for the Western market. Europe was completely unaware of the political conditions in China and imagined a fantasy of China totally unlike the real thing. They reveled in the birds, butterflies, bright flowers, and graceful maidens having tea and playing exotic instruments. The "traditional" Chinese motifs incorporating birds and flowers were popularized during the Song dynasty (1127–1279) and made up the repertoire of decorations for both textiles and other objects. This adoration of Chinese styles in Europe gave rise to the imitation of it called chinoiserie. But China also came to know its market and often created specialty textiles for export to Europe incorporating Spanish heraldry and other Western motifs.

Although the trade was very profitable for the Qing dynasty, it kept very strict control over Western contact. Even so, elements of European decorative art and textiles began to infiltrate Chinese style. Clocks brought by merchants and emissaries were especially popular. The Yuanming Yuan Summer Palace even bears distinctly Rococo architectural styles.[65] With traders came missionaries, hoping to bring the very large population of China over to Christianity. For most of the seventeenth century, European merchants were not allowed beyond the limits of the port cities, although some Jesuit missionaries managed to acquire posts within the Qing court as philosophers, advisers, and astronomers.

With this accelerated commerce came the need to expand the *jizaoju*, the imperial silkworks. Although these silkworks were originally instituted in 1399 by the Ming dynasty, in 1662 the Manchu expanded the industry from one factory in Beijing to three more in surrounding cities, plus cocoon reeling centers, dye facilities, and workshops for embroidery. It is interesting to note that some of the highly skilled specialists that were employed in these embroidery workshops were women.

The silkworks churned out yards and yards of silk for trade to Europe, but most of its production was still primarily used to create the sumptuous textiles for the imperial family. The silk workshops of Beijing had the weighty responsibility of creating, in addition to imperial garments, the official insignia badges of the imperial family and ranking nobles. Known in China as *buzi*, these badges were an important part of the Qing hierarchy and were strictly regulated. They were never exported legally until after the fall of the Qing dynasty in the twentieth century.

A dragon motif was used to indicate the imperial rank and that of the highest levels of nobility. The imperial dragon was known as the *long* and had five claws. Its use was reserved exclusively for the emperor and his immediate family.

The shape of these badges was also important. These shapes had religious connotation. In the ancient religion of China predating Confucianism and Taoist practices, the worship of *Shangdi*, the supreme celestial deity, was conducted on a round altar. The emperor and his close family were thought to have a heavenly lineage and therefore their buzi not only featured the five-clawed dragon but were also round in shape. Lesser deities were worshipped on square altars and so the lesser nobles, even those deserving of dragon insignias, were assigned buzi that were square. The dragons used for the nobles ranking just below the imperial family featured four claws and were called *mang*. Lower nobles and military commanders usually took animal symbols; the lion was the most popular of these. These buzi were always made square.

Ranking women who resided in the Forbidden City Palace—usually the daughters, wives, or concubines of the emperor—were assigned buzi according to their fathers or husbands. Most women, even among the nobility, did not have buzi. Women who attended court functions regularly often wore surcoats emblazoned with badges that were inspired by the official insignias of their fathers or husbands. These insignias helped to identify them by family and rank but were not considered official buzi.

Women's dress inside and out of the Forbidden City was very indicative of the ethnic differences between the Manchu and Han. The native Han retained their short coats that opened at the center front, called the *ao*. Under these knee-length coats, the Han women would wear leggings or narrow trousers, *ku*, or a straight, pleated skirt for formal occasions called a *qun*. The Manchu women dressed in *pao* robes, which were full length, falling from the shoulders to the floor, and had an overlapping front opening held closed by the toggle-and-loop closures. At the end of the seventeenth century, these two fashions began to merge. The Han women incorporated the overlapping center front and toggle closures, while Manchu women loved the colors and motifs used by the Han and decorated their clothes with them.

Colors have always had a special significance in China and were considered to have aesthetic, political, spiritual, and symbolic meanings. Different shades were thought to contain various properties of the five components of nature: wood, metal, fire, water, and earth. This notion is known as *wuxing*.[66] Red, for example, contains mostly the element of fire and therefore is connected to ideas of life, joy, and summer. Red is used primarily for weddings, births, and other joyful and life-affirming occasions.

In the 1650s, the bright yellow of sunlight became the official color of the imperial family. Called *minghuang*, it was said to call to mind the celestial nature of the imperial bloodline, and it was forbidden for anyone not of the emperor's immediate family to wear or possess anything that shade of yellow. But even the emperor was expected to don the proper colors for particular ceremonies, such as sky blue for the festival of the winter solstice.[67]

In the seventeenth century, garments of one color of silk decorated by multiple shades of embroidery and/or trim were favored. But soon after the Qing dynasty came to power and began to set the style, additional pieces on the cuffs and hems to contrast became very popular. With the ever-expanding silk industry under the Qing, specialty piecework for decorative trimmings was far more accessible. Traditional motifs were very popular. The phoenix was reserved for the empress only. Waves, rocks, and cloud designs, which date back to the Tang dynasty (618–907), became very fashionable for Qing court attire. Han designs of butterflies, peonies, and birds were in high demand for women's wear, as well, and Taoist, Buddhist, and Confucian motifs were used by both genders and across ranks.

Buddhism was not only an inspiration for decorative inspiration on secular garments but also a part of the textile industry. Halls of worship and temples needed special textiles and hangings for draping the walls, and the celebrants were dressed in exquisite vestments. These vestments were called *jiasha*, from the Sanskrit word *kasaya*, a monk's mantle. *Kayasa* originally meant "impure colored" and was in reference to the original patchwork robes worn by the earliest devotees in the first century. These garments were made of unbleached and undyed cotton scraps, as well as rags of other existing garments. These patchwork robes were cobbled together of castoffs to symbolize the renunciation of worldly trappings and the willingness to live solely off of charity. By the seventeenth century, these vestments had become elaborately pieceworked and embroidered—very far from their original meaning.

China had the greatest impact on seventeenth-century decorative arts and textile design. All across Europe, craftspeople strove to create adequate replicas of Chinese styles to keep up with the insatiable demand. Chinoiserie would not fall out of fashion until well into the twentieth century.

SEVENTEENTH-CENTURY EUROPEAN MENSWEAR

In the seventeenth century, menswear evolved from the highly stylized and recognizable fashion of the Renaissance into the celebrated frock coat and vest combination that would linger in the popular culture for more than a century and eventually evolve into the modern three-piece suit. These changes in clothing were fueled by and part of the great political and social upheavals of this century, as well as being highly influenced by the prevalent artistic movements. The changes in fashion were slow in coming, but once those changes began, they were far reaching and profound. Also, for the first time in history, men were at times more actively participating in fads and fashions than women. In France, these early dandies were known as the *muguets*, "lilies-of-the-valley." They were young men of good breeding who pursued each and every novelty and nuance in fashion to the point of impoverishing themselves. But even when these style chasers were forced to abandon some of their frivolities, they ended up creating a whole new fad. One such example was the rise in popularity of linen boot-hose over silk which came about after the Parisian muguets were no longer able to afford silk and were forced financially to choose linen.[68]

At the century's opening, men still wore the stiffly tailored doublet with a bulging "peascod" belly: the padding of the doublet was centered at the belly, mimicking the shape of armor. The doublet was often thickly padded and often boned. By the end of the first quarter-century, the padding ceased to be concentrated in the belly and was more evenly distributed up through the pectoral area. The waistline was situated below the natural waist with either a rounded or a slightly pointed line. Sleeves were highly decorated, often contrasting with the main fabric of the doublet body. Just as in the previous century, the sleeves were tied into the armseye beneath the decorative *picadils* or wings on the shoulders of the doublet. The jerkin, a sleeveless vest popularly worn over the doublet in the previous period, was no longer part of the look of this early part of the century.

The short, full trunk-hose previously popular were only worn for formal court occasions. For everyday wear, the trunk-hose were no longer stiff and rolling outward like the "pumpkin" or "onion" pants, but full and spilling over the band buttoned just above the knee. These trunk-hose were known as "Venetians." These Venetians were fashionable in Italy in the early years of the Renaissance and grew popular all over Europe in the later years of the sixteenth century. Venetians were not considered formalwear and were worn for everyday purposes. In the seventeenth century, though, Venetians became increasingly accepted in more formal situations, except for court functions.

Beneath these Venetian trunk-hose, two pairs of stockings were usually worn. The first was a regular knit stocking that was worn gartered up to the knee bands of the trunk-hose. The second was a thicker stocking known as *boot-hose* that had originated as an extra layer worn only with boots to cushion the foot. These boot-hose became highly decorated and were worn for fashion instead of function. They were usually heavily trimmed with lace and rolled down over the boot-top to be shown off to the best advantage. The boots themselves were very close fitting to the leg and were of supple leather, able to be turned down to show off the decorative edging of the boot-hose. Spurs were also quite fashionable, worn strapped to the relatively high heels of the riding boots.

Stiffly starched neck and wrist ruffs were still worn on formal court occasions. Informally, a falling band collar edged in lace was very popular, as were turned-back shirt cuffs, which were also usually edged in lace.

Elderly men, as well as merchants, bankers, and scholars, still wore the type of gown that had made its debut in popularity in the late fourteenth century. This garment evolved decorative effects, including densely figured sleeves that were slit down the front and often worn trailing. This post-Elizabethan, Spanish-influenced style lasted in England until after 1625. In France and across Europe, the look was quite similar, holding onto the fashions of the previous era.

In the French court of Louis XIII, it became impossible to tell a man's rank from his attire. The various ranks of gentlemen seemed to be equally well dressed, and everyone aspired to carry a sword, even though in the past that privilege had been reserved for those of noble birth or those who had earned a knighthood. A contemporary observed that "the Parisians no longer seemed able to live without ribbons or laces or a mirror."[69]

Although many sumptuary laws were passed in France, forbidding excess in design, fabric, and decoration of clothing, these laws were rarely adhered to. Young men of good breeding who became very adept at keeping up with the constant flux of fashion gave themselves over to fashionable excesses of satin, silk panne plush, and beaver hats, regardless of the impact on their personal fortunes. Many members of the French nobility all but impoverished themselves to keep abreast of the ever-changing fashions.

Both the English and the French courts sought to make a display of splendor of their courtiers and lead the parade of style. In France, Cardinal Richelieu deprived the ranking nobility of their political powers, so to remain influential, these nobles surrounded the king and indulged him in every whim and fancy of fashion, thus creating a reputation of excess, but also of style. After the mid-1630s, Spanish and Italian influences vanished almost entirely as France took center stage as the fashion leader, an honor it would hold for centuries to come.

Undated copy of van Dyck's portrait of Charles I and Henrietta Maria, 1632, shows excellent examples of men's and women's clothing. © Victoria & Albert Museum, London / Art Resource, NY.

In England, after the death of James I, his son Charles I took the throne. Charles's court was not known for the excesses of his father's, but during his reign, the silhouette that was beginning to take shape in previous decades began to solidify. His marriage to Princess Henrietta Maria of France brought Continental influence to England and began France's monopoly on seventeenth-century style.

Long hair was still in vogue, as well as wide falling band collars edged in rich lace. These collars were often as wide as the shoulders of the wearer, although smaller, lace-edged linen collars were also popular. The doublet was tight fitting to the body with deep skirting panels at the waist that overlapped. The padding vanished, replaced with thick, quilted layers that added stiffness without as much bulk. Ribbons were used to tie the doublet and breeches together with decorative bows, often of a complementary or contrasting color. The doublets were slashed, with contrasting fabrics showing behind the slits cut in the body fabrics both on the front and the back of the doublets. The fabrics contrasted often not only in color, but in weave or design as well. The sleeves were also often slashed and tied into the doublet with ribbons tied in bows. The shoulder wings were very wide, making the silhouette exaggerated and emphasizing the narrowness of the waist.

In the 1630s, the doublet loosened. It was still tailored, but no longer tight fitting to the body. By 1633, the skirting around the hem of the doublet had disappeared and the shoulder pieces had become very subdued. The doublet front was often left partially unbuttoned to show the linen shirt beneath. Collars also shrank in dimension, worn upright and close to the throat but not starched and dimensional as they had been in years past. Doublet sleeves went from being very full and paned to being very fitted with a slit down the top seam to show the shirt sleeves beneath. Shirts were made with wide, lace-edged, turned-back cuffs. Satin was highly fashionable for doublets and sleeves, but other fabrics such as wool, linen, and other weaves of silk were also popular.

The Venetian trunk-hose retreated in yardage, becoming tight fitting and ending about the knee with voluminous ribbons on the band and garters. The term for this garment changed from "trunk-hose" to "breeches" in the late 1630s. Rosettes, bows, braid, and cording were employed to decorate the bottoms of the breeches. In the following decade, the decorated bands were often worn below the knee and sometimes left loose.

Following Louis XIII to the throne was his son, Louis XIV. He would come to be known as the "Sun King" and establish a court that was the most opulent and outlandish the world had ever known. Louis XIV's courtiers were expected to be fully and formally dressed for each and every court occasion. This required them to have a vast wardrobe so no ensemble was ever repeated, further straining the assets of the nobility as they spent more and more time, energy, and money on their clothing. This tendency for the extravagant gave rise to this century's most recognizable fashion fads for men, the "petticoat breeches" or *rhinegraves*. These breeches were very voluminous and were much more like a divided skirt than trousers. In the most extreme varieties, each leg measured almost two yards (2 m) in circumference. This fashion began with the loosening of the Venetians at the knees in the late 1630s and snowballed into a fashion phenomenon. These already elaborate breeches were made even more extravagant by the use of *canons* at the knees. Canons were a band of ruffles and ribbons that were attached to the bottoms of the petticoat breeches. They were often made in a contrasting color and, at the height of this particular mode, were several inches (15+ cm) in depth.

To accompany the flamboyant petticoat breeches, the doublet changed immensely. Now no longer tailored much at all, the doublet became boxy and shortened quite dramatically, rising several inches above the natural waist and displaying the front of the white linen shirt. The doublet was too short now to tie to the breeches, but the ribbons that had been used for the purpose remained, as a purely decorative element. Fashionable young men trimmed the hem with yards of long loops of ribbons to match the canons on their breeches. In England, the short doublet became known as the "jackanapes."[70] The collar of the shirt evolved into a bib-like construction. The collars could be attached to the shirt or tied on as a separate piece. Although for the most part these bib-collars were left plain, lace-edging was still used for formal occasions and by the aristocracy.

Fashion in England encountered a massive split in 1642 when civil war broke out, pitting the Catholic king and his supporters the Royalists (nicknamed the "Cavaliers") against the Protestant Puritans (known as the "Roundheads") who backed the Parliament. This political divergence became a fashion statement. The Royalists were known to be extravagant in their dress, but that did not mean the Puritans were entirely devoid of style. Although the Puritans were known for their less opulent attire and tall-crowned hats, some Parliament supporters were known to dress as outlandishly as their Royalist enemies. Still, by and large, the dress of Puritans was described as being "sad-colored."[71]

Two major fashion trends grew out of this conflict. One was the wearing of a buff leather jerkin by the Royalist armies. This fairly simple vest was of natural tanned hide not dyed, embossed, or glazed and was worn over the armor or, in many cases, *as* armor. This fashion was quickly picked up by others in England and was eventually copied throughout parts of Europe in all levels of society.

Charles's queen, Henrietta Maria from France, dubbed the Parliamentary supporters "Roundheads" for their short-cropped hairstyles. Natural, long curls were the height of fashion, so in defiance of the Royalist decadence, the most extreme and dedicated Puritans sheared their tresses.

While the French had a new shining star to guide them, England's monarchy was about to be destroyed. In 1649, Charles I was executed and the Parliament ruled England as a Commonwealth under the guidance of Oliver Cromwell. Styles in England further diverged, as old battle lines remained drawn. Some of the ranking English were known to wear the short doublet and voluminous petticoat breeches, but overall, true high fashion did not make it into the country, and England gained a reputation as being an unrefined backwater when it came to costume. Many Royalists continued in the style of wearing the military-inspired buff leather jerkin with a decorative sword belt or sash worn across the shoulder in spite of their defeat. Some Royalists still wore boots, but the bucket tops were so wide when turned down, that it was often very cumbersome. This fashion had been out of style in France for some years.

It is also worth noting that at this time sleeves began to be sewn into the arm-seye of the doublet rather than tied in or fastened in a way to make them removable. Tailors were changing the way they constructed upper body garments, enabling a smoother, less bulky appearance. Contrasting sleeves and slashing were no longer popular, as trendsetters looked for ensembles with matching breeches and doublet, often in satin or velvet.

After the Restoration of the monarchy in England, one of the greatest and most far-reaching innovations in men's fashion would come to the fore. Although Charles II had been raised by a French mother and lived for many years in that country, the development of this style would ultimately be traced back to England, dispelling the belief that England had no taste in clothing. In 1666, the king introduced a long, sleeved garment that was plainly cut and modeled after a Persian garment, and it was similarly called a "vest." Originally it was worn to the hips, but later it was long to the knee. The vest was worn beneath a long coat. The doublet would not be worn again after 1664. With the advent of this new style, petticoat breeches immediately fell out of favor in England, primarily because they were too full to be worn comfortably beneath the vest-and-coat combination. A slimmer cut of breeches were worn beneath the vest instead. This fashion migrated to France in the 1680s and caught on with great fervor there. This style of a vest and very full coat over narrowly cut breeches would remain in vogue, albeit with many alterations, throughout the seventeenth and eighteenth centuries, carrying over even into the early years of the nineteenth.

Originally, the new garment was called a *vest* or a *waistcoat*. These terms were used interchangeably throughout the period all over Europe, although eventually *waistcoat* would prevail; *vest* would not be used in regular description of menswear again until the nineteenth century. The waistcoat was worn long, but always shorter in length than the coat. The overcoat was known as a *justacorps* in France and a *cassock* in England; *justacorps* became the standard name for this item in the seventeenth century. These coats eventually became so long that they entirely hid the breeches worn beneath. At first, the coat was fairly simple. It had a loose, smooth silhouette that fell to the mid thigh. But soon the torso began to be made more fitted, flaring out over the hips. The skirting of the justacorps now hung to the knee instead of stopping at mid thigh. The skirting also began to expand with the use of gores and pleats, and it was also often slit up the back to the hip line. Occasionally, side slits were used as well.

The justacorps was all but begging for surface decorations. Buttons and buttonholes decorated with braid and embroidery lined the opening of the coat, and the colorful silk and brocade sword belts were transformed into bright sashes worn at the shoulder across the body. The coats themselves were made in the same variety of textiles as the doublets of earlier years had been—wool, brocade, satin, and other weaves of silk. Pockets were introduced, but it was not long before they became purely decorative, placed so low on the coat's skirt that they could not be reached by the wearer. Both the coat and vest continued to feature dozens of buttons from collar to hem, most of which were left unbuttoned and used only as ornamentation. The cuffs of the coat were worn turned back, and the depth of the cuff and the lining fabric went through many changes depending on geography and time period. Early on, in both England and France, the cuff was rather wide and matched the coat. In the 1680s, the cuffs became smaller and were made in a contrasting fabric. In France, cuffs were often lined with not only a contrasting color but usually a contrasting type of fabric for added texture and visual interest.

The justacorps sleeves were quite fitted, and the turned-back cuff often showed the sleeve of the waistcoat beneath. This would also be a contrasting color and/or fabric. Additionally, the sleeves of the shirt now ended in lace-edged frills that fell over the hands. The breeches beneath the waistcoat and justacorps were rarely seen, but a new mode emerged from them: By and large, they were constructed of black velvet. The cut of the breeches was slimmer than in earlier decades, but still very voluminous by modern standards and worn gathered to the knee. Rich, heavy colors such as brown, gray, dark blue, and brick red were all very popular for breeches, as well as for the waistcoat and justacorps, but the most fashionable color of all was black.

At the close of the century, menswear had taken on the silhouette that would see it through to the next epoch. The coat was very long now and often worn unbuttoned. The sleeves were no longer straight and snug to the arm, but almost flaring outward from the armseye and ending with deep, contrasting cuffs that often reached nearly to the elbow. The skirting was quite voluminous and made with deep box pleats. Embroidery in metallic and colorful silk threads was lavished on the pockets, buttonholes, and lapels. Beneath the justacorps, the waistcoat remained simple in design and cut, still reaching past the hips, but falling far shorter than the coat. It could button down the length but most often was worn unbuttoned from the waist down. Most waistcoats at this time were being made without sleeves, although in colder climates the sleeves may have remained for warmth. But the sleeve of the waistcoat was no longer seen at the cuff of the justacorps.

By 1690, breeches were being worn very tight in the legs. While still full at the waist and in the seat, the thighs were made to fit snugly. Stockings were worn gartered at the knee, then pulled up and over the hem of the breeches. The fabrics chosen for the breeches came in one of two categories: a match to the justacorps, or black satin or velvet. Black breeches were acceptable with any color justacorps, but a matching ensemble was considered appropriate for very formal occasions. Colors for the justacorps and breeches became very subdued at the end of the period. The waistcoat was the central point of interest and color in the male wardrobe. It often contrasted greatly with the coat and breeches in color, texture, and decoration.

With the justacorps becoming the mode for indoor wear, men searched for a sensible and fashionable outerwear topcoat. While some men still indulged in capes, most gentleman took to wearing a thick wool coat that was cut and trimmed in a similar manner to the justacorps. Soldiers fancied a version made of leather. The coat came to be called the *Brandenburg topcoat* after the German province where the braided loop fasteners had originated.

Throughout the period also, elderly men and men of certain professions (bankers, scholars, clergy) were known to wear full-length robes. These robes went through remarkably few changes during the century but eventually became the basis for a quasi-fashionable casual robe known as the *banyan* in the eighteenth century. By the end of the seventeenth century, it grew less and less common for merchants to wear robes unless it was a special occasion. By and large, the wearing of long robes fell into the purview of the clergy and scholars only.

During the latter half of the seventeenth century, casual wear began to take a form unto itself. This happened simultaneously in womenswear and menswear. One major factor in this shift was importation from India and China and the new ideas in garments brought from abroad. *Pyjamas* were introduced to Europe early in the century from India by the East India Company. Influenced by the availability of printed Indian cottons, these were a luxury item intended for private use. Seen in artwork as early as the 1630s, the pyjama suit became a hallmark of wealth, indicating a connection with the lavish importation from India. Pyjamas began to be worn outdoors by men for very casual outings.

The overall look for men through the seventeenth century changed drastically from start to finish, but following a certain theme. The century began hard on the heels of the sixteenth-century fashion, and looking forward, the eighteenth century would ride the coattails of the seventeenth for quite some time. The justacorps became the basis of the fashionable silhouette across Europe both for its comfort and its ease of wear. What's more, the potential for personalization of the coat and waistcoat beneath were nearly endless. Men took a serious and unprecedented role in the determination of fashion in the seventeenth century that would last for many, many more years to come.

Accessories

Early in the seventeenth century, the ruff was the accessory of choice. Throughout the first quarter of the century, wide, starched standing neckruffs were still very popular. Wristruffs were slowly being replaced by a cutwork or lace-edged turned-back cuff. The first change in ruff wearing for men came when they stopped starching them to a crisp state and allowed the ruff to wilt onto the shoulders. In addition to the ruffs, which were an additional piece worn with the shirt, the shirt itself began to develop a fashionable collar to be worn without a ruff. The *falling band collar* began to become popular among the middle class in the late sixteenth century. By the time it reached the fashionable upper classes, the collars had grown wide and were decorated with cutwork or edged in lace. The starched ruff was still worn on formal court occasions.

The shirt itself became an important item of clothing for the fashionable man. In previous eras, the collar and cuffs were the most important attributes to a good shirt, but with the fashion of paned sleeves and slashed doublets, the shirt itself could be seen. More attention was paid to the fineness and whiteness of the linen. Common fabric types for gentlemen's shirts included holland, frieze holland, cambric, batiste, lawn, and plain linen. Working-class shirts were made from a coarse linen known as *lockeram* or *linsey-woolsey*, a linen-wool blend. Fine shirts took, on average, three *ells* of fabric to make—an ell is equivalent to approximately forty-five inches (114 cm) in length. A gentleman's shirt was far more voluminous than those of the modern era and usually even fuller than those reproduced for period costumes.

The basic shape of the shirt was relatively unchanged throughout the century. Additions of collars, cuffs, ruffs, and bibs and changes in fullness did not affect the essence of the garment itself. The neckband was narrow, and the material of the shirt's yoke was gathered to it. The shirt opening down the center front was closed by means of ribbons, strings, or buttons. Sometimes a collar was attached to a neckband, and other times the collar was tied on or otherwise attached as a separate piece. The ruff vanished almost entirely by the end of the first twenty-five years and was replaced by the falling band collar. These collars were edged in lace, often several inches (15+ cm) deep, or were made entirely from lace. They were worn from the high neck of the doublet spilling across the shoulders. For less formal occasions, a smaller collar with a more subdued lace edge was worn. Much attention was also paid to the cuffs. Pains were taken to match the cutwork and lace of the cuffs to the decorative elements of the collar to add detail to the ensemble. The lace on the cuffs could also be several inches in depth and lay back as far as midway up the forearm.

But the shirt had its heyday when the short doublet and petticoat breeches came into fashion. The shirt was integral to the look of the fashion, since it was now the most visible it had ever been in history. The doublet stopped high above the waist and the shirt was left to puff out between it and the waistband of the very full petticoat breeches. Attention to detail was imperative, as the shirt had to be uniformly white, of fine and soft linen, and voluminous enough to puff adequately between the doublet and breeches. The collars became even longer, although not as wide as they had been previously. They hung down the front, like a bib. These bib-collars were mostly left plain, although on formal occasions they could be edged with lace. Some were connected to the shirt, but a large number of them were tied on as had been the ruffs of years past.

The shirt's priority as a fashionable garment soon gave way with the arrival of the waistcoat and justacorps. The waistcoat was high collared and closed to the hips, so once again only the collar and cuffs of the shirt were to be seen. In 1666, the bib-collar was no longer worn with the shirt; instead, a strip of linen was worn wrapped around the neck and tied in a bow at the throat. With long, full-bottomed wigs now in fashion, the wide collars previously worn were no longer fashionably viable.

This was the first incidence of the *cravat* or, as it was known at this early date, the "neck-cloth." The cravat was introduced to France by Croatian mercenaries hired into the French army by Louis XIV. Adapted from traditional Croatian linen neck scarves, the cravat itself was always white, but occasionally a colored ribbon was tied into the bow with it. Scarlet ribbon was very popular. By the next decade, the cravat was usually simply looped rather than tied. One particular style was called the "Steinkirk." Supposedly, in 1684, French soldiers were surprised at Steinkirk and did not have time to properly tie their cravats, so they hastily knotted them and tucked the twisted ends through a buttonhole on their coats. Although there is some truth to the tale, evidence in artwork already shows the cravat ends tucked through a buttonhole on the justacorps prior to 1684.[72]

The cravat would remain the fashionable neckwear for men for centuries to come, although it would go through some subtle changes. Sometimes the cravats were edged in a fine, thin lace, fringing, or even pearls, but for the most part they would be worn plain. The width and length of the cravat would remain consistent for the rest of the century.

Cuffs would become a focal point of men's costume again at the end of the century. After vanishing while the "jackanapes" style of doublet was popular, cuffs returned with the justacorps. While the coat cuffs were turned back, the sleeves were not. Instead of ending in a plain band as they had in the earlier decades, the sleeves were now gathered to a band that sported deep, lace-edged frills spilling over the hands. A similar fashion became the mode for women's chemises as well during this time. The lacy sleeves became an integral part of the justacorps look, contrasting the substantial turned-back coat cuff, which was often highly decorated, with the softly falling riffles of linen pouring out from beneath. This, too, would be a major mode of shirt fashion well into the following century.

Men of all social classes wore hats. Most of the hats popular in the early part of the century were beaver felt and high crowned with one side pinned up, or "cocked," by a jeweled brooch. Feathers were popular to be worn in hats, especially trailing plumes, but the amount was not nearly as much as what was seen in later years. By the end of the first quarter-century, the brims of the hats had grown very wide and the plumes had also become dramatically large and full. The brim was still worn cocked to one side.

Men of all social classes wore wide-brimmed hats, trimmed with myriad plumes and ribbons and cocked. The Puritans' hats were extremely high crowned, but much slimmer in the brim. Usually black, brown, or gray, these hats were mostly unadorned save for a plain black hatband and possibly a simple buckle.

As the century drew to a close, the brims remained wide, but the crowns started to shorten. The abundance of feathers diminished only slightly for the fashionable male. The brims were still worn cocked up on one side. By the end of the century, the crowns were very flat, but rounded. Pinning up the sides would remain popular through the 1790s, but now men often pinned up the entire brim in three places creating the "tricorned" hat that would be the hat of choice throughout the eighteenth century. The hat was often trimmed with braid or lace and a bunch of feathers. As the color schemes became subdued in the justacorps and breeches, so did the decorations on the hats. Focus was now on the waistcoat instead of the headwear. The growing fascination with wigs took even more attention away from hats. As periwigs became the dominant mode of hairdressing, hats began to lose popularity. Most often the hat was not worn but simply carried as a status symbol.

Daggers had been the accessory of choice throughout the sixteenth century, but by 1605, rapiers had become the hallmark of a distinguished gentleman. Sword belts, worn across the body, became a popular accessory from 1630 through 1700. Often these sword belts were brocaded and highly decorative. But even the gentleman's swords soon fell from fashion, replaced by elegant canes with highly decorated and stylized handles. The use of canes and walking sticks replaced the sword or rapier for status. And all men of station used snuff, which was kept in highly ornamented little snuffboxes usually in the pocket of the coat or waistcoat. Although swords were no longer carried except for matters of state, the sword belts worn across the shoulder survived as a colorful sash draped across the justacorps.

Cloaks remained popular in some form or another throughout most of the period. At the outset of the period, cloaks were full, circular, and worn long to the knee. By the mid-1620s, cloaks became very fashionable again, worn short and flared. Older gentlemen as well as merchants, bankers, scholars, and clergymen still wore their cloaks long, however. They also persisted in the wearing of ornamented long gowns or robes with highly decorative hanging sleeves. But by mid century, cloaks had gone entirely out of fashion, save for travel and wearing outdoors during inclement weather.

Stockings were an important part of the men's ensemble—not only plain knit stockings, but also the thicker and more decorative boot-hose. Knit silk stockings were very popular, although they were also very expensive, often costing more for one pair than a person might earn in wages for a whole month. The boot-hose were usually made of linen and were still highly decorated with ribbons and lace. They remained popular even when boots were not in fashion. After 1655, the boot-hose was worn over the plain silk stockings, gartered below the knee, and folded down with the deep lace hanging over the calf. But when the justacorps came into fashion, the boot-hose was gone forever. At the tail end of the century, stockings were white silk and often embroidered at the calves and/or ankles. This embroidery was called a "clock."

Footwear

Men's footwear went through a variety of changes over the century. At the outset, shoes were rounded at the toe and fastened at the front with a bow. These bows were usually oversized and decorative but were not quite the flamboyant shoe rosettes that would be in vogue in later years. Men's shoes were made with a thick heel of about an inch (2.5 cm) in height. Riding boots were also popular, both for riding and for everyday dress. These boots were thigh high and could be worn that way for riding or fashionably turned down to show off the decorative edging of the boot-hose. The boots were very close fitting to the leg and were of supple leather. Spurs were also quite fashionable, strapped to the relatively high heels of even the boots that were made for riding. A gentleman was not fully dressed without his spurs. In the 1620s and 1630s, boots were the ultimate in fashion. They were worn even at court with turned-down tops decorated with the flounces of lace from the boot-hose. Boots were square toed and became flat soled.

By the 1650s, the turned-down boot-tops grew to enormous proportions. They were very cumbersome and were often mocked by the satirical cartoons of the time. This style was particularly popular among the Royalist supporters of Charles II. The heels were high in boots once again, and the showiest of gentlemen wore "slap-soles" attached to the bottoms designed to slap against the bottom of the heels. Toes were still very squared off for both boots and dress shoes. Dress shoes featured high heels and flat, wide rosettes.

Louis XIV is credited for popularizing the style of painting the heels of the shoes red. Although this trend was seen earlier in England, it did not catch on with mainstream style makers until the Sun Court in the 1640s. This popular treatment of the heels would remain in vogue throughout the century.

Boots started to fall out of fashion with the coming of the petticoat breeches. When the justacorps became popular, boots were immediately discarded, except for riding. High-heeled shoes were worn and often decorated by stylized ribbon rosettes. Toes were square and rosettes were not as large as they had been previously. An overshoe called a *galosh* came into use for men during this period.

The huge rosettes of shoes were replaced by elaborate buckles for both fashion and function. Shoes were still high heeled, with those heels painted red. The tongue of the shoe had grown very tall and wide and hung over the instep, and the toes were very squared off. Heavy leather jackboots replaced the supple turned-down boots of decades previous, and although they gained popularity in daywear, they were still primarily used for outdoor activities and not acceptable for formal occasions. Stockings were primarily worn alone without boot-hose. If boot-hose were worn, it was as they had been originally intended, beneath the boot and not visible. The highly decorative ruffles had disappeared. The shoe buckles were very elaborate at the end of the century, often jeweled or enameled. Although boots were no longer popular for day-to-day wear, separate leather leggings were sometimes worn with leather shoes to achieve the look of a tall boot. These were made of lightweight leather and were very close fitting. But in general, white stockings and black shoes with metal buckles were what most fashionable gentlemen were wearing at the close of the century.

Hair

Men's hairdressing took on many forms through the century. And like many aspects of male dress, the attention paid to the male coiffure was intense and unprecedented. Male hairdressing also became a tool for political and social character, announcing one's standing and position. Wigs became an integral component of noble breeding.

> It is common to regard the wig of the seventeenth and eighteenth centuries as an aristocratic ornament of Old Regime Europe, an exclusive marker of high birth and status worn by the privileged few. Indeed, the wig enjoyed the most noble of pedigrees, its origins stretching back to the seventeenth-century French courts of Louis XIII and Louis XIV, where fashion had become part of an aristocratic world of power and display. By the end of the Sun King's reign, wigs had spread well beyond France, crowning kings at royal courts across Europe and becoming an essential feature of European noble costume.[73]

In fact, the word *wig* itself was coined during this century as a short form of *periwig*, which was based on the French word *peruke*. Although the fashion for wig wearing began in France, evidence shows that it had reached Venice by

1665, where it was outlawed by an edict of the Council of Ten in 1668.[74] Forced underground, wigs then became an even more sought-after commodity. The edict was revoked several years later.

At the outset, hair was worn naturally long, covering the ears. Facial hair was neatly trimmed. By the first quarter of the century, hair was worn to the chin near the face, lengthening to fall in curls at the shoulders. Moustaches and trim, pointed beards were also extraordinarily popular due to the painter van Dyck. Some men also liked a small, trim goatee on the lower lip.

In England, hair became an essential part of the political identity. Supporters of the king wore their hair in long, fashionable curls, while Parliamentary supporters sheared their locks in an act of austerity and thus became "Roundheads."

Louis XIII had been a major consumer of wigs after he began to go bald later in life. His son Louis XIV continued the popularity of long, curling hair, and men all over Europe strove to emulate his luxuriant dark auburn curls. The styling of hair rose to a new level of chic. Curls became more defined, as were their positions on the head or arrayed across the shoulders. Each curl developed a name, a position, and a meaning. The curls were often tied with colorful satin ribbons. One such fashion came to be known as the *cadenette*. It added a jeweled ribbon to an already existing style known as the *moustache* that called for one long curl to be separated from the rest and combed forward over the shoulder.

Men who were unable to achieve their own head of curly locks turned to periwigs. Soon, the periwig caught on, as it was much easier maintenance than having to style one's own hair. Initially, Louis XIV was terribly reluctant to cut his own hair, as he was very proud about it. In the end, his desire to be fashionable outweighed his vanity about his own hair and he shaved it and adopted wig wearing. Beneath the wig, the hair was cropped very close to the scalp.

Wigs became a big business in France. By the end of the century, wig production and export was one of France's greatest tax commodities. In 1673, there were more than two hundred wig makers in Paris, enough to begin an independent wig makers guild. Some of this popularity carried over into England, but the center of the fashion for wig wearing was in France. Fine wigs were made from human hair, but lesser-quality wigs were created out of wool or horsehair. However, in the seventeenth century, wigs were primarily worn by monarchs, nobles, and high-ranking state officials—or by those wishing to curry favor with the aforementioned. Wigs were seen as a marker of social status. Michael Kwass writes in his essay concerning seventeenth- and eighteenth-century wig wearing in France:

> Long hair was a mark of honor and liberty among the ancient Gauls.... Among the first Franks, and in the beginning of our monarchy, it was a characteristic of princes of the blood.... Whereas long hair was the mark of royal blood, other subjects wore their hair cut short around their head. Some authors claim that haircuts were more or less short, depending on the degree of inferiority in the ranks; in such a way that the monarch's head of hair became, so to speak, the yardstick of social rank [*l'étalon des conditions*].[75]

Kwass also mentions the use of long hair in Classical artwork, depicting rulers and gods with abundant locks and speculates on the need to display a luxurious head of hair as a claim to elevated social rank. Samuel Pepys, a low-ranking noble and diarist of the time, writes of finally giving in to the pressure of fashion and purchasing a wig for himself. Although he complains about the discomfort of wig wearing, he is so socially ambitious that he persists in wearing it as often as possible to attempt to be connected with the social strata associated with wigs. Pepys also laments about wig lice, which infest his hairpiece, as well as the origin of the hair—rumors were circulating that the hair had been cut from those who died of the plague and other contagious diseases.[76]

The French periwig was a large mass of fat curls falling over the shoulders and down the back. These "full-bottomed" wigs were large, heavy, and expensive. They were meant to emulate the ideal head of hair as closely as possible, but it was an ideal that no mortal could ever attain. At the height of their popularity—and size—full-bottomed wigs required more than ten heads of human hair to achieve the thick fluff of curls. The simple amount of hair needed to make one of these wigs, adding to the challenge of matching the different contributions into a homogenous whole, is what drove the cost of these wigs upwards of a thousand *écus* (roughly 5,000–6,000 *livres*).

It was not long before these carefully "casual" wigs became stylized and formal. By the 1680s, structured ringlets were arrayed across the back in a smoother line than the riotous tumult of the earlier style, but the size and volume of the wig had not decreased. At the end of the century, periwigs were not natural looking at all. The curls were very sculpted. The hair was parted in the middle, with two piles of curls on either side of the part, small ringlets at the front to frame the face, and two tufts cresting forward over the temples. The length would often reach to the waist in back. This particular style was called the *binette*. Louis XIV had ten personal wigmakers and stylists in his personal household. With wigs being so costly, wig theft became a common crime in Paris.

Some early powdering of the wigs occurred at this time, but it was not a stark white powdering. This dusting only tended to give the wigs a matte grey appearance. It would be several more years before bright white powdered wigs would come into fashion.

Military Dress

Military uniforms were prevalent over armor for the first time in the seventeenth century. The metal *cuirass* was replaced by the buff leather jerkin. Although not as adequate for protection as the cuirass, the buff jerkin was more comfortable and gave the wearer more range and freedom of motion. The look of the military man was pared down from the outlandish puffs and padding and shining armor to a utilitarian mode. Decorative elements were kept to a minimum, and accessories were devised to be useful rather than aesthetic. Belts, bandoliers, and other accoutrements were better outfitted for use with the developing weapons of the time.

But with the streamlined look of troops, identification became a problem. This was addressed with the use of colorful sashes worn across the shoulder. In the Thirty Years' War, different colors corresponded to the various countries: red for Germany, white for France, blue for Sweden, orange for Holland, and red and yellow for Denmark.[77] In the English Civil War, battlefield soldiers used colored sashes to tell friend from foe; white sashes indicated Parliamentary soldiers and red was for Royalists. Commanders were identified by their battalions by use of colored scarves and sashes. This was also a useful tool in identifying the bodies of fallen soldiers.

Military uniform was fully developed across Europe by the middle of the seventeenth century. The more spare silhouette was useful in the new mode of warfare. With the rising use of muskets and bayonets, less bulky attire was crucial to the proper function of the weaponry. The fact that the uniforms were wool helped countries regulate their wool industries. The refined and uniform look of the military that developed in this century became the basis for modern military attire and established a societal paradigm.

Undergarments

The use of undergarments as a tool of class distinction was as common for men as it was for women. For the first time in history, undergarments had cultural significance. Men's shirts became an integral part of the costume. Shirts showed more than ever during the seventeenth century; between the paned and open-seamed sleeves and the short "jackanapes" doublet, a fine and white linen shirt was an absolute must-have for the well-dressed man.

The "day-shirt" was the full, linen shirt that was worn beneath the doublet. Men also had a "night shirt" that was more elaborate, often with lace insets at the neck, sleeves, and wrists. It was constructed with a flat, falling collar and a deep center front opening that fastened with ribbons or strings. Nightcaps were also common. Like the nightshirts, they were made of fine linen and often lavishly trimmed with lace. It was customary for newlyweds to give one another nightclothes for their wedding night. Gentlemen in mourning often wore black linen nightshirts and caps.

Men of station also wore drawers. This habit, like the introduction of the waistcoat, is attributed to Charles II. It is recorded that he wore silk trunks that measured about thirteen inches (33 cm) from the waist. They tied at the center front and were very full through the seat. This fullness was pleated to the narrow waistband. Another important and prominent feature was a slit at the center back seam. These male underpants were very popular throughout England and France.

Men also wore long drawers, especially in the winter. These could be silk or fine wool but were usually a very soft linen. They also featured a tied front opening with a full seat that was pleated to a waistband and a rear slit. But like their modern counterparts, these drawers covered the entire leg and were often worn with a stirrup under the foot to keep them smoothly in place under the breeches and stockings.

For the first time, men's undergarments were considered erotic. Men are featured *en dishabille* in contemporary artwork with doublets open and shirts showing. They are also painted in their pyjamas and house robes. When the waistcoat was first introduced, it was as an undergarment. Originally, it was considered salacious to open up the coat and show off not only the shirt, but the waistcoat as well. In the seventeenth century, men found themselves amid sensation and scandal about their undergarments—an arena that had previously, and almost exclusively, involved women.

Working-Class Clothing

The working-class man of the seventeenth century would have tried his best to emulate the silhouette of those of station. Overall, men wore a well-fitted jacket that buttoned up the front over plain breeches that reached the knee or mid-calf. Half in an approximation of ranking nobles and half for genuine sun shading, working-class men adopted the wide-brimmed felt hat.

Fabric was primarily wool and linen, textiles easily homegrown and homespun. Hemp was also used in certain regions for men's shirts. Linsey-woolsey, a linen and wool blend, was very popular for jackets and breeches. Stockings for the working class were usually knit from wool, when they were worn at all. The colors for lower-class costumes were limited to what was available; for farm families, that would depend on the color of their sheep's wool or the local vegetable dyestuffs.

Merchants and aspiring middle-class men could afford to purchase finer materials, including velvet, silks, and gold and silver buttons. These items of dress were very expensive and worn only for special occasions. Garments such as these might also be passed from father to son and adopted into the wardrobe of the next generation, therefore obscuring the delineations in the different fashions of the century among the lower classes. By the beginning of the last quarter of the century, menswear among the working class was an amalgam of older styles such as rhinegraves, waistcoat, bib-collar, and cocked hat all worn at the same time. But by the century's end, trade and advances in industry began to make some of the luxuries of the rich accessible to the working class.

EUROPEAN WOMEN'S CLOTHING

The seventeenth century began for women as it had for men, under the heavy shadow of the Elizabethan court. The stiffly formal brocades and decadent velvets would remain in fashion for the first quarter of the century. In England, King James I's bride, Anne of Denmark, was simply mad for the late Queen Elizabeth's fashions. She insisted that the French, or "wagonwheel," farthingale that was popular at the end of the sixteenth century continue to be worn at formal affairs at court throughout her lifetime. Anne was also known to have altered and worn many of Elizabeth's gowns both for her personal use as courtly dress and to participate in the many masques and fêtes thrown by the Jacobean Court.

The farthingale, in the first part of the century, began to evolve a different look from its Elizabethan predecessor. At the close of the sixteenth century, the farthingale—a series of wood, reed, or metal hoops—had a wide, cylindrical shape giving the impression of a flat table over which the gown would fall in deep pleats. Moving into the opening years of the 1600s, a deep ruffle at the waistline came into fashion, which accentuated the wide, flat, tabletop-looking structure. In the 1610s, the farthingale grew wider and flatter, losing the full cylindrical shape and focusing the width onto the top hoop. Queen Anne was very fond of the silhouette and single-handedly responsible for keeping it in vogue into the seventeenth century, no matter how loud were her dissenters, both women and men. An observer at court noted that the queen wore "so expansive a farthingale that ... it was four feet wide at the hips."[78]

By the opening of the second decade, the farthingale began to be pitched forward. The bottom center point of the bodice was lengthened and pressed into the hoop at the waist, forcing the back of the farthingale to rise. The effect was almost like that of a peacock's tail fanning out from behind. Large crescent-shaped pillows known as "bum-rolls" were used to help support this wide and full silhouette. Bum-rolls had been in use during the Elizabethan period, but the Jacobean bum-rolls far outstripped those in size. The skirts were still often split at the center front to display a heavily ornamented petticoat beneath. King James I tried to forbid the farthingale at court, saying that it was too ungainly, but Anne of Denmark refused. In 1617, Lady Anne Clifford records in her diary that she went without her farthingale to court,[79] but the farthingale remained an important part of courtly fashion until Anne's death in 1619.

Although the French had begun the fashion of the wide farthingale, it did not last into the seventeenth century in France. In Spain, however, an almost architectural style of dress developed for court ladies. Called a *guardinfante*, it was between the cylindrical wagonwheel shape of the farthingale and the wide, horizontally full silhouette of the eighteenth-century *panniers*. Elsewhere, the whole of Europe was characterized by a French style of costume, but women's court dress in Spain was unique. In addition to the guardinfante, the Spanish were known to use *passementarie* and other surface applications to mimic the richly patterned textiles available elsewhere on the Continent. Such patterned textiles would not be produced in Spain until much later in the century, after the country recovered from the expulsion of the Moorish weavers.[80] The neckruff remained in high fashion in Spain until well into the 1620s, not disappearing from the clothing of the wealthy until after 1630.

An elaborately embroidered women's jacket from England, made from silk and linen, c. 1616. © The Metropolitan Museum of Art / Art Resource, NY.

The bodices of this first quarter-century all across Europe moved from being cut high to the throat and worn with a very broad neckruff to being low cut with a plunging neckline. The sleeves were full and padded, but also slashed and paned to show the chemise sleeves below or a contrasting color of lining fabric. This sleeve styling remained a popular carryover from the Elizabethan period. The headrail or whisk, a stiff, standing collar supported by a wired structure, remained fashionable for women, again echoing the silhouette of Elizabeth's court. Women of station also still wore neckruffs at formal functions at this time, although wrist ruffs for both women and men had been replaced by a highly decorative lace or embroidered turned-back cuffs.

After the death of Anne of Denmark, fashion for women in England stalled. The court became a man's domain, vice ridden and decadent. Women did not appear at court as often as they had previously. It was not until 1625 when Queen Henrietta Maria, wife of James I's son Charles I, came from France that new life was breathed into women's clothing. Isolated in their island kingdom, the English were separated from the trends of fashion elsewhere in Europe. But with the arrival of the French queen also came fashion influence from France, which would last for centuries.

Henrietta Maria got rid of farthingales, even for formal affairs. She also changed the fashion for the ultralong "stomachers" that had pressed the farthingale up into the fanlike appendage swooping up from the waist. Away went the ruffles and flounces that helped define the very rigid look still carrying vestiges of the Elizabethan court.

The queen instead introduced a high-waisted style of soft petticoats and thinly paned sleeves called *virago sleeves*. There was still an abundance of surface decoration as well as layering. Petticoats were still very ornamental, but now more of them were seen, as the fashion became to tuck up the overskirts. In France, where this fashion originated, the overskirt was known as the *modiste* and the petticoat, the *secret*. The bodices and overskirt could match or be complementary. The underskirt never matched the rest of the fabric, and any of the items could be made from satin, silk plush, velvet, damask, or taffeta.[81] A standing collar was also still popular, but it was much smaller in scale and known as the *Medici collar*. A wide lace falling band collar reminiscent of menswear was also adopted by some women. This gave the appearance of great shoulder width.

Shoulders appeared to grow wider as the waistline rose. The start of the century saw a deeply pointed bodice, extending below the hips. But as the second quarter of the century came around, just the opposite happened, and in the 1630s the waistline was high and just under the breasts. The high-waisted bodice was tabbed along the bottom with six to eight wide pieces. It "diminished in length as it increased in width—the increased size of the sleeves and wide, pointed collars adding several inches to the shoulders of the wearers."[82] The deep décolletage also carried on into the second quarter of the century, first deep and rounded, then squared off, and finally a V shape. The low, spreading collar was very popular, further accentuating the wideness of the shoulder. Height was no longer an aspiration—the focus now was drape.

Moving through the 1630s, the area of decorative attention began to shift from the bodice to the collar and cuffs. These were highly detailed pieces executed with the finest embroidery, drawnwork, cutwork, and lace and were known as "raggs." As necklines plunged, sheer and embroidered modesty scarves, known in this century as a "tucker" or "fichu," became fashionable. Sleeves were no longer paned but generally very full and puffed above the elbow. The sleeves of the chemise were pulled forward and fluffed. These frilled raggs replaced the turned-back cuff. The sleeves were short, pulled above the elbow in the three-quarter sleeve look that would come back into vogue later in the seventeenth century and into the eighteenth century.

Henrietta Maria eventually became very involved in the rearing of her children and lost interest in fashion. Subsequently, both in France and in England, the look became more subdued. The high waist of the bodice lowered to an almost natural level, but the center front area, the stomacher, extended below the waistline into a U shape. The tabbing along the bottom of the bodice became smaller, and overall the look became less extreme. Necklines became very square and deep, and women across Europe adopted the French fashion of wearing the sheer modesty scarves.

The English Civil War in the 1640s brought women's fashion there to a near standstill. Two distinct political groups emerged each with their agendas tied to their dress. Those in support of the monarchy continued to wear the lavish and detailed fashions of the time, with wide collars and full sleeves puffed above the elbows. Satin was the most popular choice for gowns, and the tucker shawl draped across the shoulders and neckline was still very popular. Aprons made of silk and fine linen were worn, often decorated with embroidery and lace. The continuation of this fashion mode can usually be traced to those nobles who stood in support of Charles I and the monarchy.

That is not to say that the Parliamentary supporters, the Puritans, did not dress according to their rank in society. Silks and velvets were still used by the upper classes, although the use of embroidery and other ornamentation was more restrained. Similarly, the Parliamentary supporters favored less flamboyant colors, such as grays, browns, amber yellows, and other earth tones, even though high-class Parliamentary supporters still continued to wear fashionable colors such as blue, violet, and white. Although it was a color that bespoke great wealth, black was often used by the Puritans. Fine linens and wools were also popular fabrics for them. Puritan women wore less makeup, did not employ the use of patches, and preferred hats with a narrower brim and tall crown. They also wore the long, narrow aprons of the time but preferred an unadorned linen or cotton apron.

But all in all, most women on either side of the conflict did not differ from one another in too obvious a manner. Only those already on the extreme edges of the different factions engaged in the dress stereotyped as Royalists and Puritans.

Elsewhere, fashion continued to evolve, the overskirts becoming pleated and folded to drape better when tucked up into increasingly decorative belts that were often jeweled or chased with gold or silver. All over Europe, a tighter-fitting bodice with a pointed waist was introduced. Stiff corseting set off the full, soft skirts draped up to show off the petticoats and the puffed sleeves with the chemise sleeves showing from beneath. Necklines remained wide and deep, covered with lace-edged sheer fichus or wide linen collars.

As Oliver Cromwell settled into his role as the Lord Protector of the English Commonwealth, the divisive clothing modes in that country did not change. Those who opposed Cromwell's politics still continued to dress in a more colorful and decorated manner, although they weren't as flamboyant as they were before they lost the civil war. In France, fashion continued on without faltering. The opulent French court took in English exiles. For women remaining in England, satin gowns remain highly fashionable, but colors and surface ornamentation become more subdued.

With the Restoration of the monarchy in England in 1660, interest in fashion swelled anew. England and France were once more in communication regarding the latest trends and technologies. England rushed to catch up to the surge of fashion emanating from France and spreading across the rest of Europe. Bodices were stiffly corseted through to the waist. Skirts were still worn gathered into the bodice and full to the ground. They were still split at the front and tucked up, but now the look was more swept back, forming a bustle effect over the behind. The bustled overskirts were held back by ribbons and jeweled clips. Necklines were daringly low and wide across the shoulders and edged with a decorative frill of lace from the chemise. Sleeves continued to be worn puffed and short to the elbow. By the later 1660s, sleeves became more uniformly loose fitting and slightly longer. Satin still predominated as the favored fabric for dresses.

From the mid century and onward for several decades, the Dutch jacket was a popular item of women's dress. Featured in scores of paintings by Dutch and Flemish artists, this short coat was immediately coveted by women elsewhere in Europe looking to emulate the rich Dutch styles. Usually worn indoors, the Dutch jacket was worn long, falling past the hips with a full cut but slim through the waist. The sleeves were straight but wide, and the cuffs, neckline, and edges were trimmed in fur. The neckline was rounded and could be worn closed to the throat or open and back on the shoulders. There was no collar or lapel. The jacket body was usually made from velvet dyed a rich jewel tone, although in some paintings the jacket appears to be made from heavy satin. Judging from contemporary paintings, the most popular colors for these jackets were a vibrant yellow and varying shades of blue from teal to sapphire, possibly because of the popularity of the colors yellow and blue used in Vermeer's artwork. The fur trimming was always white. These jackets remained in fashion in the Netherlands until the end of the century but had gone out of vogue in France and elsewhere by the 1680s.

In the 1670s, women's fashions began to change throughout Europe. Waistlines had been steadily sinking over the previous decades, and now the cut of the bodice was deep and narrow, below the natural waist. The stomacher piece was often laced with yards of colorful ribbons called *eschelles*. The swept-back skirts began to be shaped to achieve maximum effect and lengthened in the back to form a train. The petticoat was often a contrasting color and weave, most often a richer fabric than the overskirt. Both women and men of this time loved to mix and match various types of fabrics in their ensembles. The sleeves were small and close fitting in comparison to the very full sleeves of previous decades. The bodice sleeves were worn rather short so that the frilled chemise sleeve could be seen. Flowered fabrics became very popular as weaving techniques improved and imports from India and elsewhere in Asia became more widely available.

But it was at the end of the century that women's fashions changed considerably, a few years after the major changes in menswear. The most important change was the *mantua*. Previously, the bodice and skirt had been cut of their own pieces of fabric, constructed and sewn together or otherwise attached. The mantua, which is thought to have originated in a Middle Eastern type of women's robe, consisted of lengths of fabric from shoulder to floor that were pleated into the waist and held with a belt. The top of the bodice was conventionally sewn with the requisite shoulder seams and sleeves, but it fell into deep pleats to the floor that could be worn loosely or belted, as the wearer desired. The fullness of the split overskirt was pulled back over the hips into a bustled train, and padding was often worn on the hips to accentuate this fullness. As in previous eras, the petticoat beneath was highly ornamented and might or might not match the mantua. Frills from the neckline and sleeves of the chemise showed amply at the sleeves and neckline of the mantua. The neckline was a deep V shape, with the mantua closing over a decorated stomacher, which was often finished in a rounded shape below the natural waistline. This type of gown also featured comparatively straight and loose sleeves that were fully gathered into the arm-seye of the bodice. Although this look began as comparably loose and free flowing, it soon gained a stiffness and structure that governed the look from the very tall and elaborate headwear to the layered, bustled, and trained skirts. Corsetry became very important during this time period to maintain the long, narrow torso required by the fashionable mode.

In addition to the structured look that the mantua achieved in the last quarter of the century, a very softly draped gown known as *dishabille, negligée, battante,* or *robe de chamber* came to be worn. Originally, these gowns were worn only as eve-ningwear in the privacy of the home, but soon they became high fashion and were even worn at court. It was also in vogue to sit for portraiture wearing this type of gown. Often, the bodices were cut and boned like a daywear gown, but the sleeves and skirt were generally left loose, billowing, and open. Sir Peter Lely was renowned for painting late-century ladies in their dishabille, such as the famous actress, courtesan, and mistress of King Charles II, Nell Gwynne.

The decadence and luxury of the close of the seventeenth century was cen-tered on the opulent palace of Versailles in France. Influences from Versailles affected every part of Europe and even echoed across the seas to distant shores as worldwide trade made for an exchange of ideas, designs, and tastes between Europe, Asia, and North America. This is reflected in the richly figured textiles, vibrant new colors, and lavish embroidery, printing, ribbons, and jewels that were used to decorate the gowns of the wealthy. The nature of this new society was one of broadening horizons that would eventually end up at odds with the traditional roles of the court and the ruling classes and lead to the tumult of the eighteenth century.

Accessories

Seventeenth-century accessories for women were often considered equal in sta-tus to the clothing itself. Hats, hoods, muffs, and masks all marked the class and status of a woman and were part of the entire fashion picture.

Headdress went through several changes throughout the century but always remained one of the most important emblems of station and, in England during the civil war, affiliation. Little lace-edged caps, common at the close of the six-teenth century, declined in popularity for women of fashion, although matrons continued to wear them for many more years. Felt hats with long, curling plumes entered the sphere of female fashion. While having been popular for men since the middle of the previous era, women's interest in wearing felt hats had not been a constant one until the seventeenth century. Although not appropriate for court, women wore jeweled and feathered felt hats for myriad other activities, both indoors and out. By the 1620s, the hats that women wore mimicked those of men almost exactly, down to the wide brims and thick floun-ces of feather plumes. It was nearly impossible to judge the gender of the owner simply by looking at a hat. For court functions, however, smaller, more elegant headwear and veils became de rigueur.

All across Europe, after the close of the Thirty Years' War in 1648, the broad-brimmed, plumed felt hat became a major fashion staple for both genders. Women wore the "cavalier" hats with almost the same ornamentation as did men. Masses of large, full feathers were preferable to jewels and adornments. In England, it became more than fashion—the wearing of the soft plumed hats declared allegiance to the king and marked the wearer as a Royalist; the female Parliamentary supporters, in contrast, wore the stiff, high-crowned, narrower-brimmed hat that became synonymous with the Puritan movement. While the Royalist hats were often worn in a variety of colors—black, brown, gray, buff, and white—the Puritans' hats were nearly almost always black, or occasionally gray.

By century's end, women's headwear had climbed to extreme heights. Begun as hair ornamentation, the *fontange*—or *commode* in England—was a towering array of ribbons, pleated lace, and frills over a wired understructure at the front of a relatively simple lacy cap. This cap also had lace lappets that hung down over the shoulders. After a period during the 1660s and early 1670s where hats of any kind were not popular, the fontange had humble beginnings: Angélique de Fontanges, a mistress of Louis XIV, began a trend of pulling her hair into a small knot at the top of her head with curls all around and decorated with lace and ribbons. She is said to have pulled up her long curls and bound them with her lace garter after losing her hat out on a hunting ride. When she returned to court wearing her hair in such a fashion, she created a scandal and a sensation. Women throughout Versailles and all over Paris immediately began twining their long ringlets into a loose bun at the top of their heads and decorating it with ribbons and lace.

The fontange style was initially just a band of lace holding back the hair and worn high on the head. Women emulating her style soon added more ribbons and artfully arranged their curls. A small lace-edged cap was usually worn just behind this confection. The style was immediately popular and continued to be called the fontange after the original trendsetter, Madame Fontange, even after it no longer resembled the original style.

"This top knot of curls and ribbon evolve[d] into the tall headdress of lace, wire, and ribbons which was so essential a part of lady's attire from the 1680s into the eighteenth century."[83] Like most fashions of the seventeenth century, the fontange had a multitude of variations and specific names for each piece. For example, in England, the foundation top-knot was referred to as the fontange, while the standing, fan-shaped frill of pleated lace was called the *pinner*; the lace-edged cap was a *bonnet*, and called the pinner-and-bonnet combination was called the *frelage*. The entire headdress with the hanging lappets and all the trimmings was collectively called the *commode* and did not differ very much from the fontange worn in France. When hoods were worn in the winter, they were specially designed to come up just behind the tall, standing frill of lace and be pinned in place without mussing the mass of curls and ribbons. Early on, the fontange sat back from the ears, revealing them. This style was known as *effronte* or "shameless."[84] By century's end, the fontange had lost all of its softness and organic feel and become not only very tall, but forward tilting in a style that became known as "palisade." The three or four tiers of standing frills were starched and wired and stood a foot or more (30+ cm) from the crown of the head.

A pale complexion continued to be in vogue, aided by the fondness for veils and a mask known as a *loo*. From early in the century, it was common for most women of rank to go outside, in both sunny and overcast weather, wearing this half-mask that covered the face from the forehead to the mouth. Combined with a veil in the summer and a scarf and hood in the winter, the loo helped to shield a woman's delicate complexion from the elements. Another important piece in the fashionable lady's wardrobe was the umbrella or parasol. Introduced from China through Portugal, the parasol was primarily used as a decorative sunshade for ladies. Another import from the East that made a great impact on women's costume was the folding fan.

Pearls remained the most popular choice for jewelry, especially pearls that were pear shaped. Both women and men often wore a pear-shaped pearl dangling from their ears. Pierced ears became fashionable. "The origin of the fashion of piercing the lobe of the ear has been ascribed by many authorities to the common belief that it was a cure for weak eyes. Tradition also associates the fashion with navigators and seamen."[85] It was also a common opinion that a single pear-shaped pearl-drop hanging from the ear "was the most advantageous way of displaying a pearl of more than usual beauty."[86]

In addition to the pearls worn on the ears by both men and women, women in the early part of the century wore slender black silk cords strung through the earlobes.[87] These black strands were also often incorporated with a dropped pearl. This fashion, although not spoken of in great detail in texts, can be seen in several well-known pieces of artwork, including the 1615 portrait of Mary Throckmorton, Lady Scudamore, by Marcus Gheeraerts, and "Sir Thomas Lucy and His Family" by Cornelius Johnson from 1625. "Musical Ensemble with Cockatoo" by Jacob Duck, painted around 1660, also depicts black strands and teardrop-shaped pearls hanging from the girl's earlobes. Pearls remained in high fashion for the entirety of the century and in later years were often worn not just as jewelry but also as accessories of dress in long strands roped around the waist or draped across the shoulders and pinned to the bodice.

In addition, women covered themselves in an array of unique and clever enameled brooches and hair ornaments. These were often fantastical shapes wrought in gold or silver and then enameled with rich colors and sometimes set with small jewels. These items were pinned to bodices and sleeves, to hats, and often directly into the hair.

Attention to cosmetics and facial adornment took a new precedence during the time of the Restoration in the 1660s. All eyes were on England as a fashion leader as the country emerged from the dourness of Cromwell's Commonwealth and erupted into a showy court culture that attempted to rival Versailles. Women in England finally got caught up on the Continental fashion for cosmetics. Since the opening years of the century, the Spanish, Italian, and finally the French had access to and made use of fine cosmetics such as rouges and facial powders. In England, the favored lily-white complexion was still being augmented by use of pasty chalks and white lead, both of which were detrimental to the skin. Lead was also used to darken the eyebrows, and contemporary plays and satires comment on the use of furred mouse skins by women to augment their eyebrows.

In earlier times, makeup was used only by prostitutes or to cover a facial disfigurement, but after the Restoration, as trade of ideas, fashions, and goods flowed between England and the rest of Europe, women of all social classes began to paint their faces. the English face became far more natural in its

FACIAL PATCHES

Patches first became popular in France in the 1620s. These were small rounds of velvet or some other fabric that could be adhered to the face. They were given names depending where on the face they were placed: "Passionate" meant a patch at the corner of one eye, while "kissing" was a patch at the corner of the mouth. "Majestic" indicated a patch on the forehead; "saucy," one on the nose; and "gallant," one in the middle of the cheek. A "murderous" patch was placed just below one eye, while a "playful" one sat on a dimple in the cheek.

Although patches would come and go as a fashion, they saw their greatest popularity in the 1670s. No longer just rounds placed on the face one or two at a time, patches in this period were cut in a multitude of more intricate shapes such as diamonds, crescent moons, stars, hearts, spades, and clubs. Women also wore them in multitudes on the face and across the neck, chest, and shoulders as well. These black bits of felt or velvet made a vivid contrast with the powdered white skin of the wearer.

paleness, and more skin-friendly cosmetics were introduced onto the market. The paleness of the flesh was not limited to just the face but also the throat, chest, shoulders, and hands. Women covered themselves in veils, masks, scarves, shawls, and gloves to keep their skin soft, smooth, and white, and employed makeup where nature failed them. A woman's foundation makeup was called *ceruse* and was made of white lead in a base of vinegar. It was thick and heavy, able to fill pockmarks, wrinkles, and any facial disfigurements. Unfortunately, this concoction was toxic and caused the premature death of many a lady.

Early in the century, scented leather gloves were very popular, another sixteenth-century carryover. Moving through the first quarter of the century, lace or silk mittens took precedence. These were lighter and more elegant and were able to match to the woman's various ensembles. Long, tight gloves made a comeback in the 1670s, as wider and shorter sleeves were fashionable. But by the end of the century, dainty lacy gloves returned to the fore in connection with the fashionable frilled caps.

Beginning in the 1660s, a cherubic, rosy face was the ideal for women. Against their pale, powdered flesh, therefore, they rouged their lips and cheeks. To achieve the round and jovial facial silhouette that was popular in the decade, small balls of wax or fabric were pressed into the cheeks. These were called "plumpers" and gave a woman the fashionably round face that was expected of her.[88] Although a pale complexion would remain the height of fashion until the twentieth century, the fad of plumped cheeks did not last more than a few years.

Footwear

Footwear for women closely mirrored the shoe fashions of men. Heeled slippers with rounded toes had become very popular at the close of the sixteenth century and remained so for many years entering the seventeenth. The line of women's shoes became increasingly long and narrow at the outset of the century, but with a squared-off toe. Heels were somewhat low, often painted red like men's shoes, and the tongue was exaggerated and long. Buckles became very elaborate and fashionable for women as for men; they were often jeweled, but the buckles for women's shoes were never as ornate as those that men wore, because the buckles were hazardous to the hems of the petticoats and gowns. Neither did women wear the overblown shoe rosettes that were fashionable for men.

By midcentury, women's shoes had remained very slender and relatively low in the heel but were reported by many women to be very uncomfortable.[89] Because of this, softer backless slippers became very fashionable for casual wearing.

By the third quarter of the century, the shoes lost the squared-off toe and became very pointed. Shoes also began to be made from not only leather but also brocades, silks, and velvets so they could match any outfit, and women of station often owned a pair for each gown. These slippers frequently came with matching overshoes called *pantofles*. Originally, these backless heeled shoes served only as overshoes to the finer and more delicate slippers of the time, but soon they became a fashionable option in their own right.

Knit stockings had been available since the sixteenth century, but when William Lee invented a knitting machine in 1599, stockings became more readily available and less costly. Nevertheless, a pair of knitted stockings around 1610 cost between two and five pounds. This was a large investment of income. In fact, all across Europe, prices of fabric, trims, and accessories were extremely high in comparison to income. People spent the vast majority of their money on dress. Although a gentlewoman's feet were never seen, fashion demanded that she wear knit silk stockings, often decorated with the embroidered or knit decorations called "clocks." While stockings were usually made of silk, some were of fine wool. In the later years of the century, knitted silk stockings were more widely available and relatively less expensive than they had been at the start. No lady's wardrobe was complete without several pairs.

Fur stoles and tippets were other highly prized accessories. Fur was very popular, and trade with North America and Russia made it an available, if pricy, commodity. Europeans made the most of fur, using it in trimmings, gloves, stoles, and—one of the most popular of ladies' accessories—muffs. The muff served not only to keep the hands warm but also as a reticule to hold small items and as a fan to hide behind and use as a tool in flirtation. Muffs were originally made out of cloth and decorated with ribbons, ruffles, and frills, but by the middle of the century, they were commonly made of fur. Muffs were considered a very important part of a lady's wardrobe but were also used extensively by men.

Hair

At the opening of the seventeenth century, hair was still worn in a predominantly Elizabethan fashion, and in England, red hair was still coveted. On the Continent, the dominating style of hairdressing began to emerge, although for the most part it was a scarcely modified copy of what had gone before. Hair that was upswept, brushed back over shaped pads, and decorated with jewels remained fashionable for several years. Often a roll was formed at the hairline, then brushed back flatly across the top. Occasionally, small fringes were cut across the forehead, and short curls were pulled down to frame the face and the nape of the neck.

But overall, the look was rigid, stiff, and almost severe. Bound hair was symbolic of modesty and propriety. Only young and unmarried girls were ever allowed to wear their hair down. The very act of loosening one's hair from its bonds was considered risqué and sometimes carried supernatural connotations. In 1633, for example, Bessie Skobister was convicted of "taking off her kerchief, shaking her hair loose and causing vehement and continual pain to Margaret Mudie."[90] In Scotland particularly, but also in other predominantly rural and superstitious countries, shaking one's hair loose was tantamount to hexing someone and often punishable by death.

Like the newest modes in clothing, new fashions for hair came primarily from France. England was the last to catch up with the latest style changes, not having close ties to France until Charles I married Henrietta Maria in 1625. As necklines simplified into a wide, sweeping décolletage, hairstyles followed suit. Women began to part their hair across the crown of the head, ear to ear. The hair in back was then coiled into a bun or rolled into a chignon. The hair in front was cut into short, feathery bangs, and the sides were left long, hanging past the ears and curled into small ringlets. Jeweled clips were still used to decorate the chignon, but not in the profusion seen in previous years.

The structured curls eventually gave way to frizzled puffs that had the look of a halo around the face. The delineation between the bangs and side curls was blurred into one continuous line of fluffed, teased hair. But this fashion was short lived, and more artfully arranged curls began to appear. The side areas were grown out much longer and consisted of larger ringlets rather than tiny, frizzled curls. Often these side-locks were allowed to grow to shoulder length. Short fringed bangs were also out of style and were grown out slightly and curled. The bulk of the hair was still left long and bound at the back of the head in a chignon or bun. Instead of jewels, ribbons began to be thought of as the hair accessory of choice. The chignon was often beribboned, as were the draping ringlets. This hairstyle was very complimentary to the lacy linen caps that were still favorable at this point in the century, but women were drifting toward the previously male-dominated fashion of wide-brimmed felt hats. The structured chignons made wearing these hats uncomfortable and required them to be cocked forward onto the forehead.

The desire to indulge in fantastically feathered hats soon got the better of fashionable women, and they began to forgo the structure of the chignon-and-side-curls hairstyle in favor of something less refined. Instead of parting the hair from ear to ear over the top of the head, women began to part their hair from front to back, usually stopping at the midpoint of the crown. The sides were brushed out widely from the center part, framing the entire face in an array of curls. The back was usually drawn up into a snood (a small netlike cap) or a more casual, lower chignon. This allowed the more comfortable wearing of the popular cavalier hats.

By the 1670s, this look had relaxed even more into a long stream of ringlets no longer bound back but allowed to cascade down the back and over the shoulders. This fashion was called the "hurly-burly," or in French, the *hurlu-berlu*—translated as "scatterbrain"—and was fashionable until nearly the end of the century. Like the hairstyles of men, each curl in the hurly-burly had a name, a position, and a meaning. And again copying the men, one ringlet was grown out longer than the others and worn pulled up over the left shoulder and tied with a long piece of ribbon. This was called the *moustache* on either gender. The basic lines of this hair fashion reverberated across Europe but were never executed with as much flamboyance as in France.

Near the end of the decade, lace-edged caps come back into fashion, bringing with them lots of ribbons. If a woman chose to wear her hair up, she bundled it into a loose roll called the *choux*, French for "cabbage," presumably named for its large, rounded shape. This hairstyle was far more popular in France than it was anywhere else.

Hats were not as fashionable for women as they had been in previous years. While still worn outdoors, hats became unfashionable for evening and indoor occasions. Thus, ribbons, combs, and clips became popular hair ornaments; jewels were seen as too heavy and formal. Often the hair was piled onto the top of the head in the top-knot of curls decorated with ribbons and lace that was known as the fontange. This almost intimately casual style was to give rise to one of the most restrictive styles of headdress in European fashion history. The hair framing the face was worn curled up and away, falling back along the ears in a cascade. The curls left to fall becomingly across the forehead were called *fripons* or *guigne-galants*, referred to in English as "kiss-curls." Often, false hair was used to augment the fullness of this facial framing style. And as if that was not enough ornamentation, in roughly the middle of the fontange era, jeweled pins and clips began to be used in a multitude all over the exposed hair as well as the stiffened lace scaffolding. These were called *guepes et papillons* by the French, literally "wasps and butterflies." It often took several hours to complete this intricate hairstyle, and women slept on wooden neck supports to try to keep their style fresh. Many women would often go as long as three weeks between sessions at the hairdresser; this practice led to rampant infestations of lice and other scalp parasites.

As the fontange style evolved, more and more lace and ribbon was added to the original top-knot, eventually building up into several standing layers of finely pleated lace held aloft by a series of wire supports. More ribbons and more lace trimmed this structure, and long lace *lappets* or *cornets* hung down the back. Usually, a small bonnet was worn at the back of the head in conjunction with the tall fontange. The focus on hairstyling faded to secondary as even the fashionable curls and small ringlets around the face gave way to more layers of lace and ruffles on the headpiece. Although this fashion of hairdressing was most extreme in France, this style would not entirely fall from fashion in Europe until well into the following century.

Undergarments and Underpinnings

Beginning during the Renaissance and growing in significance during the seventeenth century, underwear "began to assist the external costume of both sexes in expressing class distinction."[91] The chemise began to seen at the necklines and at the wrists and shoulders in the early years of the Italian Renaissance. Over the years, a variety of different names have been used to describe this garment, which was usually made of fine linen and worn next to the body beneath the dress. In England and North America, the word *smock* was commonly used in this period. Italy called it the *camicia* or *camisa*, which is the derivative of the modern Italian word for "shirt." In other areas of Europe, and among modern scholars and historians, the word *chemise* is used.

Originally very plain and functional, the chemise began to evolve decorative elements such as embroidered neck and wrist bands as early as the late fifteenth century. But by the seventeenth century, the chemise was a fashion statement all on its own. Early in the century, the chemise was, like most aspects of fashion, nearly indistinguishable from its sixteenth-century predecessor. It was made of holland, a fine, plainweave linen, and was often perfumed. The adornment of the chemise was focused on the neckline and cuffs, which were frilled. The neckline was cut low with a V-shaped opening for ease of dressing and was closed by way of a drawstring. The drawstring allowed the neckline of the chemise to be adjustable to almost any taste in dress from modest to daringly low. This style was predominant for the first half of the century. Cuffs were still frilled and sleeves were voluminous from shoulder to wrist, where they were fastened by a band or a drawstring.

By the 1650s, necklines had plunged deeply, and chemises were cut to accommodate. The frills around the neckline disappeared as the fashionable silhouette called for a very low décolletage covered by a tucker, the sheer scarves draped across the shoulders and tucked into the front of the bodices. Sleeve styles changed as well; now, instead of being gathered to a cuff and frilled or trimmed with lace, sleeves were funnel shaped with wide, turned-back cuffs.

In the 1660s, a lace border begins to reappear along the neckline. While never reaching the depth of the earlier frills, the lace edging varied in size throughout the remainder of the century but never went completely out of style. Changes in the bodice again necessitated changes in the chemise. In the 1660s, the long dress sleeves fell out of fashion in favor of shorter sleeves. This heralded a return to the frilled or lace-edged chemise sleeve. The frills at this point were softer and less full than in earlier incarnations. The sleeve was gathered into a narrow wristband, and the frill was often edged in lace. Occasionally, no frill was used, and the sleeves would be tied off at the elbow, with the great volume of chemise fabric left to puff down over the forearm.

Near the end of the century, as sleeves grew narrower, the amount of cloth used in chemise sleeves decreased, but the frill was left full and softly falling. Dress sleeves were often three-quarter length and featured a "spill"—lace-edged frills from the chemise that draped over the arm. This would evolve into the layers of frills at the elbows that characterized eighteenth-century sleeves.

In Italy, from the time of the Renaissance, many women took to wearing "silk or linen breeches under their gowns."[92] These drawers were popular among Italian women, particularly with the famed courtesans of Venice, and were introduced into French society by Marie de' Medici. Usually made of silk or fine linen, and later, cotton, drawers were not as popular in France as they were in Italy and were not worn at all in England except by those from the Continent. There are some references to drawers in English literature, but never as everyday wear. One particular verse states: "In half-shirts and drawers, these Maids did run, / But bonny Nan the race hath won."[93] From this poem, it would seem that the drawers were used as a novelty costume as part of a country fair. Wearing of drawers would not become typical across the entirety of Europe until the eighteenth century.

The term *petticoat* referred to both an object of dress and of underpinning. It is used contemporarily almost exclusively as a term for an underskirt that is not seen, but women of the seventeenth century also recognized it as a term for the underskirt that was meant to be shown when the overskirt was tucked up. The outerwear petticoat was probably referred to by fashionable women by its French name, the *secret*.

The underpetticoat was described as using only 1¼ to 2 yards (1.1–1.8 m) of silk or linen, and early in the century was most likely another level of modesty beneath the farthingale. When farthingales went out of fashion, the underpetticoat served the same purpose as a modern slip and also added an extra layer of warmth during the winter. Winter underpetticoats were often made from wool, and later cotton, flannel.

However, the underpetticoat of silk or linen began to gain a social significance and became a symbol of class distinction. Silk underpetticoats were said to be less likely to harbor lice than wool and were also considered far more sensual. "The petticoat soon became the recognized symbol of feminine charm."[94] In paintings, the chemise and petticoat began to be depicted more prominently and often in a suggestive manner. In many cases, slits were made in the layers of petticoats to reach the "pockets," the narrow purses tied at the waist beneath the gown and skirts.

Corsetry was still in its infancy in the seventeenth century. The first actual corsets emerged as important items of female dress in the sixteenth century. During that period, bodices were stiffened and known as "a pair of bodies." Bone, wood, and metal were used to stiffen the bodice. In the 1500s, wealthy women often wore a set of boned stays beneath their stiffened outer bodices. The corsets, called "stays" in the sixteenth through eighteenth centuries, came in many forms for both outerwear and underwear, laced up the back or the front, and were made from a variety of fabrics, from velvet to brocades to sackcloth.

Stays (corsets) were constructed in six pieces, plus the shoulder straps, using heavy canvas. Whalebone was then cut into strips of uniform length and thickness, precisely positioned, and sewn into channels all the way around the stays. The number of bones varies by the style of the stay, and they are arranged to maximize the pull on the waist to narrow it. Tabs at the base of the stays allowed the garment to flare out over the hips. Extra boning was often used under the breasts to push them up into the fashionable low décolleté but keep them also restrained through the center front to ensure the popular flat-fronted look.

"The ladies call a whalebone (or something else, in the absence of the latter) their stay, which they put under their breast, right in the middle, in order to keep straighter."[95] The strong center-front piece is commonly known as a *busk*. They were able to me removed from the stays, and in the seventeenth century, busks were commonly made from metal, wood, bone, or ivory and usually decorated in some fantastical way. They were painted and/or carved with hearts, crowns, cherubs, fleurs-de-lis, goddesses, or text. One such piece is inscribed with the words: "How I envy you the happiness that is yours, resting softly on her ivory white breast. Let us divide between us, if you please, this glory. You will be here the day and I shall be there the night."[96] The busks were often personified with messages such as that and others like "Love joins them" and "The arrow unites us."[97]

Young girls were trained in the wearing of stays as early as two years of age. Sometimes, young boys were put into stays as well, at least until they were breeched at age six. There were even stay makers in France that specialized in children's stays. But tensions between tailors, dressmakers, and stay makers ran high in Paris. Women were not allowed to join tailors' guilds but female dressmakers were not allowed to make stays. Yet female customers were not fond of men measuring and fitting them for so intimate a garment. As a compromise, women were allowed to fit the customers, but not to actually construct the garments. It would not be until 1776 that women were allowed to make their way into a hitherto male-dominated industry.

Drama and literature of the time ridiculed the fashion of tight lacing. Stays were blamed for asthma, consumption, suffocation, foul breath, and injuries to the skin, rib cage, and muscle, as well as encouraging vanity and artifice. In the late seventeenth century, stays—or more particularly, the lack thereof—became an important element in art. A woman depicted with her stays unlaced or on the floor was understood to be sexually promiscuous. Still, "the underclothing of the period was sufficiently uncomfortable to tempt ladies to discard some of it when circumstances permitted."[98]

The increased use of undergarments helped to control personal vermin such as lice and fleas, creating a more healthful atmosphere for the people of Europe. But for the first time, women's undergarments had grown beyond functionality, being not only for fashion but also a means of attraction. In the seventeenth century, the idea of women's underwear as erotic was born.

Working-Class Women's Clothing

Women not of the privileged class tried their best to emulate the silhouettes of the wealthy ladies around them. The men of the working-class dress was a mix of traditional folk costume, elements from past eras, and watered-down aspects of contemporary fashion, usually several years out of style.

A working-class woman's bodice was boned and worn tightly laced up the front, much like the peasantry of the previous century. Most women of this station could not afford and would not want to bother with an additional corset to wear beneath their bodices. The stiffened bodice was usually square or rounded in the neckline, cut low for young women and considerably higher for matrons.

In the Netherlands, a large bosom spilling over the top of the bodice was the ideal of working-class beauty. Dutch women were renowned for their impressive breasts and helped launch a new vogue for ample bosoms throughout Europe with the work of Rubens and other Dutch and Flemish painters. Even well-to-do middle-class women were not shy about showing off their bosoms in the seventeenth-century Netherlands. Not even the strict teachings of the Calvinists could dissuade the Dutch from their near obsession with the well-fed and well-endowed female form. This pastoral ideal of the buxom and charming country lass permeated Europe and drew visitors to Holland. Foreign tourists were soon to find, however, that the visible curves and seemingly available nature of the female form was not synonymous with the sexual license that would have been expected from women similarly dressed in their own countries.[99] But among the lower classes, the elevation and display of the cleavage would remain a favorite fashion of young women looking to catch male attentions.

The chemises of the working class were cut in a similar manner to those of the wealthy, but the cloth was less fine. Working women usually wore homespun linen or hempen chemises that were not very voluminous or frilled but made every fashionable approximation possible. More often than not, women rolled their sleeves back to the elbow to facilitate their work and to keep their cuffs clean and in good repair. The neckline of the chemise could have a drawstring, or the chemise could have the entire center-front seam open with a simple closure at the bosom.

Women usually wore two skirts, with the top one tucked up to show a patterned underskirt. Or, if both skirts were of plain woolens, a bit of trim, braid, or contrasting stripe of fabric would be used as a decorative band around the bottom of one or both of them. Most often, skirts were made of wool or hemp and dyed with local vegetable dyes or left the natural color of the fiber. Aprons were not just a fashion statement, but a necessity for the working woman. Usually made from linen or hemp, an apron that was clean and well kept was a matter of personal pride for most women. Given enough income and leisure time, women would often trim or embroider their aprons for special occasions such as weddings or festivals.

Linen and hemp were also used for the simple kerchiefs worn by married women. As with aprons, if a woman had the time and resources, she might embroider her coifs for special occasions. These kerchiefs were worn folded back from the hairline and covered the hair entirely. Most women of this class wore their hair twined into a simple bun or rolled into a plain chignon. Young girls and unmarried women usually kept their hair tucked away while they were working for the sake of ease.

Stockings were almost always woolen, unless the woman was the wife or daughter of a silk merchant, in which case she might have a few pair of silk stockings of her own. But most of the peasantry wore homespun and hand-knitted stockings during the winter and during the summers went without. Shoes were homemade, utilitarian, usually made of buckskin, and low heeled.

Little pieces of luxury often found their way into the dress of those in the rising merchant class. Items such as silver buttons, silk stockings, velvet and satin ribbons, printed cottons, and fur trims were treasured among the middle class and often passed down through generations. Those merchants involved in the luxury goods trade were able to best emulate the wealthy.

By the end of the century, the most of the merchant class had gathered an impressive amount of wealth through lucrative trade with the East. Although they could not achieve the full fashions of their social betters, they were no longer limited to plain wool, linen, and hemp for their attire. Colors were still fairly narrow in pallette; the earth tones and drab colors available with vegetable dyes were the norm. The elegantly dyed goods worn by the upper classes were out of the financial reach of those who often worked hard to create them.

The end of the century brought with it many changes in fashions and more availability of fabrics and colors for a wider array of consumers. But fashion was so closely tied to social standing that societal conventions had a large and profound influence on the distinction between the upper and lower classes.

CHILDREN'S WEAR

Throughout history, children have been dressed as miniature adults, even if only in a basic approximation of high fashion. Beginning in the early days of the seventeenth century, a separate fashion for young children began to emerge as its own mode. Young children of both genders were dressed identically in long gowns as infants and similarly styled dresses as they grew older. Young boys in artwork are depicted in this style of dress and are often confused for young girls. The "breeching" of a boy when he came of age was quite an event in the household. This age varied from five to eight years old, at which time the boy would be dressed as a miniature version of his father, wearing fashionable breeches, a shirt, a coat, stockings, a hat, and even a miniature sword. Girls, however, remained in their childhood gowns until about age ten, when they were allowed to graduate into replica adult dresses, including not only the layers of skirts fashionable at this time but also the rigid underpinnings as well.

Newborn babies, both girls and boys, were swaddled. The baby would be dressed in some small garment, a shirt or short gown, then strips of linen would be wrapped around the length of its body from neck to toes in a spiral. A *biggin* or some other close-fitting cap would then be placed on the baby's head. Swaddling was very restrictive but was thought of as necessary to comfort the baby by reminding it of the womb as well as ensuring that the baby's limbs and body grew straight.[100] Periodically throughout the day, the swaddling would be unwound so that the baby could be washed, have its *tailclout* (diaper) changed, and stretch its muscles. Over the swaddling, babies were often wrapped in a mantle of costly fabric. A bib or handkerchief was often pinned to the front of the swaddling; this was known as a *muckminder*.

Infants in the seventeenth century were given pieces of coral as both a good-luck charm and a teething aid. It was a tradition thought to be handed down through Roman times. "Coral had been thought to have magical power to ward off evil. It also provided a cool, hard surface for babies to bite on to relieve the pain of teething."[101] Often this coral was set in gold or silver and worn on a ribbon around the neck, usually with a bell. This served not only as a teething ring and good-luck charm but as a rattle as well.

The most important point of a baby's life came at christening. The christening robes and accoutrements were lavish, even for those families not among the wealthy. Families of station bestowed extravagant robes, bibs, caps, and opulent lace-trimmed and embroidered christening gowns. Children were commonly baptized as infants in this time period in the mainstream Christian faiths. Baptism was performed as early as possible to ensure that the child's soul would go to heaven in the very real fear of the child dying in infancy.

At the age of one to three months, the tight swaddling was loosened somewhat, and the baby was dressed in a long gown called a frock. As the baby aged, the swaddling was discarded altogether. The

INFANT BAPTISM

The idea of infant baptism was very common in the Catholic Church, as it was a widely held belief that the souls of unbaptized babies were barred entry to heaven and would linger in limbo. "Unlike purgatory, a sort of waiting room to heaven for those with some venial faults, the theory of limbo consigned children outside of heaven on account of original sin alone" (Ian Fisher, "Limbo Reconsidered as Catholicism Grows in Countries with High Infant Mortality Rates," *New York Times*, January 1, 2006). Although a popular belief in earlier centuries, the belief in the concept of limbo and original sin are weakening in modern times.

muckminder was replaced by a pinafore apron for toddlers and young children in the seventeenth century. The term *pinafore* came from the practice of pinning the top portion to the front, or fore, of the garment.

As toddlers and young children, both girls and boys were dressed in gowns known as "going frocks." These dresses were quite full, with long gathered skirts and petticoats, but were short enough to allow the child to walk freely.

The "ribbons of childhood" were long strips of cloth attached to the shoulders or armseyes of the child's gown. The most popular theory has it that these were stylized leading strings for assisting the toddlers who were learning to walk and making a convenient "leash" for older children. Some scholars disagree about the originally intended purpose of these strips, citing numerous works of art from an earlier period that show both leading strings and the ribbons of childhood. The ribbons seem to be vestigial sleeves and may not serve a purpose other than to symbolize the stage of childhood. It was not until the seventeenth century that childhood was seen as its own important stage of life and given accoutrements and symbols to mark it. Although the ribbons most likely came in handy in assisting a toddler learning to walk, it is fairly evident from most portraiture that they would not be made of a textile durable enough to withstand repeated use in this manner.

As the children continued to age, their costuming changed slightly. While the girls still wore the frock, it became shaped more like the popular ladies' fashion of the day. Boys wore a different look: they continued wearing petticoats but often had a top shaped like a doublet or waistcoat, depending on the prevalent styles at the time, and sometimes wore a long robe over all. "The distinctive item of clothing for small boys was the robe, which was not worn by adults or by girls. Here ... was a clear example of a costume exclusively for a child and it had its origins in costume of the past."[102]

At approximately age seven, although the age could range from as young as five to as old as ten, a boy would begin to wear breeches and a doublet or waistcoat, depending on the fashion. This was known as "breeching" and was cause for celebration among the wealthy. It usually called for the tailor to come and measure the child and then create a special suit for the occasion. This account from 1697 related in Ashelford's *The Art of Dress* (1996) gives an especially good idea of the excitement of the event:

> You cannot believe the great concerne that was in the whole family here last Wednesday, it being the day that the taylor was to help dress little Frank in his breeches in order to the making of his everyday suit by it. Never had any bride that was to be drest upon her wedding night more hands about her, some the legs, some the arms, the taylor butt'ning, and other putting on the sword, and so many lookers on that had I not a finger amongst them I could not have seen him. When he was quite dreste, he acted his part as well as any of them.... They are very fit, everything, and he looks taller and prettyer than in his [petticoats].[103]

From then on, the boy would be dressed as a miniature adult man.

For girls, the process was more gradual. As noted in the diary of Lady Jane Clifford in 1617, her daughter began to wear frocks when she was three years old. The child was also fitted with her first "bodie" (stays) later that same year and had her "leading strings" cut from her clothes (it is not evident whether Lady Jane means true leading strings or the ribbons of childhood, as the ribbons have been pictured on children as old as age five or six). At age five, the diary exclaims that the little girl is finally old enough to wear "the first velvet coat she ever had."[104] From that point on, the little girl would be dressed as fashionably as her mother.

Children had to be dressed as befitting their station, with all the necessary accessories such as hats, gloves, muffs, jewelry, cravats, shoes with decorative rosettes or buckles, fans, and even such things as miniature swords, walking sticks, and parasols.

Rather unfortunately for historians, the theatricality and neo-classicism in the Baroque style of painting in the second half of the century makes drawing conclusions about the dress of the period even less accurate. Both women and men of the period were often depicted in a very casual state. Women were often painted in their nightgown and in a state of formal undress, *en dishabille*. It can also be seen that children were dressed in this inflated style as well. Although the contemporary silhouette is still visible amid the sweeping billows of satin, it is nearly impossible to draw any logical conclusions about what children actually wore in latter half of the century. Extant garments provide the clearest evidence that the progression from swaddling through frocks to breeching or full-fledged dresses remained unchanged into the eighteenth century, when swaddling was abandoned and boys were breeched with much less ceremony at about age four.

Beginning in the seventeenth century, children's fashion took on a larger social significance expressing a family's rank and station by dressing their rapidly growing children as sumptuously as they dressed themselves.

SERVANTS, MOURNING, AND SPECIALTY CLOTHING

Servants

The term *livery* comes from the Old French term for the feeding and clothing of servants, *livrer*. The wearing of a certain set of colors and styles to connote to what household a servant belonged has been important since the medieval era. It was no different in the seventeenth century. As grasping and fawning nobles jockeyed for position in the elegant courts of Europe, a well-turned-out company of servants was imperative. Although many sumptuary laws were passed over the centuries, nobles continued to find ways to appoint their staff in such a manner as to be a living advertisement of their wealth and power.

Although only the servants of the monarch could wear silk, the servants of lower nobles were allowed silk badges or bands to denote their rank. Even among the serving class, there was a hierarchy and an entire social class structure. In the household of one English lord, his personal servants were allowed to wear a badge of an embroidered peacock on velvet to announce their station, while the lower servants were allowed the heraldic device embroidered on satin.

New liveries might be ordered for special occasions or seasonal use. By and large, the cost of these ensembles would come out of the servant's wages. But by mid century, some of the higher servants, such as personal attendants, stewards, butlers, valets, clerks, and others that dealt directly with the master or mistress of the household, were promoted out of livery and wore clothes very much like that of their employers, but made of less costly materials. The badge of the household would be worn if the servant was to go outdoors, but normally they were allowed freedom in their clothing choices. Livery became the standard for grooms, coachmen, footmen, groundskeepers, and other lower servants. In smaller and less affluent households, adherence to the structures of livery wearing was not as commonplace, although it was not unheard of to purchase a set of livery or specific garments to be worn on important visits or special occasions. When Samuel Pepys was given his first important official post, he bought his personal retainer an expensive and impressive full set of livery so as not to look uncouth when he appeared at court.

Mourning

Until the seventeenth century, there were no rules of etiquette governing the wearing of specific mourning dress. White was considered a color of mourning, especially for the widowed queen mourning the death of her husband the king, but in general, violet was the official color of mourning for monarchs.[105]

In the seventeenth century, the beginnings of the elaborate rituals of mourning were born. At court funeral ceremonies, princes were required to wear black gowns or robes and over this a heavy black robe. Black crepe bands replaced colorful ones on hats. Princesses were expected to wear long black cloaks with full trains as well as *mantes*—wide black crepe streamers that attached to the headdress, sleeves, and belt and trailed along the floor behind. All official mourning visits paid by courtiers were made in full black cloaks with deep trains, regardless of gender. If not taking part in the funeral ceremony, mourners wore plain black garments that featured deep, white linen cuffs called "weepers" in English and *pleureuses* in French.[106] These were shortened when the official period of half-mourning was reached. White stockings, colored ribbons, lace, and powdered or beribboned wigs were not allowed to be worn during mourning periods.

In coming eras, mourning would become a strict and complicated custom, culminating with the Victorian fervor for mourning in the nineteenth and early twentieth centuries.

Specialty Dress

The people of the seventeenth century were very fond of spectacle, but the political turmoil brought on by the Thirty Years' War made it difficult to engage in the lavish festivals so common in preceding centuries. In the early years, before the war, the court of James I of England was renowned for its masques, fêtes, and festivals. Inigo Jones was famous for his fantastical and allegorical costume designs for the masques that often accompanied major court functions. He drew his inspirations from Classical Greek and Roman statues, Elizabethan fashions, and contemporary styles. Jones often clothed the ladies of the court, including the queen, in semitransparent gowns and draperies. His creations were brilliant, scandalous, and expensive. The bill for the costumes for the fête to commemorate the installation of Prince Henry as the Prince of Wales in 1610 was more than £2,000.[107]

In France, Louis VIII held many court ballets and masquerades, urging his courtiers to attire themselves in all manner of exotic and fantastic dress. Louis

XIV continued this tradition, engaging his court in theatrical masquerades at which they dressed as Persians, Turks, Chinese, and Native Americans. Contemporary accounts describe the lavish events full of rich costume, vivid pageantry, and sumptuous foods. Gowns for the ranking ladies were often made of cloth-of-gold and set with diamonds, emeralds, rubies, sapphires, and precious gems of all kinds. The trains of these gowns could measure several yards in length. This extreme opulence characterized the court of the Sun King for his entire reign.

Theater also flourished during this time, with great names such as Ben Jonson and William Shakespeare early in the century and playwrights creating clever and bawdy Restoration comedies after 1660. Costumes for the theater and opera were fairly uniform, allowing a largely illiterate audience to recognize the stock characters by their outfits alone.

Jean Bérain was the "Designer to the Chamber and the Cabinet"[108] in France, serving in the same role as Inigo Jones did many years earlier in England. Bérain not only designed and created costumes for the various court events but also oversaw the costuming of all plays and operas put on for the king's pleasure or in the king's presence. He utilized the usual basic designs: for women, a tight-fitting bodice that flared over the hips, a trained skirt, and an upswept hairstyle with tiara; the men dressed in a justacorps over a kilt with tall boots. Differentiation in characters came with the use of color, fabric, trim, embroidery, slashing, ribbons, and cut of the garments themselves. Bérain was very inventive in his costuming skills and created a type of sleeve to flatter an opera singer who was known to have unsightly arms. It created a brief fashion sensation and was called the "Amadis sleeve" after the actress for whom it was made. It was said that "the French surpass the Italians in opera by their costumes: these are of a richness, a magnificence and taste that outstrip anything one can see elsewhere."[109] This reputation helped to cement France's reputation for opulence and luxury in the rest of Europe.

The role of drama and costume in courtly life, especially at Versailles, helped to distance the courtiers and the monarchy from political upheaval as well as influence the day-to-day fashions of the time. The love of allegory helped balance the sumptuous theatricality with the solemnity and ceremonial formality of the court by adding a level of morality, history, and social relevance to the masques and fêtes.

NOTES

1. Robin W. Winks, *A History of Civilization: Renaissance to the Present* (Upper Saddle River, NJ: Prentice Hall, 1996), 307.

2. Winks, *History of Civilization*, 307.

3. Winks, *History of Civilization*, 309.

4. Jane Ashelford, *The Art of Dress: Clothes in Society, 1500–1914* (New York: H. N. Abrams, 1996), 56.

5. Winks, *History of Civilization*, 317.

6. Nancy Bradfield, *Historical Costumes of England, 1066–1956* (London: George G. Harris, 1958), 95.

7. Winks, *History of Civilization*, 320.

8. "Kings and Queens of the United Kingdom: The Stuarts," *History of the Monarchy*, http://www.royal.gov.uk/output/page76.asp.

9. David Plant, "Instrument of Government," *British Civil Wars, Commonwealth and Protectorate*, http://www.british-civil-wars.co.uk/glossary/instrument-government.htm.

10. "Government, Instrument of," *Encyclopedia Britannica Online*, http://www.britannica.com/eb/article-9037548.

11. Winks, *History of Civilization*, 322.

12. "Stuarts: The Test Acts, Titus Oates, and the Popish Plot, 1673–1681," http://www.bbc.co.uk/history/timelines/britain/stu_titus_oates.shtml (accessed June 15, 2006; site no longer available).

13. "Stuarts: Charles II and the Restoration of the Monarchy, 1660," http://www.bbc.co.uk/history/timelines/britain/stu_charles_ii.shtml (accessed June 15, 2006; site no longer available).

14. "United Kingdom," *Encyclopedia Britannica Online*, http://www.britannica.com/eb/article-44872.

15. House of Commons Information Office, *The Glorious Revolution* (London: House of Commons, 2002), 3.

16. "Stuarts: James VII and II and the Monmouth Rising, 1685–1688," http://www.bbc.co.uk/history/timelines/britain/stu_james_mon.shtml (accessed June 15, 2006; site no longer available).

17. John Rickard, "Thirty Years War," http://www.historyofwar.org/articles/wars_thirtyyears.html.

18. Winks, *History of Civilization*, 333.

19. Philip D. Curtin, *Cross-Cultural Trade in World History* (Cambridge: Cambridge University Press, 1984), 149.

20. Curtin, *Cross-Cultural Trade*, 157.

21. Curtin, *Cross-Cultural Trade*, 150–51.

22. Curtin, *Cross-Cultural Trade*, 150–51.

23. Curtin, *Cross-Cultural Trade*, 151.

24. Curtin, *Cross-Cultural Trade*, 154.

25. Curtin, *Cross-Cultural Trade*, 158.

26. Stephano Zuffi, *Rembrandt*, trans. Anna Bennett (London: Dorling Kindersley, 1999), 8.

27. Winks, *History of Civilization*, 329.

28. Winks, *History of Civilization*, 328.

29. Anne Hollander, *Seeing through Clothes* (New York: Viking Press, 1975), 93.

30. Judikje Kiers and Fieke Tissink, *The Golden Age of Dutch Art* (London: Thames & Hudson, 2000), 198.

31. Grand Rapids Art Museum, *A Moral Compass: Seventeenth- and Eighteenth-Century Painting in the Netherlands* (New York: Rizzoli International, 1999), 1.

32. "Any of several kinds of pottery, especially earthenware made of coarse clay and covered with an opaque tin-oxide glaze. The term is particularly applied to the ceramic ornaments and figurines of the ancient Egyptians" ("Faience," *Columbia Encyclopedia*, 6th ed. [New York: Columbia University Press, 2001–2005]).

33. "Delftware," *Encyclopedia Britannica Online*, http://concise.britannica.com/ebc/article-9362477/delftware.

34. Kiers and Tissink, *Golden Age of Dutch Art*, 275.

35. Anthony Geraghty, "Christopher Wren and St. Paul's Cathedral," http://www.bbc.co.uk/history/society_culture/architecture/gallery_st_pauls_04.shtml (accessed June 22, 2006; site no longer available).

36. Cosgreve's line is a variation on "We shall find no fiend in hell can match the fury of a disappointed woman,—scorned, slighted, dismissed without a parting pang" from *Love's Last Shift* (1696) by Colley Cibber (http://www.bartleby.com/100/214.html).

37. Jansenism is defined as "the theological principles of Cornelis Jansen, which emphasize predestination, deny free will, and maintain that human nature is incapable of good. They were condemned as heretical by the Roman Catholic Church." *American Heritage Dictionary*, 4th ed.

38. "Music whose texture is formed by the interweaving of several melodic lines. The lines are independent but sound together harmonically" ("Polyphony," *Columbia Encyclopedia*, 6th ed. [New York: Columbia University Press, 2001–2005]).

39. "The use of two or more melodies at the same time in a piece of music; [counterpoint] was an important part of baroque music" ("Counterpoint," *New Dictionary of Cultural Literacy*, 3rd ed. [New York: Houghton Mifflin, 2002]).

40. Toby Musgrave and Will Musgrave, *An Empire of Plants: People and Plants That Changed the World* (London: Cassell, 2000), 64.

41. *Merriam-Webster's Dictionary* defines *fustian* as "a strong cotton and linen fabric" or "a class of cotton fabrics usually having a pile face and twill weave" and *dimity* as "a sheer usually corded cotton fabric of plain weave in checks or stripes."

42. John Guy, *Woven Cargoes: Indian Textiles in the East* (New York: Thames & Hudson, 1998), 22.

43. Joyce Storey, *The Van Nostrand Manual of Textile Printing* (New York: Van Nostrand Reinhold, 1974), 16.

44. Guy, *Woven Cargoes*, 21.

45. Storey, *Van Nostrand Manual of Textile Printing*, 21.

46. Guy, *Woven Cargoes*, 187.

47. Musgrave and Musgrave, *Empire of Plants*, 68.

48. Guy, *Woven Cargoes*, 32.

49. Jennifer Harris, ed., *Textiles: 5,000 Years* (New York: H. N. Abrams, 1993), 225.

50. Virginia Hencken Elsasser, *Textiles: Concepts and Principals*, 2nd ed. (New York: Fairchild, 2005), 32.

51. Elsasser, *Textiles*, 33.

52. Harris, *Textiles*, 167.

53. Harris, *Textiles*, 176.

54. Greenfield, *Perfect Red*, 14.

55. Amy Butler Greenfield, *A Perfect Red: Empire, Espionage, and the Quest for the Color of Desire* (New York: HarperCollins, 2005), 2.

56. Greenfield, *Perfect Red*, 3.

57. Greenfield, *Perfect Red*, 39.

58. Greenfield, *Perfect Red*, 138–39.

59. Greenfield, *Perfect Red*, 140.

60. Pamela Warner, *Embroidery: A History* (London: B. T. Batsford, 1991), 105.

61. Warner, *Embroidery*, 97.

62. Muriel Baker, *Stumpwork: The Art of Raised Embroider* (New York: Charles Scribner's Sons, 1978), 24; Warner, *Embroidery*, 98.

63. John E. Vollmer, *Clothed to Rule the Universe: Ming and Qing Dynasty Textiles at the Art Institute of Chicago* (Chicago: Art Institute of Chicago, 2000), 14.

64. Vollmer, *Clothed to Rule*, 15.

65. Vollmer, *Clothed to Rule*, 30.

66. Vollmer, *Clothed to Rule*, 49.

67. Vollmer, *Clothed to Rule*, 35–36.

68. François Boucher, *20,000 Years of Fashion: The History of Costume and Personal Adornment* (New York: H. N. Abrams, 1987), 254.

69. Boucher, *20,000 Years of Fashion*, 254.

70. Iris Brooke, *English Costume of the Seventeenth Century* (New York: Barnes & Noble, 1934), 60.

71. Phyllis Tortora and Keith Eubank, *Survey of Historic Costume: A History of Western Dress*, 3rd ed. (New York: Fairchild, 1998), 204.

72. C. Willet and Phillis Cunnington, *The History of Underclothes* (New York: Dover, 1992), 56.

73. Michael Kwass, "Big Hair: A Wig History of Consumption in Eighteenth-Century France," *American Historical Review* 111, no. 3 (2006): para. 8 (available at http://www.historycooperative.org/journals/ahr/111.3/kwass.html).

74. Boucher, *20,000 Years of Fashion*, 264.

75. Kwass, "Big Hair," para. 24.

76. Lynn Schnernberger, *Let There Be Clothes: 40,000 Years of Fashion* (New York: Workman, 1991), 204.

77. Boucher, *20,000 Years of Fashion*, 286.

78. Willet and Cunnington, *History of Underclothes*, 51.

79. Willet and Cunnington, *History of Underclothes*, 51.

80. Boucher, *20,000 Years of Fashion*, 278.

81. André Blum, *Costume of the Western World: Early Bourbon, 1590–1643* (London: George G. Harrap, 1951), 11.

82. Brooke, *English Costume*, 28.

83. Brooke, *English Costume*, 70.

84. Boucher, *20,000 Years of Fashion*, 263.

85. Elisabeth McClellan, *History of American Costume*, vol. 1, *1607–1800* (New York: Tudor, 1969), 51.

86. McClellan, *History of American Costume*, 51.

87. Ashelford, *Art of Dress*, 12.

88. Brooke, *English Costume*, 68.

89. Brooke, *English Costume*, 50.

90. Schnernberger, 201.

91. Willet and Cunnington, *History of Underclothes*, 34.

92. Willet and Cunnington, *History of Underclothes*, 52.

93. Willet and Cunnington, *History of Underclothes*, 65.

94. Willet and Cunnington, *History of Underclothes*, 53.

95. Valerie Steele, *The Corset: A Cultural History* (New Haven, CT: Yale University Press, 2001), 7.

96. Steele, *The Corset*, 11.

97. Steele, *The Corset*, 11–12.

98. Willet and Cunnington, *History of Underclothes*, 67.

99. Marilyn Yalom, *A History of the Breast* (New York: Alfred A. Knopf, 1997), 104.

100. Tortora and Eubanks, *Survey of Historic Costume*, 219.

101. Tortora and Eubanks, *Survey of Historic Costume*, 220.

102. Tortora and Eubanks, *Survey of Historic Costume*, 219.

103. Ashelford, *Art of Dress*, 227.

104. Ashelford, *Art of Dress*, 276.

105. Boucher, *20,000 Years of Fashion*, 286.

106. Boucher, *20,000 Years of Fashion*, 286.

107. Ashelford, *Art of Dress*, 59.

108. Boucher, *20,000 Years of Fashion*, 285.

109. Boucher, *20,000 Years of Fashion*, 285.

FURTHER READING

Ashelford, Jane. *The Art of Dress: Clothes and Society, 1500–1914*. New York: H. N. Abrams, 1996.

Boucher, François. *20,000 Years of Fashion: The History of Costume and Personal Adornment.* New York: H. N. Abrams, 1987.

Bradfield, Nancy. *Historic Costumes of England, 1066–1956.* London: George G. Harrap, 1958.

Brooke, Iris. *English Costume of the Seventeenth Century.* New York: Barnes & Noble, 1934.

Harris, Jennifer, ed. *Textiles, 5,000 Years: An International History and Illustrated Survey.* New York: H. N. Abrams, 1993.

MacQuoid, Percy. *Four Hundred Years of Children's Costume, 1400–1800.* London: Medici Society, 1923.

Tortora, Phyllis, and Keith Eubank. *Survey of Historic Costume: A History of Western Dress.* 3rd ed. New York: Fairchild, 1998.

WEB RESOURCES

http://www.royal.gov.uk/output/Page13.asp
http://www.bbc.co.uk/history/british/civil_war_revolution
http://www.bbc.co.uk/history/british/launch_t1_british.shtml
http://www.mystudios.com/gallery/dutch/praxedis.html
http://girl-with-a-pearl-earring.20m.com/
http://www.npg.org.uk/live/search/person.asp?search=ss&stext=queen+ann&linkid=mp
    00111
http://www.kipar.org/baroque-costumes/costumes_fontanges.html
http://www.wga.hu/support/viewer/z.html

MOVIES

All the Mornings of the World (1991)
Cyrano de Bergerac (1990)
Dangerous Beauty (1998)
Draughtsman's Contract (1983)
The Girl with the Pearl Earring (2003)
The Last King (2004)
The Man in the Iron Mask (1999)
Restoration (1995)

North American Colonial Costume

Suzanne Buchanan

TIMELINE

1565	Spanish colony founded at St. Augustine, Florida
1605	French establish Port Royal in Nova Scotia
1607	Jamestown, Virginia, founded by English
1613	Dutch colonists establish trading post on lower Manhattan Island
1619	Dutch traders bring Africans to Jamestown for sale as indentured servants
1620	*Mayflower* lands at Cape Cod; Plymouth Colony established
1621	English settlers bring cotton seeds to America
1630	John Winthrop and several hundred English colonists arrive in Massachusetts Bay
1634	English settlers arrive in Maryland
1641	Slavery becomes legal in New England
1643	Louis XIV ascends the throne in France and begins promotion of French silk industry via exports and trade restrictions
1651	Massachusetts Bay Colony passes its first sumptuary laws to curb the use of gold lace and other lavish clothing
1660	English Navigation Acts require exclusive use of English ships for trade with English colonies, prohibiting colonists from trading directly with non-English states or colonies; emergence of first three-piece suits for men: trousers, vest, and jacket
1667	Dutch cede New Amsterdam (New York) to England
1670	Hudson's Bay Company founded to wrest control of the Canadian fur trade from French
1681	Pennsylvania founded by Quaker William Penn
1682	La Salle claims the lower Mississippi Valley for France
1685	Revocation of Edict of Nantes forces many French silk manufacturers to move to England, prompting the importation of more English silks by the English colonies
1699	Woolens Act forbids exportation of any woolen goods by any English colony

1715	Death of France's Louis XIV ushers in a new artistic sensibility throughout Europe and the colonies
1721	Wearing of cotton garments banned in England; France had already banned cotton; ban does not apply to the colonies
1733	Iron Act forbids attempts to develop American industry and continues to protect the British iron manufacturing industry
1736	Cotton ban repealed in England
1742	First cotton mills open in England
1756	French and Indian Wars begin when England declares war on France
1760	Women's hairstyles begin to gain enormous height
1763	English defeat the French in the French and Indian Wars
1764	First recorded bales of cotton exported to England from South Carolina
1770	Printed textiles begin to gain popularity; stomachers gradually replaced by bodices that come together at center-front edges
1773	Boston Tea Party
1774	Quebec Act reasserts Canadian loyalty to British rule
1775	Revolutionary War begins
1776	Declaration of Independence; Benjamin Franklin travels as U.S. ambassador to France and forever links plain, pious dress with American identity
1783	Treaty of Paris ends Revolutionary War; introduction of chemise dress or *chemise à la reine* by Marie Antoinette; tall hairstyles gradually replaced by a wider, frizzy style

In today's America, people mask their social differences behind current fashion trends, and it is difficult to tell one person's social status from another. In this democratic fashion landscape, it is hard to imagine that the first European settlers in the New World were far from liberal in their attitudes about dress. In fact, when the first waves of European settlers arrived on the shores of North America four hundred years ago, every aspect of a man's or woman's social identity was revealed by their clothes. Through custom, birthright, and sometimes law, men and women wore clothing that clearly identified their status, their gender, their national identity, and often their occupation and religion.

If many of the men and women forging a new life in the New World did so in search of liberties not granted to them in Europe, the liberty to dress as they pleased was rarely a stated part of that quest. It would be a mistake, though, to believe that dress was not an important factor in the early colonization of America. There were many parties interested in what Americans wore in these early years of settlement. The textile industries in France, England, and Holland encouraged settlement in the colonies in order to boost dependence upon their silks, woolens, and linens, thus increasing profit and production in the home country. So great was their interest in expanding colonial markets that they clamored for the enactment of trade laws to protect and increase their profits, which in turn benefited their national economies. Religious leaders in the new colonies had an interest in clothing habits of the new arrivals, as well. Attempting to create God's kingdom on earth, they used restrictive sumptuary laws to enforce religious notions of godliness in dress. Finally, colonists themselves held a great personal interest in what they wore. Hoping to maintain the traditions of their native countries in a strange and sometimes hostile new land, they clung to the traditional dress of their homelands as a way to maintain their identity. Once in a while, though, they might stumble upon a happier identity in a new culture with an entirely new form of dress.

While early colonials were distinguished from each other individually by class, gender, religion, and clothing, the early colonies themselves were separated from each other by wilderness, language, religion, politics, and customs. Combined with laws that forbade trade with other countries, these conditions at first helped to enforce a colonial allegiance to the fashions of their native countries. Occasionally, the hardships of life in the New World forced the settlers to bend or break the law. When French settlers in Canada, for example, had difficulty obtaining enough clothing from France, they happily traded with the Native Americans for textiles and clothes—which they, in turn, had obtained from the better-supplied English colonies further south.[1] These common experiences of hardship and resourcefulness helped to initiate a gradual chipping away at the colonists' national and cultural differences.

By the later decades of the seventeenth century, the differences among some colonies would be further eroded by shared religious beliefs. Calvinist leaders of Dutch and English colonies, for example, shared a dislike of excessive finery, at least for certain classes of people, and they enacted numerous sumptuary laws to enforce public piety and conformity. The arrival of Quakers in New Jersey and Pennsylvania brought more like-minded souls who disapproved of fashionable excess.

For all their laws and fiery sermons, however, the religious leaders of early colonial America merely laid the

Benjamin Franklin, J. Elias Haid, after the 1777 portrait by N. Cochin. Courtesy of the Library of Congress.

groundwork for the first defining moment in the history of American dress. In the end, it was Benjamin Franklin, a nonsectarian religious moderate, who forever linked plain, pious dress with American identity when he famously landed on French shores in 1776 wearing his simple brown suit and signature coonskin cap. This clever act of sartorial diplomacy, which both shocked and delighted the finery-loving French, did more to further the reputation of the virtuous, plain-dressing American spirit than all the rules and regulations imposed by high-minded clergymen in the generations before. True to the ideals of the Land of Liberty, however, individual Americans would continue to respect or ignore the tone set by Franklin according to what their pocketbooks and personal taste allowed, yet the national dialogue about virtue and dress remains an important topic in America even today.

By 1785, the end of the period covered in this chapter, costumes that identified a person's religious convictions or occupation became more the exception than the rule, and the sumptuary laws that had guided the costume choices of Europeans for centuries were a thing of the past, at least outside of a religious context. The only thing preventing a free laborer's wife in the newly minted United States from wearing a gold-trimmed purple silk gown was her income and her access to shops and materials.

Other changes during this time were equally significant. Overall, clothing for both men and women became much simpler in construction, although for women this was only a temporary respite. Men, on the other hand, gradually abandoned the fancy trimmings and fabrics that had brightened their clothing for hundreds of years. The growing restraint in men's fashion toward the end of this period also widened the visible differences between men's and women's costume generally—differences that wouldn't recede again until the late twentieth century.

JACOBEAN COSTUME

As of 1620, the Spanish, Dutch, English, and French had all established settlements in North America: The Spanish had outposts in Florida and holdings from the isthmus of Panama to the future states of New Mexico and California; the Dutch had established footholds in New York; the British had colonies in Virginia, Massachusetts, and New Hampshire; and the French had settlements in Quebec. There are few pictorial examples of colonial clothing from this time, and even fewer surviving costumes, but it is known that as each settlement developed, the clothing types of its native country were still worn.

Broadly speaking, fashions in 1620 were dominated by the soon to be out-of-fashion Spanish-style costume. For men, this consisted of a short, padded, broad-shouldered shirt called a *doublet*, which had narrow sleeves and a tight waist and sometimes flared out at the hips. On their legs, they wore short, puffy breeches called *trunk hose*, which were bound above the knee by a ribbon or garter to hold up their stockings. Lacking elastic, that modern-day marvel of fashion ease, these baggy bottoms were held up by a drawstring or by means of *points*, metal-tipped ribbons that laced them to the doublet. An example of this costume can be seen in the print depicting Sir Walter Raleigh, explorer and sponsor of the ill-fated Roanoke Colony in Virginia.

Before their departure for the new colony of Jamestown, the Virginia Company tried more or less successfully to prepare its mainly upper-class volunteers for the rigors of frontier life with a list of recommended clothing items to bring with them on their journey. These included:

A Monmouth cap
Three shirts
One suit of canvas
One pair of garters
Three falling bands
One waistcoat
One suit of frieze
One suit of broadcloth
Three pairs of silk stockings
One dozen pairs of points.[2]

The Monmouth cap was a simple, close-fitting, knitted wool cap. The canvas, frieze, and broadcloth fabrics recommended for the suits were sturdy fabrics of varying weights that could take the settlers through the colder seasons. The list leaves out the silks and fine linens that the many gentlemen in the group would have been used to, and which they no doubt

Portrait of Sir Walter Raleigh, 1909. Courtesy of the Library of Congress.

brought along anyway.[3] The recommendation to bring falling bands (flat collars that lay on the shoulders), rather than elaborate Spanish-style ruff collars, was perhaps an acknowledgment that starching and pressing were luxuries that would have to be dispensed with by all but the most important members of the community. For all the Virginia Company's sensible recommendations, it didn't address heat and humidity of Virginia summers—there is no mention of broad-brimmed hats or lightweight breeches and stockings, for example.

Had there been a list for female settlers, it would have been similar, with petticoats substituted for the varying weights of suits, and perhaps a gown or two added. The undergarments—stays, shifts, and farthingales—that were integral to the shape of dress in this era would have been taken for granted. While the Virginia Company list may be interpreted to suggest that it was okay for some English colonists to dispense with the high-maintenance ruff collar, practicality did not always trump the need to maintain a colonist's national identity. Mid-century depictions of soldiers in the Spanish settlements show that the starched ruff, for all the work it entailed, was maintained throughout the Spanish colonies long after it went out of style in the other colonies.

A print of John Endicott, c. 1903. Courtesy of the Library of Congress.

The comparatively wealthy and fashion-conscious English colonists in Virginia quickly became known for the richness of their dress, importing the new larger far-thingales, along with silk doublets and gowns. Surviving early court records, a valuable source of information about Virginia costume, indicate that soon after settlement, Virginian women were also importing the fashionable new printed cottons whose elaborate floral patterns imitated the extraordinary English embroidered textiles that could only be had by the very wealthy in England.[4]

The Virginians were by no means the only fashionable colonials in the New World. Farther north, a large group of industrious and tolerant Dutch citizens on the island of Manhattan soon established itself as another prosperous colony with ready access to the most trendy European styles.[5]

Guided by religious idealism, the Puritan settlers in the Massachusetts Bay Colony demanded more restraint than their English cousins in Virginia, whose settlements were primarily commercial ventures. As early as 1634, the Massachusetts General Court issued an edict prohibiting lace, embroidered caps, and beaver hats, among other vanities.[6] For all their condemnations of finery, however, Puritan leaders usually didn't frown upon a stylish cut of suit. A portrait of Massachusetts Bay Colony cofounder John Endicott shows him wearing a fashionable falling collar of the 1630s. In keeping with his Puritan beliefs, Endicott's collar is unadorned with lace but is nevertheless made of fine quality linen and perfectly pressed. The Puritan also wears his hair in the shoulder-length style that so many more radical Puritan ministers railed about as a sign of vanity and decadence. The skullcap on his head was newly fashionable and became popular among both English and Dutch leaders in the early settlements. Endicott's black cassock is also significant. Although the taste for black originated in Catholic Spain, the modern stereotype of Puritan dress erroneously equates black with all Puritans. In fact, black dyes were very expensive and rarely worn by common folk, Catholic or Protestant. In the Puritan worldview, such luxuries were a sign of God's favor toward the wealthy few.

WORKING CLOTHING

A few miles south of wealthy Puritan Boston, the lower-class Pilgrims of the Plymouth Colony were discernibly less fashionable. Poverty and sumptuary law combined to enforce many similarities in the dress of laboring classes all over the

Pilgrim Fathers, the Puritans who settled in Plymouth in 1620, founding the first permanent colony in New England. Engraving after "Pilgrim Fathers on Their Way to Church," by George Henry Boughton. © HIP / Art Resource, NY.

colonies. Servants and slaves, laborers, and lower tradesmen were traditionally restricted to a limited range of colors in their costumes, generally blues, browns, russet, gray, and unbleached white. Working clothes needed to be durable, so the most common textiles used were wool, heavy linen, and mixtures of the two.

Variations in men's clothing were dictated by their particular occupation, and they were rarely seen in public without the tools of their trade.[7] Underneath his apron, a laboring man's clothes consisted of a rougher, less fashionable version of the costumes of his superiors, and sometimes were even the very castoffs once worn by the wealthy gentlemen. Workingmen's smocks were of coarser material and lacked the lace and ruffles of the well-to-do, and they were never white. The smock could be tied at the neckline or left undone, depending on the weather, which was both hotter in summer and colder in winter than that of England or western Europe. Over the smock, workingmen often wore a jacket or vest-like garment, to which sleeves could sometimes be attached with points. For poor men as well as wealthy ones, the smock was one of the few garments that received regular washing in seventeenth-century colonial America, unlike the wearer or his outer garments.

Like the laboring men, working-class women's clothes in the colonies were partly dictated by the demands of their trade. Women wore a smock-like low-necked shirt. Called a *shift* or later a *chemise*, this long garment functioned as both blouse and slip. Over that, a women laced her stays around her torso and then donned her petticoat, an ankle- or shin-length skirt that tied around the waist. While a workingwoman might only rarely own a nice one-piece gown, she generally had at least two petticoats and two bodices, one each of heavy wool for winter wear, and lighter linen ones for summer. Over this foundation, she donned a bodice and an apron. Her winter bodice was often equipped with detachable sleeves, making it function like a jacket. For both sexes the jacket was a convenient, useful garment that could be added or removed as the weather dictated.

Working-class men and women wore hats of various styles to protect their faces and necks from sun and rain. The form of these hats was often dictated by regional customs. Well into the eighteenth century, working-class immigrants from Holland were identified by their brimmed, conical hats. Farm women in New France were recognizable by their *bavolettes*, linen caps that had a flap on the nape of the neck to keep out the sun. They also wore characteristically short, shin-length skirts. Chronically undersupplied with clothing and footwear during the seventeenth century, workingwomen in the French colonies went barefoot in summer and were quick to acquire the beautiful quill-decorated moccasins from the aboriginal peoples when winter set in.[8]

Like the apron, the *kerchief* or *neckerchief* was a universal element in the costume of working folk throughout the colonies. Made of cotton or linen, kerchiefs were worn on the head or around the neck to soak up sweat and keep off the sun. African slaves, male and female, usually wore them wrapped around their heads. Kerchiefs served as napkins, towels, sacks, and sunshades. Also like aprons, few if any original examples of seventeenth-century neckerchiefs remain: they were used until they wore out.[9]

Since free laboring men and women might have to make do with castoffs and what they could afford to purchase, their clothing tended to lag behind the current fashion. Slaves and indentured servants in the colonies sometimes fared a little better. In the seventeenth century, before slavery became a Southern institution almost exclusively linked with the African slave trade, any non-Christian captured in an armed conflict could be enslaved. Thus Native American children and elders could be found working alongside Africans as slaves in colonial households. Slaves in turn frequently worked alongside indentured servants, who came from all regions of Europe to learn and to teach trades in the New World while they worked off the terms of their contract. In any given household, these servants and slaves retained aspects of their native dress, such as jewelry, tattoos, headscarves, or a particular type of bonnet or cap.

In this era, especially in Northern households, slaves and servants were customarily treated as subordinate members of a household and sometimes loosely defined as family members. It was the obligation of the master or mistress of the household to nurse them when sick, ensure they had enough to eat, and supply them with serviceable clothing. It was common for a prosperous citizen to hire a dressmaker to make dresses for the entire household, slaves and servants included. Thus a female slave could regularly obtain a reasonably fashionable gown, though constructed of an inferior textile.[10]

With the growth of large-scale tobacco and cotton plantations in the eighteenth century, clear-cut divisions emerged in slave costume. Household slaves were dressed either in brightly colored livery costumes or in visibly less fashionable versions of the clothes worn by the master or mistress of the household. Field slaves, on the other hand, were reduced to the bare essentials. Men wore simple trousers and a shirt, women a petticoat and chemise. Once or twice a year plantation owners bought cheap textiles in bulk and hired a tailor to make basic garments for the field slaves.[11] The resulting uniformity of dress made runaways easy to identify and may account for why they often stole clothes when they fled.

BAROQUE COSTUME

By the middle of the seventeenth century, colonists in the New World were producing increasing quantities of goods—furs, cod, tobacco, indigo dye—for export to Europe, while still importing the vast majority of their clothes and finished textiles. France, England, and Holland eagerly supplied their wants, while vigilantly enacting tariffs and trade laws to prevent the colonists from establishing their own factories to produce finished goods.

Having seen its imperial fortunes decline at the beginning of the 1600s, Spain no longer dictated the world's fashionable attire. Instead, interest shifted to the court of the young and ambitious King Louis XIV of France. A taste for French fashions, with their shiny silks and abundant laces, ribbons, and frills swept the colonies as it did Europe. The fashion-conscious English and Dutch in Virginia and New York were the first to adopt the new French look, which for men comprised the knee-length baggy *petticoat breeches* and a vest, or *waistcoat*. Fancy ribbon bows (called *rosettes*) adorned knees and shoes, and clothing was sometimes decorated with more than a hundred yards (90+ m) of ribbon on the elbows, waists, and shoulders. Large lace falling band collars allowed wealthy men to show off a large piece of fine white linen and lace fabric. Broad flat collars also allowed them to indulge in the new taste for shoulder-length hair. A new item of fashionable wear, borrowed from the military, was the high, square-toed boot, which was favored by Virginia plantation owners who spent a large portion of their day on horseback.

Fashionable colonial ladies of the mid-seventeenth century wore a lavish costume. As with men's outfits, the bodice grew shorter, with a higher waist and a lower neckline. The sleeves on the bodice grew wider and shorter, too, in order to show off wide lace cuffs on the shift. The detailed portrait of a fashionable young colonial woman from the early 1670s indicates how successfully wealthy colonists could stay in touch with current styles from Europe. The olive green of the young mother's gown in this portrait was a popular color at midcentury.[12] Women wore deep linen lace collars, called *wisks*, and held their sleeves up with ribbons. They also wore the new *mantua* gown, a one-piece garment that was cut to provide extra fullness in the skirts. This extra volume of fabric was sometimes hitched up at the back of the hips in order to better show off an embroidered petticoat underneath.

For headwear, women wore hoods, tied loosely around the head, and these appear frequently in the few American portraits of this era. This modest, graceful head covering was sometimes topped with the fashionable new *sugar loaf hat* when the lady went out. Sugar loaf hats, with their broad brim and conical crown, later became identified with the classic Puritan costume, but they were yet another item restricted to the wealthy. Imported from London at great expense, sugar loaf hats were made from the beaver pelts so eagerly hunted in the part of the New World now called Canada, as beavers had become extinct in Europe. They symbolize one of the great tragedies of New World colonization, for in the beaver trade Americans first depleted one of their natural resources in order to satisfy the whims of fashion.

In New England, Puritan colonial leaders looked upon the new French fashions with dismay. English colonists were especially prone to its temptations, as

petty merchants in England hawked a wide array of affordable imported ribbons, garters, laces, and trimmings to the lower and merchant classes and happily shipped such trifles to the growing markets in the colonies.[13] To curb
these vanities, the Massachusetts Bay Colony established new sumptuary laws
in 1651, which penalized persons with a net worth *below* £200 for wearing "gold
or silver lace, or gold and silver buttons, or any bone lace above 2s. per yard, or
silk hoods, or scarves."[14] The number of fines levied on overdressed men and
women in the Boston court during these years suggests that it may have been
an unending struggle, but it also indicates the zeal with which the authorities
enforced their ordinances. Even the Puritan authorities could not eliminate
temptation entirely, however. One historian has described the catcalls and com-
motion and no doubt the secret admiration that met a traveler decked out in
this latest fashion as he stepped ashore in sober Boston.[15]

NATIVE AMERICAN DRESS

As the seventeenth century drew to a close, Native Americans coexisted uneas-
ily with the newcomers from across the ocean. Yet, from their earliest encounters, they were enthralled with the ever-changing array of novel garments and
textiles brought by the Europeans. At the same time, second- and third-generation
colonists were undoubtedly less shocked by the appearance of the Native
Americans they came in contact with than their predecessors. Indeed, European
commentators regarded with admiration many features of Native American
dress, such as the warm and beautiful turkey-feather capes woven by Eastern
Woodland tribeswomen.[16] They also admired the Natives' traditional beadwork
embroidery, an early example of which survives on the cloak of Chief Powhatan,
now housed in Oxford's Ashmolean Museum.

Depending on where colonists lived along the coast, they encountered different costumes among the Native Americans. Native men and women of North
Carolina and Virginia, for example, wore belted fringed skirts around their loins
and went bare on top in the warm weather. They kept their hair long and
adorned themselves with tattoos and metal jewelry.

Farther north, French explorers and missionaries noted the fur-lined animal-
skin leggings worn in cold weather. They also described how Iroquois men
shaved their heads up to the top of the crown and attached bird feathers, and
sometimes entire wings, to their remaining locks, and they were astonished to
find that some Native men wore live snakes as earrings.[17] Even more discon-
certing to European eyes was the fact that within a community, Natives all wore
more or less the same costume, with no distinctions made for the different
social ranks within the group. A chief or his wife might be distinguishable only
by a few extra bits of beadwork or jewelry.[18]

From the earliest years of contact, Europeans predicted that goods manufactured abroad would be eagerly sought by Native Americans. Many of the financial sponsors of colonization efforts expected the colonists to help build
markets for European goods by distributing among the Natives cheap wool
blankets and cotton shirts made expressly for this purpose.[19] Treaty arrangements often included direct exchanges of land for clothing.[20]

As trade between Natives and colonists flourished, influences went both ways. Native American women often adapted the European trade shirts as dresses, which they adorned with their traditional belts and jewelry. Native American men and women also made mantles, or cloaks, from the wool blankets obtained from trade with Europeans. French trappers trekking the wilderness of Hudson Bay and the Great Lakes may have been the first Europeans to adopt the rugged, warm garb of their Native guides and partners. Spending long months in the wilderness, these *coureurs des bois* were recognizable by their fur caps, long leather leggings, moccasins, and fringed shirts, as well as their *ceinture fléchée*, a red, yellow, blue, green, and black woven belt. Sometimes it was only their beards that distinguished them from Native men. Many colonials who spent time with the Natives, such as those who had been taken captive, found the moccasins given to them by their captors to be far more comfortable and sturdy for frontier life than European shoes. English children in particular were reluctant to give up their Native costume after they were repatriated, for their captors treated them with as much affection and indulgence as they did their own children.[21]

In 1710, artist John Verelst recorded a dashing example of the hybrid costumes that resulted from trade among the colonials and Natives. His portrait of Mohawk king Tee Yee Neen Ho Ga Row reveals a costume of both Native American and European elements. Among the clearly identifiable European features are a cotton or linen smock shirt, buckled square-toed leather shoes, and a trade blanket worn as a Native-style mantle. The chief's belt and open-fronted overshirt are Native American fashions rendered in European materials.

LATE BAROQUE ERA

By 1700, the settlements of the East Coast of North America had begun to thrive, becoming full-fledged small urban centers. These included Montreal, Boston, New York (formerly New Amsterdam), Philadelphia, Williamsburg, and Charles Town. Each was respectably cosmopolitan, but each had its own character: New York, with its mix of worldly English and Dutch traders, was especially attuned to the latest European fashions.[22]

Urbanity, however, did not always translate into modishness. Montreal, a French town, had a large population of Catholic missionaries, laborers, and farmers and their more recently imported wives who retained the colorful country fashions of their homeland. Their more fashionable cousins in Quebec thought them very provincial.

Under the continued influence of the Puritan leadership, Boston retained a reputation for somber, conservative dress. A portrait of wealthy Bostonian John Freake shows him wearing a newly fashionable long-waisted suit and *justacorps* vest adorned with dozens of buttons, although his broad lace collar suggests his conservative inclinations. By the date of this portrait, the falling band collar had been replaced in fashionable circles by a small gathering of lace called a *cravat*, which hung at the throat. Freake also declined to wear a *periwig*. Piling curls high on the head and down past the shoulders, the periwig accentuated the long, lean lines of late Baroque-era fashion, but it was also hot and heavy.

Ever attentive to changes in European fashions, wealthy colonial women began to sport mantuas with open-fronted skirts that revealed a matching or contrasting petticoat underneath. The bodice was closed at the front by a triangular closure called the *stomacher*. Stomachers were often embroidered or decorated with ribbons, and they represent some of the oldest and best-preserved colonial costume items to be found in American museums. Fancy lace continued to be an important element in women's costume, appearing at necklines, cuffs, and apron hems. A new headdress, the *fontange*, replaced the soft, rounded kerchief of previous decades. Made of elaborate bits of lace mounted onto tall wires, the fontange sat front and center on a woman's head. Delicate and impractical, the fontange was one fashion element that could not be readily adapted by workingwomen.

In the midst of the seventeenth century's sartorial excess, models of restraint continued to insist on modesty and piety in colonial dress. The establishment of a Quaker colony in Pennsylvania in 1681 brought fresh voices to this chorus. Quakers disapproved of finery in general and tried to adhere to a philosophy of plainness in both speech and dress. They took their doctrine seriously and were also careful to avoid grabbing attention by appearing *too* plain. White Quakers refused to wear anything dyed with indigo blue dye in protest of the terrible conditions slaves endured in its production.[23] Importation records indicate that the bold patterned silks so popular in other colonial centers were rarely even carried to Philadelphia.[24] With time, Quaker fashion gained a recognizable look, and late into the eighteenth and nineteenth centuries, it was easy to spot a Quaker man by his broad-brimmed hat and conservative gray or brown coat.

Adherence to the doctrine of plainness was essentially voluntary. Wealthy Quakers were known to keep to the letter of the doctrine while still making sure that their clothes were made from the finest materials available, and young Quakers were sometimes castigated, though rarely punished it seems, for wearing ribbons and fashionable hairstyles. The famously tolerant environment of Quaker-led Pennsylvania drew other religious minorities to the colony, such as the German and Swiss Ammonites, who ironically imposed very strict dress codes on their adherents. Their costume has changed little through the centuries and can still be seen today in the Amish and Mennonite communities of rural Canada, Pennsylvania, Ohio, and elsewhere.

To their long-term benefit, Pennsylvania Quakers didn't adhere to the isolationist practices of their more radical guests from the Rhineland. They mingled in society as farmers, bankers, merchants, speculators, and tradesmen of all sorts. Many Quakers, such as Thomas Paine and Dolly Madison, became respected and influential citizens in the colonies and thereby extended Quaker influence over the direction of American colonial life, including fashion. It was from Philadelphia, after all, that Benjamin Franklin set sail when he left American shores to court French support for the Revolution.

Also emerging in this era were environmentally or climatically motivated differences in costume. For all but the most formal occasions, the increasingly prosperous tobacco growers of Maryland and Virginia sometimes did away with their waistcoats because of the heat. Workingwomen in the South favored separate skirts with easily removable bodices that allowed air to circulate around their chemises.[25] In the north, quilted petticoats filled with wool fibers were popular and kept the women warm in the harsh cold winters. Demand for these useful garments was high in the drafty houses of New England, so when they couldn't be imported, women were forced to make them themselves.

The fabrics worn in the South were different from in the North. Plantation owners in the Carolinas and Louisiana began to discard the traditional wool and wool-linen blended fabrics of their homelands in favor of suits made of linen. Their wives favored silk, linen, and the increasingly popular cotton prints known as *chintzes*.[26]

EARLY ROCOCO ERA

The death of France's Louis XIV in 1715 ushered in a new artistic sensibility throughout Europe and the colonies. Baroque formality and heaviness were replaced by a love of playful asymmetry and a fascination with curvilinear lines. The Rococo era coincided with a flourishing of arts in the American colonies, as wealthy merchants, statesmen, and plantation owners commissioned grand houses, portraits, and furniture in the new taste from both local and recently immigrated craftsmen. The happy result for students of costume is a rich visual record, which suggests that Rococo fashions, with their whimsical lines, delicate patterns, and soft, rich colors, were embraced enthusiastically by American colonists.

Men's costume expressed the new style through wider, flared coat skirts and deep, generous coat cuffs, which reached almost to the elbow until about 1760. Patterned fabrics were popular for men, as was floral embroidery around buttonholes and on pocket flaps. Waistcoats began to shrink in length and became a focus of ornament when the overall fabric of a suit was plain. While older men continued to wear long wigs in this era, the younger generation adopted a smaller powdered wig, which was tied at the back of the neck with a black bow and adorned at the temples with stiff sausage curls.

For women, mantua gowns remained popular in the colonies well into the eighteenth century. Part of the appeal of mantua gowns was that they were cut from one piece of fabric and enabled the wearer to show off yards of expensive, glossy French or English silk. Necklines remained low and square for fashionable ladies, and sleeves crept back up to the elbow, where they were adorned with layers of lace ruffles. The long, pointed bodice fashionable in this era gave the wearer's torso the shape of a cone and made it difficult to sit down. At the French court, where this fashion originated, men and women were in fact rarely permitted to sit down. For them, this restrictive construction was actually a necessity. The stiff bodices helped women maintain an erect posture through sometimes ten- or twelve-hour days. Many examples of this type of dress are found in American museums, but given how impractical they were, it's not clear how popular this fashion was in the workaday lives of American women. While French fashion also dictated a tightly curled hairstyle, with their hair pulled up high in the back, many contemporary portraits of colonial women show a style with softer curls pulled back at the nape of the neck.[27]

LATE ROCOCO AND REVOLUTIONARY ERA

As the eighteenth century passed the halfway mark, the British Empire consolidated its power in North America. Having already routed the Dutch in New

York, the English went on in 1763 to take New France and Florida in the French and Indian War. Meanwhile, colonists in North America grew increasingly dissatisfied with the Navigation Acts and other trade laws that seemed to always work in the favor of the British crown and domestic British industries and against the colonies and their progress. Laws such as the Molasses Act, which required sugar to be imported through Britain, forced the colonists to pay more than necessary for basic goods. Other laws, such as the Iron Act of 1733, forbade attempts to develop American industry in order to protect iron manufacturing in Britain.

These restrictions on colonial growth spurred some activists in the 1760s to call for boycotts of British textiles while promoting the production of "homespun" textiles and garments. These efforts met with mixed success. Northern colonists had a long tradition of spinning and weaving textiles for home use, but Southern plantation life had never favored the development of such household industries—it was more profitable to devote their slave labor force to tobacco cultivation, while importing all other necessities. In either case, the colonies did not yet have the industrial resources to meet their demand for textiles.

While France continued to dictate the newest fashions throughout Europe, England, and the colonial world, the French themselves were increasingly influenced by the elegant restrained attire of the English gentry. It is a testament to the tenacity of English influence that American colonists enthusiastically joined the French in embracing the new English taste, even as the war to declare their independence from England erupted in 1776. People proudly fashioned their clothing from homespun cotton and wool yet nonetheless imitated the latest English styles.

The collared frock coat, formerly identified only with laboring classes and the military, made its way up the social ladder and became fashionable for wealthy civilians as well. At the same time, men's fashions grew more restrained. Colors were more somber, and embroidery and trimmings were relegated to ever smaller portions of the waistcoat, which continued to shrink in length. Breeches, meanwhile, grew longer and remained close fitting to the leg. Coats changed drastically in this era: they were cut very close to the body, with the front closure buttoning only over the chest and cut away falling to the sides at the waist. The coat's wide, flared skirts of previous decades shrank in the 1760s and 1770s, beginning their evolution into the tails that still cling to the modern formalwear designs. Coat cuffs grew smaller and less ornate. In a last show of extravagance, though, a fad for oversized buttons took hold and persisted through the 1780s.

It was in this era that young men who weren't in the military began to abandon the wigs that had been fashionable for so many decades. Perhaps these were among the few articles of British attire tainted by association, for as early as the 1760s, the gun-toting British soldier with his red coat and white wig was a target of colonial resentment. One of the many forms of mischief perpetrated by anti-British mobs in the colonies was to knock the wigs or hats off the heads of unwary Loyalists. Such acts of insolence had been considered deeply humiliating and insulting since the Middle Ages.[28]

When the Continental militias began to assemble, officers and soldiers fashioned their own uniforms according to their means. Many Continental soldiers went to war in their own homespun coats. Despite the variations in military style among the colonial officers, it would have been inconceivable for officers such as Charles Lee and Benjamin Lincoln to use anything other than British models for their own uniforms. Native American men joined the war effort on both the British and the American side and frequently served in uniforms that were characteristically hybrid combinations of Native costume and European dress. Comdr. Robert Rogers of the Queens American Rangers is shown in a contemporary engraving wearing a British uniform adorned with a Native American fringed sash.

On the eve of the American Revolution, the most fashionable gown seen on colonial women was a *sacque gown* adorned with an elegant drape at the back. Dresses with this feature were known as *robes à la française* for their origins in the French court. Rococo sensibility and its fascination with curves emerged in the serpentine trimmings and meandering floral patterns frequently found on the skirts of the sacque gowns.

Around 1780, at the height of the Revolution, a new English-inspired gown became popular. Dubbed the *robe à l'anglaise* in the French fashion magazines, this new form kept the open-fronted skirts and pointed bodice of previous decades, but the waistline was higher, and the long drape formerly falling from the shoulders was drawn back into the waistline, allowing the fullness of the back draping to emphasize the rear end.[29] To balance the fullness at the back, necklines were draped with large kerchiefs puffed out in front of the bosom. This fashion arrived on colonial shores unscathed despite British blockades of French imports. Moreover, it was especially popular in the British printed cottons that were rendered scarce by the American embargo of British goods. Fashion, it seems, was indifferent to politics.

For a time during the Revolution years, French taste again prevailed, as

General Charles Lee, 1780. Courtesy of the Library of Congress.

An etching of General Benjamin Lincoln, 1782. Courtesy of the Library of Congress.

An etching of Commander Robert Rogers, 1778.
Courtesy of the Library of Congress.

women's wigs grew to enormous heights, following yet another lead set by the French court. The tall wigs needed their own special hoods, called *calashes*. The many calashes that survive in American museums indicate the popularity of these towering hairstyles in colonial America. Powdering was also popular with young and old women alike.

By 1780, English influence again held sway, and women's hairstyles were reduced somewhat to a wide, frizzled arrangement that held up nicely the new broad-brimmed straw hats formerly associated only with workingwomen.

As the Revolutionary War drew to a close in 1783, a new and daring fashion was introduced by the queen of France. The *chemise dress*, as it was known, was a relatively unstructured gown by contemporary standards, being essentially a fancy shift that was cinched above the waist with a satin ribbon. It was so informal looking that conservative critics thought it looked like a nightgown. For others, the chemise dress's unstructured, more natural-looking form may have been part of its appeal.

To contemporary eyes, this new, less constricting shape brought the female costume silhouette one step closer to the lightly draped idealized statues of Roman goddesses that were emerging from the exciting new archaeological digs at the ancient Roman sites of Pompeii and Herculaneum. Eagerly acquired by both European and American collectors, these remnants of the Classical world deeply inspired eighteenth-century revolutionaries everywhere. For the newly independent American Republic, the Classical ideals embodied in these ancient artworks gave ready-made form to their republican ideals and aspirations. This fascination with all things Classical laid the foundation for the Empire style, the vastly different look that ushered out the turbulent eighteenth century.

DRESS AND THE NEW REPUBLIC

By 1785, the landscape of American dress had changed radically from the socially restrictive codes of dress observed by the early settlers. Most free Americans could dress as their inclinations and income allowed.

The American colonial world had enabled successful tradesmen like Paul Revere to earn enough wealth and self-regard to have their portraits painted, while still taking pride in the badges of their labor. In a portrait by John Singleton Copley, Revere chose to be depicted as a proud, hardworking artisan. Revere's smock is untied at the neck, and it has no lace or trimming. He hunches forward, his waistcoat unbuttoned, to contemplate the fruits of his labor. The nearby tools indicate that whatever wealth he possesses is due to his own handiwork.

FASHION DOLLS

French and English fashion illustrations were avidly consumed by colonists eager to remain up to date, but they weren't widely published or distributed until the later eighteenth century. Before that time, imported fashion dolls, dressed in the current mode, were the main source of detailed information about European fashion.

CHILDREN'S COSTUME, 1620–1785

From the beginnings of colonial America through the middle of the eighteenth century, many beliefs known to be erroneous today dictated the clothing worn by infants and children. It was thought, for instance, that extending their legs helped babies to grow straight and tall, so newborns in the colonies were straightened out and swaddled tightly in broad bands of linen called a *bed*. This was a practice shared by their Native American neighbors, who bound their newborns in moss-lined beds slung on their mother's backs.

From toddlerhood onward, colonial children were often dressed nearly identically to adults, as they were in Europe. Little girls wore the tightly laced stays that were expected to give them an erect posture. The daughters of Madame Riverin are depicted as tiny versions of herself, with identical costumes, while her son is dressed in the standard male attire of the period.

There were admittedly a few details that took into account the erratic and active behavior of these miniature adults: at the walking and crawling stage, toddlers often had sturdy ribbons, called *leading strings*, attached to the shoulders of their costumes. These kept adventurous little ones from wandering too far away and helped their bodice-bound mothers pick them up when the nursemaid wasn't around. Another protective device for toddlers just beginning to walk was the *pudding cap*, a padded design to protect the skull from tumbles and collisions with furniture.

With the 1762 publication of his famous treatise on childrearing, *Emile*, philosopher Jean-Jacques Rousseau turned centuries-old childrearing practices upside-down. Under Rousseau's influence, children were no longer viewed as simply untrained sinful adults in miniature, but as unformed beings, naïve and innocent, requiring mental and physical freedom to grow to their fullest potential. Cities and other "civilized" environments came to be seen as bad influences, capable of stunting a child's natural inquisitiveness and honesty.

Rousseau himself was influenced by the new concept of the "noble savage"—an idea whose seeds had been sown with the discovery of the New World. Rousseau and other Enlightenment thinkers eagerly read published accounts of Native American life and closely followed the fanfare that surrounded the visits made to Europe by Native American dignitaries. Rousseau and his fellow philosophers were intrigued by accounts of the tall stature and strapping builds of Native American men and women. Barring the diseases introduced from the Old World, Native children tended to be healthier, and they were treated with deep affection and indulgence by their parents, who let their toddlers freely run about unhampered by restrictive clothing.[30] Rousseau reasoned that if the godless natives, so close to nature themselves, could raise such healthy children, then perhaps the laws of nature had more to teach about childrearing than the laws of man or God.

In this new era of more sympathetic childrearing, both boys and girls were dressed in little loose dresses cinched around the chest by a wide sash. This garment allowed young children more freedom of movement. Unfortunately for modern students of costume, these unisex garments can make it a difficult to tell the difference between boys and girls in contemporary portraits. There are clues that sometimes reveal the gender of the sitter: Boys are commonly depicted with particular items such as toy guns or soldiers, whereas girls will often be depicted with their hair parted on the side and are sometimes accompanied by a basket of flowers or a doll. In addition, girls' dresses rarely had buttons on them, and they were sometimes depicted wearing an apron or bonnet.

Sometime between four and seven years old, boys graduated from their dress to pants. To accommodate their active play, they were sometimes dressed in a "skeleton suit," an outfit of long pants attached by buttons to a long-sleeved, short-waisted jacket worn over a white blouse. Skeleton suits first appeared in the last decades of the eighteenth century and remained popular well into the nineteenth.

CONCLUSION

While costume in the colonies closely reflected the fashions and styles worn all over Europe, gradually as the colonies developed their own set of rules and settled into a life reflective of the climate and environment, adaptations to dress occurred. This left a distinct record of clothing that is different in detail and sometimes purpose from fashions worn by both men and women in the Old Country.

Early in the colonial period, Spanish fashions gave way to fashion from France and England. These countries continued to hold influence throughout the first century and a half of colonization in the New World. With trade tightly controlled, drastic changes to fashion were discouraged, as raw materials were only shipped, not further refined for colonial use. Yarns and fabrics were not locally produced from the cotton grown in the South, and the beaver that was trapped in the Far North by the courreurs du bois was shipped to fashion markets in Europe, refined, and then shipped back at great expense.

Along with the independence sought with the American Revolution at the end of the eighteenth century, fashion changes were more local in flavor and allowed the now well-established colonials to express themselves through their clothing and make decisions that suited both the environmental climate as well as the political and social situations they lived with. American fashion never went back to the direct imitations that had first been attempted upon arrival in the New World, and American style became (and remains) unique and much copied throughout the world.

NOTES

1. Diana de Marly, *Dress in North America*, vol. 1, *The New World: 1492–1800* (New York: Holmes & Meier, 1990), 63–66.

2. Elisabeth McClellan, *History of American Costume, 1607–1870* (New York: Tudor, 1937), 46.

3. McClellan, *History of American Costume*, 45.

4. Alice Morse Earle, *Two Centuries of Costume in America, 1620–1820* (1903; reprint, New York: Dover, 1970), 1:113.

5. McClellan, *History of American Costume*, 104.

6. Earle, *Two Centuries of Costume*, 61.

7. As the colonies grew, coopers became valued tradesmen, since they filled the increasing demand for the large barrels or "hogsheads" in which the colonists shipped cod, tobacco, indigo, and furs back to England and the Continent.

8. McClellan, *History of American Costume*, 40.

9. Linda Baumgarten, *What Clothes Reveal: The Language of Clothing in Colonial and Federal America* (Williamsburg, VA: Colonial Williamsburg Foundation in association with Yale University Press, 2002), 138.

10. Laurel Thatcher Ulrich, *The Age of Homespun: Objects and Stories in the Creation of an American Myth* (New York: Vintage Books, 2001), 205.

11. Baumgarten, *What Clothes Reveal*, 135–37.

12. Earle, *Two Centuries of Costume*, 114.

13. Margaret Spufford, *The Great Reclothing of Rural England: Petty Chapmen and Their Wares in the Seventeenth Century* (London: Hambledon Press, 1984), 84–100.

14. Colonial Laws of Massachusetts, Sumptuary Laws, 1651.

15. Earle, *Two Centuries of Costume*, 182.

16. Earle, *Two Centuries of Costume*, 127; Ulrich, *Age of Homespun*, 45.

17. De Marly, *Dress in North America*, 21.

18. Gregory A. Waselkov, "Indian Maps of the Colonial Southeast," in *Powhatan's Mantle: Indians in the Colonial Southeast*, ed. Peter H. Wood, Gregory A. Waselkov, and M. Thomas Hatley (Lincoln: University of Nebraska, 1989), 337–35.

19. Ulrich, *Age of Homespun*, 55.

20. Ulrich, *Age of Homespun*,, p. 95

21. James Axtell, *The Invasion Within: The Contest of Cultures in Colonial North America* (New York: Oxford University Press, 1985), 309.

22. McClellan, *History of American Costume*, 104.

23. Debora E. Kraak, "Variations on 'Plainness': Quaker Dress in Eighteenth-Century Philadelphia," *Costume* 34 (2000): 56.

24. Kraak, "Variations on 'Plainness,'" 52.

25. De Marly, *Dress in North America*, 92–93.

26. De Marly, *Dress in North America*, 78.

27. See also John Smibert's "Bishop Berkeley and His Family" (c. 1729) and the portrait of Deborah Glen in the Abby Aldrich Rockefeller Art Center, Colonial Williamsburg, Virginia.

28. Earle, *Two Centuries of Costume*, 347–48.

29. Stella Blum, ed., *Eighteenth-Century French Fashions in Full Color: 64 Engravings from the "Galerie des Modes," 1778–1787* (New York: Dover, 1982), 43.

30. Axtell, *Invasion Within*, 307.

WEB RESOURCES

http://www.history.org/Foundation/journal/Winter03-04/clothing.cfm
http://www.worcesterart.org/Collection/American/1963.135.html
http://www.iht.com/articles/2007/05/04/arts/melik5.php
http://www.worcesterart.org/Collection/American/1963.134.html
http://www.brooklynmuseum.org/collections/american_art/42.45.php

FURTHER READING

Axtell, James. *The Invasion Within: The Contest of Cultures in Colonial North America.* New York: Oxford University Press, 1985.

Baumgarten, Linda. *What Clothes Reveal: The Language of Clothing on Colonial and Federal America.* New Haven & London: The Colonial Williamsburg Foundation in Association with Yale University Press, 2002.

Blum, Stella, ed. *Eighteenth Century French Fashions in Full Color: 64 Engravings from the "Galerie des Modes," 1778–1787.* New York: Dover Publications, Inc, 1982, p. 43.

De Marly, Diana. *Dress in North America: Vol 1: The New World: 1492–1800.* New York, London: Holmes & Meier, 1990.

Earle, Alice Morse. *Two Centuries of Costum in America 1620–1820.* Vol. 1. New York: Dover Edition, originally published Macmillan Co., 1903.

Kraak, Debora E. "Variations on 'Plainness'; Quaker Dress in Eighteenth Century Philadelphia." In *Costume, the Journal of the Costume Society*, 34, 2000.

McClellan, Elizbeth. *History of American Costume, 1607–1870.* New York: Tudor Publishing Company, 1937.

Spufford, Margaret. *The Great Reclothing of Rural England: Petty Chapmen and their Wares in the Seventeenth Century.* London: The Hambledon Press, 1984, pp. 84–100.

Ulrich, Laurel Thatcher. *The Age of Homespun: Objects and Stories in the Creation of An American Myth.* New York: Vintage Books, A Division of Random House, Inc, 2001.

Waselkov, Gregory A. "Indian Maps of the Colonial Southeast." In *Powhatan's Mantle: Indians in the Colonial Southeast*, edited by Peter H. Wood, Gregory A. Waselkov, and M. Thomas Hatley, pp. 292–343. University of Nebraska, 1989.

MOVIES

Amistad (1997)
Black Robe (1991)
Jefferson in Paris (1995)
Last of the Mohicans (1992)
The Patriot (2000)
Roots (1977)

Clothing in Edo Japan

Mary Pluckhahn Masilamani

TIMELINE

794–1185	Heian period
1185–1333	Kamakura period
1333–1573	Muromachi period
1573–1615	Momoyama period
1615–1868	Edo period
1688–1704	Genroku era
1868–1912	Meiji Restoration

The convergence of more than 250 years of political stability, economic growth, unprecedented urban affluence, inventive textile dyeing techniques, and artistic creativity produced the beautiful *kosode* of Edo-period (1615–1868) Japan. Named for their narrow wrist openings, these exquisite garments are not merely fashionable clothing. They are true works of art and were recognized as such by their owners and by succeeding generations who carefully preserved some of the most exceptional kosode of the time. The Edo-period kosode is the culmination of centuries of changes in the basic clothing of the Japanese elite. During the Edo period, the kosode was the basic garment of all women, men, and children of all classes in Japan's strictly segmented society. Kosode communicated the wearer's class, wealth, aesthetic sensibility, awareness of fashion trends, and knowledge of classical Japanese culture to the inhabitants of the often-brash and exuberant society that was Edo Japan. The urban style of the time was unfailingly the newest, the best, and the most fashionable, and the rest of the land was quick to adopt whatever was the latest favorite in Edo, the new capital city that is now called Tokyo.

To fully comprehend the clothing of the period, it is necessary to appreciate the environment in which the Edo-style kosode developed. Because the Edo period began almost four centuries ago, it is essential to understand the sources of clothing information used to study this form of dress. Looking at the origins and inspirations for clothing worn by the elite of the period helps place the garments in context.

Clothing of the wealthy *chōnin*, the townsmen, was new and daring. The styles they wore existed within an isolated and controlled society politically dominated by the military elite. In spite of the many restrictions, fashions and fashion setters constantly evolved during the period. In contrast to the varied fashions of the townsmen, clothing worn by the nobility remained conservative. The clothing of military families varied more than that of the nobility but never achieved the innovation or importance of the clothing of the leading chōnin.

Before examining the fashions of Edo-period Japan, we must be familiar with the basic universal garment of the period, the kosode.

THE KOSODE: CONSTRUCTION AND MEANINGS

The *kosode* of Edo Japan was almost identical to its descendent, the current Japanese *kimono*. Through time there have been slight but significant changes in details such as body length, sleeve length, and the width of the fabric used to create the garment. The name *kosode* ("small sleeve") was used until the end of the Edo period, when it was replaced by *kimono* ("thing to wear").

Like the kimono, the kosode made very economical use of a narrow woven length of fabric. It consisted of two long panels of cloth that formed the front and back of the body of the garment. They were joined with a narrow center-back seam and had no shoulder seams. Two sleeves each—like the body panels, cut from the full width of the fabric—were joined to the body. The front opening of the kosode had a neckband and two pieces for front overlaps and bands. The kosode was always worn with the left side lapped on top of the right side. It had no fastenings and was held in place with an *obi* (waist wrap or sash). The elegance of the garment came not from its shape or structure, but from the skillful selection of colors, themes, and designs and the suitability of the complete costume for each occasion.

Kosode sleeve choices indicated the wearer's age and position in society. Custom dictated that the swinging *furisode* sleeves of a kosode should be worn only by a young, unmarried woman. These sleeves hung free of the body of the kosode, and their length increased during the Edo period. At marriage, a woman would shorten her sleeves. As she aged, she wore clothing with more subdued colors and less conspicuous patterns. *Osode* (sleeves with a wide wrist opening) were part of a stiff, wide garment that was part of formal court wear and were worn only by the most aristocratic members of society.

TRACING EDO FASHIONS: KOSODE, HINAGATA-BON, UKIYO-E

The best way to understand clothing history is to look at examples of actual garments. Although few items of Japanese clothing have survived from before the last quarter of the seventeenth century, a number of garments worn by the elite of Edo society were preserved. Many of these were associated with major events in the owner's life. Some of these surviving garments were carefully preserved by generations of imperial and *samurai* families, and most of these were articles of clothing that belonged to men. Frequently the garments were received as gifts from military or noble superiors. These gifts were recorded in family records. Unlike women's clothing, men's garments were less likely to be reworked into other styles.

Partly because of the relatively low status of even the highest ranking Japanese women, women's garments were less likely to be kept as treasured mementos. Women's clothes were more likely to be reworked into styles more suited to the wearer's age and status in life or simply put away because their shapes or colors were no longer suitable. Many of the women's garments that have survived intact were kosode that were donated to temples at the owners' death in return for prayers to smooth the route to salvation. Kosode given to temples were usually marked with the owner's name and date of death. Unfortunately, the date inscribed in the garments is not an accurate record of the person's age; the donated kosode might have been a garment that an elderly owner wore in her youth. Many donated kosode were cut apart and reassembled into altar cloths, temple banners, and robes for temple priests.

Written and printed records of Edo garments are another major source for information about the fashions of the time. In addition to brief descriptions in literature, a number of published design books (*hinagata-bon*), the equivalent of fashion magazines for the style-conscious women of the time, have survived. The first of about 120 surviving hinagata titles appeared in 1666; the last volume was issued in 1820. By then, designs for kosode were standardized and no longer the vibrant, dynamic creations of the best of Edo clothing.

Initially the design books merely contained verbal descriptions of garments. As kosode designs became more elaborate, each garment was illustrated with a simple outlined view of the garment. Text suggested the color and dyeing techniques to be used for the garment and often also gave suggestions about the suitability of the garment for women of different ages. Some surviving garments can be matched to hinagata illustrations that may have inspired their creation.

The arrangement of the illustrations in the books varies. Some include garments arranged by the age and social standing of the potential wearer. Others are organized by the wearer's occupation. At least one example is divided into categories designated for occupations of the pleasure quarter, including clothing for the top courtesans, lower-ranked courtesans, and other denizens of the floating world such as the girls who worked in the bathhouses and young male prostitutes. Changing designs in the hinagata-bon help the historian trace changes in Edo fashion through time.

Another invaluable resource is the surviving order books of the Kariganeya dry goods dealers based in Kyoto. Their order books have drawings of nearly five hundred garments ordered by its customers between 1661 and 1678. Although it was not designated as an official supplier to either the imperial palace or the shogunate, Kariganeya supplied clothing to leading members of both households. Dated sketches and dyeing instructions tell us what women of the highest classes chose to wear at the time.

Later members of the family that ran Kariganeya included some of the leading artists of Edo-period Japan. Among them was Ogata Kōrin, a leading artist of the *rimpa* style of painting. Because Japan does not make a distinction between fine arts and crafts, textile design and designs for kosode were frequently created by artists like Kōrin, who painted the lovely balanced autumn flowers and grasses on the kosode. Kōrin is best known for his paintings and painted screens but, like most leading artists of the time, he also created calligraphy and ceramics in addition to this refined kosode.

Paintings and *ukiyo-e* (woodblock prints of the pleasure quarter) also help us understand the clothing worn in Edo-period Japan. These items are useful because they have been preserved in large numbers, they show people from all levels of society, dates based on artistic style can relatively easily be assigned to them, and the pictures represent clothing as it was actually worn by individuals. Starting around 1660, after the great fire that destroyed much of Edo, woodblock prints of stylish inhabitants of the floating world helped people all over Edo Japan keep up with the rapidly changing fashions of the period. Beautiful courtesans and favorite kabuki theater performers were popular images for the residents of Edo's urban centers. A favorite subject of the woodblock prints of the pleasure quarter were series of prints of beautiful women. These subjects tended to be erotic and sensual, not individual likenesses. They represented idealized types of women.

The early polychrome woodblock print made by Suzuki Harunobu (c. 1724–1770) in 1760 shows a fashionable woman taking a walk accompanied by two young attendants. The fashionable woman has a large, elaborate knot tied in the front of her obi. The artist was the first to make multicolored prints called "brocade prints." He is also known for his rather dreamlike depictions of women, all with very similar facial expressions.

At the same time, many paintings and prints are not the most reliable of sources for costume history for the period. Many of the illustrations look stylized and flat. Although detailed textile patterns are included in many paintings, the artists often seemed to be unfamiliar with textile dyeing techniques. Some artists took liberties with the types of patterns actually used on kosode. Patterns produced by weaving techniques sometimes replace representations of the elaborate dyeing techniques used for Edo clothing. Other paintings or prints show women wearing overly elaborate designs more suitable for theater costumes than for even the most flamboyant courtesan. Designs often cross-draped portions of the garment, ignoring the irregularities caused by folds in the fabric.

Some of the most useful Japanese artwork from this period is the genre scenes favored by the newly affluent townsmen. Unlike Japanese genre paintings of court activities from before the sixteenth century, the ones from the Edo period feature commoners going about their daily activities. For example, Katsushika Hokusai (1760–1849) included many commoners in his series of prints called *Thirty-six Views of Mount Fuji*. In "Nakahara in Sagami Province," the foreground shows a pilgrim traveling to or from a popular nearby shrine, a peasant woman carrying her baby on her back, a fashionable young man traveling with his servant, a fisherman, and a laborer carrying a heavy load on a long pole across his shoulders. Both the location and the individuals would immediately be familiar to chōnin from nearby Edo.

This style of design even appeared on garments like one early-nineteenth-century kosode, patterned with the stages of rice cultivation. Genre scenes are especially useful for examples of clothing worn by people who were not members of the most elite circles of Edo society. These kosode and other garments, the books that elite women all over Japan pored over when selecting new garments, order books recording the choices the women, prints, and paintings all help to reconstruct the clothing worn in Edo-period Japan.

KOSODE ORIGINS

The kosode has a long history in Japan. Like many aspects of Japanese culture, the kosode developed from models derived from China, Japan's neighbor to the west. Throughout its history, Japan repeatedly and selectively adopted new ideas and products from both China and Korea. This borrowing had long-lasting effects on Japanese society.

By the seventh century, Japanese court dress was closely based on contemporary Chinese styles. Both men and women wore similarly styled clothing: an upper body garment and a skirtlike garment from the waist down. Men wore the round-necked *agekubi*, which was derived from northern Chinese garments, and women wore the wrapped-front *tarikubi*. The tarikubi was derived from southern Chinese clothing and is a likely ancestor of the kosode. Underneath the outer skirt, men wore trousers and women wore a second skirt, the *mo*.

Two hundred years later, during the Heian period (794–1185) in a period of relative isolation, what is now known as classical Japanese culture developed. At the same time, formal Japanese court garments were established, and the kosode became the innermost garment of the aristocracy. The kosode was made of white silk in either a plain or twill weave. Women topped the kosode with multiple layers of additional garments in the *kasane shōzoku* style. Some women wore as many as twenty layers made of hundreds of yards of silk fabric. Such excesses led eleventh-century officials to restrict court wear to five layers, the standard that persisted through the Edo period for the most formal court occasions.

The fabric used for these robes was silk with small-scale, allover patterns that were woven into or embroidered onto the fabric. Noblewomen selected their clothing colors carefully. The ability to coordinate the layers of an ensemble communicated the wearer's sense of subtle aesthetics through both prescribed color families and classical allusions. Lucky individuals received special permission to wear particular colors as an esteemed award.

Simultaneously during the Heian period, commoners also wore kosode made of various bast fibers, but as their daily clothing, not just as inner garments like the nobility. Commoners were not allowed to wear silk, and the patterns on their kosode were also carefully restricted.

During succeeding periods, clothing styles changed slowly. The military class, the *samurai*, and their elite military leaders, the *daimyō*, became increasingly prominent. In the Kamakura period (1185–1333), the wives of the military elite set a new style for everyday wear. They tucked their kosode into their *hakama* trousers. This style of dress was less restrictive and was well suited for their serious and active lifestyle in a time characterized by simplicity and austerity. Women of the imperial court also adopted this style of dress for everyday wear, while the most formal court clothing continued to be very conservative.

TRANSITION TO THE EDO PERIOD

Less than a century after the end of the Kamakura period, Japan entered a period of intense political instability and unrest. During the Muromachi period (1333–1573), the social and economic changes that eventually led to the intense urban culture and artistic flowering that characterize the Edo period began. The central government was weak, class boundaries became less rigid, and the chōnin, the lowest class in the Japanese hierarchy, began to assert themselves through formations of guilds. The imperial court and religious centers were no longer the only patrons of the arts.

Clothing for the elite became less elaborate. By the end of the fifteenth century, the kosode was the main outer garment for men and women of all classes of Japanese society. Demands for both imported and domestic silk fabrics woven in patterned designs increased. A new, uniquely Japanese dyeing technique, *tsujigahana*, appeared, possibly at least partially in response to this increased demand for silk textiles. Although the dyeing techniques used in Japan sound extraordinarily complex and luxurious today, at the time dyeing was generally considered a less prestigious patterning technique than either woven designs or allover embroidered patterns.

Tsujigahana dyeing is characterized by use of a combination of patterning techniques, including two types of *shibori* (resist dyeing employing various clamping, stitching, and tying methods): *nuishime*, which uses a running stitch to create the resist, and *kanoko* (fawn spot), shibori created by tying off small square or round pinches of fabric before dyeing. *Shibori* is often translated into English as "tie-dye," a phrase that is reminiscent of gaudy hippie T-shirts from the 1960s, but this is too simple a concept to represent the complex, varied, time-consuming, and expensive dyeing method practiced in Japan. Shibori had a long history in the country but only became truly popular when it was used as part of the tsujigahana technique. Kanoko shibori was especially popular in the Edo period and eventually was restricted by sumptuary regulations.

Tsujigahana also employs *kaki-e* (painting), *haku* (application of metallic leaf), and *nui* (embroidery). Embroidery, used in Japan as early as the seventh century, was prized for its ability to embellish textiles and garments with designs that traveled across surfaces, moving independent of the restriction of the warp and weft of woven designs. Tsujigahana was done on a thin, lightweight, plainweave silk that allowed very clear, sharply defined, small designs. The distinctive combination of dyeing methods persisted through the succeeding Momoyama period (1573–1615) into the Edo period.

The Momoyama period was a period of consolidation of military and political power. Military designs, such as the arrow feather border in a man's short *dōbuku* jacket patterns, became more common in clothing. People from rural areas moved into Kyoto and Osaka, Japan's urban centers, where they became artists and merchants. Luxurious clothing began to cater more to the taste of the warrior and merchant classes, as these markets became more important to dry goods purveyors. A new type of woman appeared in sixteenth-century Japan, the *asobime* (playgirl), who has been described as stylish or fashionable and as a courtesan. These women were the first to wear their hair up in the Chinese style, and they wore their kosode with a narrow *nagoya* obi cord wrapped several times around their hips. In addition to all of their other embellishments, tsujigahana-dyed kosode were enhanced with fine lines drawn in ink. All of these changes during the Momoyama period hinted at the great social upheaval to come during the Edo period.

STRUCTURE AND CONTROL IN EDO-PERIOD JAPAN

At the end of the Momoyama period in 1615, Japan had a single military leader, Tokugawa Ieyasu, the first Tokugawa *shōgun* (literally the "general who quells barbarians") at the head of the *bakufu*, the military bureaucracy that controlled the country. Edo was his provincial headquarters from 1590. When Ieyasu became shogun in 1603, previously insignificant Edo became the capital of Japan. At the same time, Kyoto, the imperial city, remained the center for the most exquisite craftsmanship, and Osaka was the center for trade and commerce. The scene was set for the artistic triumph that was Edo-period Japan.

By the 1630s, the shogunate, always concerned about losing control of the population, instituted strict policies restricting international travel by Japanese citizens and limiting foreign access to the country. Although not a complete prohibition of foreign contact, the restrictions did tend to isolate the general population of the country from outside influences. During the same period, the shogunate introduced an alternate-year residency program for the daimyō, the elite samurai leaders. These leaders were required to spend one year in residence in Edo and one year at their provincial headquarters. When the daimyō were away, their wives and families remained in Edo as comfortably housed hostages of the shogunate, ensuring that their spouses remained loyal to the central authority. The complexly scheduled annual trips to and from the capital were the second highest single expense in the daimyō's budget. A bit more than a century after Edo became Japan's capital, the city had become one of the largest cities in the world with more than one million residents.

The shogunate enforced a strict, inflexible, four-class system. The samurai were the highest class, followed by agriculturists, artisans, and finally merchants. The artisans and merchants together made up the chōnin, the townsmen, who, in spite of Tokugawa efforts to control their behavior, became the fashion leaders of Edo society. Certain segments of society were not part of the class system. The imperial family and the aristocracy, Shinto and Buddhist priests, medical doctors, and some teachers were not included. People who practiced certain disreputable professions, including acting, prostitution, leather working, and grave digging, were also outside the class system.

Japan during the Tokugawa shogunate became an urban, cash-based society. In spite of their high social standing, samurai often had financial difficulties in the Edo period. Most taxes were paid in bales of rice, but the samurai needed cash for the majority of their purchases—and during the Edo period, most of the available cash was in the hands of the townsmen and the agriculturists. Lower-order samurai often found themselves in debt to merchants and, on occasion, merchants lost large amounts of money through loans that were never repaid by the military class. As the Edo period progressed, many samurai could no longer afford to spend lavishly on new clothing styles.

The chōnin, especially the leading merchants, could and did spend heavily on clothing and artwork during the Edo period. The strict class system kept merchants, especially those from the wealthiest families, from spending money to enhance their political and social roles. Instead, they reinvested in the family business or spent on the entertainments of the pleasure quarter and on an unending stream of lovely art objects, including beautiful clothing carefully selected from the latest fashions of the day. Even the household staff of the wealthiest chōnin wore elaborate garments made of fine textiles enhanced with embroidery, woven patterns, and appliqué work, in a further demonstration of their master's affluence and taste. Fashion and style in Edo Japan reflected the economic power of the chōnin. Meanwhile, the conservative imperial court at Kyoto remained the center for classical Japanese culture. The leading samurai were torn between the urban styles of the elite among the chōnin and the respected, conservative imperial style.

CULTURE AND BEAUTY IN THE FLOATING WORLD

The famous pleasure quarters of Edo, Kyoto, and Osaka were the only places where the strict class system of the shogunate was ignored. A man's status in the *ukiyo* ("floating world") was based on his ability to pay, not his position in the class system. By about 1660, wealthy merchants had replaced samurai as the area's chief patrons. The activities of the floating world were confined to a section of the city enclosed by a wall with a single gateway. Visitors to the pleasure quarter found teahouses, public baths, theaters, brothels, and other diversions. Outside of the floating world, the pressures of family and society weighed heavily; inside its boundaries, visitors were free to play and enjoy themselves.

Visitors to the ukiyo were eager to demonstrate their knowledge and understanding of traditional classical Japanese culture. They aspired to the ideal of the cultivated amateur. At the same time, they were careful to present their finely trained taste in a subtle and refined manner. Cultured men, no matter what their class background, gathered as equals for a pleasurable, stimulating evening that perhaps ended with a sexual liaison with one of the great beauties of the pleasure quarter.

Leading courtesans were not simply beautiful, well-dressed sex workers. They were experts at cultured pursuits like the tea ceremony, flower arranging, poetry, and calligraphy. They were entertaining conversationalists, as well. Their customers included both wealthy individuals and the leading artists, craftsmen, authors, and poets of the time. Men who had relationships with leading courtesans followed customary rules for such encounters. The distinguished Edo man-about-town needed to demonstrate his ability to dress correctly for every meeting and occasion. The courtesans were not the only desirable creatures in the floating world. *Onnagata*, the beautiful young men who played lovely courtesans in popular kabuki plays, were also sex objects for many visitors to the ukiyo.

The aesthetics of the cultured visitor to the ukiyo made no distinction between fine art and fine craftsmanship. The effort expended on the creation of a fine garment was as highly valued as any other artistic endeavor. All of the decorative arts were closely intertwined during the Edo period. Artists rarely worked on a single type of project. Those who painted scrolls also designed kosode and decorated ceramics.

Calligraphy, a long-respected art form in Japan, was frequently used as part of kosode design. The literate resident of Edo would immediately recognize the characters and most likely be amused by the clever interplay of language and design. The characters that appear on garments frequently copied the style of highly appreciated calligraphers of the period. Kosode could feature wordplay, rebuses, and puns, all to the amusement of both the wearer and the observer.

The proper garment for a special occasion contributed to the overall experience of the event. The total experience was important to the cultured person's enjoyment of the occasion. Designs used for kosode referred to seasons of the year, literary passages, and poetry. These references were always subtle and nuanced, simultaneously displaying the wearer's refinement and the observer's ability to recognize the intent of the garment. Artistic effect was communicated by resonances, not by crude or blatant statements that, if they occurred, were unfailingly considered improper and uncouth.

The Japanese appreciation of restrained, subtle motifs has a long history dating back to classical concepts of refined taste suitable for the imperial court from the Heian period. Throughout Japanese history, naturalistic depictions were preferred. Irregularity and asymmetry were appreciated. Perishability and impermanence were frequent themes. Observers were charmed and fascinated by shifting shadows and light. Ideally an object would always be able to change and alter. The garments that illustrate this chapter are beautiful as depicted here, but all of them were meant to be animated by a living person. This clothing was designed to be in motion, continually exhibiting the subtle, changing character so valued by the aesthetics of the period.

By contrast, and perhaps in reaction to so much restraint and refinement, designs of the Edo period sometimes exhibited extreme brashness. Designs could be boldly graphic. Kosode could be flamboyant and over-the-top. Sometimes the playfulness that characterized the pleasure quarter also appeared in the clothing of the day.

TRANSITION INTO EDO-STYLE KOSODE

Early Edo kosode were in the *Keichō* style, which developed late in the Momoyama period and continued well into the seventeenth century. Favorite new designs of the period were dyed with dark colors in zones or bands of color, Early Edo period kosode were sometimes made with tsujigahana patterning. They were often heavily decorated with gold leaf of especially high quality and fine embroidery in delicate patterns of cherry blossoms, clouds, waves, and geometric designs. The *surihaku* (gold leaf) patterns were small, repeat patterns that were derived from the woven repeat patterns associated with court robes since the Heian period.

The Momoyama period dobuku jacket, also dyed using the tsujigahana technique, is said to be part of a gift from the great military leader and unifier of the Momoyama period, Toyotomi Hideyoshi (1536–1598), to Nanbu Nobunao in 1590. The three-part pattern is a graphic example of tsujigahana at its best. The entire garment was dyed using only shibori techniques. No additional painting, embroidery, or metallic leaf enhances this garment.

Earlier tsujigahana kosode were colored in paler colors. The background colors were divided into abstract shapes or zones by fine rows of shibori. Through time, the background of the kosode fabric was increasingly left unpatterned, anticipating later kosode styles. Embroidery tended to be done on a relatively small scale, with short stitches in designs that were relatively delicate.

Rinzu (figured monochrome silk) replaced the plainweave *nerinuki* silk first used for tsujigahana kosode. Nerinuki silk, with its warp threads made of unglossed silk (with its sericin left in) and its wefts of glossed silk (with its sericin removed) was a relatively stiff fabric. Garments made from nerinuki were therefore less pliable and tended to stand away from the wearer's body. Nerinuki continued to be used for *koshimaki*, summer robes, where its crisp quality helped keep the aristocratic wearer cool in Japan's intense heat and humidity.

Made completely of glossed silk, rinzu was a softer, more supple material well suited to dyeing with various shibori techniques. Textured rinzu was not a good base for surihaku with its stenciled adhesives and applied gold leaf. Gradually, couched embroidery with restrained application of metallic threads replaced surihaku work on most luxurious clothing. Similarly, fine lines of embroidery replaced the ink drawing used in some tsujigahana designs. It was difficult to apply ink accurately on the patterned rinzu. Surihaku continued to be used on lavish costumes for *Nō* theater plays, where its reflective quality and glamour were assets.

The new textiles also encouraged new designs more suitable to the softer, flowing fabrics. Clothing of the elite of the early Edo period began to move more with the wearer's body. Carefully executed rows of white "fawn spots" of kanoko shibori, each with a tiny central dot of the ground color, became the preferred resist technique for patterning expensive garments, replacing the thread resist lines of nuishime shibori.

KANBUN STYLE AND FASHION SETTERS

During the first sixty or so years of the seventeenth century, designs on kosode changed. They became asymmetrical and often reached diagonally from one shoulder to the opposite hem. The wearer's body animated the garment that was draped around it. Negative space became a significant design element. Designs were often large and graphic. The entire garment became a single, unified design field. Undoubtedly the skills of the dyers of Edo were constantly challenged by the need to make kosode designs match perfectly once the lengths of dyed fabric were cut apart and assembled into finished garments. All of their complex, flowing patterns had to align perfectly at each seam and between the body and the hanging sleeves of furisode.

The Keichō kosode became passé, and the Kanbun style was born. Bold patterns, such as drying fishnets, were used in a sweeping pattern across the wearer's shoulders and down the right arm and right side of the garment. Garments were patterned with *nuishime, kanoko,* and *mokume* (woodgrain-patterned) shibori. Through time, the colors used for Kanbun garments became lighter and brighter. Patterns slowly covered the negative space of the garments, gradually filling in the entire body of the kosode. Patterns popular with the chōnin included familiar objects like musical instruments, books, fans, and other man-made items like the dramatic fishnets of the garment.

The portrait of Lodovica Tornabuoni inside this religious painting depicts her wearing a rich giornea; in her hands is a fringed linen handkerchief, an accessory that was just beginning to become a status symbol. © Scala / Art Resource, NY.

The detail shows the gathered and ruffled over-sleeves called "baragoni," but also the elaborate camisa, the simple jewels and the black detachable sleeves slashed by decorative cuts. The beads on the belt probably kept aromatic paste. © Scala / Art Resource, NY.

The two central figures of the painting are wearing the despised short farsettini that left the underwear in plain view, while at the sides the men watching the game are wearing giornee and mazzocchi on the head. © Erich Lessing / Art Resource, NY.

The hair is parted in the middle; the masculine look is confirmed by the beard and moustaches. His giubbone reaches the waist, where it joins the puffed braghe; the codpiece is made in two different colours. The outfit is completed by the black vesta worn open on the front. The most evident character is the fabric used to sew the outfit; a stratagliato slashed in a random fashion that lets the underneath fabric show. © Erich Lessing / Art Resource, NY.

This noble warrior shows a rather short haircut, the characteristic Renaissance beard, and is wearing body armor rounded at the chest, paired with a rather thin waistline. The armor is embellished by a striped decoration and completed by a helmet, while the lower part of the armor is missing and underneath are clearly visible the usual braghe with the coordinated braghetta, the scandalous codpiece that soon become the object of severe criticism by ladies and preachers. © Scala / Art Resource, NY.

F. Barocci, Federigo, duke of Urbino, swaddled in typically ornate Renaissance fabrics. © Nimatallah / Art Resource, NY.

The children all wear miniaturized replicas of the adults' outfits; the boys especially wear pointed giubboni and puffy brache alla sivigliana, the Spanish–style pants made with stratagliati fabrics, garments that give away the provincial origin of the family (they came from Bergamo, where clothes were more strongly influenced by Spanish fashions than in Venice). © Erich Lessing / Art Resource, NY.

Portrait of Henry VIII in typical Northern Renaissance doublet and jerkin with puffed, slashed, and ornately decorated sleeve. His hat is adorned with a feather. Courtesy of the Library of Congress.

"Las Meninas," Diego Rodriguez Velázquez, 1656, shows typical Italian Renaissance children's clothing, which was generally in the same style as adult clothing, only in minature. © Scala / Art Resource, NY.

Elaborate seventeenth-century jacket made with linen and silk, c. 1616, paired with a full, structured skirt. © The Metropolitan Museum of Art / Art Resource, NY.

"Nakahara in Sagami Province" from *Thirty-Six Views of Mount Fuji*, Katsushika Hokusai, ca. 1830–1832, shows various styles of Japanese dress. © Victoria & Albert Museum, London / Art Resource, NY.

A lady holding a flower wears Indian dress, eighteenth century. © Victoria & Albert Museum, London / Art Resource, NY.

"The Maya chief Zingari presents his sister to Hernan Cortes." A variety of colonial and native Latin American dress styles can be seen. © Erich Lessing / Art Resource, NY.

High-ranking woman of the Inca culture around the time of the Spanish colonization. The borders of her dress and mantle show the geometric symbols some scholars believe convey specific information about rank and lineage. Courtesy of Karrie Porter Brace.

"La Marquise Visconti" is wearing an
eighteenth-century dress of the empire style.
© Erich Lessing / Art Resource, NY.

"The Baillie Family," by Thomas Gainsborough, c. 1784, shows typical late-eighteenth
century dress for women, men, and children. © Tate, London / Art Resource, NY.

These new patterns indicated that the wealthy merchants were well on their way to becoming the main patrons of the leading courtesans of the pleasure quarter. Fashion no longer led the lower classes to emulate the clothing of the upper classes. By the middle of the seventeenth century, the origin of fashion in Japan changed: The chōnin set the styles, and the styles they embraced changed constantly. By the end of the century, an instruction manual for women noted that clothing designs rose to prominence and became outdated in as little as five years.

Their choices were often inspired by the high-class courtesans and actors of the floating world who were pictured in prints and paintings. Outcasts of the strict Tokugawa class system became the ideal for respectable women. Individual courtesans and onnagata from the kabuki theater became so well known that their names were immediately recognizable outside of the pleasure quarter, rather like the names of leading performers and models today. As shown in the woodblock prints that chronicle the pleasure quarter, for the only time in Japanese art history, it was sometimes difficult to tell males and females apart. Especially during the Genroku era (1688–1704), sexual identity in the floating world was not always obvious, at least to the twenty-first-century eye. At the time, both sexes sometimes adopted fashions from the opposite sex. Fashionable male actors who performed female roles set styles for chōnin women.

Kabuki performers, also frequent subjects of woodblock prints, were popular favorites. Kabuki was a popular floating world entertainment form that developed from vaudeville-like entertainment into theater during the seventeenth century. Performances lasted all day. Wealthy audience members used the theater as a venue to display their fashionable taste. By the last quarter of the century, rich theatergoers regularly left the kabuki theater several times during the performance; each time they returned from the retiring rooms at the local teahouse, they sported new outfits for the examination and enjoyment of their fellow attendees.

The shogunate repeatedly restricted kabuki and its performers, but the form was too popular with the public to ever be completely eliminated. Kabuki costumes and their wearers were often emulated. Fans adopted motifs from clothing worn by favorite performers and wore new obi knots named for the performers who first wore them. Dye masters, designers, and performers collaborated on new colors, dyeing techniques, and patterns. Performers displayed design innovations on stage in costumes that immediately inspired the audience to order outfits like those of their favorite star. New colors were named for the actors who first wore them. A dark, yellow-brown color was named *rokōcha* after a favorite male performer of female roles. The color was in vogue from 1766 until the middle of the next century. Chōnin color preferences both influenced kabuki costumes and were, in turn, shaped by the costumes. During the eighteenth century, costumes were often in rather dull, grayed shades of greens, browns, and similar hues. Gray itself was not used, because it had a negative connotation—it meant "rat," a dirty, unsavory animal. Female characters, the onnagatas' forte, wore touches of red.

In any case, the hinagata-bon and woodblock prints of these famous individuals informed the merchant class about the newest styles of the period. Young men, whether dandies or tough characters, wore the latest kosode style tucked into their hakama trousers for a night on the town. Rich townsmen constantly balanced their family and business needs against their yearning for the playful, sensual, and intellectual pleasures of the floating world.

Women of the merchant class did not limit their purchases of new kosode to selections for special occasions like spring cherry blossom viewings and outings to view the beautiful colors of maple trees in autumn. Many of the expensive garments they purchased were so elaborate that they looked like they were meant for important events and not simply for daily wear. As noted Edo-period novelist Ihara Saikaku (1642–1693) observed, not only prostitutes but also high-ranking individuals and wives of commoners wore increasingly ostentatious clothing during the seventeenth century. Some observers complained that respectable women followed fashion so slavishly that it was impossible to recognize the difference between them and prostitutes. Occasionally merchant families were actually driven to bankruptcy by the high cost of garment purchases.

GENROKU-ERA FASHIONS AND SUMPTUARY LAWS

Influences from the floating world may account for some of the boldest Edo patterns. Denizens of the ukiyo often needed to be recognized easily at a distance and therefore wore flamboyantly patterned garments. In any case, the new cultural elite of urban Japan followed a concept of fashion and beauty that was evoked by their perception of stylized images of beauties of the floating world. Designs in the Genroku era had strong patterns featuring chrysanthemum flowers; an intense, dark, geometric, netlike design created by kanoko shibori; and heavy use of metallic embroidery and would be difficult to miss in a crowd. In addition to exhibiting the wearer's wealth, such as kosode indicated its owner's familiarity with Japanese culture. Blossoms subtly referred to a literary theme: the story of Kikujidō, the Chrysanthemum Boy who drank dew from the flowers' petals and became immortal.

Just before the turn of the eighteenth century, women's kosode proportions resembled those of more modern garments. Bodies were narrowed and longer. The swinging sleeve of the younger woman's furisode style became distinctly longer. Fabric used to make kosode changed in width and length to accommodate the changing proportions of the garment without wasting expensive fabric. The woman's obi, like the kosode a carefully selected fashion item, reached six to seven inches (15–18 cm) in width.

Just before the beginning of the Genroku era, the Tokugawa shogunate made one of its repeated attempts to restrain the chōnin. Sumptuary rules and regulations were not new in Japan. Before the Edo period, restrictions had limited use of silk and selected colors to particular ranks of the population. The shogunate instituted sumptuary laws that restricted styles, dyeing methods, and colors of clothing. However, the authorities' attempts at control were often futile. The laws were erratically enforced; often they were ignored by the shogunate, but sometimes they were enforced extraordinarily harshly. As an example for other chōnin, a man named Ishikawa Rokubei was banished and all of his property was confiscated as punishment after his wife and her attendants were charged with wearing exceedingly flashy clothing in public.

In 1682 and 1683, early in the shogunate of the conservative fifth Tokugawa leader Tokugawa Tsunayoshi (R. 1680–1709), seven laws that placed restrictions

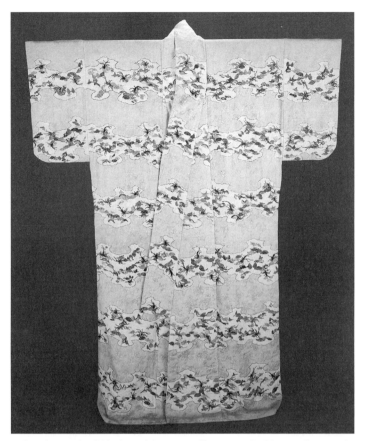

Embroidery and gold leaf on plain-weave silk patterned with warp floats, early seventeenth century. © The Metropolitan Museum of Art / Art Resource, NY.

on clothing were issued. These included controls on the use of gold thread embroidery, gaudy-colored silk embroidery, and kanoko (fawn spot) shibori. The target of these laws was the perceived excesses of the height of the exuberantly patterned Genroku kosode. Tsunayoshi issued a total of fifty-nine sumptuary laws during his administration.

The laws were frequently ignored or circumvented by the invention of new dyeing techniques. Kanoko shibori was simulated with the *kata kanoko* technique, in which a stencil and paste resist were used to make a pattern similar to that of true kanoko. The stencil created a small, even pattern of fine lines of white spots, and frequently the central dots of the dye color characteristic of true kanoko were added by hand after the resist was removed. However, kata kanoko lacked the pleasing and prized texture created by the many tiny knots used in true kanoko shibori.

Dyers also found new methods to produce restricted colors. Purple dye was prized, costly, restricted, and produced by new methods during the Edo period. New shades of red replaced the favored and restricted scarlet red produced by petals of the safflower plant. Fashion also changed to accommodate sumptuary laws.

The restricted kanoko shibori technique was extremely expensive and time-consuming to create. Some surviving kosode are patterned completely in kanoko with extraordinarily even patterns of dots on a dyed field. Saikaku describes similar garments in a novel he wrote in the last quarter of the seventeenth century. The uchikake was a formal outer kosode worn unbelted. It was patterned, often with motifs such as bands of flying cranes across the center of the body and the lower portion of its swinging furisode-style sleeves. The ground color of the upper and lower fawn-spotted sections is red, and the bands with the cranes are on light brown. This uchikake is a luxurious garment that required months of skilled work to complete.

YŪZEN-ZOME

Around the time of the sumptuary laws of the early 1680s, a new dyeing technique allowed creation of dramatic new kosode designs. The technique was perfected by painter Miyazaki Yūzen, whose name is used for the method. *Yūzen-zome* (resist dyeing in the style of Yūzen) appeared at a time when the chōnin eagerly sought out new styles that would not violate the sumptuary laws.

Like shibori, yūzen is a resist-dyeing technique. The exact methods used for early yūzen dyeing have been lost, but the process began with the application of a paste resist used to outline design areas. Dyes were brushed onto the areas delineated by the resist, the textile was washed to remove the resist, and the fabric was processed to set the colors. The resist left a distinctive fine white undyed line separating the various painted areas. Additional enhancements as required by the pattern were added, either during the coloring process or after dyeing was completed. Yūzen could incorporate shibori techniques, embroidery with silk and metallic threads, hand painting, and stencilwork.

Yūzen dyeing let patterns flow across the body of the kosode and allowed much finer detail in garment patterns. The technique was also considered easier, faster, and possibly less expensive than large areas of kanoko shibori. The 1688 *Yūzen hinagata* touted its colorfastness and flexibility, implying that both qualities were a problem with other competing patterning techniques. Around this time, kosode became somewhat narrower, possibly influenced by the increased flexibility of yūzen-dyed textiles.

Early yūzen kosode designs were characterized by the use of framing devices like circular medallions. The kosode retained the asymmetrical sweep of the Kanbun-era kosode style, but the use of the framing device, filled with delicate natural motifs, is characteristic of Genroku fashion. Other popular framing devices included geometric shapes, fans, poem papers, and familiar household objects. The framing devices, like the dyeing technique, were closely associated with Miyazaki Yūzen. Hinagata-bon of the late 1680s stated that they featured garments in the style of Yūzen. Yūzen dyeing was used to pattern all sorts of garments and accessories, from obi and other sashes to *yokui* (bathrobes), *furoshiki* (wrapping cloths), and even long handkerchiefs.

The flexibility of yūzen dyeing allowed many new kosode styles. Popular patterns were more restrained than the full-blown Genroku style. Early yūzen patterns from the end of the seventeenth century tended to be more abstract, with controlled touches of embroidery in silk and metallic threads. Novelist Saikaku was instrumental in spreading the popularity of yūzen dyeing and reminded his readers that the use of characters on garments was dowdy and old-fashioned, a fashion faux-pas that none of his readers would want to commit. Beginning in the early eighteenth century, the most fashionable yūzen designs were painterly. Hinagata-bon featured yūzen-dyed kosode designs around the turn of the century, with the number of yūzen designs peaking around 1714.

Among the painterly yūzen designs, landscapes and cityscapes were favorite motifs. Paintings of landscape scenes have a long history in Japan. They were used on aristocratic women's garments as early as the eleventh century, but during the Edo period, the themes of landscape scenes on garments changed, reflecting the popular taste of the chōnin.

The extreme flexibility of yūzen dyeing allowed the creation of finely detailed scenes on garments. Kosode with city scenes, such as recognizable locations in the city of Kyoto, were placed all over the fabric of the garment. The requirement for the alternate-year residency in Edo meant that daimyō and their associates were constantly moving about Japan. Transportation was easy by the standards of the day. Members of merchant families frequently traveled between their scattered suppliers and outposts of the family business. Increased affluence and leisure time made tourism possible. Numerous guidebooks led tourists to the best spots. Paintings, prints, and other depictions of famous places and religious pilgrimage destinations were popular with everyone who could afford them and were also a favorite design for clothing.

Other popular painterly yūzen designs featured naturalistic or narrative scenes. More classical such scenes were especially favored by the nobility and samurai, but the townsmen preferred genre scenes showing people going about their daily activities. Each vignette on a garment was placed where it best enhanced the design of the piece. Only the control of color, as was possible with yūzen dyeing, allowed for the creation of intricate detail. Unlike earlier genre scenes executed as curiosities for samurai patrons, scenes were treated in realistic detail because the chōnin who acquired them were more intimately familiar with the occupations depicted.

Another popular image was horse races like those held at the Shinto Kamigamo Shrine in northern Kyoto. The race was an annual competition between two carefully selected animals chosen from among the best available mounts owned by leading religious centers and the aristocracy. It had been held on the fifth of May since the Heian period. The race began at a cherry tree and ended with a stirring finish at a maple tree at the far end of the shrine's grounds.

ANIMATED PAINTINGS

In addition to the painterly yūzen-dyed garments, very special kosode were painted by leading artists of the Edo period. Called kaki-e ("brush painting on fabric"), some painted garments survive from before the Edo period, so the technique was not new. Early painted garments were strictly something that only the upper levels of society could afford, but that changed during the Edo period. Some of painted garments from the period are clearly part of particular schools of painting; some can be attributed to individual artists, and some are even signed by the artists who created them.

Ogata Kōrin painted a kosode with fall flowers and grasses at the height of his fame. Historians believe that the artist painted the garment at the request of a member of a timber merchant family named Fuyuki who lived in Edo. This costly purchase demonstrated the refined taste and extraordinary wealth of the leading merchants of the time. Kōrin painted this kosode after the fabric was already assembled into a garment. This means that he designed the entire garment, much as he would any other type of painted composition, without having to contend with the interruptions and alignments that dyers constantly faced when working with fabric.

Roughly one hundred years later, in the early nineteenth century, another artist, Sakai Hōitsu (1761–1828), studied Kōrin's painting style and produced a painted kosode, possibly worn unbelted as an uchikake, that represents the peak of the merger of painting, textiles, and garments. Sakai's kosode painted with a blooming plum tree is beautifully designed to move with the wearer. Imagine how the garment looked when worn. The gnarled trunk of the tree moves up the wearer's left leg and its upper branches curve across the shoulders and down the wearer's arms. When the arms are bent, the wearer is enveloped in the blossoming tree limbs. The tree trunk sways with each step. Sakai placed his signature on the right underlap at the front of kosode. The hem of the garment includes blooming violets and dandelions, highlighted with gold pigment, and the tree trunk may have originally been detailed with silver pigment that is now oxidized—luxurious additions to a splendid work of art.

EDO CHIC

Eventually, as the novelty of yūzen dyeing wore off and harsh sumptuary laws were instated around 1720, fashion changed and, although yūzen dyeing continued to be used for kosode, other dyeing techniques became popular. *Shiroagari* (white-reserved designs) and *shiroage nuiiri* (white-reserved designs enhanced with embroidery) became more popular with the public and in hinagata-bon. Design motifs became smaller, and monochrome grounds were stylish. Use of embroidery was restrained. Grounds in dark shades of blue or green were preferred. Women's obi were wider, and kosode designs reflected the increased importance of the waist wrap: they became divided at the waist—effort was not wasted on areas that would not be seen by the public. Patterns were smaller and less graphic. Designs often featured bilateral symmetry. Gradually, patterns were restricted to the lower edges and front opening of the kosode. Sumptuary laws during the administration of Yoshimune (R. 1716–1745), the eighth Tokugawa shogun, influenced these changes. By the second half of the eighteenth century, trends in art and culture no longer originated in Kyoto; once-tiny Edo became Japan's arbiter of taste and style.

The truly cultured person of the late Edo period followed the fashion of the capital city and practiced the restrained chic that was *iki*. *Iki* connotes restrained, unpretentious, understated elegance. The leading representatives of iki style were the *geisha* for women and the *tsū* for men.

The *tsū* was the sophisticated, cultured urban man who never flaunted his taste, learning, or money ostentatiously. Obeying the increasingly strictly enforced sumptuary laws of the late eighteenth century, he wore sober, quietly patterned clothing. Favorites of the time were grays, browns, and blues. Garments often used two or more shades of a single color. Stripes and *komon* (small-scale repeat patterns) replaced flamboyant designs. Forbidden to wear bright colors and flashy clothing, the fashionable chōnin left those styles to samurai and prostitutes and, most often, wore plain black on visits to the pleasure quarter.

By the beginning of the nineteenth century, another round of harshly enforced sumptuary laws were enacted, and the use of silk fabric was prohibited. The power of the shogunate was weakening. Increasingly fearful, the shogunate established networks of spies in the cities. In this environment, the townsman had to conceal both his true feelings and his taste for luxurious clothing. His garments, dark and sober on the outside, might be lined with luxuriously patterned or embroidered fabric that showed only in brief flashes as he walked down the street. Outer clothing might conceal undergarments made of expensive printed cotton imported from India. Even though silk fabric was forbidden, silk embroidery was not, so an observer might catch a quick glimpse of a cotton *juban* (inner garment) heavily embroidered with scenes of Edo in bright silk floss as it peeked out of the neck of the man-about-town's kosode.

Special occasions could still be celebrated in ostentatious clothing. Wedding garments were often decorated with auspicious motifs. A favorite design was pairs of mandarin ducks that signified marital happiness.

The ideal of feminine beauty changed. The geisha became the embodiment of all that was iki. Originally, in the seventeenth century, geisha were male entertainers hired to work at parties. Female geisha first appeared in 1751 in Kyoto and soon were also entertaining in Edo. By 1780, there were more female than male geisha, and two decades later the term was used strictly for female entertainers.

Geisha were usually associated with unlicensed, unregulated areas, not with the licensed pleasure quarters. The geisha exemplified the refined iki style. She made the flashy courtesan of the licensed pleasure quarter old-fashioned. During the second half of the eighteenth century, as the number of geisha increased, high-class courtesans, the previous style setters for Edo Japan, gradually disappeared and the number of lower-class prostitutes in the pleasure quarter increased. Geisha were hired for stylish parties, where they sang, danced, played musical instruments, and conversed with guests. They were not sex workers, although they might, on occasion, form a relationship with a special client. These unconventional women occupied a unique position in late Edo society.

Iki ideals indicated that a beauty should be tall and thin. One 1813 advice manual encouraged women to wear vertical stripes to visually elongate their bodies. Her stylish kosode would puddle on the floor around her feet indoors, and she needed a secondary obi, the *shigoki obi*, to hitch her kosode up and off of the ground when outdoors. This was a major change from the early Edo period, when any woman in vertical stripes was immediately recognizable as a prostitute.

By the early nineteenth century, the woman's obi became as important as her kosode. By then, the standard woman's obi was twelve inches (30 cm) wide and covered the entire center of her body from below the bust to below the abdomen. As the obi's width increased, its original simple knot moved from the front to the side and eventually to the back. The sleeves of women's kosode were no longer stitched into the side seams of the kosode so that the wide obi could be wrapped around the her torso. Styles for knotting obi and obi patterns were as important as kosode designs for fashionable women. Undoubtedly a practiced eye could easily tell if a woman was wearing the correctly coordinated obi with her kosode and could also tell if her choices were appropriate for her age and position in life. Overly large and elaborate knots became objects of ridicule. At least one contemporary observer complained that the wide obi with its large knot favored by respectable women was more appropriate for prostitutes. Woodblock prints show courtesans dressed for work in kosode belted with wide obi tied in the front with large knots, an extremely awkward style. Both the wide obi and the trailing kosode restricted the women's movement.

In contrast to the extreme restraint of iki style, certain garments like clothing for weddings and for certain individuals like the prostitutes of the pleasure quarter were patterned in extravagant designs with bright colors and elaborate dyeing techniques.

Prints show women wearing garments made of *katsuri*-dyed indigo cotton, previously something worn only by peasants and the urban poor. In katsuri (often known by its Malaysian name *ikat*), patterns are dyed into threads before they are woven into fabric. Bundles of threads are tightly wrapped and dyed, creating the design that appears during weaving. These fabrics were made in rural areas.

Near the end of the eighteenth century, the brightest color that women were allowed to wear was a medium blue. Sober garments often featured designs at the hem and along the front opening on a solid-color ground unbroken except for *mon*, seals placed at the center back and the fronts and backs of both sleeves. This design was to be worn open because the embroidery flows up both edges of the front opening.

An early nineteenth-century fashion for kosode decorations limited primarily to the edges of the lower-front bands and opening of the kosode gave a new twist to women's clothing, eventually earning the name *Edo-zuma* (Edo skirts). Its popularity was short lived, and the rather static kosode design of plain body, *mon*, and decoration at the hem became so standardized that hinagata-bon ceased publication. Kosode designs became so entrenched that fashion was no longer an issue. Even older women wore kosode of plain fabric with a narrow band at the hem. The formal kimono of the twentieth century followed the same style.

SAMURAI ASPIRATIONS AND FASHIONS

The consolidation of power in the shogunate changed the lives of the samurai. No longer fighters, by the early Edo period they were members of an urban feudal aristocracy who lived in close contact with each other at the capital for most of their lives. Gift giving was a necessity, and clothing often was a prized present that helped strengthen interpersonal relationships. The samurai competed with each other in ostentatious displays of their cultured refinement and taste.

At the beginning of the Edo period, the shogunate established regulations called the "laws for military households" that included prescribed clothing styles for various levels of samurai men and women. These regulations made it easy to tell high-ranking individuals from their underlings. The military often ignored the rules, especially for clothing worn for major life events like the celebration of the birth of an heir or a child's coming-of-age ceremony.

In addition to kosode, men also wore special garments like the *jinbaori*, an outer garment possibly derived from imported European surcoats, once worn by fighting men for warmth and protection from the elements. During the peaceful Edo period, they became fashionable samurai apparel. Their bold patterns, like European sailing ships, were no longer needed to recognize individuals on the battlefield. For formal occasions during the late Edo period, military men wore the *kamishimo* (literally "upper-lower") over the kosode. The kosode was tucked into hakama trousers that tied at the waist, and the "upper" portion of the set, the *kataginu*, was worn much like a vest. The kataginu was sleeveless and was held away from the body by whalebone supports along its wide shoulders. As a reward, commoners sometimes were allowed to wear the kataginu for special occasions like weddings.

Samurai women favored closely patterned designs at the beginning of the Edo period. In general, their clothing was always more conservative and less tied to mainstream Edo fashion than the clothing of wealthy chōnin women. Appropriate designs for elite samurai women's clothing included various poems, tales, and well-known locations, all associated with traditional imperial and court culture dating from the classical Heian period. Their clothing was always luxurious but patterns were often rather stale.

Strict rules dictated what type of garment could be worn by military wives. On the first of April, they donned the summer kosode called the *katabira*. It was often made of the finest cool, crisp ramie, one of several bast fibers used in Japan. Like all bast fibers, the preparation of ramie for weaving was a time-consuming process.

Most surviving katabira are women's garments patterned with indigo dye in a complex stencil-and-paste resist technique called *chayazome*. Only the most elite samurai women wore garments patterned by the chayazome process, because the chayazome stenciling technique was the most expensive and time-consuming dyeing method used in Japan. Each garment required multiple exacting applications of resist and multiple trips to the dye vat. Resist was applied to both sides of the fabric. Areas treated with resist before dyeing began stayed white. After dyeing began, additional resist was added to some areas to keep them a lighter shade of blue than other parts of the pattern. Chayazome dyers specialized in particular steps of the process, so many individuals participated in the creation of a costly garment like the furisode-style katabira shown here. A garment this complex could easily take two years to complete. It undoubtedly belonged to a young, high-ranking samurai woman and survives today as a treasured example of the dyer's art. Its cool blue and white colors highlighted with refined touches of red silk, delicate gold threads, and rustic autumn garden scenes reminded its wearer and her companions of the cool, breezy countryside that they rarely visited even at the height of Japan's oppressive summer heat and humidity.

For formal summer occasions, a woman would wear a *koshimaki* over her katabira. The koshimaki was shaped like a kosode. It was originally worn with its sleeves slipped off of the wearer's shoulders and tied around her waist, but by the Edo period, instead of tying the sleeves at the waist, a belt was used to hold the koshimaki in place. The long, stiff ends of the belt were passed through the koshimaki's sleeves. The sleeves stood out from the woman's body rather like wings that were attached at waist level instead of at the shoulder. The garment undoubtedly made movement awkward for the wearer.

Koshimaki were frequently patterned with small, allover designs. Assorted auspicious symbols were thought to bring good fortune and good luck to the wearer. The classic winter combination of pine trees, bamboo, and plum blossoms represented long life, resilience, and purity, respectively. Together, the koshimaki and katabira made a dramatic garment, contrasting fine, dark, allover patterns with light, crisp, almost monochromatic, refreshing landscape scenes.

On September 9, samurai women resumed wearing their winter garments, including silk *aigi* (middle robes) sashed at the waist with a special obi called the *kakeshita*. Kakeshita were usually made of relatively stiff, heavy fabrics, including velvet and densely embroidered satin. Over these garments, the women wore the outer, unsashed kosode called the *uchikake* that originated in the Muromachi period. The uchikake, the original source garment for the koshimaki, became part of samurai women's formal dress before the Edo period. During the Edo period, it also became a favorite of courtesans and wealthy chōnin.

The elaborate clothing required of the samurai class was a constant financial burden throughout this time period. Protocol at the capital required proper attire; any departure from accepted standards was immediately noticed. The attendants in daimyō households dressed conservatively as well. Like their superiors, they wore designs that reflected classical themes dating from the Heian period. A lady-in-waiting considered herself lucky if her lord gave her permission to wear his *mon* (crest) on her kosode as a reward for exceptional service.

CLOTHING OF THE NOBILITY

From the fourteenth century on, samurai and court culture blended into each other. Members of both groups practiced Zen Buddhism and subscribed to the austere ideals of Confucianism. The two elite groups favored sedate woven patterns and looked down on dyed and embroidered textiles, cheaper alternatives to figured weaves. Members of the nobility consistently dressed in the most conservative garments. During the Edo period, they were virtual prisoners in Kyoto.

Court clothing for formal occasions for the nobility changed little from the Heian period in the eighth century. For the most formal court occasions, men and women wore very similar court robes with wide wrist openings (*osode*, the opposite of the small openings of the *kosode*) in the sleeves. Men's garments were double breasted. The casualwear of the nobleman included special jackets and trousers for playing sports and jackets worn for hunting. Emperors and retired emperors could wear special long, trailing robes called *ohiki nōshi* (long *nōshi*), which originated in the Muromachi period. The specific names and cuts of all of these garments quickly let courtiers know exactly what place the wearer held in the court hierarchy.

Noblewomen had more choices in their clothing styles by the middle of the Edo period. Historians often credit Tōfukumon-in (1607–1678), the daughter of the second Tokugawa shogun and wife of emperor Go-Mizunoo, with the introduction of samurai women's fashions into the imperial household. Tōfukumon-in's name and descriptions of the garments she ordered appear in surviving order books belonging to the Kariganeya dry goods shop in Kyoto. Beginning in the middle Edo period, imperial women wore kosode and unbelted uchikake (called *kaitori* by the nobility). Embroidered designs were preferred over less-expensive dyed patterns. Favorite patterns included seasonal flowers, cranes, and other naturalistic designs.

CHILDREN'S CLOTHING

During the Edo period, the children of the elite wore clothing much like that of their parents. Adult-size garments were temporarily altered to fit small children. Some children's garments from the period survive with tucks running front to back across the shoulders showing how the adult-size clothing was altered to fit a growing child. Other children's garments survive with intact protective back guards made of a specially patterned line of running stitches going down the center of the garment from the neck to the shoulder blades, ending in dangling threads.

Children wore special clothing for events like haircutting ceremonies. Special woven designs were worn only by young imperial princes. Younger princes wore smaller versions of the designs than their older brothers. The auspicious kosode designs protected their young wearers and made them part of the complex interplay of taste and play of the Edo period. An infant's kosode with a design of the seven good-luck deities only shows six gods. The seventh, the god of happiness and contentment, is represented by the baby boy who was wrapped in the auspicious garment. Bold, sophisticated scenes like a horse race on the boy's kosode in must have delighted the lucky children who wore them.

CONCLUSION

By the end of the Edo period in 1868, Japan had changed again. Continual economic problems worsened because of the negative impact of heavily restricted foreign trade. External pressure from potential trading partners like the United States and domestic interest in subjects like science, medicine, and industry could no longer be ignored. The Tokugawa shogunate ended, and imperial power was restored. Before the end of the Edo period, Western-style clothing was used for uniforms for certain occupations, including police, train conductors, and members of the military. Some modern urban Japanese men combined Japanese and Western clothing after the restoration of imperial power. Gradually Western clothing styles spread among urban men. Women and rural populations were slower to change.

Fashions inspired by the garments selected by influential courtesans, geisha, and actors and adopted by affluent townsmen of Japan's main cities passed into history. Their beauty endures in selected surviving garments, books, and prints and paintings of the floating world and the bustling streets of Edo. During the period, the courtly, conservative garments of the nobility and the leading samurai continued to depend primarily on classical designs that referred back to Heian standards of fashion. Meanwhile the wealthy townsmen and their families experimented with new forms of dyeing and creative designs that continue to inspire today. The best of the often brash and exuberant, always innovative styles of urban Edo period Japan still fascinate us.

FURTHER READING

Dalby, Liza Crihfield. *Kimono: Fashioning Culture*. Seattle: University of Washington Press, 2001.

Four Centuries of Fashion: Classical Kimono from the Kyoto National Museum. San Francisco: Asian Art Museum of San Francisco, 1997.

Gluckman, Dale Carolyn, and Sharon Sadako Takeda. *When Art Became Fashion: Kosode in Edo Period Japan*. New York: Weatherhill, 1992.

Ishimura Hayao and Maruyama Nobuhiko. *Robes of Elegance: Japanese Kimonos of the 16th–20th Centuries*. Raleigh: North Carolina Museum of Art, 1988.

Shimizu Yoshiaki, ed. *Japan: The Shaping of Daimyō Culture, 1185–1868*. Washington, DC: National Gallery of Art, 1988.

Stinchecum, Amanda Mayer. *Kosode: 16th–19th Century Textiles from the Nomura Collection*. New York: Japan Society, 1984.

Swinton, Elizabeth de Sabato. *Women of the Pleasure Quarter: Japanese Paintings and Prints of the Floating World*. New York: Hudson Hills Press, 1996.

WEB RESOURCES

Kyoto National Museum. http://www.kyohaku.go.jp.

Tokyo National Museum. http://www.tnm.go.jp/en.

(http://www.tnm.jp/en/servlet/Con?processId=00&ref=2&Q1=&Q2=&Q3=&Q4= _65_&Q5=&F1=&F2=&pageId=E15&colid=I721)

(http://www.tnm.go.jp/en/servlet/Con?processId=00&ref=2&Q1=&Q2=&Q3=&Q4= _65_&Q5=&F1=&F2=&pageId=E15&colid=I4070)

National Museum of Japanese History, Nomura Collection http://www.rekihaku.ac.jp/ e-rekihaku/110/cover.html

Clothing in Mughal India

Mary Pluckhahn
Masilamani

TIMELINE

1527	Babur defeats the Lodi sultanate at Delhi, introducing Mughal rule to present-day India
1530	Babur dies; his son, Humayun, loses control of northern India
1555	Humayun, with the help of Persian forces, regains control of Delhi
1556–1605	Reign of Akbar, first of the three Great Mughals
1605–1627	Reign of Jahangir; period of refined patronage of the arts
1628–1658	Reign of Shah Jahan, connoisseur and builder of the Taj Mahal
1658–1707	Reign of Aurangzeb, a conservative, reactionary leader who brings decline to the high period of Mughal arts
1858	British crown takes direct control of India; last Mughal emperor, Bahadur Shah II, exiled to Burma

The King appeared seated upon his throne, at the end of the great hall, in the most magnificent attire. His vest was of white and delicately flowered satin, with a silk and gold embroidery of the finest texture. The turban, of gold cloth, had an aigrette whose base was composed of diamonds of an extraordinary size and value, besides an Oriental topaz, which may be pronounced unparalleled, exhibiting a lustre like the sun. A necklace of immense pearls, suspended from his neck, reached to the stomach.

—François Bernier, *Travels in the Mogul Empire,*
A.D. 1656–1668

At its height in the sixteenth and seventeenth centuries, the Mughal court in northern India was without a doubt one of the most luxurious in the world. Today its former capitals at Agra, Delhi, Fatehpur Sikri, and Lahore retain many of the splendid buildings that housed the imperial household and hosted the formal activities of the court, but without the thick carpets, satin draperies, lush gardens, flowing water, bubbling fountains, splendidly dressed courtiers, and visitors from much of the known world, they are but pale shadows of their former grandeur. Three early Mughal rulers, Akbar (R. 1556–1605), Jahangir (R. 1605–1627), and Shah Jahan (R. 1627–1658), were collectively known in Europe as the Great Mughals. During their reigns, a uniquely Indian style of dress made of the finest cottons, silks, and wools and embellished with gold, silver, and precious stones emerged as part of an unprecedented aesthetic and artistic flowering.

The Mughals invested their vast wealth in personal adornments. Each individual's clothing reflected his social, economic, and political standing within a highly codified society. Ostentatious display was their birthright. The Mughal aesthetic gave the world some of its best-known masterpieces, including some of the finest and most complex textiles ever woven, exquisite jewels and jewelry, architectural wonders like the Taj Mahal, and lively and individualistic miniature paintings that accurately present the court and its residents. All of this developed at a center that controlled much of the world's trade in fine textiles, fragrant spices, gemstones, and other valuable goods through an administrative system that ensured a stable and secure environment.

HISTORICAL BACKGROUND

Throughout much of its history, the northern portion of the Indian subcontinent was repeatedly raided and invaded by peoples coming from Central Asia and the Middle East. By the eighth century, Islamic peoples were settled on the far western edge of the region. Four hundred years later, at the end of the twelfth century, they occupied Delhi, the chief city of north-central India. In 1526, a new invader, a Muslim of Turkish and Mongol ancestry named Babur, defeated the last of the Islamic Delhi sultanates. Babur (R. 1526–1530) began the Mughal dynasty that ultimately controlled the subcontinent from Kabul in the west to Bengal in the east and as far south as the Deccan Plateau in central India.

Babur died shortly after he began his rule and was succeeded by his son Humayun (R. 1530–1540 and 1555–1556), who lost the throne to the Afghan Pashtun Sher Shah. Humayun fled to the west, taking refuge at the Safavid Persian court. Later Mughal design, art, and culture was heavily influenced by the highly refined aesthetic sense the early Mughals honed during their years in Persia. Both Babur and Humayun were well trained in the art of poetry. Humayun planned to establish a royal atelier including two Persian artists on his return to India. Humayun regained control of northern India but, like his father, died shortly afterward.

Babur and Humayun set the stage for the Great Mughals. Humayun was succeeded by his son Akbar, often called the greatest of the Mughals. Although only about thirteen years old when he took the throne, Akbar quickly established strong central control of the territory regained by his father and enlarged the empire. Like his contemporary Queen Elizabeth I of England, Akbar ruled for almost fifty years. Recognizing the importance of retaining the support of the diverse religious and regional groups over which he ruled, Akbar practiced tolerance as statecraft. Trained in the Safavid tradition, Akbar was also intellectually curious. He established royal workshops staffed with both Persian and local master craftsmen. Ultimately a distinctly Mughal style developed from melding of these varied traditions.

Akbar's successors refined this style through their passionate, discerning artistic patronage. During the rule of Akbar's son Jahangir, Mughal miniature paintings portrayed and recorded the people and events of life at the court in a lively, accurate fashion. Jahangir's personal interest in art lead to increased realism. Colors were softer than those used during his father's reign. Court life became more formalized and codified. This trend intensified during the rule of Shah Jahan, who showed less interested in painting than in architecture. He built the Taj Mahal as a tomb for his favorite wife Mumtaz Mahal. A connoisseur of gemstones, he collected them assiduously.

Ultimately, in an apparent conservative reaction to the profligate lifestyle of many members of the royal family, Shah Jahan's son Aurangzeb (R. 1658–1707) defeated his older brothers, imprisoned his father, and seized control of the empire. Patronage of the arts declined at court as the treasury was depleted by repeated attempts at expansion of the empire into the Deccan Plateau. Aurangzeb's rule marks the end of the great artistic flowering of the Mughal court. The skilled craftsmen who created the finest paintings, textiles, garments, jewelry, and weapons gradually scattered to smaller patronage centers throughout northern India, spreading and preserving Mughal artistic sensibilities throughout the region.

COSTUME RESOURCES

Almost no clothing from the court of the Great Mughals has survived. Textiles are extremely fragile, and the heavy, complex metallic thread embellishments and garment silhouettes favored at the court made Mughal garments even less likely to survive than most. The Indian climate's extreme heat and wide fluctuations in humidity contributed to the destruction of Mughal garments, and clothing that includes precious metals was often destroyed to recycle the metals into new uses.

Of the surviving garments that have been reliably dated to the early Mughal period, by far the most common is the man's sash, the *patka*. This is not surprising because patkas are relatively small pieces that were easily stored. They were often treasured symbols of the court honors awarded to the original recipient. Rulers stored garments in royal storerooms, which were favorite destinations of invaders, such as Nadir Shah who sacked Delhi in 1739—among other plunder, he carried the Mughals' fabled Peacock Throne and the Koh-i-Noor diamond home to Persia. Ironically, similar storerooms at courts in India's independent Hindu states in areas like Rajasthan protected many of the surviving early Mughal textiles.

Luckily there are many other reliable sources for information about the clothing worn at the courts of the Great Mughals. The Mughal administrative system relied on excellent recordkeeping and communication. The early rulers kept detailed inventories of events and court proceedings, including elaborate ceremonies; distribution of gifts such as special garments, sashes, and other symbols of status and honor; and gifts and tribute received from vassal states. Descriptions of these events and gifts are invaluable for understanding the role of costume at court and the styles worn there. Emissaries from European trade organizations and monarchs were frequent visitors to the Mughal court; their detailed observations and descriptive letters to their sponsors are dependable resources, as well.

The court histories of the Mughal rulers include numerous miniature paintings that are the most reliable sources for information about court dress. The royal artists created detailed images that, along with the written records, chronicled court proceedings. Emperors are shown during the regular public audiences that played a major role in the daily activities of the court. These *darbar* scenes show who was present at court and what clothing and symbols of rank they wore. Other paintings show such royal activities as hunting expeditions and warfare, with the appropriate clothing for each activity. Individual portraits are especially valuable because they show details of garments. Predictably, these paintings are primarily records of men's activities and their associated clothing.

MEN'S CLOTHING

Clothing worn at the Mughal court changed through time and reflected both the Mughals' Turkish and Central Asian origins and adaptations to the Indian subcontinent, ultimately arriving at a consistent northern Indian court style that persisted with minor changes well beyond the rule of the Great Mughals.

When Babur arrived in India, he was shocked to find the local population dressed in minimal clothing. Babur and his associates wore clothing derived from Turkish, Persian, and Central Asian styles, including a *chaftan* or *kaftan* (a long coat), an overcoat made of sheepskin (*postin*), and a turban head-wrap similar to those worn in Timurid paintings from the late fifteenth and early sixteenth centuries. The nomadic early Mughals came from a much colder climate than the plains of northern India and quickly learned that their clothing was unsuitable for the extreme heat of the subcontinent.

The grooming of the early Mughals was also very different from the styles that prevailed in India. To the amusement of the local population, Mughal men wore long moustaches and long, thin beards that hung from their chins. They also kept their hair closely cropped, a fashion that continued at the court of the Great Mughals.

Babur's successor Humayun and his court continued to wear the early style of clothing introduced by his father. Humayun, though, introduced a new style of turban seen in a dynastic portrait completed for Shah Jahan about ninety years after Humayun's death. The ruler wears the *taj-i izzati* turban, a style unique to Humayun's court and, if the painted record is to be believed, not used after his reign. This unique head covering includes a brimmed high cap with a rounded point made of a blue fabric with a small repeat pattern in gold. The brim has been cut into points that are turned up and intertwined with a multicolored striped turban cloth heavily decorated with gold. Humayun holds a *sarpech*, a turban ornament, made of gold with a large red spinel or ruby surrounded by pearls and topped with a feather. Jewels like this large red gem were treasured possessions within the Mughal dynasty; many of the largest stones were engraved with the names of their previous royal owners. Humayun's outer coat is made of red fabric, perhaps silk or velvet, brocaded in gold. A bit of green lining shows at the coat's front opening, and its sleeves appear to be made of two layers of cloth, a shorter outer sleeve in the same red as the outer body of the coat, and a longer green-and-gold sleeve that matches the coat's lining. Beneath the coat, he wears a golden yellow, long-sleeved garment with a wrapped front overlap that may tie under his right arm in the style of the *jama*, a garment that would soon become part of the typical Mughal court costume. This inner garment is held close to the body at the waist by a bejeweled golden belt buckle.

At Humayun's death, Akbar took the throne and began the synthesis of Mughal ancestral customs with local Indian practices there by safeguarding the stability of the empire and ultimately creating a uniquely Mughal court style. By the close of Akbar's reign, the standard Mughal court costume emerged. This costume was adapted to the Indian climate and, through the use of elaborately woven and lavishly embellished fabrics, contributed to the display of imperial power at court. Akbar himself wore a Mughal court ensemble in an ancestral portrait done in 1630, early in the rule of his grandson Shah Jahan.

The court costume consisted of an unlined outer coat (*jama*), trousers (*paijama*), and a turban. These garments were worn with a sash (*patka*) at the waist, ceremonial weapons, and elaborate jewelry, often including a turban ornament. The term *jama* is a generic name for coat or outer garment and can be used for many different garments. In Govardhan's painting, Akbar wears the typical Mughal jama made of a fine, somewhat transparent white fabric depicted with a faint regular allover pattern of flower sprigs in gold. The long sleeves are close fitting, and the jama has a lapped front closing that ties under the ruler's right arm with several lengths of fabric that match the jama. The inner layer of the jama front closes in a similar way under the other arm. The jama's full skirt extends below Akbar's knees. The crumpled legs of his paijama extend from below the jama to his ankles. This crumpled look is probably created by cutting the snug lower leg of the paijama longer than the wearer's leg length and then crushing the excess fabric into small folds around the ankle. Although not visible in this painting, the waist and thigh areas of the paijama in other paintings appear to be cut quite full and gathered around the waist, perhaps by a drawstring. This general shape is much like the *churidar* style of trouser worn in modern India. Akbar's paijama is probably made of silk brocaded with another gold floral pattern, a favorite design that became synonymous with Mughal decorative arts.

Akbar wears a relatively flat red-and-gold-striped turban wrapped around his head. One end of the turban forms a fanlike cockade at the front. This shape is often described as a "conch shell" and may be derived from the Hindu Rajput-style *pagri*, an indigenous turban of non-Muslim design. Akbar has two multicolored, gold-embellished patkas at his waist. These two sashes are the most elaborately patterned textiles in the outfit the painter created for the ruler. Secured to his patkas are several objects, including an embroidered bag of red and blue velvet, several small objects that are suspended by fine cords, and, most importantly, his *katar*, a ceremonial thrusting dagger. Akbar's katar is carried in a sheath made of gold that is set with rubies, emeralds, and diamonds. The brilliant red, green, gold, and white of this katar is typical of the extravagant jewelry and ceremonial weapons worn by the Mughals. The same gems and colors are seen interspersed with pearls in the necklace he holds in his outstretched hand, in his bracelets, and in the thumb ring he wears on his right hand. To complete his outfit, Akbar wears red-and-green velvet slippers on his feet and holds a sheathed sword with his left hand.

The katar and other ceremonial daggers continued to be important Mughal court accessories throughout the rule of the Great Mughals. The most breath-taking Mughal dagger to survive is made in the uniquely Indian *kundan* gold-working technique. Dating from the reign of Jahangir, it is set with more than 2,400 separate gemstones and is found in the Kuwait National Museum.

As part of the incorporation of local customs and culture into the Mughal empire, Akbar reportedly invented a number of new names for existing garments. For example, the girdle worn around the waist became the *katzeb*, from the Sanskrit word *kati* meaning "waist" and the Persian *zeb* meaning "adorning." These name changes most likely were used at court only until his death and never spread into general use.

A garment seen in paintings from the Akbar period but rarely depicted in later periods was called the *chakdar jama*. It may be derived from the Rajput court's *takauchiah*. The chakdar jama was shaped much like the standard Mughal jama except that the skirt fell in four to six long points instead of in the circular hem of the jama. Perhaps most importantly, Akbar reportedly introduced the convention of Muslims tying the jama under the right arm and Hindus tying theirs under the left. This practice made it possible to tell an individual's religion quickly and easily.

At the Mughal court, textiles were extraordinarily important. The Indian subcontinent had been known for its cotton production since Roman times, and silk weaving was well established in northern India before the Mughals arrived. Indians were also masters at printing and dyeing cotton with colorfast dyes—skills much appreciated by their trading partners. The region was a major exporter of fabrics to markets as diverse as Europe and Southeast Asia.

The most exquisite fabrics produced in India stayed at the court, and court demands for fabrics of all types drove producers to ever greater heights of creativity. Akbar set up royal workshops, *kharkhanas*, patterned on the workshops of the Safavid Persian court, over much of his empire. Specialized kharkhanas produced textiles, embroidery, clothing, and a whole range of other goods. Court demands for clothing and textiles were so high that the court often ordered goods from independent workshops. Indigenous textiles for the court were produced in Bengal, Gujarat, and Kashmir and at the various Mughal capitals.

Some of the most complex textiles ever made were produced during a fifty-year period from the late seventeenth century into the early eighteenth century during the reign of Aurangzeb. The complexity of the weaving techniques that produced these patkas is difficult to comprehend. Nevertheless, the skill and attention to detail needed to create such intricate double cloth weaves is truly exceptional. The court also acquired textiles from many other countries but, for sheer beauty, none of the imports could outshine the local production.

The court costume shown in Akbar's portrait continued to be the standard dress during his son Jahangir's rule. Clothing, like the court itself, became increasingly elaborate, formal, and codified. An aesthete known for his exquisite taste and always involved in the design process, each of Jahangir's garments was expressly designed for him and, like all garments worn by royalty, was worn only once, no matter how many months and how much labor went into its creation. The court followed his fashion dictates closely. Jahangir decreed that certain textiles and garments should be made for his use alone. As a reward of high honor, the emperor rewarded selected courtiers with gifts of clothing or jewelry. One of these garments, the *nadiri* (rarity), was a special sleeveless overcoat designed by Jahangir himself. The emperor is also credited with a number of innovations in *qaba* (overcoat) decoration, including embroidery at the hems of the garment's long sleeves and a new folded collar style. The *tus* shawl, made of the finest wool from Kashmir and introduced by his father Akbar, was another garment that could be worn only if received from the emperor. Jahangir also introduced the *salimshahi*, a slipper with a finely pointed toe, that was still in use during the late twentieth century (in his youth, Jahangir was called Prince Salim and the salimshahi was named for him).

The official memoirs of Jahangir's reign, the *Tuzuk-i Jahangiri*, include a miniature painting showing the emperor

"Emperor Jahangir Weighs Prince Khurrami," from the *Tuzuk-i Jahangiri (The Memoirs of Jahangir)*, 1615–1625. © Werner Forman / Art Resource, NY.

weighing his son Prince Khurram, who later succeeded him as emperor Shah Jahan. This painting dates to the early seventeenth century and depicts the wealth of clothing, textiles, and jewels at the court. Manohar, the artist credited with the painting, was an expert at reproducing the details of every object in a scene, from the densely knotted carpets covering the floor of the audience hall to the extravagant textiles and jewels worn by each of the individuals present at the ceremony. Jahangir valued this attention to detail in artwork and recognized the artists most capable of recording scenes accurately.

In this painting, we see Prince Khurram seated on a red velvet cushion in one pan of a bejeweled golden balance. He wears a sleeveless garment, probably a *nadiri*, so heavily brocaded with gold that, in this painting, it is difficult to tell what colors are interwoven with its gold threads. Its slightly extended shoulders are trimmed with a row of pearls. Underneath the vest, the prince wears a long-sleeved white jama patterned in a fine design in red and gold. The jama's skirt is very sheer and is most likely made of the very fine Bengali *mal mal* cotton for which India was famous for centuries. The faint green tint of the jama skirt indicates that the prince wears green paijama trousers. His conch-shaped, Mughal-style turban is made of red cloth patterned in gold. It is wrapped in strings of pearls, a gem associated with Mughal royalty, and he wears an aigrette as well. His ear studs, necklaces, and bracelets are also made of pearls, with occasional emeralds and red spinels or rubies. Prince Khurram, like most of the relatives and military officials in the painting, wears a double patka wrapped once around his body and knotted in front at his waist in the Mughal style. Emperor Jahangir stands to his left, wearing similar but less elaborately embellished clothing. The skirt of his mal mal jama clearly shows the transparency of the fine cotton cloth. Other members of the party wear striped, patterned, or solid colored jamas and paijamas.

Prince Khurram is shown being weighed against bags that probably represent the gold or silver coins that would be given to charity in his name. Other precious goods against which the prince would be weighed include the beautiful brocaded textiles, jewelry, and ceremonial daggers spread out on presentation trays on the white cloth in the foreground of the scene. A clerk stands to the right, keeping careful record of the proceedings. One European emissary observed that, in a 1665 weighing ceremony, Aurangzeb actually received personal gifts valued at significantly more than the donations he made to the poor that day.

All of the Mughals continued the ancient Islamic court tradition of gift giving. As can be seen from the goods at the weighing ceremony, textiles and clothing played a major role in this practice. Clothing worn by the emperor became *malbus-i khass*, a special costume, which was permeated with his royal essence. *Khil'at*, robes of honor, came in sets of three, five, or seven pieces, depending on the rank of the recipient. These sets were *sarapa*, covering the recipient from head to foot. A three-piece set consisted of a tunic, a turban, and a ceremonial *shash* (sash). At Humayun's coronation, twelve thousand robes of honor were given out, but these garments were probably not all equally fine. Wool shawls from Kashmir were also used as gifts of honor. Jewels, including turban ornaments, finger rings, and brooches as well as ceremonial daggers and swords, were also given as royal gifts of honor.

Clothing could also be used to humiliate and degrade. Aurangzeb disgraced his defeated eldest brother Dara Shikoh and his young nephew by dressing them in dirty rags of the poorest quality and parading them through the streets of Delhi mounted on a filthy and bedraggled elephant that lacked all of the proper ostentatious royal trappings. This public disgrace preceded Prince Dara's execution.

The only surviving garment that has been reliably identified as a court garment from the rule of the Great Mughals is a man's silk coat. It is variously dated to the rule of either Jahangir or Shah Jahan, somewhere between 1605 and 1658. The coat's fine chain-stitch embroidery shows a complex scene in the Persian style. Lions prey on bounding antelope or doze contentedly and birds fly through the air, all in a fabulously blooming landscape full of tulips, daffodils, poppies, and iris embroidered on a soft, cream-colored satin ground. The trim around the neck and partway down the garment's front opening is the only part of the exterior of the coat that is not embroidered, indicating that it may have been expressly made to be worn with a narrow fur collar, a style that was frequently worn in cold weather.

The cut and basic garments of court costume changed little following the rule of Jahangir. Fashionable textiles used during the reign of Shah Jahan were perhaps even more finely woven and refined. Patkas became shorter and the patterning on them became much more complex and dense. Illustrations from the *Padshahnama*, the official record of Shah Jahan's reign, continue to show scenes with all of the grandeur associated with a wealthy and powerful court at its height. These depictions serve to reaffirm the status of the emperor and his nobles.

A double-page picture from the *Padshahnama* shows Shah Jahan receiving his three eldest sons and Asaf Khan, the father of the new emperor's wife Mumtaz Mahal and brother of his father's favorite wife, Nur Jahan. This *darbar* scene showing a formal audience during Shah Jahan's ascent to the Mughal throne was painted early in the emperor's reign. The scene was painted by the artist Bichitr who, like Manohar, excelled at exact depiction of details and originally worked in Jahangir's the royal atelier. This rather static miniature shows Shah Jahan dressed in all his imperial splendor. He wears a multicolored turban adorned with a long feather and a deep purple or blue silk brocade jama with a narrow strip of unstitched cloth that passes under his right arm with its long ends draped over his left shoulder, first the back to the front and then

Court coat or "hunting coat," made out of white satin and embroidered with colored silks in fine chain stitch, ca. 1630–1660. © Victoria & Albert Museum, London / Art Resource, NY.

the front to the back. Most interesting in this picture is the vast range of textiles worn by the courtiers arranged in their carefully ordered and prescribed ranks below the area where the ruler is being greeted by his elaborately dressed sons and the gift-bearing Asaf Khan. We see bold stripes on the two attendants who flank the ruler's throne with the imperial yak tail whisks, and more stripes on the jamas, coats, and turbans of various courtiers. Each garment, turban, and face is unique. Almost without exception, each person can be identified by name, and almost all of them are immediate relatives of the new emperor and his father-in-law.

A close-up view of a court coat or "hunting coat," made out of white satin and embroidered with colored silks in fine chain stitch, ca. 1630–1660. © Victoria & Albert Museum, London / Art Resource, NY.

The second panel of the accession scene, ascribed to the artist Ramdas, shows a host of lower-level courtiers—many, but not all, of them wearing the typical Mughal conch shell–shaped turban. All of the officers in the back row wear two-tone leather boots, many with light tan uppers and some in a bright red. This type of boot was also worn by soldiers shown in battle scenes. All of these officials wear ornately patterned patkas at their waists, and many of them wear densely brocaded coats over their jamas. The officials who precede the gaily appointed horses all wear the complexly patterned textiles that typify the reign of Shah Jahan. Together, these two pictures give a feeling for the grandeur of the Mughal court at its most magnificent.

Dara Shikoh never inherited the Mughal throne. Instead, his younger brother, Aurangzeb, wrested control of the empire from their father. During Aurangzeb's long rule, court patronage of all of the arts decreased and the craftsmen responsible for making all of the magnificent goods slowly scattered to smaller regional courts in areas like Rajasthan and the Punjab or to centers for textile production. This helped to spread the Mughal aesthetic style throughout much of northern India but also reduced the grandeur of the court itself.

Scholars disagree on exactly what changes occurred in clothing worn at Aurangzeb's court. Some see an increase in the fullness of the turban, jama, and paijama. Others say that turbans became smaller and caps became more fashionable and continued to be popular after his rule ended. Relatively unadorned caps may have appealed to Aurangzeb because of his turn toward Muslim orthodoxy as he aged. This ruler actually owned a business that made and sold caps. Elaborate patkas also are attributed to Aurangzeb's reign, so in at least some cases, craftsmen continued to produce some masterpieces for the court.

WOMEN'S CLOTHING

Accurate portraits of noble Mughal women are rare because they were sequestered in the royal *zanana*, the women's quarters within the court compound. Most women depicted in miniature paintings tend to be idealized and lack the individuality of the best Mughal portraits. Male artists were not allowed into the women's quarters, and scholars have identified only one significant female artist, Sahifa Banu, who was active during the rule of Shah Jahan in the early seventeenth century. Occasional paintings of women appear to be more recognizable portraits of specific individual women, but these paintings are rare. Written descriptions of women's clothing are also rare. In non-Mughal descriptions of women's dress, the careful reader must question exactly which women of the court the foreign male visitors were allowed to see, meet, and describe.

In Akbar's time, the royal entourage included five thousand wives, concubines, and prostitutes, all living in the women's quarters. The women of the royal household led complex lives. Some note that the roles and rights of the royal women grew out of the traditions of the Mughals' Mongol ancestors and not from the more restrictive traditions of Islamic Central Asia. Although the women were sequestered in the royal zanana, they traveled with the court, observed battles from a safe distance, and participated in ceremonies, including weddings, royal births, circumcisions, and weighing ceremonies. They also played powerful roles behind the scene at court, where they were often as powerful as their husbands. They were wealthy patrons of art, architecture, and science in their own right. The practice of having royal children nursed by multiple women within the zanana contributed to complicated webs of interrelationships between the men and women of the court, giving women many paths to individual power.

The clothing worn by these women went through several changes that were similar to those of the Mughal men's costume. The early Mughal woman wore clothing in the Turkish style, including long gowns, trousers, the *kartiji* (a short bodice extending to the hips and worn under the gown), and the *nimtana* (an outer jacket, similar to a vest). The memoirs of Babur's daughter Gulbadan Begam include a description of wedding gifts to a young bride. She received nine jackets, each trimmed with jeweled balls, and four shorter kartiji, also embellished with ball trimmings. The early Mughal women also wore tall, cone-shaped Turkish hats that were sometimes decorated with a long plume or a small veil attached to the top of the hat. These hats persisted into the reign of Akbar.

Because of the stylized depictions of women in paintings and the general lack of reliable written descriptions of women's clothing, exactly what royal Mughal women wore, and when, is a bit confusing. Once the standard men's court costume of jama, paijama, and turban was firmly established, illustrations of women show two types of clothing that apparently coexisted. Both styles are shown in "The Birth of a Prince." This painting is regarded as one of the most reliable depictions of Mughal women. The painter, Bishan Das, was a favorite of Jahangir, and this painting is from the *Tuzuk-i Jahangiri*, the official history of the emperor's reign.

In the painting, the infant swaddled in white cloth and with a faint royal nimbus behind his head is most likely Jahangir. His mother, the Rajput princess Maryam az-Zamani, reclines next to him. She is wrapped in a beautifully embroidered shawl and wears a jeweled band around her neatly oiled and combed hair. She also wears strings of pearls around her neck and multiple rings, many with dangling pearls, along the outer edges of her ear. The elderly woman sitting in the highly decorated chair beside the mother is probably Hamida Banu Begum, Akbar's mother. As befitting the highly respected mother of the ruling emperor, she wears a tall, heavily embellished, Turkish-style cap over a fine white cloth head covering, a blue shawl around her upper body, and green trouser legs peeking out from below her inner robe. Her feet rest comfortably on a small pillow. These two women exemplify the first style of women's court clothing. Many of the other women who crowd around baby, mother, and grandmother wear clothing similar to what these prominent women wear. The women in this style of dress tend to wear either tall Turkish caps or the conch-shaped Mughal turban.

The second most popular woman's clothing style of the Mughal was the Rajasthani. Woman in this style covered their heads with an *odhani*, an unstitched cloth wrapped around the upper body with the loose end drawn over the back of the head. The rest of her clothing was more revealing. They wore a snug short-sleeved *choli*, an abbreviated blouse that emphasized and supported the breasts. With the choli, women wore the full skirt worn by Rajasthani Hindu women, the *ghagra*. Over this ensemble, they wore a shawl. According to Akbar's biographer, Abul Fazl, trousers were considered more elegant court attire than the long ghagras.

Muslim and Hindu court styles frequently came into contact with each other, because the court included many Hindus, and women from outside the zanana often attended special women's functions at the court. A favorite was the zanana bazaar, the *khushroz*, where female entrepreneurs of the zanana sold goods to the emperor—the only male allowed to shop there—and to other women associated with the court. This bazaar was also a prime place to see and be seen. Many marriage arrangements began at the khushroz. It was held on a varying schedule within the palace complex. Here women could buy the finest textiles and see the latest fashion styles. The men held a similar bazaar the following day. Nur Jahan, the wealthy trader and skillful political manipulator who was the favorite wife of Jahangir, probably sold some of the special fabrics she is credited with introducing at this bazaar. These include a silver thread brocade called *badla*, a lace made of silver thread called *kinari*, a very lightweight flowered muslin called *dudami* that was used for gowns, and *panchtoliya*, a fine fabric for veils.

Certainly Mughal women who went out in public were hidden from prying eyes. Records state that Mughal women wore white veils over their faces when outside of the zanana. Written sources also say that their public clothing was very similar to that worn by the men: trousers and coats. Women wore an outer robe called a *pairhan* in public. The pairhan was made of relatively heavy cloth and would be removed in the privacy of the zanana.

The nobility also apparently wore less substantial garments. Akbar's biographer Abul Fazl describes the woman's *peshwaz* as being similar to the *takauchiah*, except that it tied in the front with strings or simply was left to hang open. The peshwaz resembled a long-sleeved, high-waisted, *choli*-like blouse with an attached skirt that was open down the front. It was often made of the fine, transparent Bengali mal mal. Women are frequently shown wearing a patka underneath the peshwaz, with its long ends hanging down in front covering the point where the legs join the torso. Underneath the peshwaz, women wore trousers cut in the paijama style, with tight-fitting lower legs that were longer than the wearer's legs. The trouser legs were crushed into small folds around the ankle. These were made of heavier, less revealing fabric than the peshwaz.

The transparency of the mal mal *khas*, the special muslin fabric, was both a wonder and a modesty issue. Early Greeks and Romans marveled at the beauty and delicacy of Bengali cottons. Mal mal was called "woven wind," "flowing water," and "evening dew." Records say that Shah Jahan chastised one of his daughters for the indecent transparency of a particular outfit and she responded by proving that she was actually wearing seven layers of the gossamer fabric. European traveler François Bernier repeats a story he heard at court about women's beautifully embroidered paijamas that were so delicate and fragile that they often did not survive one night of wear. Painters loved to show women wearing this transparent cloth while bathing. Many of the more standardized pictures of women painted during the Mughal period show dancing girls wearing clothing that clearly showed the snug cholis and trousers worn underneath their sheer outer garments. Cholis often rode up a little to expose a seductive bit of the woman's lower breast. The costumes of the dancing girls often are reminiscent of Hindu women's clothing from the same period.

Mughal noblewomen led very active lives in spite of being housed in the zanana. Some played polo among themselves and also went hunting. Nur Jahan, Jahangir's favorite, loved to hunt. She is portrayed hunting in clothing very much like the Mughal man's standard garments, including a sheer muslin jama worn over a modest undergarment, trousers with tight-fitting crushed legs, a conch-shaped Mughal turban, and gold-embellished slippers with turned-up toes topped with pompoms. The backs of the slippers are folded down beneath her heels, revealing the red henna coloring the soles of her feet. Around her waist, she wears a patka from which hang a powder horn, a small pouch that may hold extra shot for her long rifle, and several cords terminating in jeweled tassels.

COSMETICS AND JEWELRY

No noblewoman's costume was complete without makeup and jewelry. The Mughal woman wore significantly more types of jewelry than her bejeweled male counterpart. She had rings for her toes and her fingers, ankle bracelets and other foot decorations, bangles for her wrists, rings for her earlobes, studs for her nose, and ornaments for her hair, neck, and waist. Her clothing was also decorated with jewels and precious metals. One European doctor, Niccolao Manucci, who visited the court of Aurangzeb and was allowed to treat the women of the zanana, wrote that its inhabitants wore so many bracelets on their wrists that it was difficult for him to find a free space to take a patient's pulse.

Women colored their hands and feet with elaborate patterns made with henna paste. As she aged, the noblewoman used henna to hide the telltale gray strands in her long dark hair. She wore *kohl* around her eyes and used *masy*, a rice dentifrice, to turn her teeth an attractive black color. Heavy perfumes were popular with both men and women. These included scents like musk, jasmine, and attar of roses. However, these oil-based fragrances could be dangerous—Jahanara, the oldest daughter of Shah Jahan's wife Mumtaz Mahal, survived extensive burns after her heavily perfumed clothing caught fire.

CONCLUSION

As we have seen, although almost no clothing survives from the early Mughal court, other, less transitory sources give an excellent feel for the relatively simply shaped garments made of superbly crafted textiles worn by Mughal nobility.

The record for men's clothing is especially rich in descriptions, illustrations, inventories, and accounts of newly invented and renamed garments. Clothing including the robes of honor were prized status symbols, and patkas became treasured mementos of royal favor. Representations of Mughal women's garments are less reliable, but there is enough description of their clothing and accessories to tell us that their garments were no less luxurious than those of their male counterparts.

Ultimately the Mughals were able to combine their own clothing traditions with indigenous Indian clothing styles into a unique style of dress well suited to the heat and monsoons of the Indian subcontinent. Indian master weavers, embroiderers, dyers, jewelers, and metalsmiths created extraordinary costumes for a knowledgeable clientele well versed in the art of personal display. The floral motifs and basic clothing shapes of many Mughal court garments became a familiar and enduring style that continues to this day in much of the subcontinent.

FURTHER READING

Bernier, François. *Travels in the Mogul Empire, A.D. 1656–1668*. Trans. Archibald Constable. London: Oxford University Press, 1916.

Goswamy, B. N. *Indian Costumes in the Collection of the Calico Museum of Textiles*, vol. 5, *Historic Textiles of India at the Calico Museum, Ahmedabad*. Ahmedabad, India: Calico Museum of Textiles, 1993.

Keene, Manuel. *Treasury of the World: Jewelled Arts of India in the Age of the Mughals*. New York: Thames & Hudson, 2001.

Okada, Amina. *Indian Miniatures of the Mughal Court*. New York: H. N. Abrams, 1992.

Schimmel, Annemarie. *The Empire of the Great Mughals: History, Art and Culture*. Trans. Corinne Attwood. London: Reaktion Books, 2004.

Untracht, Oppi. *Traditional Jewelry of India*. New York: H. N. Abrams, 1997.

WEB RESOURCES

Metropolitan Museum of Art. http://www.metmuseum.org.

Victoria and Albert Museum. http://www.vam.ac.uk.

http://www.asia.si.edu/collections/zoomObject.cfm?ObjectId=22373

http://www.mfa.org/tours/package.asp?key=684

www.designerhistory.com/historyoffashion/mughal.html

MOVIES

The Great Moghuls (six half-hour segments, distributed by Landmark Films, Falls Church, VA, 1990)

India: From Moghuls to Independence (Films Media Group. 1975)

Warrior Empire: The Mughals (History Channel, 2006)

Korean Clothing

Aleasha McCallion

TIMELINE

HISTORICAL KOREA

Despite struggling to keep an independent cultural and political identity, the Korean people have one of the longest national histories in the world. They are a single ethnic family anthropologically distinguished from both their Chinese and Japanese neighbors and claim descendants from several Mongol tribes. The Korean language has long been spoken, but a uniquely Korean written alphabet wasn't developed until 1443 by King Sejong the Great.

Old Choson, the earliest known state in Korean history, spanned a legendary age between 2333 and 108 BCE on the Korean Peninsula. Taken over by the Han Chinese, Old Choson would not be the last Korean kingdom to be influenced by China. In the first century BCE, the Korean kingdoms of Koguryo, Paekche, and Silla rose in power, bringing about the Three Kingdoms period (57 BCE–668 CE). Depending on their political or geographical circumstances, all three kingdoms were influenced by alternating alliances with China and Japan, including socially, aesthetically, and religiously.

Buddhism was brought into Korea through China in the fourth century and grew to a powerful force by the sixth. The nature-aligned and respecting practice was successful because it paralleled an older philosophy of relating humans with their natural surroundings. The Korean cultural expression is influenced by this awareness of nature and is reflected in the costume classifications of beauty of nature, personality, evil, and tradition.

After five hundred years of warring among the kingdoms, Silla emerged dominant in the seventh century with the assistance of Tang China. Prior to unification, the Silla Kingdom held a distinctive native culture that had developed due to its greater distance from the seat of power in China, and it is credited as a strong basis for the independent Korean culture. By the tenth century, a united Korean state was firmly established, and Buddhism, the official state religion, had inspired much of Silla's intellectual and artistic achievement.

Silla fell in 935 to the Koryo dynasty (918–1392), and a period of increased northern pressure from Mongol invasions ensued; their influence was intense and invasive. Even so, Koryo revealed a time of civil sophistication, Buddhist publications, and cotton cultivation. It was in the later thirteenth century that Korean royalty submitted to the encouragement to marry Mongol princesses, and the style of Korean women's costume was greatly influenced by the northern invader.

The Choson dynasty (1392–1910) was a period of extensive Chinese influence, but also of the revival of the Silla-developed Korean identity. The Qing-style code of Confucianism was integrated into social life by the fifteenth and sixteenth centuries, and the Choson dynasty regulated costume based on status, including fabrics, colors, motifs and accessories.

However, in the seventeenth century, after surviving several invasions from the Manchu and Japan, the Korean identity became a national project. The sporadic exposure to Western ideas through China and Japan encouraged the study of Korea's own history and geography. Soon there was a movement away from Chinese themes in art as artists started to focus on the Korean common people rather than Chinese characteristics.

The artistic expression of Korea, despite other Asian influences, has refined in a unique and identifiable style. Paintings by Cho Yongsok (1686–1761) and Kim Hongdo (1745–before 1818) exemplify this trend of portraying Korean people in representative costume and surrounding landscapes rather than Chinese settings.

Korea became a vassal state to Qing China, and this increased the exporting and paying of resources and goods as tribute. However, even though there was extensive economic and scholarly trade, with political cooperation evident throughout the eighteenth and nineteenth centuries, the export of resources diminished the economic strength of Korea. At a time when the class structure was strictly polarized, in that the *yangban* or aristocrats held elite social positions of power and had influence over the king, Catholicism spread among artisans and farmers. The last years of the Choson dynasty were tumultuous, with isolationist policies against foreign influence and trade, internal Catholic persecutions, and peasant wars (1812 and 1862). This era was the last of the independent neo-Confucian Korean society state before the annexation by Japan in 1910 and direct Western influence in 1943.

KOREAN COSTUME: THE HANBOK

The Choson dynasty is the time period where the costume of the Silla Kingdom was gradually altered into the recognized traditional Korean *hanbok*, or costume, in the forms known today. The basic hanbok was designed and made in the home by women, until the influence of Western clothing production. Modestly covering almost all of the body, the colors, fibers, and ornamentation of the hanbok were purposely selected to reflect themes of cultural belief and the wearer's particular guild or position in society, and they adhered to sumptuary laws that were present during the Choson dynasty.

The origin of the hanbok is traced to Manchurians and northern Koreans, who regularly wore white gowns or robes with large sleeves and pants; on special occasions, they would wear adorned silk brocade or embroidered clothing. The art of the Koguryo tombs of the Three Kingdoms period is the strongest reference to early forms of costume, even though it is portrayed within a Chinese-influenced art aesthetic. The women are dressed in waist-length or longer V-neck tops and generous long skirts over pants, while the men are shown wearing a similar-style top garment with wide-leg pants.

The costumes of men of the later Silla court, on the urging of royalty, were adaptations of the Tang style of official costumes brought back from China in 647. Women's clothing in court and eventually royalty themselves would also adapt styles of the Tang, Yuan, and later Ming dynasties. However, the traditional Korean clothing aesthetic persisted among the common people, who were less affected by such fashion trends.

The basic hanbok for women is the *ch'ma-chogori*. *Ch'ma* refers to the high-waisted full skirt, with narrow shoulder straps, that wraps to overlap in the back and flows in slight pleats to the ankles. The *chogori* top is a jacket or blouse with long curved sleeves (*sohme*); it has evolved to a short bolero length that is overlapped to close to the right of center front and ties above the bust line with two long sashes (*korum*) in a large loop. The collar (*kit*) has a thin, replaceable outer layer (*tongjong*) of white woven material—hemp, cotton, or ramie—to protect the garment from wear at the neckline. The ch'ma-chogori was worn over undergarments, a remnant of the earlier pant underlayer, and could be accompanied by an overcoat (*dooroomakee*) or outer cloak/veil (*chang-ot*). Delicately ornamented hairpins were worn, and in place of pockets, small geometrical pouches (*yeomnang* or *gangnang*) hung on ties and were embellished with the embroidery of auspicious symbols.

The ch'ma has changed little over time, except originally tying at the ankles and later demonstrating class or marital status, but the chogori has undergone many alterations to the shape of the main body (*kil*), hem, and sleeve arc. Also, the characteristics of the collar, armhole, panel positioning, sashes, and component measurements changed in the garment over time. Controversially revealing, cropped lengths were popular in the seventeenth and eighteenth centuries even when women's rights were limited by the Confucian state (the Principle of Three Obediences constrained a women's locus of control to a man her entire life).

The Korean chogori has basic form similarities to the Chinese robe and the Japanese *kimono*, but also unique characteristics reflecting Korean style and aesthetics. Stylistic norms demonstrated in Korean costume are natural, soothing lines and gracefully exaggerated human shapes. In the sixteenth century, the shape was more similar to the Chinese robe, in A-line or fan shape and sleeve structure, especially in the garments for men.

The hanbok for men, the *paji-chogori*, includes the wide leg trouser *paji* and an earlier longer version of the chogori. The men's chogori length has remained more constant over time, reaching to just below the waist. Additional layers—long coats (*turumagi*) or overcoats (*dopo*)—had wider sleeves and collars and were generally considered more formal wear. The dopo's tie position was adjusted above that of the chogori in order that the two ties would not overlap on a man's chest; however an additional tie belt (*tti*) was fastened around the outside of all the jacket layers. Women, especially women of status, also wore overcoat styles that originated from men's garments.

During a time of extensive hierarchical organization, class-based costume was dictated by sumptuary laws. Costume colors, materials, motifs, and accessories reflected the status of the owner and the occasion or function. This is still true in modern times for special occasions and festivals. Although children's clothing reflected in miniature the attributes of adult garments, including the padded socks (*beoseon*) and *heukhye* footwear with pointy toes, the head ornamentation styles were extremely different. Children wore a bonnet-style embroidered hat (*gulle*) with a number of dangling ribbons or tails, depending on the region. Women in warm weather wore a peaked hat (*gokkal*) made of paper or cloth folded repeatedly and fixed to the hair; dark fur- and silk-detailed *nambawi* hats were worn by fashionable women and offered warmth in the winter.

The men's hats were the most intricate and diverse; there were different designs for nobles and officials, as well as Confucian scholars and religious leaders. The nobleman's headgear (*gat*) was stacked onto a headband (*mangeon*) and high cap (*tanggeoun*) and then fastened to the head with a tie around the chin. The wide brim was position carefully to sit lower in the front. The *samo* or *coronet* hat of the official was woven with side wings out of bamboo or horsehair, which like the *jegwan* of the Confucian horsehair hats, were architecturally tiered upward from the crown of the head in geometrical shapes and points. Royal men wore a silk, taller, black cylindrical *coronet*, and some kings wore the Confucian *jeongjagwan*.

The most exquisite examples of traditional Korean costume are royal costumes of the Choson dynasty. The queen and noblewomen had the pick and privilege of wearing luxurious fabrics of silk, cotton, hemp, or ramie, all of

The most exquisite examples of traditional Korean costume are of the Choson dynasty royal costumes. Courtesy of the Library of Congress.

which were available in abundance from royal gifts, imports, or domestic production. Noblewomen wore the *Samhoejang* chogori, which would have been worn by the upper-class women on special occasions. The queens of the Choson period layered several embellished garments, including an outer ceremonial jacket (*hwangwonsam*); in this manner, the chogori was not the outer layer, as it would have been for women of lower status.

The Choson king's robes changed slightly with each to reign, but the *hongnyong-po*, or official costume, included a long, wide-sleeved robe in red, blue, or yellow, decorated on the chest, back, and shoulders with large elaborate golden crests with the royal motif of a dragon with five claws. The footwear of the king was the same basic design of a pointy toe and thick elongated ankles but was eloquently made of dyed black deerskin with a prominent sole.

Although the elite classes and royalty were not restricted in fabric choices, the lower or laborer classes were limited to hemp, and to some degree ramie, which were produced in great amounts at the beginning of the period. Later, ramie increased in value and quality, declined in production, and was attainable only by the upper classes. The dominant fiber production for the general population of the late Choson period was cotton, which was in widespread cultivation after being introduced in 1367. Garments of choice for everyday use continued to be predominantly the natural cellulose white; however, with natural dyes, there were a number of colors that were used to ornament costume and demonstrate social class.

The five colors of blue, red, yellow, white, and black have powerful natural, elemental, and spiritual interpretations in Korean aesthetics and tradition; various meanings assigned to them include the four directions and their center, the annual season changes, and the five elements of wood, fire, metal, water, and earth. These colors can be seen on the sleeves of ceremonial robes and communicate a distinctly Korean style. Alternating positive and negative color

A detail of *Meeting Between a Notable and Three Women in the Street*, shows a variety of hanbok and accessory styles. © The Art Archive/Musée Guimet Paris/ Gianni Dagli Orti.

placements are seen within the sleeves of upper garments, as well as in an ensemble combination of the upper and lower garments.

Colors reserved for those of status or special occasions varied; purple and pink garments can be found in the royal collections of queens, while courtesans' or princesses' jackets were green. Prior to marriage, a high-status woman wore an attractive combination of a yellow chogori and red ch'ma; once married, women wore colors that reflected their husband's social station.

Throughout the history of Korean society, the traditional costume characteristics have reflected the social, political, national, and economic changes of the society yet have maintained the religious and spiritual preferences and practices of the Korean people. The simplicity and uniqueness of the Korean traditional costume is a recognizable symbol of the Korean aesthetic within an extensive and world-renowned Asian textile culture, thus reflecting the historic pattern of an independent people thoroughly influenced by their geographic neighbors yet still established as a distinguished culture.

FURTHER READING

Kwon, O-Ch'ang. *Korean Costumes during the Chosun Dynasty*. Trans. Kim Eun-ok. Soul-si: Hyonamsa, 1998.

Kwon, Yoon-Hee Suk. *Symbolic and Decorative Motifs of Korean Silk, 1875–1975*. Seoul, Korea: Il Ji Sa, 1988.

Roberts, Claire, and Huh Dong-hwa. *Rapt in Colour: Korean Textiles and Costumes of the Choson Dynasty*. Sydney, Australia: Powerhouse Museum, 1998.

WEB RESOURCES

Korean National Folk Museum. http://www.knfm.kr.
Seoul Museum of History. http://www.museum.seoul.kr.
Pacific Asia Museum. www.pacificasiamuseum.org/calendar/exhibitions/kcostumesmore/
    html
http://bosp.kcc.hawaii.edu/Horizons/Horizons2001/63Handbok.html

MOVIES

Blood Rain (2004)
Hawangjin-i (2006)
Wang-ui namja (*The King and the Clown*; 2005)

Clothing in Latin America

Karrie Porter Brace

TIMELINE

1487	Dedication of the Great Temple of Tenochtitlán, the capital of the Aztec Empire
1492	Columbus arrives in the New World
1493	Inca emperor Huayna Capac expands Inca domain to Ecuador and Colombia, establishing the Tiwaninsuyu from northern Chile to almost the Isthmus of Panama
1502	Moctezuma II becomes Aztec emperor until his death at the hands of his own subjects in 1520
1516–1700	The Habsburg dynasty controls Spain
1519–1522	Hernando Cortez and his conquistadores land in the Gulf Coast region of Mexico ande take over the Aztec Empire
1531	Virgin of Guadalupe appears to Juan Diego on a hill outside of Mexico City
1532	Atahualpa becomes Inca emperor; after an extended civil war, Spanish conquistador Francisco Pizzaro takes the empire
1535	Maya force the Spanish out of the Yucatan Peninsula
1542	Bartolomé de las Casas (later named bishop of Chiapas in southern Mexico) writes *Devastation of the Indies* to push the "New Laws" to reform treatment of Indians
1615	Felipe Guaman Poma de Ayala of Cuzco finishes *Primer nueva corónica y buen gobierno* for King Philip III of Spain
1621	Mirra, a Hindu princess, arrives from the Philippines and becomes the "China Poblana"
1697	Last of the independent Maya conquered by the Spanish at Flores in Guatemala (although many continue to live in seclusion throughout Quintana Roo in Mexico)
1740–1781	Inca uprisings against the Spanish in the Andes
1799–1803	German geographer Alexander von Humboldt explores Mexico and South America

The textile and clothing traditions of Latin America during the Pre-Columbian, Late Post-Classic, European Contact, and colonial periods (i.e., through the eighteenth century) represent a

Portrait of Don Marcos Chinguan Topa, Inca elite in fine clothing reflecting a combination of indigenous and Spanish influences after the arrival of conquistadores, clerics, and civil servants in western South America. Courtesy of Karrie Porter Brace.

time of great change in the New World. European kingdoms of the fifteenth century sought more natural resources and territories for expansion, and Christopher Columbus's voyages to the Caribbean and Latin America established the connections between indigenous American peoples and Europeans that, among many other changes, would lead to new ideas, styles, and ways for people to make, use, and wear clothing.

The arrival of Spanish soldiers, clerics, and settlers in the Caribbean, Mexico, and Central and South America introduced new concepts, ways of life, materials, and styles to both the settlers and the indigenous peoples. The Natives were amazed by the fair-skinned, bearded strangers with their alien technology, religion, horses, cattle, and sheep. Conversely, Spanish explorers' accounts described in equal amazement the busy New World cities that rivaled European ports or commercial centers. The hierarchical culture ranged from common working-class people to high nobility, and each of these groups had a distinct sartorial culture with extensive histories, technologies, and resources.

The Spanish colonists, soldiers, and clerics in the early sixteenth century naturally wore the current fashions of Europe. All the men wore shirts, hose or leggings with breeches over them, and doublets or *jubones*, which were tight-fitting jackets or tunics that were longer in the front than the back, with short upright collars and detachable sleeves. The *jubon* had originally served as padding beneath a chain mail hauberk or leather cuirass, but it later became increasingly elaborate and a fashion statement itself.

Although armor was passing out of European fashion, the early *conquistadores* frequently wore metal breast plates and heavy metal helmets. Pieces of Spanish armor have been found in archaeological contexts throughout the New World, from the Carolinas and the south-central and southwestern United States throughout Mexico and on down to South America.

As the heat of the tropics caused many Spaniards to reconsider their wardrobe, Spanish armor gave way to the heavy cotton quilted or leather armor styles utilized by the native peoples of Latin America. The colonial elites, however, wishing to maintain and display their social position, continued to wear silk brocades, velvet, and lace. Ladies wore full skirts supported by a farthingale,

Cortez and Malinche meeting with Mesoamericans. The Old World clothing styles contrasting with New World indigenous clothing styles seen in *El Lienzo de Tlaxcala*. Courtesy of Karrie Porter Brace.

a round bell-shaped hoop skirt of Spanish origin. Clerics wore the long black robes of the Spanish Catholic Church.

The major geographic areas of indigenous Latin American cultures include Mesoamerica and the Andes. The region of Mesoamerica, as defined by Paul Kirchoff, is bound by central Mexico on the north and Costa Rica on the south. While this area spans many different ecological zones, the complex cultures that rose and flourished there share common cultural traits, language families, and agricultural practices focusing on maize (corn), beans, and squash. Included in the major cultural groups of Mesoamerica are the Maya (Quiche, Chol, Kanjobal, Tzeltal, Yucatec) in the southern Central American lowlands and highlands; the Aztec (Mexica) and other groups such as the Tepanec, Acolhua, and Tlaxcalas in central Mexico; and the Zapotec-Mixtec of Oaxaca, Puebla, and Guerrero in the highlands of western Mexico.

Andean civilization was primarily centered in the northwestern highlands of South America but had connections from the headwaters of the Amazon River to the Pacific shores of Chile. The Inca were the dominant culture in the Andes at the time of European arrival; however, their empire included multiple ethnic groups that spoke a variety of Quechua and Aymara languages.

By the early sixteenth century, the major Post-Classic, Pre-Columbian Latin American cultures had reached such levels of complexity as to be considered true empires. The Aztec Empire controlled much of Mexico through its *pochteca* or trading armies. They produced vast amounts of manufactured goods, raw minerals, semiprecious stones, exotic animals, and food to send to the Aztec capital of Tenochtitlán from ethnic groups as far away as the American Southwest, the Caribbean, and Pacific Ocean. Similarly, the Inca Empire held sway in the Andes, although Cuzco preferred *mit'a* or courvée labor. The Inca economy relied on a complex trade network that connected commercial communities from the Pacific seashore over the mountains to the Amazon rain forest. Textile and clothing production were vital in both these imperial economies.

Before the arrival of Europeans, garments were obviously created only from materials available in the New World, such as white cotton (*Gossypium hirsutum*); Mexican brown cotton (*Gossypium mexicanum*), which the Maya called *ixcaco* or *ixcay* and the Spanish called *cuyuscate*; various other plant fibers such as agave and ficus bark cloth; animal skins; and feathers. An additional material available only in the Andes was camelid wool fiber from llamas, alpacas, guanacos, and vicuñas. The ancient Andean peoples also had cottons, but of a wider variety of colors, including the chocolate-brown, long-staple *Gossypium barbanense*. A wide variety of naturally occurring colors of plant fibers were used; however, many of the textiles recovered from archaeological sites have a surprising variety and sophistication of dyed colors from New World color sources such as minerals, cochineal, and indigo. The Spanish, and the rest of Europe, would come to value the red dye derived from cochineal, the cactus louse, so highly that its production and export was second only to Latin American silver.

Indigenous women dominated sixteenth-century Latin American garment technology, production, and design. Textile and clothing production in Latin America was highly valued by indigenous peoples, who deemed the work more important than the production of precious metals. Entire courts of elite or sacred women were employed to supply the needs of the ruling class or the state trade of fabrics and garments in Aztec and Inca society.[1] Elite Aztec women considered their work a source of pride and dedicated countless hours to the task. The Inca brought in weavers from Bolivia and the southern Peruvian highlands to Cuzco, where they were cloistered in workshops. These weavers were part of the class of women called the Sun Virgins (*accllacuna* or *accllawasi*), who served specifically in the temples and courts. Their weaving and textiles were reserved for elite use. Although indigenous Latin American women were the masters of weaving in provincial and elite society, there were also Andean men who were known as *cumbicamayos* or *qunpikamayuq*, "makers of *cumbi*," who wove only the finest tapestry-style textiles, or *cumbi*, specifically to be used as garments for the *Sapa Inca*, the king, or the *Coya*, the queen.

Indigenous weavers in both Mesoamerica and the Andes spun fibers using simple spindle whorls and wove fabric on backstrap looms. These looms and spindle whorls were in use at the time of culture contact and are in continued use today, but evidence of their existence is found archaeologically in both Mesoamerica and the Andes dating well before the Common Era. Archaeologists have found spun cotton yarn in the Tehuacán Valley in Mexico dating to 1200–1500 BCE. Spindle whorls are ubiquitous in Mesoamerican archaeological contexts and range from reworked shards of pottery to elaborately crafted pieces of art. Clean and combed cotton or wool fibers were hand spun onto reed spindles weighted with clay whorls. Often women would spin as they performed other chores; they also used ceramic bowls to support the spindles as they twirled.

Models of backstrap looms dating to the Late Classic period (600–900) have been found interred with deceased Maya elite women on the island of Jaina off the Mexican coast of Campeche. Andean use of the spindle whorl and backstrap loom was documented in Felipe Guaman Poma de Ayala's *First New Chronicle and Good Government* (1615). Inca elite portraits painted in the mid-sixteenth century show the *ñustas* with their spindles in hand. Spindles and backstrap looms were easily portable and could be set up in any work or living space. The only drawback to using the backstrap loom was that it limited the width of fabric to that of the warp. For wider garments, woven sections had to be sewn together, but the seams frequently were embellished as a part of the garment's adornment. A variation of the backstrap loom was the "toe loom" used by Andean highland weavers to produce even narrower strips of fabric to be used as belts, sashes, straps, or other parts of garments.

The Maya are the best known of the Mesoamerican weavers, producing textiles ranging from the lightest gauze to thick blankets. Images of ancient Mayan clothing found in stone carvings and on ceramics from the Late Classic period show elite women in fine garments woven in ornate brocades and fine lacy gauzes. Fragments of these textiles and garments have also been found in archaeological contexts or the bottoms of *cenotes*, sinkholes formed in the porous limestone of the Yucatan Peninsula. In the Late Post-Classic period, weaving was so integral to Mayan cosmology that many important buildings at the large urban centers of Chichén Itzá and Uxmal have architectural facades decorated in Maya weaving patterns.

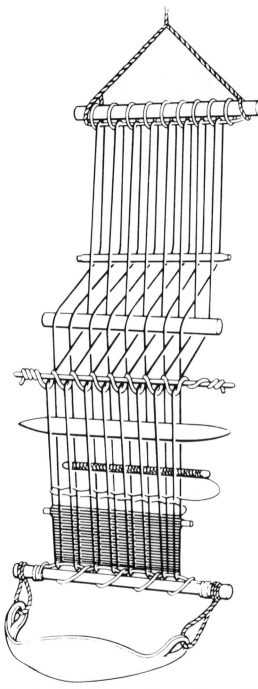

A good example of a backstrap loom like those used in early Latin American textile production.

Most brocaded fabrics, in the past and present, are created in indigenous patterns symbolizing natural elements found in the local environment. Many designs included flowers, stars, snakes, amphibians, people, and lightning bolts.

Over time, designs brought by European elites were incorporated with the Maya's natural motifs. Women's blouses or *huipiles* in the Guatemalan villages in the department of Sacatepéquez incorporated designs of peacocks, rampant lions, rearing horses, and double-headed eagles. Early textile colors were limited to natural dyes produced from vegetable and mineral sources. With the arrival of Europeans, the Maya gained access to new dyes or more brightly colored silk and wool fibers. The weaving tradition in the highlands has continued through today with finely woven and brightly colored Maya huipiles, *tzutes*, and *cortes* that utilize the most durable and colorful natural and synthetic fibers.

Historically and archaeologically, the weaving tradition of the Andes is as colorful and complex as the textiles themselves. New World cotton and wool were used to create long mantles and tunics used by almost all indigenous highland peoples. Complex weaving and designs from the earlier cultures such as the Paracas, Chimu, and Wari still influenced Inca weaving at the time of European contact. Andean designs, like those of the Maya, were taken from their natural environment. Some contemporary textile experts believe the Inca also developed a geometric design pattern that may convey information in ways similar to a written language. Although the Maya could weave more complex brocade patterns, the Inca produced stronger textiles and more colorfast dyes that were well preserved even from ancient times. The Inca created sturdy fabrics using a cotton warp framework, through which softer and more colorful wool wefts were woven. Strong yellow, red, magenta, tan, brown, blue, green, and black dyes were used. Some cloth was even painted.

Cloth and clothing in the Andes was differentiated between simple fabrics made for home use in the outer provinces and the finer cloth sent as *mit'a* to Cuzco. Cloth for the home was referred to as *awaska*, made from llama wool at a thread count of about 100 or more per inch (40+ per centimeter). Better cloth and clothing was made of alpaca fibers and used as fulfillment of the *mit'a* or in the exchange of gifts among the Inca elite. Clothing for the Inca royalty was called *qunpi* or *cumbi* and was frequently made of the finest fibers of the wild vicuña, the smallest of the Andean camelids, with textile thread counts of 500 or 600 strands per inch (200–240 per centimeter). To the Inca people, cloth and clothing were so highly valued that gifts of garments were made to adolescents at the time they were recognized as adults and to conquered tribes by imperial armies, conveying an understanding that clothing and proper dress was an integral part of being Inca. More elaborately woven clothing and textiles were worn and used by the Andean elite. Members of the Inca army were believed to have their own garment design of a black-and-white checkerboard-patterned tunic with a red inverted triangle at the center front.

Many textiles and garments from the Inca period before the conquest have survived in well-preserved condition throughout South America. Sacrificial and funeral mummy bundles found in Andean archaeological contexts frequently comprise multiple layers of finely and elaborately woven cloth wrapped over and around the deceased, not necessarily a person of elite descent but dressed in ritual clothing.

Clothing was gender specific for adults. Throughout Latin America just before the time of European contact, most basic indigenous menswear consisted of a simple loincloth, over which tunics, mantles, capes, or kilts were worn. Women wore a broader variety of garments, from a sarong-style wrap to blouses over wrapped or belted skirts. Clothing for infants and toddlers ranged from simple knee-length shifts to complex garments identical to those of adults except smaller in size.

For the average person of Tenochtitlán in the sixteenth century, Aztec clothing was simple white cotton garments that fitted loosely over the torso. Illustrations from Spanish colonial-period documents and indigenous codices show the Aztec people and their roles in society, with clothing being consistent across most of the population. Men wore a basic loincloth at the hips and mantle around the shoulders. Women wore a long and wide sleeveless tunic over a skirt tied at the waist. The Aztec of higher social status displayed more ornately adorned and colorful garments but built of basically the same construction. The Aztec so strongly identified their gender with clothing that men and women could be referred to by their garments, either as ''a blouse'' or ''a skirt'' or as ''a loincloth'' or ''a mantle.''[2]

The Maya had a broader variety of clothing, as their culture was spread over both the cool highland and hot lowland areas of southern Mexico, Guatemala, Belize, and Honduras. Before conquest, Maya men wore a loincloth but had different garments that covered the upper torso. Elite Maya men wore short capes

Aztec costumes during Montezuma's reign, early sixteenth century. © HIP / Art Resource, NY.

High-ranking Aztec noble wearing loincloth and mantle from Codex Ixtlilxochitl. Courtesy of Karrie Porter Brace.

over their shoulders, or longer mantles and tunics in the higher elevations. Kilts or short pants were worn over their loincloths at the hip. The Maya crafted heavy greenstone jewelry of jade or related semiprecious stones, including heavy necklaces, ear plugs, broad collars, and bands of beads at the wrists and knees. In battle, the Maya fighters wore a heavy sleeveless tunic of padded cotton, which was extremely protective in pre-Columbian indigenous warfare.

The full ensemble or complex array of clothing and accessories that made up a Maya woman's traditional garb (*traje*) included the *huipil*, or blouse; the *tzute*, a head cloth or turban; and the *corte*, or skirt. Maya women wore skirts tied or belted at the waist with broad sleeveless tunics or huipiles woven or embroidered in elaborate patterns. Full-length huipiles were woven, sewn, and worn in more formal ritual settings or by elite women.

The vast differences in climate throughout Latin America determined appropriate dress for survival. In the warmer climate zones, garments were made of light cotton or ficus tree fiber, loose fitting and simple, allowing movement of cooler air next to the skin. In the highlands, the climate ranged from mild to colder temperatures, requiring people to wear heavier garments to maintain body temperature. Before the arrival of European sheep, highland Mesoamericans wove or quilted heavy cotton outer garments. Andean peoples wove heavy wool tunics and mantles, which women fastened with a *tupu*, a long metal straight pin with a large flat head, frequently made of silver, copper, gold, or *tumbaga*, a combination of these precious metals.

Western Mexico has variable lowland and highland climate zones, as well. Zapotec women wore long, heavy tunics, similar to the Maya huipil, over longer, thicker skirts. Zapotec men wore longer loincloths and heavier mantles than those of the Aztec. Mixtec women wore wrapped skirts under a *quechquemitl*, a long fringed, diamond-shaped, poncho-like blouse.

Inca women wore a long dress that reached from the neck to the ankles and was belted with a sash at the waist. A mantle was worn over the shoulders with

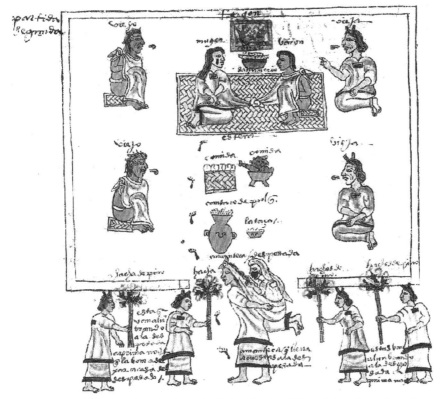

Typical male and female attire taken from the *Codex Mendoza*. Men in loincloths and mantles, women in long huipiles and skirts. Courtesy of Karrie Porter Brace.

the corners worn over the shoulders and fastened at the front. The women of higher social rank had increasingly elaborate belts and hems, either of intricate geometric or stylized natural designs.

Footwear was less gender specific in general, although it differed in the Northern and Southern Hemispheres, as well as according to climate. If footwear was worn at all, Mesoamericans preferred "heel cup" sandals with thongs through the toes. Andean people also wore sandals, but the high, cold, dry climate of the *altiplano* required them to wear boots that reached the knees.

Appropriate clothing for indigenous people was also determined by social and ritual parameters from the Late Post-Classic period on. Imperial and colonial sumptuary laws regulating the use of clothing and adornment limited the display of finery and jewels to elite Mesoamerican and Andean groups.[3] Jade jewelry and fine featherwork were restricted to people born in higher-status wealthy families such as the nobility and merchant classes. The elite indigenous men of western Mexico also wore obsidian *labrets* (lip plugs) and ear plugs.

Native garment styles and symbols woven or embroidered into the garments in both Mesoamerica and the Andes identified the wearer by group affiliation and status. The Maya, who had garment styles and symbols dating back to the Classic period (200 BCE–900 CE), continue to use them as a way to maintain their group identity during times of culture change.[4] So, too, do Andean highland peoples attempt to conserve their traditional clothing styles to affiliate people by village and lineage.

Indigenous Latin American headwear varied by membership within local groups and status. Elite headwear was extremely complex and was worn as an indication of status. Mesoamerican provincial men wore headbands, wraps, or woven straw hats, while Mesoamerican women braided or wrapped their hair. Some groups used strips of bright fabric like turbans or ribbons for colors and patterns identifying them by village or family affiliation. Many Mesoamerican women used a folded multifunctional utility cloth as headwear. Inca women also used the folded cloth, but among royal and elite women it had ceased to be used as anything but a head covering. Inca men's headwear ranged from simple headbands with feathers to caps with turban-like wraps to domed hats fringed with feathers and decorated with gold or silver disks.

Because colonial Spanish friars held strong opinions regarding native dress and behavior, life for indigenous peoples became increasingly strict and modest. Spanish friars at first attempted to restrict native peoples from adopting Spanish dress to curtail the mixing of European and indigenous lineages. Men were expected to wear short pants rather than loincloths.[5] Although many indigenous women were already modest in dress, the friars required women in the warmer lowland climates to keep their upper torsos covered when working or nursing infants. European clerics—warned of Old World courtesans in rich, colorful dress and unbound long hair—mistakenly assumed that Aztec and Inca elite women with their long hair and fine garments held similar roles in their societies.[6]

As European and indigenous people continued to interact over time, there was an inevitable exchange of clothing resources and styles between groups. Similar to European life, the ladies of elite Mesoamerican and Andean households took great pride in their weaving skills. New materials were adapted to changing traditional sartorial patterns as the different groups assimilated. Indigenous ritual clothing for elite men and women in Mesoamerica and the Andes maintained many native elements as people continued to participate in their own civic and religious activities as well as the liturgical activities of the Spanish Catholic Church.

Indigenous men's clothing changed more than women's attire as they integrated with the colonial infrastructure, adopting the silk coats and lace-trimmed shirts of Spanish grandees in religious, civic, and commercial settings. Women's clothing remained more traditional in style but adapted introduced materials and elements into use. The colors and textures of new fibers and fabrics such as sheep's wool and silk became popular. Merino and *churro* wool were especially valued among the Andean and Mesoamerican highland women for its insulating qualities, color variety, and ability to hold dyed colors. Andean women had highland metalsmiths adapt silver spoons into *tupus* by pounding and honing the utensil handles into long sharp points and engraving or elaborating the spoon bowl for fastening their long woolen mantles.

Although weaving and cloth production had already been a large part of the lives of Latin American indigenous women, they significantly increased during the colonial period.[7] European women, who were similarly skilled in spinning, weaving, and embroidery, brought freestanding looms to the New World. Finely woven textiles were highly valued by the elite in both indigenous and colonial societies, as lighter-weight cottons began replacing silks and wools in the hotter tropics. While in Pre-Columbian times Andean and Aztec imperial demands caused many women to make a cottage or cash industry of cloth and clothing, colonial clothing and textile production became another means to feed the new cash economy, as indigenous long-distance exchange and craft specialization previously controlled by the empires were now assumed by the Spanish crown. As textile production became increasingly important, indigenous men also started producing textiles and garments in the colonial period.

For the European colonists, adaptation of dress for warmer climates began replacing the restrictive garments of Imperial Spain. The heavy wools, leather, and thicker cotton flannels were replaced with finer wools, lighter cottons, and changes in style to allow heat to be carried away from the body. The heavy brocade finery used by the Spanish elite gave way to lighter silks and cottons. The men's garment styles abandoned more restrictive styles of the jubon or doublet for a simpler vest or a cotton tunic over breeches. Although Latin American indigenous fabrics and styles were better adapted to the tropical climates, most high-born European women were reluctant to modify their long skirts and proper attire until almost the eighteenth century.

In addition to the Spanish and indigenous clothing, styles, and resources, trade with East Asia also came to Mexico, Guatemala, and South America. Spanish merchants were circumnavigating the globe by the late sixteenth and seventeenth centuries. Rather than wait for Asian goods to be shipped overland through Asia to the ports of Europe and then on to Latin America, those who could afford imported goods started getting them directly from port cities along the Pacific coasts of New Spain, such as Acapulco. Fabrics from India, China, and the Philippines were imported, along with spices and other exotic luxury items. Fine silks were extremely popular, because they were seen as prestigious material yet were comfortable in the tropical climates.

Asians themselves also came to Latin America with the Spanish merchants, bringing with them unique clothing styles and color combinations. One colorful style of seventeenth-century dress is attributed to "La China Poblana," a woman who migrated to the Mexican city of Puebla. Although the Spanish colonial legend refers her as *La Chinita*, or "the Little Chinese Girl," Jesuit church records from Alonso Ramos, Francisco de Aguilera, and Jose del Castillo Grajeda recount that she was actually an India-born Hindu princess named Mirrha. Her story is an amazing tale—from her capture by pirates as a child, transfer by galleon from India to Manila and on to New Spain, then being sold or given to an elite Spanish colonial household in Mexico. After being baptized as Catarina de San Juan, she became popular for her charity, deep spiritual nature, and exotic dress.[8]

Local women from Puebla adopted Mirrha's colorful embroidered clothing and full skirts, in addition to adapting the popular Asian imported fabrics and fibers shipped into the port of Acapulco on the *Naos de China* from the Orient and Philippines in the seventeenth and eighteenth centuries, and came to be known as *Chinas Poblanas*. China Poblana dress comprised a white blouse overlaid by a colorful embroidered shirt, completed with a long colorful skirt in patches or sections of brightly colored cotton flannel. Chinas Poblanas braided their hair with ribbons on each side of their heads.

Eventually the China Poblana style incorporated the red, white, and green colors of the national flag and became the symbol of Mexican *mestizo* womanhood. The basic components of the style are the wide skirt called a *castor*, made of profusely embroidered red-and-black printed cotton flannel and a cotton blouse. The waist and hem of the skirt were trimmed with green satin. The white blouse was heavily embroidered at the neck and shoulders with a wide band of flowers made with thread, beads, and spangles. Wrapped around the shoulders and head was the traditional multicolored handmade *rebozo* and a headdress made of two strands of hand-braided red, white, and green ribbons. Although a few Mexican historians attribute the colorful China Poblana style to regional indigenous people, believing they wore a style that resembled Chinese dress, the earlier local clothing traditions actually used long tunics over wrapped skirts.

The Pre-Columbian, Late Post-Classic, European Contact, and colonial periods experienced great culture change in Latin America, not just for native peoples but also for the colonists themselves. As these people adapted to new cultures and climates, a rich exchange of ideas, resources, and styles became the visible markers of these changes. Indigenous people no longer wore loincloths or the dull colors of natural fibers, yet symbols and elements of their culture persisted in the style and design of their newer garments. Colonists adapting to their new lives and environments learned more about the climate and resources of their new homes. Eventually these changes would cause the elements of indigenous and colonial dress to be incorporated into the clothing and lives of the coming revolutionary times later in the nineteenth century.

NOTES

1. Carol Damian, "From Pachamama to the Virgin Mary: What the Spanish Never Saw," in *Andean Art: Visual Expression and Its Relation to Andean Beliefs and Values*, ed. Penny Dransart (Brookfield, VT: Avebury, 1995), 123; Louise M. Burkhart, "Mexica Women on the Home Front: Housework and Religion in Aztec Mexico," in *Indian Women of Early Mexico*, ed. Susan Schroeder, Stephanie Wood, and Robert Haskett (Norman: University of Oklahoma Press, 1997) 47.

2. Burkhart, "Mexica Women," 46–47.

3. Patricia Anawalt, "Costume and Control: Sumptuary Laws," *Archaeology* 33 (1980): 33–43.

4. Walter F. Morris Jr., "Maya Time Warps," *Archaeology* 39, no. 3 (1986): 52–59; Walter F. Morris Jr., *The Living Maya* (New York: H. N. Abrams, 1987).

5. Morris, "Maya Time Warps," 54.

6. Margaret Campbell Avery, "Women of Ill-Repute in the Florentine Codex," in *The Role of Gender in Pre-Columbian Art and Archaeology*, ed. Virginia Miller (Lanham, MD: University Press of America, 1988), 180–85; Cecilia Klein, "Wild Woman in Colonial Mexico: An Encounter of European and Aztec Concepts of the Other," in *Reframing the Renaissance: Visual Culture in Europe and Latin America, 1450–1650*, ed. Claire Farago (New Haven, CT: Yale University Press, 1995), 245–63; Carolyn Dean, "Andean Androgyny and the Making of Men," in *Gender and Pre-Hispanic America*, ed. Cecilia F. Klein (Washington, DC: Dumbarton Oaks Research Library and Collection, 2001), 157–65.

7. Susan Kellogg, "Gender Roles: Colonial Period," in *The Oxford Encyclopedia of Mesoamerican Cultures: The Civilizations of Mexico and Central America*, ed. David Carrasco (New York: Oxford University Press, 2001), 1:430.

8. Ronald J. Morgan, *Spanish American Saints and the Rhetoric of Identity, 1600–1810* (Tucson: University of Arizona Press, 2002), 119–42.

FURTHER READING

Anawalt, Patricia. "Costume and Control: Sumptuary Laws." *Archaeology* 33 (1980): 33–43.

Anderson, Arthur J. O., and Charles Dibble. *Florentine Codex*. Santa Fe, NM: School of American Research, 1955.

Avery, Margaret Campbell. "Women of Ill-Repute in the Florentine Codex." In *The Role of Gender in Pre-Columbian Art and Archaeology*, ed. Virginia Miller, 179–204. Lanham, MD: University Press of America, 1988.

Brown, Betty Ann. "Seen but Not Heard: Women in Aztec Ritual—the Sahagun Texts." In *Text and Image in Pre-Columbian Art*, ed. Janet C. Berlo, 119–53. International Series 180, British Archaeological Reports, Oxford, 1983.

Bunson, Margaret R., and Stephen M. Bunson. *Encyclopedia of Ancient Mesoamerica*. New York: Facts on File, 1996.

Burkhart, Louise M. "Mexica Women on the Home Front: Housework and Religion in Aztec Mexico." In *Indian Women of Early Mexico*, ed. Susan Schroeder, Stephanie Wood, and Robert Haskett, 24–54. Norman: University of Oklahoma Press, 1997.

Damian, Carol. "From Pachamama to the Virgin Mary: What the Spanish Never Saw." In *Andean Art: Visual Expression and Its Relation to Andean Beliefs and Values*, ed. Penny Dransart, 109–130. Brookfield, VT: Avebury, 1995.

Dean, Carolyn. "Andean Androgyny and the Making of Men." In *Gender and Pre-Hispanic America*, ed. Cecilia F. Klein, 143–82. Washington, DC: Dumbarton Oaks Research Library and Collection, 2001.

———. "Inka Nobles: Portraiture and Paradox in Colonial Peru." In *Exploring New World Imagery, Spanish Colonial Papers from the 2002 Mayer Center Symposium*, ed. Donna Pierce, 79–103. Denver, CO: Denver Art Museum, 2005.

Kellogg, Susan. "Gender Roles: Colonial Period." In *The Oxford Encyclopedia of Mesoamerican Cultures: The Civilizations of Mexico and Central America*, ed. David Carrasco, 1:430–32. New York: Oxford University Press, 2001.

Kirchoff, Paul. "Mesoamerica." *Acta Americana* 1 (1943): 92–107.

Klein, Cecilia. "Wild Woman in Colonial Mexico: An Encounter of European and Aztec Concepts of the Other." In *Reframing the Renaissance: Visual Culture in Europe and Latin America, 1450–1650*, ed. Claire Farago, 244–63. New Haven, CT: Yale University Press, 1995.

Morgan, Ronald J. *Spanish American Saints and the Rhetoric of Identity, 1600–1810*. Tucson: University of Arizona Press, 2002.

Morris, Walter F., Jr. *The Living Maya*. New York: H. N. Abrams, 1987.

———. "Maya Time Warps." *Archaeology* 39, no. 3 (1986): 52–59.

WEB RESOURCES

Woven Voices: Textile Traditions of the Highland Maya [website for the Woven Voices Exhibit Symposium, January 27, 2001, Appleton Museum of Art, Ocala, Florida]. http://www.anthro.fsu.edu/wovenvoices/symposium.html.

MOVIES

In Search of History: The Aztec Empire (History Channel, 2005)
In the Shadow of the Incas (1994)
Secrets of the Lost Empire (1997)

The Eighteenth Century

Jennifer Grayer Moore

TIMELINE

1709	Discovery of ruins at Herculaneum
1714	George I becomes king of England, beginning the Georgian period (through 1820)
1715	Death of Louis XIV and ascension of his great-grandson Louis XV to French throne
1737	Invention of the steam- or water-powered flying shuttle
1745	Madame de Pompadour becomes mistress to Louis XV and influences fashions at the French court and beyond; Rose Bertin becomes the first "fashion designer"
1748	Discovery of ruins at Pompeii and advent of neoclassicism in the arts
1755	Jean-Jacques Rousseau publishes *Discourse on Inequality*
1768	Steam-powered spinning jenny allows faster production of yarn
1774	Death of Louis XV and ascension of his grandson Louis XVI
1775	American Revolution begins
1776	Declaration of Independence signed; Thomas Paine distributes *Common Sense*; first steam engines in use (patented 1769)
1784	Power loom invented
1789	French Revolution; George Washington elected first U.S. president; guillotine invented
1792	Death of Louis XVI; Mary Wollstonecraft publishes *A Vindication of the Rights of Woman*
1793	Death of Marie Antoinette
1796	James Watt develops an improved steam engine
1799	Napoleon stages a coup d'état and becomes dictator of France

GENERAL HISTORY

The eighteenth century, which is roughly synonymous with the Age of Enlightenment (1715–1789), was an era of profound change and development in virtually every sector of society. The spirit of free scientific inquiry led to advancements in medicine and technology. Philosophical investigations led to upheaval and change of the extant social order and long-entrenched political ideas. It was also a period of great movement of people throughout the world, resulting in shared ideas and informed investigations. More and more people attempted to prove, in a rational way, what had until then been mysteries of the world or ideas simply accepted as part and parcel of life. Many of the uncertainties, medical and otherwise, of previous centuries became explainable, and thus less frightening, and to a great extent the powerful hold that religion had for centuries maintained on the human imagination lost some of its strength. In many ways, Great Britain and France led the way in intellectual discourse, economics, industry, literature, art, architecture, ethics, sanitation, and certainly—especially in France—fashion.

The eighteenth-century aesthetic essentially falls into two categories, one French and one English, both of which were adopted throughout Europe. The French style was delicate, charming, and light colored; it was the embodiment of an utterly refined elegance. Often the motifs found on objects of interior design were elaborately fashioned with modulating arabesques and lavishly gilded in gold leaf. This period of design is sometime referred to as the Rococo (meaning decorated with rocks and scallop shells), an extension and evolution of the heavier, though equally elaborate, Baroque of the seventeenth century. Works of fine art were frequently playful or even erotic and often included fantastic depictions of an idyllic outdoors. Perhaps the most exotic example of this style in architecture is found at the palace of Versailles, while prime examples of paintings are to be found in the works of Jean-Honoré Fragonard (1732–1806) and François Boucher (1703–1770).

In England, a different aesthetic was developing to replace the outdated Baroque. This eighteenth-century style developed to a great extent in the work of the architect Christopher Wren (1632–1723). Wren's works include St. Paul's Church in London (along with fifty other churches built after the Great Fire of London in 1666), as well as designs at Kensington Palace, Hampton Court, and Whitehall. This new style incorporated elements of Classical design with elements of Gothic and Baroque. Overall, the aesthetic was clean, spacious, and utterly modern. It was far less heavy, cluttered, and adorned than the preceding Baroque or the predominant French style of interior design. This aesthetic crossed the Channel to Europe and can be seen in many eighteenth-century edifices, including the Pantheon in Paris.

The large population of France contributed to the position of this empire at the forefront of the world. With a French population at the beginning the century that was roughly four times that of England or Spain, the workforce and productivity of the land was formidable. Intermarriages and political alliances orchestrated via the reigning kings were also key factors in positioning France at the helm of both political power and fashion. Almost all European courts, from Russia and Poland to Denmark, spoke French more often than the native language of the respective countries. The aristocracy led the way with fashion and taste making in art, architecture, and apparel, but literature, art, music, and fashionable dress were all readily consumed by the growing middle class and civil servants, thanks to increased communications in an age of widespread availability of print books, papers, and magazines.

The printed word was especially important for the dissemination of the new scientific, social, and ultimately revolutionary ideas that were being discussed, written, and printed en masse in the eighteenth century. Among the most important social theorists whose words changed the world was Jean-Jacques Rousseau (1712–1778). Rousseau, a Genevan musician, novelist, and social theorist, argued that Man had a natural goodness within him and that Mankind should thusly be ruled by the common good. Among his works are *The Social Contract* and *Émile* (also known as *On Education*), both from 1762, two books that changed the way people looked at social governance and the rearing and education of the nation's youth. Rousseau's ideas were revolutionary indeed and sparked ideas in the population at large that would frame the centuries to come.

Also fanning the flickering flame of enlightenment was François-Marie Arouet (1694–1778), known as Voltaire. Voltaire was an essayist, deist, and philosopher who criticized the institutions of his day, including both the Church and civil authorities. He was a staunch defender of civil liberties and consequently argued that human life should not be governed by a higher authority, neither god nor other man. Voltaire's writing was so incendiary that it cost him forced exile from his adopted homeland of France for much of his life (although he is known to have evaded exile by using a pseudonym).

Printed books, magazines, and leaflets also bore images of interest to the masses. Satirical cartoons of either a political or bawdy nature were the most common type. The technique of engraving upon metal or carving into wood allowed for the mass reproduction of fine art, drawings, and paintings. Perhaps the most influential satirical cartoonist of the period was William Hogarth (1697–1764). His illustrations, often done in series, poked fun (often quite viciously) at contemporary customs and political events. Among the most famous and biting social satire illustrated by Hogarth were *The Harlot's Progress* (1731), which shows the downward spiral of a country girl in the debauched city, and *Marriage à la Mode* (1743–1745), portraying the debauchery of the eighteenth-century elite, especially those who arranged marriages for the gain of money. The proliferation of these images and countless thousands of other prints of political and social satire opened the minds of the masses to a new kind of social critique that was both entertaining and informative.

Economically, Europe transformed over the course of the century from a rural lifestyle to a more urban existence. Instead of working on farms, people found themselves working in the new factories, thanks to the Industrial Revolution. Factories produced all kinds of consumer goods, which meant that people no longer had to make everything themselves. The spinning jenny helped in the production of yarns, and the factory system was ideal for production of clothing and textiles. More food was produced more efficiently with new methods of farming, and new crops were introduced. Improved cleanliness and regular bathing helped reduce the spread of disease within Europe. There was an overall increase in length of life and a decline in death rates, meaning that the overall population increased. The improvements in agriculture and industrial development meant that more people were able to make more money, and this contributed to major changes in society, wherein not only the landed gentry and titled aristocracy had money to spend, but the growing merchant class was also able to buy land, consume goods, and generally help develop a market economy. Even the common people were able to purchase all kinds of goods, including fashion.

For Great Britain, the eighteenth century was a time of increased power on a global scale. With superior sea power and the ability to travel long distances

Marriage A-la-Mode: 4. The Toilette, William Hogarth, 1743. "Marriage A-la-Mode" was the first of Hogarth's satirical moralizing series of engravings about the upper echelons of society. © Erich Lessing / Art Resource, NY.

over oceans, colonial rule allowed the English to dominate world trade, in goods as well as slave labor. In Africa, the British used their power to export labor to American colonies, where they would put the people to work on plantations. These plantations produced goods (primarily cotton) that were then shipped back to England for final distribution. Similarly, in India, under the power of the East India Company, there was increased trade as the English established widespread control. Trade in spices and beautiful cloth and clothing not only contributed to the wealth of many who went to India as soldiers and came back wealthy merchants, but also allowed for the spread of exotic ideas and designs for clothing and furniture in fashionable households all over Britain.

At the beginning of the seventeenth century, Queen Elizabeth I had granted a charter to London merchants for a trading monopoly with Asia. Soon known as the East India Company, it gained a foothold in India and the British traders quickly realized massive profits. The establishment of such a powerful company eventually led to imperial domination by the British in India. Raw materials were shipped from the colonies, manufactured in England, and then shipped back to the colonial markets. Profits were large and paid for military activity. At the same time, British economic control kept the money supply limited within the colonies. France, having once been massively powerful as a colonist, was stripped by England of its territories in North America and South Asia, and England dominated imperial trade at this time. The Dutch East India Company was similar to the British East India Company but did not yield nearly the same kinds of profits as those realized by the British.

Royalty, Power, and Court Life in Europe

For the British monarchy, the eighteenth century was a time of relative stability in comparison with previous centuries. The accession of George I and the House of Hanover marked the beginning of the German line of monarchs. European dynastic and aristocratic marriages were common at this time, allowing members of royal families of different countries to marry. To avoid conflicts, such as the Catholic and Protestant split and the Jacobean Revolution of the 1600s, English monarchs were required to be members of the Church of England, making the king a Protestant. Additionally, the Divine Right of Kings had been replaced with rule by consent of Parliament in England, and various other forms of government in other parts of Europe. Politics became more important in England as parties formed and political views became points of discussion and division among the population.

During the eighteenth century, neither Germany nor Italy was a unified nation as each is today. Dress and court customs in these regions were often characterized by archaism and regional or customary dress. However, powerful courts dominated by figures such as Prussian monarch King Frederick I (*R.* 1740–1786) engaged in international affairs and adopted the French taste at court. Portions of the Italian peninsula adopted French customs as a result of shifting political control. Naples, for example, fell in and out of Spanish control throughout the century, while Austrian influence was powerful in northern Italy. By the end of the first half of the century, it is safe to say, French fashion was widely adopted in Europe, although local customs and sumptuary laws (so greatly in conflict with the French taste) were still in place in the more remote, less cosmopolitan regions.

All the Great Powers of Europe in the eighteenth century, such as France and England, were monarchies, although the political structure in each country varied. The Holy Roman Empire and the Kingdom of Genoa boasted elected monarchs, and these both stood in stark contrast to France, Spain, and Austria, which were ruled by monarchs who yielded absolute power. While the power of the monarch varied greatly from land to land given the political structure, the glitter and the prestige of the court of each kingdom were similar in their excessive and beautiful fashions. None, however, was as decadent and vast as the court at Versailles in France.

The cost of keeping a royal court on such a scale is now unfathomable. To consider but a few components may help to illustrate the financial burden it created. The king was responsible for feeding, housing, and dressing hundreds of royal courtiers, many of whom also received a salary. Among those serving the court was a small army of footmen, chambermaids, cooks, laundresses, personal attendants, animal keepers, and governesses. Royal mistresses also proved to be costly, as the best and the brightest of these were rewarded with palaces that were fully staffed, and of course the wardrobe of the official mistress, the *maîtresse-en-titre*, was required to be the most stupendous of the entire court. So while the great machine of the French monarchy was developing an internationally lauded and mimicked taste, the cost of this endeavor was taking a negative toll on its revenue source.

It is perhaps illuminating to follow the dissemination of French style to the rest of Europe via Spain. Philippe of Anjou was born in 1683, the grandson of

The sheet music cover for *The Court of St. James* by Charles d'Albert, showing the royal court dress in London at the time of King George II, 1757. © The Art Archive / Private Collection.

King Louis XIV. In 1700, he assumed the throne of Spain that was left vacant upon the death of Charles II, and as Philip V, he reigned until his death in 1746. The Spanish court had traditionally been quite insular and *retardataire* in terms of fashion and development of style, but during the reign of Philip, Spain adopted the French taste. Portugal in turn followed Spain, in part because of several intermarriages between courts. During the first quarter of the eighteenth century, the Austrian court at Vienna followed the unique customs of Spain and was thus also put under the spell of the French taste by the changing customs at the Spanish court. In addition, marriages between members of the court at Vienna and those near Paris further reinforced this stylistic emulation.

Culture and Thought

Society turned away from a blind faith in religious doctrine, fear, and superstition that had guided every facet of their lives and instead relied more heavily on the sciences, which were assuming more importance and were thought capable of solving all problems. There was an outright rejection of religion, and the pursuit of secular knowledge gained new importance. Scientist Sir Isaac Newton and his group concentrated on what could be proven by experiment and mathematical methods and left nothing to myth and mysticism. The universe was understood like never before.

Regardless of this move toward rational thinking led by social theorist John Locke, strict class divisions within society, between the aristocracy and the common people, continued to exist all over the European Continent, in the colonies (although perhaps less so), and especially in Britain. The eighteenth century is also known as the Age of Aristocracy, a time of impeccable refinement. Great country houses with exquisite architecture and landscapes glorified the owners and reflected their material wealth. The king of Prussia, for example, built Sans Souci in Potsdam, a vast playground and retreat, where he had elaborate gardens and many different styles of buildings from all over the world (a pagoda, for instance). This undertaking is an excellent example of both the excess and the aesthetics enjoyed by the aristocratic elite; the edifices remain on the outskirts of Berlin, much the same as when they were built centuries ago.

People with money in England included the old aristocracy, the great land owners, and increasingly the lesser gentry who had been able to make vast amounts of money in businesses that were largely enabled by the fruits of the Industrial Revolution. These gentry mixed to a certain extent with the aristocracy and were expected to spend time in London as well as at their country estates. Springtime saw a movement from London to the country houses, where the landed estates could be watched and recreation enjoyed.

In France, numerous state agencies were purveyors of culture. Royal patronage of institutions represented yet another source of bills the royal coffers had to satisfy. Among these institutions were the Academie de Peinture et de Sculpture (later known as the Academy des Beaux-Arts), the Academie de Musique, and the Academie Français, which was responsible for standardizing the French language. They guaranteed that French music, plays, art, and language would dominate this era. Even the manner of dance throughout Europe was determined by the styles of dance in France at the time.

In 1685, Louis XIV revoked the Edict of Nantes, which had been in place for eighty-seven years, with the promulgation of the Edict of Fontainebleau, declaring Protestantism illegal. This affected the French Protestant minority, known as the Huguenots, who included many master craftspeople, especially in textile related arts. Mass immigration of the Huguenot craftspeople, such as embroiderers and tailors, from France to England and other Protestant countries in 1685 helped to establish French decorative traditions and essential techniques for lavish garment construction in foreign lands.

Although perhaps of lesser importance, dissemination of taste and design can be traced to colonization in America, India, and Africa. The fashions of these places, however, were also greatly influential in how Europeans dressed. Details in colonial design and accessories, for example, were readily adopted by fashionable French, English, and Dutch women whose men fought and worked in the East and imported luxurious textiles for the fashionable European women.

Revolution

The end of the 1700s was a time of upheaval worldwide, most notably including the American (1776) and French (1789) revolutions.

Starting with Louis XIV (R. 1643–1715) whose reign was the longest in European history, political and cultural preeminence became hallmarks of the nation. His tenure was followed by the rule of his great-grandson Louis XV (R. 1715–1774). Louis XV died an unpopular ruler due to his inability to reform the corruption within his monarchy and because of unsuccessful military campaigns; however, his reign corresponds to a period of profound flourishing in fine art, design, literature, philosophy, fashion, and culture in general. Despite this, Louis XV and his grandson Louis XVI governed France to the verge of bankruptcy and did nothing to prevent its ultimate collapse.

Despite the gradual breakdown of political authority at home, the authority of French culture was unwavering. The last half of the century was characterized by a certain amount of rebellion against the beauty and idealism of the early Rococo aesthetic. Some rebelled against the excesses, the beauty and reason of this era, and in the second half of the century the sublime was replaced with those artists and writers who preferred to show the ugly and terrifying. This prerevolutionary fervor led to later moments of rebellion that occurred with some frequency throughout the last quarter of the eighteenth century. The disdain of the populace came to a breaking point on July 14, 1789, and culminated in the storming of the Bastille in Paris, marking the beginning of the French Revolution. This bloody revolution resulted in the destruction of the monarchy and the beginning of democratic rule, where the monarchy was replaced by government of the people. In 1793 the last French monarchs, King Louis XVI and Queen Marie Antoinette, were dispatched on the guillotine, marking the end of an era of excessive consumption and lavish lifestyle.

The inability of Louis XV and XVI to curtail their spending can be attributed to myriad factors, some of which demonstrate the striking dichotomy of the period whereby the opulent development of high culture led to the bankruptcy of the nation. Among the entities that usurped the financial resources of the state while developing French culture were numerous academies, countless courtiers, lavish households with armies of maids, attendants, royal mistresses and lesser prostitutes, and countless extravagant practices and displays required by the court.

The Industrial Revolution contributed to both the success and empowerment of the common people. The right to personal liberty and freedom of speech and politics developed in the 1760s and were put to great use during this time. People felt freer to fight against injustices of a dominant upper class and fought for equality among the masses. In France this meant storming the Bastille in Paris, and a violent revolution that marked the end of opulence and monarchy all in one swift rebellion but ended with Napoleon Bonaparte becoming France's dictator in 1799. A desire in the colonies for independence and British mismanagement of colonial affairs led to the War of Independence in the American colonies in 1775, with the outcome of a new independent nation headed by George Washington in 1789. After this, the British were less of a world power, however the French, who had allied with the Americans against the British in the war, gained strength from the success of the colonies, especially in North America.

Fashion and what clothing symbolized in this time are very important, and the people were acutely aware of the messages they were sending in what they wore on their backs. Status was achieved in wearing certain elaborate garments, and men and women were both exceedingly fashion conscious.

CLOTHING IN THE EIGHTEENTH CENTURY

Dressing was an important affair for many of the wealthiest people in European and colonial society. In France, courtiers were expected to wear the most flamboyant and decadent clothing, characterized by extensive embellishment. Costumes were large in every sense of the word and expressed a sense of entitlement and wealth that was to come apart at the seams at the end of the century with revolutionary vigor. What courtiers wore before the revolution was beautiful and extravagant like never before or after. Meanwhile in England, aristocratic men and women wore elaborate gowns and suits that showed off new mercantile and inherited wealth and stated the wearer's place in society. Peasant dress, though difficult to know precisely due to the perennial problem of a lack of extant examples, was of similar silhouette to the elite dress, but was made of poorer-quality materials, was less embellished, and admitted little attention to detail and aesthetics. These were garments for working but shared some of the same nuances found in the clothing worn by wealthy people.

Dressing for the royal courts of Versailles and the like was both a privilege and a burden for eighteenth-century courtiers. While the rules of dressing for the court varied from place to place—for example, some courts forbid nonroyals to wear a train on a gown—regulations and hierarchies of some form existed throughout Europe. Dressing for court encouraged competition in terms of both design and expenditure, and such competition could readily escalate to ridiculous levels of expense. Clothes of the courts were often used like weapons to stave off enemies who might have designs on one's position. The garments a courtier wore spoke volumes about their wealth and power or their ability to partake of leisure, although to look now, with an eye less practiced, the nuanced distinctions are often difficult to see. The choice of color, selection of trim, or knotting of a *jabot* represented small pieces of the visual language within the hierarchy and indicated position within the social structure and belonging in general. Many minor innovations and trends in dress can be attributed to the desire of the highest ranking members of the court to distinguish themselves from the hungry mimicry of less important courtiers.

The system in which fashion was developed and manufactured in the eighteenth century is rather different than it is today. Courtiers and wealthy merchants could gain information about style in a number of ways: through careful observation of others, especially emissaries of Versailles; through reproductions of engravings, sometimes dedicated specifically to fashion; and by the receipt of fashion dolls called "Pandora" dolls or *poupées de mode*, large dolls dressed in the current mode, that were sent to the various European courts. As a result, the exact moment of innovation is rather hard to pinpoint and is often a matter of legend since the manufacture and decoration of clothes was a complex process involving many entities.

Fine clothing was an expensive commodity, but it was more readily available in this period than it had ever been before. Automation made the availability of cloth, and consequently clothing, more plentiful. Expedited production led to a reduction in production costs and was in part a response to the advancements in yarn-spinning technology, which improved rapidly in the latter half of the century, evolving from the hand-powered spinning jenny (1767) to the steam-powered spinning frame (1768) to the even more efficient spinning mule (1779). The invention of the steam- or water-powered flying shuttle in 1737 enabled the automatic movement of weft yarns, thereby expediting the weaving process. These new technologies touched many strata of society, but the poorest people and those in the most remote regions continued to make cloth using more primitive, hand techniques.

Regional specializations and mass production of textiles are most evident and best documented historically with luxury fabrics. For example, the silk-weaving industry in Lyons was subsidized by French royalty, thereby making silk products more available to those with disposable income for such finery. In the 1400s, Lyons had been a major warehouse for silk coming in from the Silk Road from China; Louis XI in 1466 declared it a city where silk could be made, and in 1536 it had a monopoly on the silk industry that carried on for centuries. It remains an excellent place for top designers to obtain their precious fabrics. Early in the 1800s, workers in the Lyons silk industry protested the conditions in which they worked, and there were two major uprisings. It is also well documented that regions such as the Italian peninsula became well known for the production of exquisite velvet fabrics. Textiles such as chintz and muslin were imported to Europe from India. Thanks to this important trade between India, China, and other Eastern states, European women were introduced to exotic designs and new styles with oriental inspiration. Often these designs were re-created on European looms, sometimes with curious errors that became innovations in design.

The manufacture of garments made of wool or silk was typically the business of men in the early eighteenth century, while the manufacture of linen garments was the domain of women. Later in the century, it was typical for men to make menswear and women to create women's attire. This segregation of activities, which extended to all aspects of the garment industry, was mostly due to strict regulations by guilds and precise segmentation of the production of garments at every step, from the preparation of cloth to making clothes. For example, there were three guilds dedicated to regulating the dyeing of cloth; each guild could handle only certain types of cloth and dye: There was a single guild for dyeing broadcloth, wool, and silk; a second guild for the dyeing of "common fabrics"; and a third for the re dyeing of fabrics that had lost their original color, which was a common problem until well into the nineteenth century because of the lack of effective mordants to set the dyes.

Fashionable garments were made to order. For costume historians, the extant examples of dress tell a lot about the segment of society that commissioned and wore them. The patron or garment maker would select the desired cloth from one or more merchants. Thereafter the garment maker would cut and sew the pieces to suit his client's form and taste. Garments in this period were typically lavishly trimmed, which was done by another person who exclusively did only trims, not garment construction—the fashion merchant. The fashion merchant (*marchande des modes* or *modiste*) was typically a woman and was involved in the decoration of garments made by other manufacturers. These merchants used ribbons, trim, braid, beads, and jewels, which were also made by other manufacturers of distinct guilds, to lavishly adorn clothes. Typically, the cost of the garment skyrocketed with the more expensive and excessive applied design.

The most famous modiste in France was a woman named Rose Bertin. While she began her career as a hat maker, she ultimately found favor with the French royal court and was responsible for the lavish decoration of the garments of Madame de Pompadour, mistress to King Louis XV in 1745. Madame de Pompadour—best remembered not for her romance with the king, which by all accounts cooled after the first few years, but for exercising a great deal of power at court—was a great arbiter of taste. Her garments, trimmed and accessorized by Bertin, strongly influenced the fashions worn by all in the French court. Bertin is often referred to as the first-ever "fashion designer." Although she was not, strictly speaking, a designer, as she did not design the clothing and concentrated only on the trim and decorations, she nevertheless helped shape the costume of the time.

Modistes were creative entities who had at their disposal a great array of trimmings, called *agreements*, through which they could shape their visions. Trimmings included a great variety of lacework, the most expensive of which was wrought of gold or silver gilded thread. Braid, typically made of silk, could be

"The Tailor," by Pietro Longhi, 1741, shows exquisite fabric and dress styles for women and young girls. © Cameraphoto / Art Resource, NY.

artfully arranged into sweeping arabesques and was often used in profusion on both men's and women's apparel. Appliqué, including long strands of hand-wrought velvet flowers in multiple colors, might also be applied by the yard to elaborate court costumes. Embroidery was a favorite mode of ornamentation, applied to garments for both genders, as were sequins, called *pailettes*, which, along with the gilded thread, had the added benefit of picking up the flickering candlelight that served to light the elegant evening activities. Paste jewels, made of leaded glass, were sewn directly to the cloth or were set into buttons. Buttons themselves were the most diversified of trims. The buttons consisted of either a wood or bone former, which was then typically covered with embroidered cloth. The range of embroidery patterns was quite varied and many were known by special names such as *Basket*, a lattice pattern, or *Death's Head*, which consisted of circles of chain stitch. Many buttons were also decorated to match or compliment the embroidery or other trim that had been applied to a garment.

It is important to clarify that the focus is on fashionable dress, which was worn by a very small percentage of the population: the aristocrats of the court and the wealthy merchant class who could afford more modest emulations of those fashions. By contrast, the majority of the population, consisting of the peasantry, wore a combination of functional clothes (some of which had hardly changed since medieval times) in combination with the cast-off fashions of the upper class. For centuries, it had been typical for a master to gift old clothes to servants, and as mass production of textiles led to less expensive, and sometimes finer, grades of cloth that wore out more readily, the rate of handing down used clothes increased.

The clothing of the commoner is poorly documented and very little evidence exists today. The lowest classes would have worn, for the most part, simple woolen clothes in styles dating back years. These garments would have essentially been worn until they wore out. Some members of the lower working classes might also have acquired clothes from secondhand dealers known as *fripiers* or *revendeurs*, who, although renowned for illegal acquisition and resale of goods, also provided a necessary service reselling clothes that had little use for the upper classes once fashions had changed. Purchase and use of secondhand clothing in this era constituted an unfashionable adaptation of *retardataire* fashions but was frequently maligned by the upper classes nevertheless, because people were expected to dress according to their station in life, and with lower-class people being able to acquire beautiful clothes, the lines became blurred and confusing.

Working-class men and women wore clothes that were characterized by functionality. Women wore a petticoat and a chemise, over which they wore a tunic, called a "short gown." Men wore breeches or pantaloons and a smock. Both genders wore functional aprons of cloth or leather. Display of layers and variations in textile depended on where they lived and the weather.

Records of the styles and manner of dress in the eighteenth century as a whole are incomplete. There is little or no documentation of intermediate social groups, nor of the many variations that existed across regions or across categories of gender, age, or the many fine gradations of rank. It should be noted that the growing complexities of urban civilization, urban–rural migration, and increasing social mobility would have provided for variations of dress that would likely have been expressed in terms of construction, fabric, color, and the amounts and types of embellishment.

It is important to note that the eighteenth century saw far more widespread adoption and adaptation of fashionable dress across larger groups of people than previously thanks to the increased economic stratification of society. As untitled merchants began to make their way, grow, and ultimately flourish, dress was used as a way of expressing their prosperity. Studying household inventories and other household records shows the up-and-coming bourgeoisie were devoting increasingly larger portions of their incomes to fashionable dress. By dressing well, new merchants could hope to buy their way into the next rung of society and satisfying their ambitions of integrating with the wealthy.

Women's Dress

Women's fashionable garments of the eighteenth century were ostentatious and elaborate, and the silhouette often proved to be unwieldy. Throughout the first three-quarters of the century, garments were designed to discipline and mold the body into exotic, yet often inhuman, shapes and fetishistic forms. Garments were used to create an idealized version of a woman who was perfectly delicate. The elegant weakness of her person was communicated through her teetering, encumbered, yet gliding gait, the short, light breaths that her restrictive stays required, and her heavily powdered skin which made the woman look pale and sickly.

By the advent of the eighteenth century, women's clothing could be classified into distinct categories: skirt with petticoat beneath it; a mantle (sometimes referred to as a *mantua*); a bodice stiffened with a whalebone *corps du robe*, and sometimes including a central panel called a *stomacher* that closed in the front. Over all of these garments, women wore an *apron*. These basic components were cut, styled, and combined in different ways and are typical of eighteenth-century women's dress.

Fashionable dress, although fairly diverse in terms of appearance, can be grouped into two main categories of construction. Many gowns of the period were closed in construction, meaning that the bodice of the garment and the skirts were connected. Sometime closed-construction garments consisted of a bodice sewn to a skirt, while other times a single panel of cloth made both the bodice and skirt and extended from shoulder to floor. Open-construction garments consisted of a bodice fashioned somewhat like a man's modern morning coat with tails where the two side of the bodice did not fully cover the upper body. The bodice was completed with a wedge-shaped stomacher that attached the two sides and closed the garment. Below the waist, the garment was typically long, but open in the front, so the petticoat showed through.

Eighteenth-century women's dresses changed over the years, with the silhouette going through modifications and accentuating different parts of body. The *panier*, which was introduced early in the century and lasted only until mid century, was a frame worn beneath the skirt that allowed for great versatility and change to the silhouette, with the volume of the skirt increasing to a staggering proportion and then decreasing by the end of the century. *Paniers*, a French word meaning "baskets," were a set of maneuverable hoops worn to give a wide front and narrow profile to the skirts of dresses such as the mantua and the *robe à la française*.

Paniers were made from wicker, metal, or whalebone and were originally a circular and domed shape referred to as the *paniers a coupole*, as it was thought that this silhouette resembled the dome on St. Paul's Cathedral in London. The shape became more ovoid over time and flattened in the front and back, extending the hips. The width of the paniers peaked in the 1740s; one dress in the costume collection at the Victoria and Albert Museum in London has a skirt so wide the figure would need roughly four feet (1.2 m) of frame on either side to properly arrange the fabric.

Englishwoman from London wearing a late-eighteenth-century gown by Sylvain Maréchal, 1787. © The Art Archive / Bibliothèque des Arts Décoratifs Paris / Gianni Dagli Orti.

The panier showed off the beautiful textiles and decorations used on the dresses, creating a sort of tableau. Cords were attached to the frame to allow the hoops to be pulled in closer to the body to allow the wearer, for example, to sit or walk through doorways and other narrower spaces. Side hoops continued to be used for formal dresses through the 1780s, but after 1770, the volume was achieved through the use of hip pads and bustles. Satiric cartoons of the period indicate that the elegance of such wide and excessive dresses and the sophistication of this silhouette was not universally appreciated, and many thought it ridiculous.

Stays, another undergarment of the time and the forerunner of the corset, are thought to have come from Spain during this period. Stays were constructed of coarse stiffened fabric that was typically reinforced with thin strips of whalebone or metal busks, sewn into narrow vertical channels. Unboned versions of stays were called *jumps* and were worn only during private encounters in one's own chamber, where comfort was more desired.

In addition to the undergarments described above, women wore a *chemise* under everything. This was a basic thin layer of fabric, in a tunic style with a wide, low neckline, that was mainly worn to protect the fine outer garment fabrics from being soiled by bare skin. It generally hung to the knees and was what women wore instead of what we now know as underwear or panties.

The mantua originated in the seventeenth century as an informal garment similar to a dressing gown. Some scholars have speculated that it was adapted from a gown of Eastern origin. In its original incarnation, it consisted of a garment made of a single piece of cloth extending from shoulder to hem that was fitted through the bodice. Some versions of this garment were open in the front and required a stomacher to close the bodice. Open-front styles allowed a petticoat to show. Over time, a train developed, gathered into folds and flounces at the back, but that seems to have gone out of style during the 1730s. At mid-century, the mantua was still popular in England and the Netherlands, where the train was replaced by a pleated flap that hung from waist to hem.

The *sack* or *saque* dress (also called the *robe battante*, *robe volante*, and *innocente*) is, by comparison to other garments of the period, an informal-looking garment. The informality is ascribed by some scholars to the fact that the rules of the court of Louis XV relaxed during his early reign when he was still a youth. Popular in the early half of the eighteenth century, the sack dress was worn for formal or full-dress occasions. It was defined by double box pleats to the front and back of both shoulders, creating a tent-like construction. The skirt was gored at the waist to allow for more voluminous gathering of cloth, and a pleated or quilted petticoat typically supported it. Its emphasis on pleating was, as we shall see, transferred to the robe à la française, which took its place after 1730.

The *robe à la française* developed in the second quarter of the eighteenth century. This dress style was composed of multiple pieces, including a petticoat, which was visible in the front; an open bodice; and a stomacher. This stomacher style was sometimes boned and was frequently lavishly decorated with a ladder of ribbons called *echelle*. This dress typically had three-quarter-length voluminous sleeves with small undersleeves of two or three layers of lace that hung out the bottom of the sleeve. These ethereal decorations were meant to draw attention to and enhance a graceful gesture of address or movement while dancing. The most obvious difference of construction that distinguished this dress from all others was the double box pleats, which started at the shoulder yoke and fell straight down the back, creating a loose flat train to the ground. This straight train produced a different view from the front and the back, with quite distinct silhouettes depending on from what angle the dress was viewed. This style of dress did not allow for the insertion of pockets into the fabric of the petticoat, so pockets were worn on strings attached under the petticoat and could be accessed through subtle slits in the skirts.

The *robe à l'anglaise* was worn more toward the middle of the eighteenth century and then found a revival in the 1780s when a trend to adopt English fashion swept through France. The robe à l'anglaise consisted of a bodice that was fitted through the back and closed in the front. To this was sewn a separate skirt, where the masses of fabric were evenly gathered around the waist to create volume. The fitted back of this garment was in stark contrast to the loose silhouette of the robe à la française or the sack gown. One panier was used to create a bustle out the back of the skirt. This bustle look could also be achieved through gathering extra fabric at the back to create the silhouette. Under the dress, women wore an ankle-length petticoat. The robe à l'anglaise was worn for informal or semiformal occasions.

The *robe à la polonaise* was a popular garment from roughly 1785 until the end of the century. It consisted of a closed bodice, worn over a petticoat that reached to slightly below the ankles. The bodice was cut to waist length in the front, in a fashion similar to the robe à l'anglaise, and was gathered into a bustle in the back. The full bustle at the back of the dress was constructed of three panels of fabric that could be manipulated with a system of pulleys to vary the bustle's size and shape. This garment, although still elaborate, allowed the wearer greater mobility than a dress with a panier, yet it still created sensuous, curvy lines, especially at the back. It was worn with a decorative apron and was intended to reference the modest petticoats and aprons of the peasantry. This simple yet highly affected style was popularized by Marie Antoinette. It is well documented that she and her entourage would escape the court society at Versailles to a minor palace, the Petit Trianon, and would put on airs of simple country living in less lavish clothing.

The *robe retroussée dans les poches* (pocket dress) was also a garment of the latter part of the century. The garment itself, which boasted a petticoat that was hemmed well above the ankle, seems to have been adopted in France in conjunction with the new custom of taking strolls through the countryside in the English fashion. Inspiration may, however, once again be attributed to the simple wardrobe of the workingwomen of the countryside, whose fitted jackets and shorter petticoats do find a place in this fancy, decadent society. The name *pocket dress* is derived from its construction. The outer skirt was attached to a fitted bodice in much the same manner as the robe à l'anglaise and was puffed and manipulated through a series of slits (pockets), loops, and rings in the underskirt, creating great volumes of fabric at the sides and back.

Throughout the last decade of the eighteenth century, the same basic garments continued to be worn, with alterations to proportions, silhouette, materials, and embellishment. As a general rule, sleeves lengthened and relaxed in their fit. The type of embellishment shifted toward less ostentatious and ornate embellishment. The vogue for cotton, which was popularized by Marie Antoinette beginning in the 1770s, persisted as cotton textiles become more readily available through increasing trade with the East. The shape and width of skirts became mush less voluminous and took on more natural shapes.

In addition to the gradual modification of women's dress, revolutionary fervor caused some specific changes in what women wore. In the 1790s, a one-piece, high-waisted, lightweight garment became fashionable. This garment, known now as the *Empire gown*, seems to have evolved out of a one-piece, closed-front chemise that was popularized by Marie Antoinette in the 1780s. The queen's garment was meant to embody an air of simple, country purity and was in part a mirror of Rousseau's "back to nature" philosophy. Perhaps this simple garment is better attributed to the *goût Grec* (Greek taste) that had gradually evolved after the 1748 excavations of Pompeii and Herculaneum (cities of the Roman Empire buried in the volcanic eruption of 79 CE), which found an increased prestige in the imagination of the liberty-seeking postrevolutionary era.

This simple dress was thought to be inspired by the ancient Greek *chiton* (see volume 1, chapter 4) and was typically made of a very lightweight, sheer, gauzy cotton. Though the Empire gown, which was named for the French political regime in postrevolutionary France, has found a lasting place in the modern imagination, in the late 1700s it was utterly impractical, leaving the wearer cold and shivering and contributing to the high incidence of tuberculosis. The need for warmth sparked new trends in accessories to complement the dress and insulate the wearer. Among these practical accessories was the *Spencer jacket*, which was cropped to just above the waist and had an upright collar that shielded the neck from the cold. Warm and beautiful Kashmir shawls were popular and, thanks to increased trade from India, were readily available to the European woman in warm fabrics with exotic designs. Bonnets also became fashionable and provided much-needed warmth. The fact that Empire dresses were not made with pockets meant that women had to carry around a purse, called a *reticule*, which was a small drawstring bag.

To brave the outdoors, women wore a *domino*—a full, long, loose, hooded cloak worn by both men and women. At Carnival time, this cloak was worn with a mask and was considered appropriate attire to wear at court. Shorter jackets were worn by women in the 1780s and appear to have been based on a garment of the peasant class called the *caracot*. Women also wore riding habits and jackets based on the design of a man's *redingote* (coat with tails).

In addition to the many varieties of formal, semiformal, and informal dresses that were worn in the eighteenth century, there existed a variety of *deshabille* (undress) for both men and women. Dressing gowns were often quite extravagant among the upper classes, as the dressing room was an inner sanctum for deal brokering and alliance forming. Dressing gowns often picked up elements of the exotic and in the eighteenth century frequently exhibited oriental motifs. Less visible, but no less ornate, was the *negligée* for women, which was called a *peignoir* in the period.

Women's Hairstyles and Hats

In the eighteenth century, hats, hairstyles, and accessories were just as large, beautiful, exotic, and elaborate as the dresses women wore, and were often equally as impractical as the large paniers they wore in this period. Hats were worn both inside and outdoors. The *bergère* was a large, flat-brimmed hat that was originally associated with servants and older women but was adopted by the young and fashionable early in the eighteenth century. The bergère became progressively larger and more lavishly decorated with feathers, flowers, ribbons, and trim of all manner as the century went on. Rather less grand was the *dormouse cap*, also known as a *mob cap*, which was worn only indoors. This was made of soft, sheer cloth that was puffed at the crown of the head and decorated with a frilled edge. Toward the end of the century, simple bonnets with lappets that imitated and interpreted the countrified simplicity of the peasantry gained vogue.

Although the adornment of hats could be quite grand, it may be argued that the outlandish and voluminous hairstyles of the late eighteenth century were grander by far. So outrageous were many of the lavish hairstyles of the 1770s that they were satirized in the press by contemporary observers. It was said that the hairstyles were so large that they housed mice and other kinds of vermin. So popular were these elaborate coiffures that they merited a serial publication by Legros de Rumingny (published 1767–1770) titled *L'art de la coiffure des dames française avec des estampes, ou sont representées les têtes coiffées.*

Hairstyles were categorized by name. The more common style was called the *tête de mouton* (sheep's head) and was characterized by large rows of powdered curls similar to sheep's coat. These were so voluminous that the hoods of coats and capes, called *calash hoods*, required wire supports to suspend the hood above the hair and protect the style. In order to achieve the height and style, women used their natural hair but also added false hair (either human or animal hair) and decorated their coiffure with exotic colored feathers, ribbons, papier-mâché ornaments, strands of jewels, or elaborate hair combs. The embellishments seen on the clothing were reflected in the hairstyles and hats. In addition, women also adopted exotic pieces from the East such as shawls, scarves, stoles (called *tippets*), parasols, and fans. In addition, women wore gloves and mittens (gloves without fingertips) for fashion as well as function.

Another somewhat anomalous but well-documented facet of dress in the eighteenth century relates to the adoption of garments of the opposite gender. There are several famous cases of women taking on military or seafaring roles, including piracy, dressed as men. These women, such as the famous pirates Anne Bonny and Mary Read, would never have been able to step aboard ship if they had been dressed as women. On the other hand, women playing men in theatrical performances were fairly common and were generally lauded and considered to be in good fun. The adoption of men's dress by women was not problematic unless it involved sexual role-playing or lesbianism. Where this was the case, women were typically exiled from the community, whereas some faced jail sentences. In circumstances that included behavior that was considered deviant, biblical references often served as the justification for persecution.[1]

Men's Dress

Opulence in eighteenth-century dress was hardly relegated to women's costume. Opulent fabrics and extravagant detailing also characterized men's dress prior to the French Revolution. In terms of construction, it is easy to trace the

A beautifully embroidered three-piece suit tailored in the Venetian style. © Finsiel / Alinari / Art Resource, NY.

evolution of the cut of men's clothes from the late seventeenth century through the eighteenth century, and indeed into the nineteenth. These changes are best described as slow and methodical if traced decade to decade, but there was drastic change from the beginning of the century when compared to the end of the century.

The formal attire of the eighteenth-century man was a full suit (*habit complet*) that consisted of a *justacorps*, or coat; a *waistcoat*, or vest, which had a long skirt at the beginning of the century; and *culottes*, or knee breeches. Virtually all men wore a version of this suit, with socioeconomics dictating how elaborate or plain the embellishments, the quality of the fabrics, and the cut would be, and thus serving to declare the status of the wearer.

The justacorps was cut of two front pieces and two back pieces, a construction technique developed in the seventeenth century to more finely fit the garment to the body. At the beginning of the century, the coat had a long and full skirt extending to the knees, or sometimes longer. For the first half of the century, the skirts were quite full in both the front and back of the garment, but over time the fullness diminished and the front was gradually cut away, leaving the breeches at the front. This coat eventually became the morning coat or *tails* we now see worn mostly by bridegrooms. At the beginning of the century, the skirts were stiffened, typically with layers of coarse wool, horsehair, or buckram and were elaborately decorated with appliqué, embroidery, and decorations. The sleeves of the coat had a large cuff, often extending to the elbow, called a *boot sleeve*. Sleeves often were also designed with back slits, contrived to display the large, ruffled cuffs that were characteristic of this garment. The size of the cuff generally shrank over the course of the century. The collar was a stand-up collar, quite narrow at the beginning of the century and gradually becoming higher near the end of the century so as to frame the ears. A slit in the side of the coat was standard and was placed with the purpose of allowing men to carry their swords comfortably and practically.

The waistcoat, or *veste*, gradually changed in subtle ways over the course of the century. Around 1700, the waistcoat matched the coat in decoration, color, and fabric (called the *veste en suite*) and hung to the knee as did the coat; near the end of the century, the length of the waistcoat was cropped to just below the natural waist and showed off the front of the breeches. In the coldest weather, men wore a second waistcoat to help keep them warm. By the 1750s,

it was more typical to alternate the heavily decorated coat, breeches, and waistcoat, with the
waistcoat and breeches complementing the coat
but not matching as it had at the start of the
century. Solids were mixed with patterns, and
the waistcoat differed from the other components of the suit.

Breeches, at the beginning of the century were
cut generously, sagging in the seat and wide in
the thigh. The seat was said to be so voluminous
in order that padding could be placed inside the
seat to cushion the as-yet unpadded chairs that
men sat on. The breeches were cut to just below
the knee throughout the century but became
more fitted in the leg and seat as the century progressed. The breeches were closed at the front
with a square flap, with buttons on the top corners that attached to the hips in the front. This
made for a flat, more refined front closure that
was wide at the beginning of the century and
became narrower by the last quarter of the 1700s.
The waist could be adjusted with ties that were
placed on the waistband in the center back of the
breeches. The knees were often closed tight with
either ties or decorated plackets consisting of four
buttons up the outside of the thigh, matching the
decorations on the rest of the suit. The knees of
the breeches were also sometimes decorated with
rosettes, especially for military dress or revolutionary costume. Breeches typically included pockets
that were artfully hidden in the side seams or
waistbands. Men wore an extra layer of linen fabric under their breeches to protect the fabric.

A simple white shirt of linen or cotton was
worn beneath the waistcoat. It was constructed
like a tunic and was not fitted or tailored. Its

A beautifully embroidered Italian three-piece
suit, c. 1740. © Finsiel / Alinari / Art Resource,
NY.

function was essentially as underwear, serving to protect the finer fabrics of the
veste and justacorps, which could not be readily laundered. The shirt was cut
longer in the back than in the front and frequently had elaborately ruffled cuffs
that showed under the large cuffs of the coat with a flash of white or cream-
colored lace adding to the elaborate look of the suit.

After 1720, a neck cloth called a *stock*, which could be fastened to the back of
the shirt, was introduced. A neckpiece of some kind was always worn and disguised the simple neckline of the shirt. Also typically of this era was the *cravat*, a
neck cloth that could be worn by a man or a woman. It could be simple or decoratively fringed or trimmed with lace. Tying and styling the cravat was the subject of great study, and the fashion changed over the course of the century, with
the most noteworthy style called *à la Steinkirk*, which left the long ends of the
cravat untied so they could be threaded through the buttonhole of the shirt.

STEINKIRK FASHION

The cravat *à la Steinkirk* was apparently named for the Battle of Steinkirk, which occurred in 1682. It is a reference to the perceived behavior of officers who were taken by surprise and were forced to dress themselves rapidly.

The knee-length breeches of this period made it necessary for men to wear hose at all times. During the early part of the century, hose were worn rolled up above the hem of the breeches, while after mid century the hose were tucked under the breeches and held in place and pulled taught by a button or a buckle. Around 1770, in response to a fad in accentuating this erogenous zone, men inserted false calf muscles in the back of their hose to make the leg look more muscular.

The use of linen increased dramatically—in both frequency and quantity—over the course of the eighteenth century. The shirt, cravat, and hose were typically made of linen. In addition, a man of means would own a *toilet* and shaving linen, as well as nightcaps, night mantles or robes, and various forms of dishabilles, all made of linen. The proliferation of such things, it should be noted, went hand in hand with increased attention to sanitation and cleanliness and was not an improvement relegated solely to the upper class but filtered to the growing middle class as well.

Dishabille and nightclothes were just as important for men of the eighteenth century as they were for women. Nightgowns, at the beginning of the century, were worn just below the knee, but over time they lengthened to reach the floor. They were often made of linen but could also be made of silk and were frequently lined for warmth, sometimes with fur. Dressing gowns or morning gowns were also commonly worn by gentlemen, as they conducted key business in their private chamber. The *banyan* was a specific type of dressing gown that was double-breasted and fairly formal. It was worn as outerwear as well.

Men's outerwear and leisurewear were somewhat diversified. There were various styles of great coats, plain coats, and sporting coats. The *roquelaure* was a formal coat worn in the first half of the eighteenth century that was cut in three pieces and essentially banished the basic draped semicircular cloak that had been in use since antiquity. The *surtout* was a plain coat characterized by a broad collar and back vent, used during the latter half of the century, that was typically quite plain and was popularized as casual walking became popular. The frock coat, a garment that existed well into the nineteenth century, was a knee-length, loose-cut garment made of plain colored cloth. Its use and its cut varied greatly over the eighteenth century, but it was typically unadorned. Men also wore capes that fastened at the neck and hung over their shoulders. These were completely open in the front and meant that the elaborate coat, breeches, and waistcoat could be visible even while wearing outer garments.

During the last decades of the eighteenth century, a notable departure occurred in menswear, not so much in the type and cuts of clothing as in terms of overall appearance. From the 1770s onward, the penchant for suits "all of a piece" (made to match) was virtually abandoned in favor of a jacket, waistcoat, and breeches made from different fabrics. In addition, there was a departure from the lavish ornamentation, light gay colors, and luxurious fabrics that had characterized the fashion of earlier decades. Whereas men before 1770 had, at times, adorned every piece of clothing with embroidery or beading, the end of the century saw a more somber palate and austere detailing. After 1780, the waistcoat became the sole piece that showed any kind of flamboyance, with a particular taste for bright stripes characterizing that garment. Beginning around 1780, there is a movement toward democratic dress that was not quite so declarative of wealth and rank. This movement went hand in hand with the revolutionary movements of the period and was seen in England well in advance of its adoption in France. The adoption of somber colors and restrained ornamentation echoed the uniforms of grooms, coachmen, and various other household employees.

After 1789, the year in which revolutionaries stormed the Bastille in Paris, shapes of garments began a huge change. Ultimately, the justacorps went out of style and was replaced by either a sleeveless waistcoat called a *gilet*, which was worn over the waistcoat, or a *redingote*, which replaced the justacorps as the sleeved coat. Long trousers or pantaloons, prior to this time, had been worn only by laborers, but they were adopted by the *sans culottes*, a group of revolutionaries who wore long laborers' trousers rather than culottes or breeches. This politically inspired dress was adopted after 1793 as a symbol of the revolution. British men of the aristocratic class led the French in the move to democratic dress and began wearing long trousers before the men in France. The English fashions were always less elaborate than those in France throughout the century, and the British wore informal sporting clothes during the entire period. This was a part of the general movement toward democratization of dress for men, although long trousers were not truly typical until the beginning of the nineteenth century.

Men's dress was markedly less ostentatious and flamboyant at the end of the century. The taste for embellishment, luxuriousness, and studied elegance dissipated with the eruption of revolutionary gunfire and the disintegration of the extant social order. Men of status, no longer finding their fortunes through the sweat and labor of the peasant class, sought new employ in the common market and found new fortunes in a world where the values of democracy reigned.

A brief fad in men's fashion between 1780 and 1800 was affected by the young in Paris known by the sobriquet as *les Incroyables*. These young men purposefully adopted an unkempt appearance and garments that embodied outlandish proportions. Jackets sported unusually high collars, ending just below the ears. Wide revers (the turned-back sleeve cuff) of ungainly proportions were the terminals of tight sleeves. The coats exhibited fronts with daring cutaways, atypical of the period. This apparel is best categorized as a subset, somewhat fetishistic in nature, of the standard garments of the period. The presence of this unusual apparel is indicative of the fragmentation of society and the fact that fashions were no longer solely and strictly governed by a unified elite.

Cases of men dressing as women have been well documented throughout the eighteenth century, especially in London and in Paris. While a case has yet to be found that indicates a man adopted the dress of the fairer sex for occupational gains, it is universally the case that these men were persecuted when their ruses were uncovered. A famous example was the Chevalier d'Eon who lived as a man in London and as a female in Paris. He was of such high standing in society that he had a wardrobe made by Rose Bertin. When he was exposed as a man in the *London Evening Post* in May 1771, his reputation was damaged and he fell from the grace in a society unable to accept his deceptions.

Men's Hairstyles and Hats

Men's hats were both functional and fashionable affairs in the eighteenth century. The most sought-after and expensive hat was still typically made of beaver skin, while less desirable and cheaper versions were made of beaver hair mounted on felt. Beaver felt was one of the commodities made available by the increasing trade with the colonies. Beaver was hunted and fetched very high prices for trappers in Canada, helping to establish this colony in North America. Indeed, the popularity of the beaver hat is said by some to be the foundation of the Canadian colonization. This black, tall, hard hat was sometimes trimmed along the edges with a fringe or some other decoration such as lace. Another style of hat that was popular in the eighteenth century was called the *tricorne* (three-cornered hat), a style of hat that is by far the most iconic of the period and was considered to be worn most fashionably when all three sides of the brim were turned up or cocked. The top hat was introduced after 1770 as part of riding costume but underwent many changes over time.

Eighteenth-century men wore wigs (*perruques*) as part of the standard fashionable ensemble. Wigs were silvery-blue in color and powdered like the women's wigs, and they could be made of horse, goat, or human hair sewn into a net cap. At the beginning of the century, wigs, which might be kept straight or fashioned into rows of curls, were rather long and tall and were called *periwigs*. These reached their largest size by 1710 and were gradually replaced by the *bob wig*, which was shorter in front and always tied at the base of the neck in a ponytail and wrapped with black ribbons. Ribbons were often long and allowed to dangle down the wearer's back; however, sometimes the ribbon was brought around to the front of the neck and threaded through to gather the frilly edge of a shirt collar. A variation on the bob wig was the *bag wig*, which was used for formal occasions and included a small black silk bag, worn at the back of the neck, into which the hair of the wig was bundled.

The top of the hair was brushed straight and given volume after 1730 and was referred to as a *toupee* or a *foretop*. In the latter half of the eighteenth century, men began to style their natural hair in the manner of the bob wig. This may be attributed to the ascendancy to the British throne of George III, for he refused to wear a wig. This act readily influenced other men to also stop wearing wigs, greatly upsetting the wigmakers.

Shoes

The cut of men's and women's formal shoes varied little in this period, while materials and ornamentation varied considerably. Square-toed shoes predominated in the first half of the century for both men and women, then gave way to rounded-toe styles in the latter half. Men's shoes were generally flat-heeled, made of leather, and ornamented with a buckle. Women's were more likely to be made of cloth, had a higher heel, and were crafted *en suite* to match the fabrics of dresses.

Both men's and women's formal shoes were built with a curved heel, which, after 1770 moved toward the instep. This forced people to walk with a peculiar

The Family of Luigi Pisani, Alessandro Longhi shows the various styles of eighteenth century clothing for men, women, and children. © Cameraphoto Arte, Venice / Art Resource, NY.

gait that was said to enhance a woman's grace while dancing. It also contributed to the overall artifice of the clothing a woman wore, from the dramatic paniers to the large hairstyles.

Travelers and workmen wore practical boots that often reached above the knee, but such boots were not a part of fashionable dress. Military men also wore black leather riding boots, often trimmed with a band of brown leather at the knees. *Gaiters* or *spatter-dashers* were knee-length, stiffened cloth coverings worn by men to cover their lower leg and protect shoes and clothes, which was a necessity for walking through the dirty streets of towns.

Servant Classes

Dress of the servant class—employees such as footmen, butlers, servers, and messengers—also constitutes a category of fashionable dress, as these paid workers on elaborate estates, in representing their masters, required beautiful clothes as testimony to the wealth and position of the household. The master of the household would order all the clothing for his servants. These were not as lavish in design as those for the family and the fabrics were of lesser quality, but all of those employed by the household were expected to look a certain way, even wearing colors of the household. The master and mistress of the household often made "gifts" of clothing to their servants, although the servant's clothing, purchased by the master, remained the personal property of the master.

Children

Children in the eighteenth century were dressed exactly like adult men and women when they reached the age of five years. Before then, infants wore swaddled blankets and eventually unisex gowns. Upon reaching the fifth birthday, it was typical for young boys to start wearing breeches. The garments for young girls' clothing gradually became more complex and more like the garments of the older women.

The concept of children wearing clothing that is comfortable and made for playing and exercising was introduced in the eighteenth century by Rousseau in his 1760 fictionalized account of the education of the young boy, Émile, in the book of the same name. While there is some evidence of relaxed standards of dress prior to 1760, the concept didn't really gain currency until the nineteenth century.

CONCLUSION

Fashionable garments of the eighteenth century marked an exciting time in the history of dress. For men, the garments of the first part of the century demonstrate the end of the extravagance and ornamentation and the beginning of the modern evolution of conservative or democratic dress. Fashion followed advances in politics and changes in culture and society, becoming more democratic at the end of the century after the American and French Revolutions and was influenced heavily throughout the century by trade and exploration in the New World. The garments of this period are among the last moments of true elitism. As such, the clothes are beautiful and are truly works of art and yet, not truly indicative of the fashions of a lower class and the masses of people. Indeed, this is one of the last times in which fashion was the domain of a very small, elite class. The message speaks of a cultivated uniformity that would be all but dead within a hundred years.

NOTE

1. Deuteronomy 22:5 forbids one gender from adopting the clothes of the other.

WEB RESOURCES

http://www.metmuseum.org/Works_of_Art/department.asp?dep=8
http://www.metmuseum.org/toah/hd/eudr/hod_2001.472.htm

FURTHER READING

Buck, Anne. *Dress in the Eighteenth Century*. New York: Holmes and Meier Publishers, Inc., 1979.
Harris, Ronald W. *England in the Eighteenth Century*. London: Blantford Press. 1963.
Koda, Harold, and Andrew Bolton. *Dangerous Liaisons: Fashion and Furniture in the Eighteenth Century*. New Haven, CT: Yale University Press, 2006.

Ribero, Aileen. *Dress in Eighteenth-Century Europe*. 2nd ed. New Haven, CT: Yale University Press, 2002.

———. *A Visual History of the Eighteenth Century*. London: Batsford, 1983.

Roche, Daniel. *The Culture of Clothing: Dress and Fashion in the Ancient Régime*. Trans. Jean Birrell. Cambridge, UK: Cambridge University Press, 1994.

MOVIES

Amadeus (1984)
Barry Lyndon (1975; many costumes were original antique clothing of the period)
Dangerous Liaisons (1988)
The Last of the Mohicans (1992)
The Madness of King George (1994)
Marie Antoinette (1938)
Marie Antoinette (PBS, 2006)
Moll Flanders (1996)
Pride and Prejudice (BBC, 1995)
Rob Roy (1995)
The History of Tom Jones, a Foundling (1997)
Valmont (1989; Oscar for best costumes)

Glossary

à la jardinière   A dress with one or more frills on the shoulder, and a wristband, ruching, or plaiting at the hand, with the fullness caught at the shoulder and/or wrist with gathering or pleating.

acetate   Generic term for a manufactured fiber composed of acetylated cellulose used since the 1950s.

acid dyes   Class of dyes used primarily for protein and nylon fibers.

aiglet   Decorative metal tip applied to ribbons and other ties used to fasten clothing.

alpaca   Long, fine, natural protein hair fiber obtained from the domesticated South American alpaca, a member of the camel family; a wool variant.

altobasso   Velvets characterized by a sculpted effect given by the juxtaposition of two (or more) heights of the velvet pile cut with velvet irons in Renaissance clothing.

anaxyrides or braka   Pants, which were rare in Byzantium. *Braka* is a German term for pants. Many images in Byzantine art show the Persian's wearing pants, but they do not seem to be a part of Byzantine dress until the 12th century. The exception may be the pants (or stockings) shown throughout the Menologian of Basil II, worn by soldiers.

angora   Goat native to Turkey from which the natural protein fiber, mohair, is obtained; a wool variant.

animal fiber   General term for natural protein fiber of animal origin, such as wool (sheep) or silk (silkworm).

apoptygma   Overfold of the peplos, formed by folding the top part of the fabric over and below the shoulders. It could be unbelted, or belted, either under or over the overfold; the excess of the *apoptygma* pulled over the belt created a pouch of fabric known as a *kolpos*.

Ara Pacis   The marble *Ara Pacis Augustae*, "Altar of Augustan Peace (13 BCE), celebrated the peace established in the Empire after

Augustus's victories in Gaul and Spain. Its elaborate relief decoration represented the actual procession that took place on the occasion of the triumph, with the realistic portraits of the priests, attendants, and members of the family of Augustus, dressed in their official costumes.

armcye   The part of the shirt or sleeved jacket where the top of the sleeve is sewn or attached.

attifet   A heart-shaped wired headdress that sat atop the hair that was brushed aside into two rolls and sat with its point just touching the forehead.

baion   A scepter held by a Byzantine empress.

baltadin   A belt with precious stones, insignia for certain offices in the Ninth–Tenth centuries.

Banyan   Eighteenth-century long robe worn as outerwear by men.

barathea   Twill variation with a broken rib weave on one side and a pebbly texture on the other.

bark cloth   A roughly woven drapery fabric with a bark-like texture, or a nonwoven material made from soaked and beaten inner bark of tropical trees such as tapa.

bast fibers   Woody fibers from the stems of plants such as flax, jute, and hemp.

batik   Resist print in which wax is drawn or blocked onto a fabric before dyeing so the color does not penetrate in the waxed area.

batiste   Fine, sheer, plain-woven cloth of combed and carded long-staple cotton.

bavolet   A loose fitting cap with a flap on the nape of the neck worn primarily by French peasant women. A large ruffle around the band helped keep sun off the face and neck.

beater   Movable frame on a loom that holds the reed and packs the filling yarns into place.

bias   Invisible diagonal line at a 45-degree angle to the grain of a fabric, popular in the 1930s.

binyeo   Long bobbin-headed hair pin.

bionda   A homemade bleaching mixture composed mostly of lemon juice, ammonia, and urine: the combined effect of the *bionda* and of the sun exposure bleached the hair to the signature Venetian blonde in the Italian Renaissance.

blackwork (or Spanish work)   A type of embroidery that creates geometric, lace-like patterns in black silk thread worked on white linen or silk, usually seen on cuffs, collars, and sleeves of shirts and chemises.

blanket   A textile sample showing a series of patterns or colors all on the same warp.

bleaching   Basic finishing process to whiten untreated fabrics (greige goods).

bleeding	A fault in which dye runs from one pattern area into another.
blend	Yarn of two or more staple fiber types spun together, or fabric containing blended yarns in the warp and filling directions.
block printing	General term for a hand-printing process using wood or other solid material blocks into which patterns have been cut.
blotch printing	Open-screen roller-printing process by which the plain background of a printed fabric can be colored.
bobbin lace	Single-element construction, originally handmade on a pillow with numerous threads.
bodice	A close-fitting woman's garment worn over the stays (later, corsets), sometimes with detachable sleeves. The bodice also describes the upper part of a one-piece gown.
bolt	An entire length of fabric, usually rolled full-width on a tube; sometimes folded before rolling.
bombasina	Cotton fabric in the Italian Renaissance.
bombazine	A mixture of silk and wool.
borzacchini	Leather ankle boots worn by people in the Italian Renaissance.
brache	Italian Renaissance trousers.
braghetta	Italian renaissance codpiece. A fabric triangle, originally created to cover the male groin area.
braid	Flat or round, woven or plaited fabric used for trimming.
breeches (or Upper Stocks)	Men's short (usually knee-length) trousers. The style of these changed drastically from period to period and were either close-fitted hose or very elaborately puffed, slashed, and structured.
broadcloth	Tightly woven, lustrous cotton fabric in a plain weave with a fine crosswise rib, or wool fabric with a close twill weave, brushed and sheared to give a uniform, slightly felted, smooth appearance. Originally describes a finely woven wool cloth used for better grades of clothing. At 29-inches wide, it was broader than most woven fabrics of the early American Colonial era.
brocade	Jacquard-woven fabric with a supplementary warp and/or filling which creates an all-over design: background is satin or twill weave.
brushing	Finishing process in which fibers are raised to obscure the construction of the fabric.
buckram	Plain-woven cotton fabric stiffened with sizing.
bulla	An amulet worn by Etruscan children as a good-luck charm, by young men on bracelets on their upper arms, and on horse trappings; or the locket worn by Roman male children as the sign of their free-born status. They were made of leather, bronze, silver, or gold, and were dedicated to the gods when the boys put on the *toga virilis*, or man's toga, around the age of fifteen, signifying the end of their childhood.

burlap	Plain-woven cloth of retted, single-ply jute.
busk	A piece of wood, metal, or bone that slid into the center front of the female dress bodice to provide stiffness and structure.
busun	Padded/quilted sock, made from specially shaped forms with a heal, thick ankle and pointy curled-up toe.
calashes	Very large hoods worn in eighteenth-century France and the colonies to fit over the large piled hairstyles. These were pulled over the towering hairstyles with specially made devices that the woman could manipulate to reach high enough to come over the hair.
calcagnini	Typically Venetian footwear that could reach the height of 50 centimeters. Fashionable in the late fifteenth–early sixteenth century in Italy.
calcei	The high-topped, laced boots that a Roman citizen wore with the toga in public; indoors he wore sandals. A patrician's calcei were dark red (mullei), the Senator's calcei had black laces and a buckle. Their basic form derived from the laced, pointed shoes represented on Etruscan monuments of the Archaic period, though the Roman calcei were not pointed.
calendering	Standard finishing process in which cloth is pressed heavily and/or repeatedly under steel rollers to produce a polished surface also used to emboss fabrics.
calico	Ancient, basic woven cotton cloth.
calze solate (or calzebraghe)	Tight-fitting footed hoses made in wool cloth with a central seam in the back. Used in the fifteenth and early sixteenth centuries in Italy.
camel hair	Natural protein fiber obtained from the undercoat of the Asiatic camel.
camise (or camicia)	Shirts, sometimes ruffled at the cuffs and neck, in which the ruffles were gathered in a short collar decorated with embroidery worn during the Renaissance period.
cammellotti (or ciambellotti, zambellotti)	Very warm wool cloth used for winter clothing in Renaissance Italy. Originally, probably made with camel hair, hence the name.
cammino	A textile pattern characterized by a horizontal sequence of lobed Italian Renaissance motifs framing the "Italian artichoke," a pomegranate, or a pinecone.
camora	A petticoat skirt worn as a feminine gown in the Renaissance. It was known in Italy under various names, according to different regions: *gamurra* or *camurra* in Florence; *camora, socha,* or *zupa* in northern Italy; and *Gonna, gonnella,* or *sottana* in the south.
candys	A long under-tunic thought to be the precursor to the caftan, developed from the Sumerian shawl.
canion	Men's leggings worn over hose and attached to the culots. Very short breeches were laced to the culots and usually came to just below the knee. They were a close fit, but not tight.

capelet	Upper part of the Greek female dress of Daedalic figures; a tightly fitting tubular dress cinched in tightly at the waist.
capigliara	Elaborate hairstyle fashionable in sixteenth century Italy that mixed the hair with postiches, ribbons, bows, jewels, and pearls.
carded yarn	Yarn spun from a carded sliver of fibers.
carding process	Used for all natural fibers, in which they are separated and brought into general alignment prior to spinning.
carrick	A long coat usually of wool broadcloth with buttons down the front and a many-tiered capelet topped by a conventional collar.
cashmere	Fine, extremely soft natural protein fiber obtained from the undercoat of the Himalayan Kashmir goat.
casque à la Minerve	A small, plumed hat styled to look like the one worn by the Roman goddess of wisdom.
casso, busto	Corset, often made with wood or metal busks in Renaissance clothing.
cassock	Long, front-buttoning gowns worn by various clergy.
caul	Hairstyle tied up in a netted *caul* and topped with a flat, very wide-brimmed hat.
ceinture fleshée	Multicolored woven belt worn by the coureurs des bois in Canada.
cellulose	Organic fibrous substance found in all vegetation that is the basic constituent of both natural and manufactured fabrics such as cotton.
cellulosic fibers	Such as cotton, linen, jute, and rayon.
chōnin	The townsmen and merchants, the lowest class in Japan's inflexible class system and the fashion leaders of the urban, cash-based society of Edo Japan.
ch'ma	High-waisted full skirt worn in Korea, with narrow shoulder straps that wrapped to overlap in the back and flowed in slight pleats to the ankles.
ch'ma-chogori	Top and bottom of Korean hanbok.
chang-ot	Outercloak/veil in Korean dress.
chatelaine	A heavy hook with a collection of small thimbles, scissors, needle-cases, scent cases, seals, patch-boxes, toothpick cases, keys, and watches.
cheesecloth	Cotton in loose, plain weave with a very low thread count, originally used to wrap cheese.
chemise dress	A simple straight shift dress made of cotton or light silk, sashed at the waist and adorned at the neckline and hem with a deep ruffle.
chemisette	An underlayer of sheer white fabric made into a sleeveless tunic; the lace decoration around the neckline was often worn to peak over the neckline of the main gown.

chiffon	Sheer fabric, made usually of silk.
chinoiserie	Objects made in Europe in imitation of Chinese styles.
chintz	A plain woven fabric, usually made of cotton, printed with colorful lively patterns such as flowers.
chiton	A Greek rectangular garment used as a basic shirt by both men and women in all periods, made from a single piece of cloth, uncut and unfitted, woven to order, straight from the loom. Its length varied. A long chiton was worn by women, old men, charioteers, and musicians. Active men wore a short or three-quarter length chiton. Also, a tunic worn by middle-rank courtiers in the early Byzantine period. Biblical figures are illustrated wearing the *chiton* throughout the history of the Byzantine empire.
chlamys	A short or long cloak fastened over the right shoulder with a *fibula* (pin). When worn for military purposes the chlamys was left plain and was usually made of felt. The civilian chlamys is decorated with a *tablion*, a trapezoidal or rectangular embroidered panel sewn onto the front and back, along the side of its opening in the knee area. By the sixth century the chlamys became part of the dress for the emperor and began to slowly lose its military connotation. It could be made out of luxury fabrics like silk or wool with embroidered decoration of high quality. By the sixth century, the empress also wore the chlamys.
chogori	Top jacket or blouse with long curved sleeves, *sohme*, that evolved to a short bolero length for women that is overlapped to close right of center front and ties above the bust line with two long sashes, *korum*, in a large loop. Men's chogori length has remained more static overtime, reaching to just below the waist.
choli	Indian woman's short, tight-fitting blouse.
city-states	Athens, Sparta, Corinth, and others, were independent Greek cities, each with its surrounding territory, characterized by different political systems, social customs, and artistic specialties but bound together by language and religion.
clavus (i)	Vertical stripes of embroidery on a tunic, usually two stripes (clavi).
cleaning	**Dry**: immersion of fabric in petroleum or synthetic solvents to remove oil or grease. **Wet**: removal of waterborne soil or stains by a soap or detergent and water process, done usually on a flat surface with a brush, not to be confused with laundering by immersion.
cloth count	*See* thread count.
cloth	General term used for any pliable material whether woven, knitted, felted, knotted, or extruded.
coazzone	Typically fifteenth-century northern Italian ponytail wrapped in ribbons and trimmed with jewels.
codpiece	A man's accessory used to connect the two legs of the breeches and cover the opening at the center front. Codpieces could be a

plain patch of cloth or very decorative, stuffed, and ornamental, often considered risqué.

coir Coarse and extremely durable fiber obtained from the outer husks of coconuts.

colobium A sleeveless or short-sleeved tunic.

color A hue, as contrasted with white, black, or gray.

color abrasion Loss of color, particularly in pigment prints or from poor dye penetration.

colorfast Term applied to fabrics colored in such a way as to prevent color fading from light or cleaning.

combing The process of making carded fibers parallel and removing impurities and short fibers before spinning.

corsaletti Upper body armor made of steel plates, worn in the Renaissance.

cotton Natural vegetable fiber from the cotton plant, grown in the southern United States, Egypt, Russia, and China.

coureurs des bois (or Voyageurs) French fur trappers of the seventeenth and eighteenth century who traveled and hunted with Native American groups in the Great Lakes and Hudson Bay area of North America. They often trapped the beaver used for fashionable hats in the seventeenth century.

courtesans Prostitutes.

courtiers The privileged who frequently attended the royal courts of Europe.

couturiers High-fashion designers.

cravat A scarf or band of fabric worn by men around the neck as a tie.

crease A line in a fabric caused by a fold, usually along the front of trouser legs.

crêpe Yarn that is overtwisted to create a crinkled profile and stretchy resilience; fabric woven of crepe yarn, which has a matte surface texture and slight stretch.

crewel A hand embroidery technique from Kashmir in which fine, loosely twisted two-ply yarn is stitched onto a cotton base.

cuirasse Named after the ancient piece of armor formed of leather that protected the upper torso. These long, figure-hugging bodices emphasized a woman's hourglass figure, created by the very heavily boned corsets of the day. By 1878 the cuirasse bodices had reached the thighs. The cuirasse bodice was corset-like-and dipped even deeper in both front and back, extending well down the hips creating the look of a body encased in armor.

culots Very short breeches often worn with canions, but could be worn only with hose. Culots were so short that they appear in contemporary images as just a band of puffed fabric around the hips.

cuoietto, coletto	Upper body garment worn in the Renaissance made of leather, hence the name.
daedalic style	An artistic style typical of the seventh-century Orientalizing period in Greece, featuring a frontal stance, flat surfaces, a triangular face with triangular, almond-shaped eyes, and a wig-like, layered hairstyle.
daimyo	The top class in Japan's strict four class system. This military class included the elite military leaders and *samurai*.
dalmatic	A wide short or long-sleeved unbelted robe or tunic, with sleeves usually cut on a diagonal and decorated with clavi (lengthwise stripes). This is an older Roman term which may have gone out of use, but this is unclear.
damask	Woven pattern based upon contrasting warp-face and filling-face cloths.
darbar	Term referring to the Mughal court. Paintings of *darbar* scenes are major records of clothing worn at the Mughal court.
ddidon	Fastener for precious metal pendants to the top of an outfit or at the waist or belt section, then a *juche* or knot, and finished with one tassel *yuso,* or three.
decating	(decatizing) Basic finishing process that includes light scouring and single calendering.
degumming	Removal of natural gums from silk yarn or fabric by boiling in a mild alkaline solution.
denim	Yarn-dyed cotton cloth woven in a warp-faced twill, usually with a dyed warp and a natural filling.
density	The measure of the set of a cloth—the total number of ends and picks.
deshabille	A type of "undress" for both men and women such as a dressing gown with often quite extravagant decoration worn among the upper classes in the eighteenth century.
Dionysos	God of wine and drama: in the fifth century Greek drama was presented at Athens at his festivals. As god of the wild, he had a retinue of maenads and ithyphallic satyrs.
direct printing	General term for a process in which color is applied directly onto the fabric.
discharge printing	Process in which pattern is obtained by bleaching portions of already dyed cloth. It may be left white or dyed another color.
disperse dyeing	Process for coloring acetate, acrylic, nylon, and polyester in which a slightly water-soluble dye is dispersed in the fiber solution. Sometimes subject to fume-fading and sublimation.
divetesion	A ceremonial, long, silk tunic usually worn in the Byzantine era over another tunic and belted. The emperor wore this tunic under a *chlamys, loros,* or *sagion,* depending on the time period.

dopo dooroomakee Korean overcoat that had wider sleeves and collar than chogori, and were generally considered as more formal; the *dopo's* tie position was adjusted above that of the *chogori's* in order that the two ties would not overlap on a man's chest.

double cloth Compound cloth based on two sets each of warp or filling yarns held together at regular intervals by a warp or filling thread passing from one fabric to the other.

double crown Emblematic of both upper and lower Egypt (the red and white crowns are combined) with the white crown (symbolizing upper Egypt) set in the red crown (symbolizing lower Egypt) called the pschent (⚱).

double knit Knitted fabric made with a double set of needles to produce a double thickness of fabric which is consequently denser and has greater stability than a single knit. Popular in the 1970s.

double weave Fabric woven with two sets of warp and filling yarns, with an extra yarn to loosely hold the two cloths together. The connecting yarn is cut, leaving two cut-pile fabrics.

doublet In each era a doublet has slightly different characteristics. It is generally a man's close fitting buttoned jacket, sometimes short and padded with broad shoulders and tight waist, usually with sleeves and flared at the hips. Worn from the fifteenth to the seventeenth centuries.

dye house Facility where greige goods are dyed or printed.

dyeing The process of applying color to fiber, yarn, or fabric with natural or synthetic coloring agents.

Egyptian cotton Fine grade of cotton known for its long staple fibers that create a smooth cotton fabric.

elasticity Ability of a stretched material to recover its original size and shape.

elastomer Elastic synthetic fiber with the physical properties and strength of natural rubber such as Spandex.

embades High boots represented on Greek hunters, for example Artemis, the huntress, or other active figures, usually with shortened chiton, folded about the waist to get it out of the way.

embroidery Basic cloth embellished with ornamental needlework.

Empire dress Essentially a tube dress with one drawstring at a round neck and another at a high waistline. The neckline was low, the sleeves short, and the waistline high, located just under the bust. Skirts were very narrow, and because of this comparatively form-fitting silhouette, a reduction of underpinnings was necessary.

ephebe A member of an adolescent age group or a social status, the age of young men of training age. At a certain point an official institution (*ephebia*) saw to building them into citizens, especially training them as soldiers, as part of the militia of citizens.

fabric	General term for any woven, knitted, knotted, felted, or otherwise constructed material made from fibers or yarns. Cloth, carpet, and matting are all defined as fabric.
fabric width	Crosswise measurement of cloth.
face	The side on which a fabric is finished.
fading	Color loss due to light, pollutants, cleaning, etc.
faldia, faldiglia, verducato	Farthingale or early hoop dress worn (origins in Spain) in Italian Renaissance.
falling band	A large, square, turned-down collar that rested on the shoulders.
farsetto, giubbetto, zuparello	Characteristically short upper body garment. Used in fifteenth and early sixteenth century Italian Renaissance clothing.
farthingale	A round bell-shaped hoop skirt of Spanish origin; a roll of padding, sometimes called a hoop, worn around the hips or waist extending the width of a skirt.
felt	Nonwoven fabric made of fibers joined through the application of heat, agitation, and moisture, or by mechanical treatment; woven fabric that has been treated with heat, moisture, and pressure to achieve greater strength and fullness.
fiber	The basic element of yarn and cloth. Any tough, hair-like substance, natural or manufactured, that can be spun or thrown to form yarn, or felted or otherwise joined into a fabric.
fibula	A brooch like a large safety pin used to fasten a variety of Roman garments. Like many devices meant to fasten or bind—the bride's belt, for example—it could have a symbolic meaning. So the mantle of the *flamen*, a priest, had to be *infibulatus*, fastened with a fibula in back. The bride's wedding dress was tied with a square knot, the Hercules knot. (*See* Herakles knot.)
filament fiber	Of indefinite length, either natural (silk) or manufactured. Silk filament is the actual thread of a silkworm's cocoon; manufactured filaments are produced by forcing a solution through a spinneret.
Filling yarn (or weft or woof)	In weaving, the crosswise yarn or yarns that interlace at right angles with the lengthwise warp.
filling faced	A term used to describe fabrics in which the filling picks predominate over the warp ends. The filling may conceal the warp completely.
finish	Any treatment given to a fiber, yarn, or fabric to alter its original or greige goods state.
flamen (plural flamines)	The highest rank of Roman priesthoods, at one point including four priests dedicated to the cult of particular divinities. Their costume is best represented on the Ara Pacis, where they wear the *laena, galerus* hat with *apex,* and *calcei.*
flannel	Medium weight, slightly napped plain or twill-woven cloth, most often of wool or cotton.

flapper	A flighty young girl of questionable morals in the 1920s who danced the Charleston and wore straight, uneven hemmed dresses that swung around while she danced—originated from a British word for a kind of fish that thrashed about when thrown into a hot pan.
flax plant	Plant from which linen is produced.
fleece	The woolly coat of a sheep, usually clipped in one large piece; fabric with a deep soft woolly pile.
float	Portion of warp or filling yarns covering two or more adjacent yarns to form a design or satin surface.
fontange	A tall headdress created by counting elaborate bits of lace and ribbons onto tall wires and placing it at the front and center on a woman's head.
frenello	Big jewel made with a central stone surrounded by pearls or diamonds; usually worn on the top of the head in Renaissance clothing.
frieze	A coarse, woolly woven cloth used for outerwear.
fringe	A kind of braid or tassel attached at each shoulder of a female figure's chiton in the fourth century BC was a sign of status, often marking her as a priestess or divinity.
frogging	Ornamental closures made of braid or cording.
fulling	A finishing operation dependent on the felting properties of wool that shrinks the fabric to make it heavier and thicker.
furisode kosode	Style for young Japanese women featuring long, swinging sleeves.
gabardine	Fabric of fine worsted yarns closely woven in a diagonal twill and finished with a high sheen.
galerus	The characteristic hat of the flamen, a helmet-like leather head covering, topped by a spike, the *apex*.
garibaldi	Renaissance style of shirt with a full-sleeve. Sometimes made in red or black lightweight wool, or flannel, but more often in white cotton, with the full front gathered or pleated at the neckline.
garters	Before the invention of elastic, garters were generally silk bands tied around the leg to hold up hose. Worn by both men and women, though rarely visible under the latter's dresses.
gat	Nobleman's hat; stacked onto a headband, *mangeon*, and high cap, *tanggeoun*, fastened to the head with a tie around the chin; the wide brim was positioned carefully to sit lower in the front.
gauze	Openly constructed sheer cloth of any fiber.
Geometric Period	The period of Greek art characterized by vases decorated with geometric patterns.
gilet corsage	A woman's garment made in imitation of a man's waistcoat, and front-buttoning jackets with short *basques* that extended below the waistline could all be softened by wearing underneath a

chemisette usually in white muslin or cambric with frills showing at the neckline and cuffs.

gin (cotton gin)   A machine used to separate seeds and impurities from raw cotton fibers.

giornea   A sort of cloak opened at the sides, with a scooped neck in the back. Worn by both men and by women in fifteenth century Italy.

gokkal   Peaked hat, worn by women in warm weather made of paper or cloth that is folded repeatedly and fixed to the hair.

gorgiera   A ruff made either of thickly pleated linen trimmed with lace or linen worn in the Renaissance.

grain   The alignment of vertical (lengthwise) and horizontal (crosswise) elements in a fabric to form a right-angle relationship.

grass fibers   General class of fibers that includes abaca, sea grass, grain straw, bamboo, rattan, and cane.

grey goods (or greige goods)   Woven fabric as it comes from the loom: unbleached, not dyed or printed, unfinished.

griccia   Vertical arrangement of vegetable motifs on fabric, many of which were inspired by Persian, Chinese, and Indian patterns and used in Renaissance clothing.

grosgrain   Heavy, corded ribbon or cloth; large-scale frieze cloth with a heavy, regular warp pile.

grottesche   Composite pattern (architectural details mixed with medallions, cartouches, festoons, mermaids, sphinxes, fountains, and other heterogeneous motifs) used especially in sixteenth-century lace and inspired by the rediscovery of the frescoed decorations of Nero's Domus Aurea, in Rome.

gulle   A bonnet style embroidered hat worn by children, with a number of dangling tassels and ribbons.

hackling   Combing process as it applies to flax.

hair fibers   Animal fibers that lack the crimp and resilience of wool, such as rabbit hair and fur fibers.

hakama   Trousers worn by both men and women in Japan.

hanbok   Traditonal Korean costume bodice, made up of the ch'ma and the chogori.

hand   The tactile quality of fabric.

hand-spun yarn   Yarn spun by hand on a spinning wheel.

handwoven fabric   Cloth woven on a hand or foot-powered loom, or woven by hand without a loom.

harness   Rectangular frame on a loom that holds the heddles through which the warp yarns pass. The harnesses raise and lower the heddles in predetermined patterns so that the filling yarns can be inserted through the shed to produce the desired weave pattern.

headrail (also *conch* or *whisk*)	A wired veil worn by women that stood up from the back of the shoulders and created a heart-shaped silhouette behind the head and shoulders.
heather	Mixture of yarn composed of fibers dyed in different colors.
heddles	Needlelike wires on a loom through which the warp yarns are threaded. They are mounted in the harness, which is raised and lowered during weaving.
Hellenistic Period	Period after the death of Alexander in 323 BC and before the rule of Augustus as the first Roman emperor.
hemp	Coarse natural cellulose fiber.
Herakles knot	A strong knot created by two intertwined ribbons, used in ancient Greece and Rome as a protective amulet, for both men and women, with a variety of symbolic meanings.
hetaira	Professional female entertainer, musician, or prostitute, slave or foreign, non-citizen, hired to work at an all-male Greek drinking party, the symposium. Similar to a Japanese *geisha*.
himation	A square, large woolen mantle worn by both men and women over the chiton, draped in a variety of ways. Both men and women pulled it over the head in a mourning gesture. Typical of a bride was the gesture of holding it out as if to cover her head. In Roman times, Greek men wore the square himation with sandals, in contrast with the costume of the Roman citizen, the toga and calcei.
hinagata-bon Kosode	Design books published in Japan between 1666 and about 1820.
Homeric Greece	The early period of Greek history, when the Greek cities were ruled by the feudal monarchies described by the poet, Homer, in the *Iliad* and the *Odyssey*.
homespun	Originally, a plain-woven, fabric from hand-spun yarns; currently, a machine-woven fabric with irregular yarns to simulate the original textures.
hongnyong-po	King's robes of Choson or official costume; a long, wide sleeved, red, blue, or yellow robe decorated with large elaborate golden crests on the front chest, back, and two shoulders with the royal motif of a dragon with five claws.
hoplites	Greek foot soldiers, infantrymen, fighting in formation, in contrast to the earlier system of hand-to-hand single combat.
hopsacking	Coarse basket-weave fabric of jute, hemp, or cotton.
houndstooth	Variation of a twill weave, with a broken check pattern.
hue	Color, shade, or tint of a color.
hwanwonsam	Outer ceremonial jacket worn by the Korean queens of the Choson period; covering several layered embellished garments.
ikat	Fabric woven with tie-dyed yarns.

Incroyables	Young and fashionable French men and women born into well-to-do families who, after the end of Robespierre's bloody dictatorship, blossomed into a subculture boldly dressing in eccentric and expensive clothing proclaiming a return of individual freedom after the revolutionary terror ended. This included both ancient regime elements with revolutionary elements blending to provoke the singularity of the sans-culottes who also elevated politics above fashion.
indigo	Natural vegetable dye from the indigo plant used to color fabric deep blue or purple.
interlining	A layer of fabric between the outer, decorative fabric and the lining.
jacket bodice	Developed during the 1840s as an alternative style for day wear. It had a loose straight fit that was more masculine than the traditional fitted bodice.
jacquard	Loom attachment that uses a punched card system to raise and lower single heddles. It permits the weaving of fabrics with complex patterns such as tapestry and brocade.
jama	Generic name for a coat or outer garment worn at the Mughal Indian court.
jangot	Woman's hooded cloak, originating from the men's style of overcoat.
Japonism	Japanese-inspired styles of art and design.
jean	Sturdy cotton twill fabric (also called denim).
jeanette	Was a necklace made of a narrow braid of hair or velvet with a cross or heart charm that was worn around the neck in the later 1830s.
jegwan	Confucian horse hair hat worn by men, architecturally tiered upwards from the crown of the head in geometrical shapes and points.
jeongjagwan	Confucian hat worn by some kings.
jerkin	Short close-fitting sleeveless vest worn over the doublet by young men.
jokdur	Women's crown or headdress, small jewelled, round corner cube or architectural shape, sits forward on the head with dangling ornaments and tassels draping down the side and forehead.
juche	Knot used on Korean clothing.
justaucorps	Knee length, elegant, close-fitting men's coat usually made of rich fabrics such as velvet or brocade and decorated with cords, often with a long slightly flared skirt. Worn in the Renaissance and rococo periods.
jute	Coarse natural cellulose fiber, used primarily in burlap.
kabbadion	A Byzantine caftan or robe with an opening in the front. In the ninth century it is noted as the costume of the *ethnikoi*, probably

referring to the fact that this was a common garment in Islam. By the fourteenth century according to Pseudo-Kodinos, it is typical for many courtiers to wear a *kabbadion*. It seems that aristocrats who were influenced by Islamic culture may have been wearing these as early as the tenth century. This is also the word for knee-length quilted coats.

kalisaris	Worn by ancient Egyptian women and men. A richly ornamented narrow shell with straps. Also worn as a shift in transparent finely pleated fabric.
kamellaukia	Felt caps worn by the infantry in the tenth century.
kanoko shibori	"Fawn spot" shibori dyeing technique in which a pattern of tiny round or square dots of undyed fabric forms a design on fabric.
kapok	Natural cellulose fiber.
katabira	Summer *kosode* worn by members of the samurai class in Edo Japan.
kerchief	A large square cloth, which when folded diagonally, was worn as a head or neck covering.
khat headdress	The Egyptian king wore head-cloths arranged in two different ways; the *nemes*-headdress and the *khat*-headdress or *bag wig*. Both were made by securing a rectangular piece of cloth with a band stretching over the brow and above the ears in the manner of a kercheif. The *khat*-headdress was generally plain, with the pieces of cloth tucked up under the band instead of hanging lose around the face as on the nemes.
kil	Main body of the Korean garment.
kit	Collar of Korean dress.
knickerbockers	Pants gathered or tied at the knee known as knickers for short in the 1860s and 1870s.
knit fabric	Textile produced by continuous interlooping of one or more yarns.
kore	A type of monumental life-size stone statue representing a standing youthful woman, beautifully dressed, presented as a gift to the gods. The best known are the sixth-century Archaic korai from the Akropolis at Athens.
korum	Long sash on the chogori top in Korean women's dress.
koshimaki	Formal summer robes made of crisp fabric worn in Edo period Japan.
kouros	A type of monumental, life-size or bigger, stone statue representing a standing youthful nude male figure, which started to be made in different Greek cities in the seventh century BCE. Emphasis was placed on their nudity. They were used as votive gifts to the gods, representations of Apollo, or funerary markers.
kranea or kassidia	Iron helmets.

lace	A decorative trim created by manipulating a fine yarn or thread into a two-dimensional fabric with an open structure, often with floral or geometric patterns.
lacis (also filet)	An Italian style of cutwork where a fine piece of netting is embroidered and cut out to form a decorative trim. It is a precursor to lace.
laena	The Roman rounded garment worn by the flamines; it was draped back to front, forming a semicircle in front, and fastened with a fibula in back.
lambswool	First fleece sheared from a young sheep. The previously unclipped fiber ends are tapered, producing a very soft texture.
lappets	Flat lace caps with tapered ends that extended into long tails or *lappets* at the sides. Worn into the 1860s, this headdress was placed far back on the head.
lattughini	Small ruffles at the cuffs and neckline worn in Renaissance clothing.
lawn	Lightweight, sheer, fine cotton or linen fabric.
leading strings	Used in the walking and crawling stage, toddlers often wore sturdy ribbons, called *leading strings*, attached to the shoulders of their clothing. These kept adventurous children from wandering too far away, and helped a bodice-bound mother pick them up when the nursemaid wasn't around.
lenza	Thin silk cordonnet that crossed the forehead and from which dangled jewels or other decorations; used in the Italian Renaissance.
line	Long linen fibers that have great luster and strength.
linen	Natural cellulose yarn made from flax fibers, noted for strength, cool hand, and luster; low resilience fabric woven from linen yarn.
lining	Material attached under the principal material of a cloth or piece of clothing to protect the outer fabric and sometimes to help give stability and shape to a garment.
livery	Comes from the Old French term *livrer*, which indicates the feeding and clothing of servants provided by the employer.
llama	South American animal of the camel family whose fleece is produced in a variety of colors.
long back braid	The typical hairstyle for women in the seventh and eighth centuries BCE.
loom	Machine that produces woven textiles by interlacing warp and filling yarns at right angles to each other.
loroi	A lighter scarf used in insignia, especially for the eparch.
loros	A heavy stole worn by both the emperor and empress as much as five meters long, often studded with precious stones. Originally this formed an X over the body, coming over the

shoulders from behind, which evolved out of the *trabea trium-phalis*, the toga of the Roman consuls. During the tenth and eleventh centuries the *loros* gained a slit so that it could be pulled over the head. The empress's *loros* wrapped around the body differently and was once thought to be a different garment called a *thorakion*.

luster   The gloss or sheen on the surface of a fiber, yarn or fabric.

Lycra®   Trade name of a spandex fiber.

maitress en titre   A royal mistress.

mandyas   In Roman times, this was a light cloak, resembling the *chlamys*. The *mandyas* came to be known as the long, dark, undecorated cloak worn by both monastic men and women. The *mandyas* was knee length and slit up the front with drawstrings at the neck and waist for closure. The Bishop wore this garment over his *omophorion* when celebrating the liturgy. The emperor wore a gold *mandyas* during coronation by the fourteenth century.

mangeon   Headband that the gat was stacked on top of in Korean men's adornment.

maniakion   A torque, or collar, worn by barbarians and sometimes associated with soldiers. In *listes de preseances* this is the word they use for collars of insignia for certain soldiers.

manikelia   Padded wool arm guards sometimes covered with mail or wood and worn by both infantrymen and cavalry.

mantle   A loose cloak or wrap, usually sleeveless.

mantua   A gown heavily gathered at the back and often open at the front bodice and skirts to reveal a matching or contrasting stomacher and petticoat underneath.

manufactured fiber   Inclusive term for manufactured fibers of natural or synthetic origin.

maphorion   A hood that covered the neck and shoulders dating back to the fourth century. Sometimes this term is used to describe the hooded part of male and female monastic garb. By the middle Byzantine era, *maphorion* were also associated with the dress of noble women. The Virgin Mary is always shown wearing a *maphorion*. The occassional man is described as wearing a *maphorion* as well. In *The Book of Ceremonies*, a member of the Senate wears a *maphorion* that covers his entire body.

maspilli   Precious buttons used in Renaissance clothing.

mauveine   William Perkin discovered mauveine, a bright purple dye synthesized under laboratory conditions in 1856.

mazzocchio   The typical Florentine headwear worn with the long scarf called *becchetto* in Renaissance clothing.

mercerization   Caustic soda treatment for cotton and linen, which makes the yarn or cloth stronger and increases luster and dye affinity.

merino	Breed of sheep yielding a high grade wool used for fine woolen and worsted cloth.
microfiber	Extremely fine fibers of one denier or less. Fibers are often spun in bicomponent form and excess material is dissolved, leaving fine, strong fibers.
mineral fiber	Natural or manufactured fiber derived from a mineral, such as asbestos or fiberglass.
Minoan	Name used by archaeologists to refer to the civilization the pre-Greek Myceneans found on Crete. The name refers to the mythological king of Crete, Minos, son of Europa and father of the Minotaur.
mitra	A gold, embroidered kerchief-like headdress or veil worn by the patriarch of Constantinople in fourteenth century Byzantium.
moccasin	Native American soft leather shoes or boots, often fur lined and decorated with intricate quill and beadwork. Worn by native Americans and settlers in the colonies of North America.
modiste	Seamstress, needlewoman, or someone who made and repaired dresses.
mohair	Processed fiber of the long, silky hair of the Angora goat.
monk's cloth	Basket-woven cotton fabric.
monmouth cap	A knitted cap, with a rounded crown and small band. Worn primarily by sailors and soldiers originally but later widely adopted.
monofilament	Single synthesized filament; fishing line is one example.
mordant	A metallic salt used to fix dyes.
motif	A pattern unit, usually repeated.
multifilament yarn	Composed of several, or hundreds, of extruded filament fibers.
muslin	Plain-woven, uncombed cotton fabric, ranging from sheer to coarse.
Mycenean	Name used by archaeologists to refer to the civilization the pre-Greek invaders brought to the Greek mainland. The name refers to the city of Mycenae in the Peloponnesus.
Nambawi	Dark fur and silk-detailed hat worn by fashionable women and offered warmth in the winter.
natural fiber	Any textile fiber obtained from an animal, vegetable, or mineral source, such as wool, cotton, or asbestos.
Nemes **headdress**	The king wore head-cloths arranged in two different ways called the *nemes*-headdress and the *khat*-headdress or *bag wig*. Both were made by securing a rectangular piece of cloth with a band stretching over the brow and above the ears in the manner of a kerchief. The *nemes*-headdress was generally made with striped fabric, and the excess fabric was left hanging at the back in a kind of tail. At the sides, two strands or lappets hung down beside the face.

new chevron	A zigzag band applied around the hem dress.
Nuishime	Japanese *shibori*-dyeing technique in which a running stitch creates lines of resist pattern.
nylon	Generic term for synthetic polyamide fiber; nylon 6,6 has 6 carbon atoms.
obi sash	Wrapped around the waist of the Japanese *kosode* and *kimono*.
off-grain	Finishing fault in which the horizontal structure is not at right angles to the vertical.
organdy	Sheer, plain-woven cotton cloth with a crisp hand.
organza	Similar to organdy but made of silk, rayon, or nylon.
ormesini	Silk fabric originally coming from Ormuz, an island in the Persian Gulf.
paenula	A short, hooded cloak worn by farmers, shepherds, and other lower-income people in late antiquity and as the cloak of a shepherd until the fifteenth century. The *chasuble*, worn by the Pope, stems from the *paenula*.
paijama	Trousers worn in South Asia. During the Mughal period the *paijama* typically was cut full through the waist, hips, and thighs and snug fitting from knee to ankle.
pajama	A loose-fitting garment consisting of trousers and a jacket, worn for sleeping or lounging; Loose-fitting trousers worn in the Far East by men and women.
paji-chogori	*Hanbok* for Korean men includes the wide-leg trouser *paji* and an earlier longer version of the chogori.
paletot	A heavy knee-length coat with three, layered capes and slit armholes; worn by young women of the 1820s.
palla	The Roman word for the square Greek *himation* worn by women over their tunics and stolas.
pallium	The Roman word for the square Greek *himation*, worn by men, usually without a tunic, when they were not dressed in the formal attire of the Roman citizen.
paludamentum	A short cloak worn by soldiers, hunters and riders. This is a Roman term and was used in late antiquity but was replaced by the term *chlamys*.
panier	Eighteenth century hoop skirts, typically very wide at the sides but flattened in the front and back.
pantalettes	Women wore long under drawers, called *pantalettes*, with lace, ruffles, or pleats at the edges that showed at the hem of dresses.
pantaloons	Very tight-fitting ankle trousers usually made from knitted jersey.
pantofle	Shoes with cork soles the name of which is derived from the Greek word *pantophellos*, meaning "cork."

parthenon	Temple of the Greek goddess Athena Parthenos, "the virgin," built on the hill of the Acropolis of Athens in the fifth century BCE (447–432), when the Athenian empire was at its height, and the goal of the Panathenaic procession. The gold and ivory statue of the goddess in the temple, and the relief frieze of a procession outside the temple, are high points of Greek art.
paternostr	Precious belts composed of large gold beads inside which are aromatic pastes and holding the hanging *pomanders*—gold or silver filigree spheres containing sponges imbued with perfumes or scented pastes—worn in Renaissance Italy.
patka	Sash from the Mughal period in India.
pattern	The arrangement of form, design, or decoration in a fabric; guide for cutting fabric.
peascod belly	The stuffing of the belly of a man's doublet. Said to derive from the shape of plate armor.
Peisistratus	Ruled as tyrant at Athens at various times (not elected), with his sons, the Peisistratids, from c. 560 to 510 BCE. He beautified the Akropolis, encouraged the Panathenaic Festival and the city's Dionysiac festival, and brought Athens to cultural prominence among the Greek city-states.
pellanda, cioppa	In Bologna called *sacco,* elsewhere *veste* or *vestito*; a corruption of the North European name of *houppelande*, indicating a garment similarly characterized by magniloquent lines, long, trailing sleeves, and decorated with precious trimmings.
pelisse	A cape-like garment with arm slits, sometimes made with a hood and worn over dresses.
peplos	Female garment, characteristic costume of Athena, and the typical dress of the Early Classical female period, though it was worn and represented in Roman times. It was made from a rectangular piece of woolen fabric draped around the body and pinned at the shoulder, usually not sewn together at the side; its simple shape contrasted with the flowing lines of the earlier fine linen Ionian chiton.
pereline	A deep cape that covered the arms to the elbows with long, broad front lappets worn over a belt.
Pericles	Political elected leader and general at Athens, active from c. 460–430 BCE, under whom Athens had its years of greatest power and influence, including the building of the Parthenon and other buildings on the Akropolis.
perizoma	Short pants worn by active males to avoid complete nudity. They are represented in Greek art, and no doubt worn in Greece before the innovation of public nudity for males, as well as elsewhere, in areas where this innovation was never accepted in real life, and only partially in art.
peruke	A wig, especially one worn by men in the seventeenth and eighteenth centuries; a periwig. French *perruque*, from Old French, head of hair, from Old Italian *perrucca*.

petticoat	An ankle- or shin-length skirt that tied around the waist or a woman's underskirt, sometimes exposed by an open-fronted robe.
pharos	A wide mantle, used as a mantle by day and a blanket by night, mentioned by Homer.
pianelle	Slippers that do not cover the heels and are characterized by a very tall wedge obtained by overlapping layers of cork covered in leather, worn in the Italian Renaissance.
picadil	A decorative trim made from a loop of fabric that was added to the hem and/or shoulder of a doublet or bodice.
pick	In weaving, a single passage of filling yarn through the warp shed.
piece dying	Dyeing of cloth after construction.
pigment	Insoluble powdered coloring agent carried in a liquid binder and printed or padded onto the surface of a cloth.
pile weave	Construction in which cut or uncut loops protrude from the ground cloth; loops may be warp or filling yarns and be produced by a double weave or with wires. The wire method uses round-tipped, removable wires to raise loops for uncut pile, and sharp-edged cut wires for cut pile such as velvet.
pinafore apron	A type of apron worn by women. It originates from "pin afore," reflecting that the bib part of an apron was earlier often secured to the chest using pins.
plaid	Pattern of unevenly spaced repeated stripes crossing at right angles.
plain weave	Simplest method of interlacing warp and weft yarns to make cloth. Each filling (weft) passes alternately under and over the warp yarns to produce a balanced construction. It is strong, inexpensive to produce, and the best ground cloth for printing; the thread count determines the fabric's strength.
plied yarn	Yarn formed by twisting together two or more single strands.
plus fours	Full knickerbockers worn by men in the 1920s and 1930s.
ply	A single strand of yarn that is twisted with one or more strands of yarn together.
points	Ribbons with metal tips that could be threaded through sleeves and attached to jackets, or could be used to lace trunkhose to doublets.
polos hat	A tall, tubular hat worn in the Orientalizing and Archaic periods in Greece by images of goddesses.
polyester	Generic term for a manufactured fiber in which the fiber-forming substance is a long-chain synthetic polymer composed on a complex ester, popular in the 1970s.
poplin	Plain-woven, warp-faced fabric with a fine crosswise rib.

posta	Silk sash worn in the Italian Renaissance.
printing	Application of color designs to the surface of cloth.
protein fiber	Natural fiber originating from an animal such as a sheep (wool) or silkworm (silk).
pteryges or kremasmata	An apron-like covering for mid-section, sometimes known as a "fighting skirt." It was generally suspended over the shoulders with leather straps and tied around the waist.
pudding cap	A padded cap, sometimes made of crossed bands, worn by toddlers to protect their heads from injury.
quilting	Compound fabric construction of two layers of cloth with a layer of padding (batting) between, stitched through all three layers.
ramie	Fine, oriental bast fiber.
raw fiber	Textile fiber in its most natural state, for example, cotton before ginning, wool before scouring.
raw silk	Silk that is not fully degummed. It is stiff, tacky, and caramel in color.
rayon	Generic term for a manufactured fiber derived from regenerated cellulose.
red crown	The royal headdress symbolizing lower Egypt called the *deshret* ($\checkmark$), this was probably made of metal.
reed	Comb-like device on a loom through which the warp ends pass.
reed mark	Vertical streak in woven fabric caused by a bent wire in the reed.
reeled silk	Continuous filament silk as it is reeled off the softened cocoon of the cultivated silkworm.
repeat	The amount of surface a single pattern covers on a fabric that is repeated over and over.
resist printing	General term for printing processes in which the motif or the ground is treated with a dye-resistant substance before dyeing the fabric.
restello	An elaborate, carved, painted, and gilded shelf that could be completed with a glass mirror and pegs used during the Italian Renaissance.
reticule	Small bags used to keep small necessary objects close at hand.
retting	Soaking of bast fiber plants to permit bacterial or chemical breakdown of the outer bark, in order to loosen the fibers.
rib	Raised ridge running lengthwise, crosswise, or diagonally on a fabric, usually formed by the insertion of a heavy thread; also formed by embossing with heated rollers.
rib weave	Modification of plain weave in which fine warp ends are closely set and two picks (or one heavier pick) interlace as one; any woven fabric construction with a horizontal rib or cord.

roba, robone	Imposing knee-length coat made of velvet or wool, completely open at the front with wide *revers* or lapels, that showed the precious furs or silk linings, worn by both men and women during the Italian Renaissance.
robe à l'anglaise	In the imported French fashion magazines this new form kept the open-fronted skirts and pointed bodice of earlier 1700s, but the waistline was higher, and the long drape formerly falling from the shoulders was drawn back into the waistline, allowing the fullness of the back draping to emphasize the rear end; often long sleeved.
roller printing	Mechanical printing of fabric with engraved rollers.
ropa (also Spanish surcote)	A long outer gown that fastened up the center front from neck to hem and could be worn open or closed. It had a high neckline and was worn unbelted in an A-line silhouette over a gown.
rotary-screen printing	A fast and accurate printing process in which the cloth moves under a series of large, patterned cylinders.
rotella	Round shield used in the Italian Renaissance.
round gown	Gowns like the Empire style dress in France, had an unstructured bodice; the shaping was provided by a drawstring around the neck opening, or by lining flaps pinned together under an apron front. The neckline shape was most often rounded, rather than wide or square. The waistline was raised to just under the bust and was formed like the neckline, by a drawstring. To support the bosom two gussets were inserted underneath the bust line at either side.
roving	Bundle of fibers that are carded and combed and arranged in parallel alignment before spinning.
ruff	A rounded, densely ruffled collar popular in the late sixteenth and early seventeenth centuries. It required extensive pleating and starching to maintain its stiff appearance. Thin strips of starched or stiffened fabric were accordion-folded or folded in a figure-eight and tacked to a band that closed at the front or the back with a hidden fastening. Ruffs were worn by men and women at the neck and wrists. Large ruffs required a *supportase* to keep them from collapsing.
sacque gown or robe à la francaise	A voluminous gown fitted tightly at the front and box-pleated at the back of the shoulders to fall in an elegant drape at the back all the way to the floor.
Sagion	A term for several types of Byzantine cloaks. Like the *chlamys*, it had a military use in its early history (sixth century are earliest mentions). But it appears to be heavier than a *chlamys* because soldiers could use it as a blanket or tent. In the middle Byzantine period it is associated with the costumes of several courtiers, such as *protospatharioi*. Monks and hermits are noted as wearing *sagia* in the twelfth century.
saio, saione	Occasionally worn by Italian women around 1520; it could have short sleeves that let the *giubbone* sleeve show. It could be made with two or more different fabrics.

sakkos	A tunic that replaced the *divetesion* for Byzantine imperial dress in Paleologan times. The origins of this garment are in the sack-cloth, worn by ascetics. In the thirteenth century it had some ecclesiastical use.
samhoejang	Chogori worn by Korean noble women on special occasions.
samjak norigai	A triple-tasselled pendant for women.
samo or coronet	Hat worn by a male public official; woven with side wings out of bamboo or horsehair. Royal men wore tall silk black cylindrical versions.
samurai	Warriors of Japan's military class who were reduced to membership in a highly controlled urban feudal aristocracy during the Edo period.
sans culottes	Men who wore full-length trousers instead of knee-length breeches in revolutionary France. The term referred to the ill-clad and ill-equipped volunteers of the Revolutionary army during the early years of the war.
sarabula, intercula	Briefs worn during the Italian Renaissance.
sateen	Filling-faced satin-woven fabric with horizontal rather than vertical floats.
satin weave	Basic weave in which the fabric face is composed almost entirely of warp or filling floats, producing a smooth, lustrous surface.
sbernie	Mantles that leave one arm free.
scarpette	Shoes that were used throughout Italy under different names; *zibre* or *zibrette* in Milan, *cibre* in other cities in North Italy, *tapine* in the South.
scarsella	A small pouch that substituted for the missing pockets in Renaissance garments.
scouring	Washing of fiber, yarn, or fabric to remove grease, dirt, sizing, or color.
screen printing	Hand- or machine- printing process in which a pattern-making stencil or screen held in a frame is positioned on the cloth and coloring agent applied.
segmenta	Gold patches or embroidery used to decorate a *sakkos* or other tunic.
selvage	Reinforced edge on either side of a woven or flat-knitted cloth, finished to prevent raveling.
serge	Smooth-finished fabric in a balanced twill weave, identical on face and back.
sericin	Gummy substance that holds silk fibers together as they are spun (in pairs) from the silkworm; removed from silk before spinning.
sericulture	Raising of silkworms and production of silk.
sex crines hairstyle	This special hairstyle, worn by brides and priestesses, the Vestal Virgins, was based on the Archaic Etruscan *tutulus* hairstyle,

which consisted of a high bun formed by separate strands or braids of hair. The ritual dressing of the Roman bride's hair included parting the strands with a spear, which were twisted on top of her head to form a kind of bun made up of six braids or coils.

shantung silk   Dense, plain-woven silk cloth with a slightly irregular surface due to uneven, slubbed filling yarns.

shaube   A sleeveless robe with a large shawl collar became a popular garment with mayors, sheriffs, and other men of rank.

shed   The space formed as the harnesses of a loom raise some warp yarns and lower others, through which the shuttle passes to lay in the filling.

sheer   Very thin, transparent, or semi-opaque fabric.

shenti   Hip skirt or loin cloth with pleats and decorations worn by Egyptian men.

shibori   General name for the Japanese resist dye technique often translated as "tie-dye." Shibori includes various resist techniques including clamping, stitching, and tying.

shift   The universal undergarment for women, rich or poor, was a smock-like low-necked shirt. Called a "shift" or later a "chemise," this long garment functioned as both blouse and slip.

shogun   Literally "the general who quells barbarians;" the head of the military bureaucracy that controlled Japan during the Edo period.

shuttle   Device on a loom to carry the filling yarn through the shed to interlace it with the warp.

silk   Natural protein fiber unwound from the cocoon of the silkworm.

siren suits   Suits that could be zipped into quickly for lightning-fast escapes to underground shelters in wartime London, 1940s.

sisal   Strong natural cellulose fiber used in making cord and matting.

sizing   Starch applied to warp threads to strengthen them for the weaving process, usually removed by scouring during finishing; starch applied to cotton or linen cloth that is removed when the fabric is washed.

skaranikon   A word mentioned in a twelfth century poem and Pseudo-Kodinos, according to the Oxford Dictionary of Byzantium. It is unclear whether this is a cloak or a hat similar to the *skiadion*.

skeleton suit   A young boy's outfit consisting of long trousers attached by buttons at the waist to a long-sleeved, short-waisted jacket, worn by eighteenth-century boys.

skiadion   A squarish hat worn by courtiers and sometimes the emperor in Paleologan times.

sliver   Continuous ropelike strand of loosely assembled fibers before twisting into yarns.

slub	Lump or knot in a yarn; may be a defect or purposely spun to produce a textured surface in cloth.
smock	Loose-fitting knee-length over-blouses worn by the working class for centuries. They were also a very practical fashion for children.
Socrates	Athenian philosopher (449–399 BCE) during the Golden Age of Athens, teacher of Plato, developed the Socratic method of question and answer, focusing on ethical problems, in contrast to the relativism of the sophistic philosophers.
sohme	Long curved sleeves on the Korean chogori.
soprarizzo, cesellato	Rich fabrics with textured appearance that was obtained with the alternation of cut and looped velvet. It was often brocaded with gold threads, and the details of the pattern could be highlighted with the *allucciolature*, very thin gold or silver plate loops threaded through the fabric, and variously twisted in order to achieve the desired decorative effect. Used in Renaissance clothing.
spandex	Generic term for synthetic elastic fibers composed of segmented polyurethane made popular during the 1980s fitness craze.
spencer	By 1804–5, a long sleeved, short-waisted, fitted jacket called the *Spencer* became very fashionable for women.
spinneret	Metal disc with numerous fine holes through which a chemical solution is extruded to produce synthetic fibers.
spinning	Drawing out and twisting fiber into yarn or thread; extruding manufactured filaments through a spinneret.
spoon bonnet	A hat with a narrow brim close to the ears, rising vertically above the forehead in a spoon shaped curve and sloping down behind to a very small crown.
spun yarn	Yarn spun from staple-length fiber, either natural or cut synthetic filaments.
staple	Natural or manufactured fiber that has a relatively short length.
stays	An early term for corset. A stiff undergarment tied or fastened around the torso to give a desired shape to a gown's silhouette.
stemma	A Greek crown that replaced the late antique *diadem*, or headband, for imperial head-gear. A crown is made of precious metals and gemstones, and sometimes has enameling or other luxury arts techniques used in its construction. *Perpendulia*, or simply, *pendulia*, are strings of pearls that hang from the stemma at the temples.
stola	The stola was a long garment worn by respectable upper-class Roman married women (*matronae*) over the tunic and under the palla; it can be recognized on portraits by the thin straps coming down from the shoulders.
stomacher	Stiff, triangular garment that attached to the front of a dress bodice. Sometimes embroidered or adorned with ribbons and bows.

Stratagliati, accoltellati	Fabrics, mostly simple silk satins, but also damasks and velvets, slashed and cut following specific decorative patterns such as little flowers, zigzag motifs, and crosses. Fashionable in the second half of the sixteenth century in Italy.
stretch fabrics	Constructed of stretch yarns to have much greater than normal stretch and recovery characteristics. "Comfort stretch" is a designation for fabrics with up to 30 percent stretch and recovery; "power or action stretch" describes fabrics with 30–50 percent stretch and recovery. These became popular in the 1980s.
stretch yarn	Yarn with a durable, springy elongation and exceptional recovery.
stripe	Narrow section of a fabric differing in color or texture from the adjoining area.
sugacapi	Hair towels used during the Italian Renaissance.
sugar loaf hat	A conical hat, rounded at the top with a broad brim. Similar in shape to the form in which bulk sugar was purchased in the seventeenth and eighteenth centuries. Later became identified with classic Puritan costume.
sulphur dye	Dye that produces heavy shades of black or brown in cellulosic fabrics.
sumptuary laws	Laws that governed how people of all classes were allowed to dress. Versions of these laws appear in most periods in history and most regions up until modern times. Purple, for example, has often be restricted by sumptuary law to be worn only by royalty.
sun rot	Deterioration caused by sun or light.
superhumeral	A collar with a mock turtleneck that extended out to the shoulders and down to the chest, usually decorated with gem stones and metallic threads, worn over a tunic. Worn by Byzantine aristocratic men, including the emperor in the eleventh century and beyond.
supportase (also underpropper)	A wired structure worn by both men and women that served to hold up the elaborate ruffs; wide ruffled bands worn at the neck.
synthetic fiber	Textile fiber made from a petrochemical rather than a natural base. All synthetic fibers are manufactured, but not all manufactured fibers are synthetic, e. g., rayon.
tabì, tabin, tabinetto, tabinazzo	Sometimes defined as a fabric similar to damask or as thick taffetas; characterized by a "wave" effect. Seen in the Italian Renaissance.
taffeta	Crisp, plain-woven fabric in which the filling is heavier than the warp, producing a fine, lustrous rib.
tainia	A purple headband worn by Byzantine children in the palace in the Palaeologan period. It was also acceptable for children to go without any hat.
Tanaquil	Etruscan queen, wife of the first Tarquin, legendary figure in Roman tradition. Her story is told by the first-century Roman historian, Livy.

tanggeoun   High cap onto which the gat was placed in Korean men's clothing.

tapestry   Jacquard-woven fabric with supplementary multicolored yarns that form an intricate design or scene. The finished products were often used to cover walls in cold castles in Europe.

tarquins   Etruscan dynasty who ruled at Rome in the sixth century BCE, whose fall brought about the Roman Republic. The last Tarquin especially, Tarquinius Superbus, brought to Rome many elements of Etruscan culture, including the Temple of Jupiter Capitoline, most aspects of the Roman triumph, music, and theater. Such important Roman symbols as the curved priestly *lituus*, the *fasces* and the axe of the lictor hark back to Etruscan models, and in dress, the toga, decorative purple borders, the *laena*, *calcei*, *sex crines*, and *galerus* with *apex*.

tea-gown   An unboned, loose-fitting afternoon gown, often with *watteau* style backs, that fell in folds from the neck to the hem.

tebenna   The rounded mantle worn by the Veii Apollo and other male figures from mid-sixth century Rome, the ancestor of the Roman toga.

terrycloth   Uncut warp-pile fabric, plain or jacquard; woven of cotton, linen, or rayon.

textile   Orginally, a general term for any woven cloth; now, a general term for any fabric made from fibers or yarns, natural or manufactured made into any fabric structure such as woven, knits, nonwoven etc.

thorax   From the sixth through tenth centuries cavalrymen wore this body armor made of chain mail, a shirt, with or without sleeves, made of metal links which sometimes was mounted on leather, or lamellar, small plates of iron or leather laced together or attached to a leather backing. These varied in length from ankles to waist.

thread   A strand of plied and twisted yarn with a smooth finish that is used in sewing and stitching.

thread count   The number of warp and filling yarns per square measure (inch or centimeter).

throwing   Slight twisting of filament yarns.

tippets   A short shoulder cape with a longer hanging front worn over dresses by women.

toga   The rounded mantle clearly distinguished a Roman from a Greek, who wore the rectangular himation mantle. The Romans' were by definition the *gens togata*, (Vergil, *Aeneid*). Different colors and decorations distinguished the various kinds of togas, all of them deeply symbolic of age, rank, status or office. The purple borders of the *toga praetexta*, for example, characterized the costume of the higher levels of office, the curule magistracies; it was also the dress of boys, who wore it until they discarded it for the *toga virilis*, the normal plain woolen toga of adult men. A bright white *toga candida* marked the wearer as a candidate for office, a dark *toga pulla*, a mourner. Most prestigious was the *toga triumphalis*, worn by the victorious general when he celebrated a triumph.

toile   Plain, coarse twill-woven fabric, often in linen. Most noteworthy were the toiles de Jouy; eighteenth-century French fabrics printed with scenes of one color on pale cotton, linen, or silk.

tondo   The circular area in the center of a Greek vase.

tongjong   A thin, replaceable outer layer on the neckline of the Korean chogori; white woven hemp, cotton, or ramie protected the garment from wearing at the neck.

tow   Short or broken fibers of flax, hemp, or synthetic materials used for yarn, twine, or stuffing; thick bundle of continuous filaments assembled without twisting into a loose ropy strand for cutting into staple length.

trade name   Name given by manufacturer to distinguish a product produced and sold by that manufacturer, for example, Lycra.

trademark   Word, letter, or symbol used in connection with a specific product originating and owned by a particular manufacturer.

treadle   Lever or pedal on a loom that activates the lowering or raising of a harness.

Trojan War   Mythological story, the subject of Homer's *Iliad*, of the siege of the city of Troy, by the united force of the Greeks, in 1200 BC.

trunk hose   Short, puffy breeches, bound above the knee by a ribbon or garter to hold up the stockings. Worn from the sixteenth to the seventeenth centuries.

tsujigahana   Complex Japanese technique using *shibori*, painting, metallic leaf, and embroidery techniques to pattern fabric for *kosode*.

tti   Additional tie belt, fastened around the outside of jacket layers in Korean dress.

tunic   Tunics are the main piece of the Byzantine wardrobe. The T-shaped garment could be long or short, with various length sleeves. They were worn as an undergarment (this is the closest item to Byzantine underwear) and as a regular garment; typically more than one tunic was worn at one time. Or, tunic is the Roman word for the shirt or chiton worn under the mantle. The vertical purple stripes that decorated it were either broad or narrow, indicating the wearer's status.

turban   Called *phakeolis* or *phakiolion*. Worn by both Byzantine men and women by the tenth century according to evidence found on Cappadocian frescoes.

turumagi   Additional layered long overcoat in Korean dress.

tussah   Brownish silk fabric from uncultivated silkworms.

tweed	Medium-weight, rough woolen fabric, usually twill woven. Named tweeds such as Donegal, Connemara, Harris, and Galashiels are produced in Ireland and Scotland.
twill	Basic weave that produces a surface of diagonal lines by passing filling threads over two or more ends in a regular progression. Denim is a common modern example of a twill weave.
twist	The tightness and direction of the twist spun into a yarn. *S* twist is a clockwise twist and is the most common; *Z* twist is a counterclockwise twist.
twistless yarn	Yarns formed by combining fibers by means other than twisting.
uccelletti di Cipro	"Cyprus birds," solid perfumes kept in small leather cases in the shape of tiny birds, used by Italian women during the Italian Renaissance.
uchikake	Formal, outer *kosode*, worn unbelted.
ukiyo	Literally the "floating world," the pleasure quarter of Edo period Japan where prominence was determined by one's taste and ability to pay, not by position in the period's inflexible class system.
underpropper (supportase)	At the height of their fashion and their width, ruffs needed more than starch to stay rigid and were worn with this wire understructure.
ungarina	Bell-shaped Renaissance dress made from precious fabrics. The gown reached the ankles and closed in the front with frogs. Usually worn by boys aged between two and four. The name refers to the heavy braiding decorations, very common in clothing of Eastern European countries, such as Hungary.
vegetable fibers	Natural textile fibers of plant origin, such as cotton, flax, or hemp.
velour	Cut warp-pile fabric, usually of cotton or wool, with higher, less dense pile than velvet.
velvet	Close-cropped, warp-pile fabric with a smooth, rich surface, produced by double weaving or with wires. Originally woven in silk, now made with cotton or synthetic fibers as well.
velveteen	Single-woven weft pile fabric with a dense-cut surface.
vicuna	Small, wild Andean animal of the camel family, from the undercoat of which is derived a fine, lustrous fiber.
vinyl	Nonwoven fabric made from a petrochemical solution; thick or thin, it is usually soft and pliable.
virgin wool	New wool; not reused, reprocessed, or respun.
viscose rayon	The most common rayon, formed by converting cellulose into a soluble form and regenerating it into a synthetic fiber.
voile	Soft, sheer cloth, plain-woven of fine crepe (overtwisted) yarns.
waistcoat	Also called a vest. A front-buttoning, sleeveless garment worn usually by men under a jacket or coat. Occasionally had detachable sleeves.

wale	A horizontal, vertical, or diagonal rib in a fabric; the vertical rib on the face of a knitted fabric.
warp	Lengthwise yarns in a fabric, running vertically through the loom, parallel to the selvages.
weave	Structural pattern in which yarns are interlaced to produce fabric.
weaving	Process of making a fabric on a loom by interlacing horizontal yarns (weft) at right angles with vertical yarns (warp).
weft	Horizontal or crosswise element of a woven cloth.
weighted silk	Silk treated with metallic salts to increase the weight and apparent value, strictly controlled and now virtually obsolete. Historic textiles treated with this finish deteriorate quickly and damage the silk fibers.
whisk	A large unstarched falling collar, often with a deep lace trim that reaches past the shoulders.
white crown	Emblematic of Lower Egypt and probably made of metal; the white crown is also known by many names, including *hedjet* (⚱).
Windsor knot	A knot for a man's necktie named for and popularized by the Duke of Windsor in the early twentieth century.
wisk	Deep linen lace collars.
woolen	Fuzzy, loosely twisted yarn spun from carded short wool fibers. Woolen cloths are generally simple weaves and show coarser finishes than wools.
worsted	Smooth, compact yarns spun from carded and combed long wool fibers. Worsted cloths are more closely constructed and have smoother finishes than woolens.
yangban	Male aristocrats in the Korean Choson Dynasty (1392–1910).
yarn	Any form of spun, twisted or extruded fibers, natural or manufactured, that can be used in weaving, knitting, or other fabric construction.
yarn dyeing	Dyeing at the yarn stage of production, as opposed to solution, stock, or piece dyeing.
yeomnang or gangnang	Small pouches used in place of garment pockets in Korean dress.
zanana	The women's quarters at the court of Mughal India.
zebellino da mane	Fur stole worn on the shoulders during the Italian Renaissance.
zetanini avvellutati	Silk velvets originally made in the Chinese city of Zayton, worn during the Italian Renaissance.
zimarra	A Turkish-inspired overcoat, similar to a kaftan. Usually made with very expensive and showy fabrics and suitable to be worn inside the house in the Italian Renaissance.
zovi	A general word for belt, girdle or sash.

List of Museums

CLOTHING COLLECTIONS

Clothing artifacts are housed in a number of different museums around the world. In fact, most museums, from large metropolitan collections to local museums, will house at least some items of textiles and clothing in their collections even if it is not devoted to the study of clothing and costume. The staffs of dedicated employees at these museums are trained in the conservation and preservation of the textile artifacts. Specific technical skills are needed to allow costume resources to survive through time, and if only these techniques had been known long ago, there would be many more examples for study today. However, at this time in history, it is well known that climate and humidity affect textiles to a great extent and need to be controlled or the textiles will rot, fade, and disappear.

Certain types of fibers are more durable and will last longer than others. Silk is a valuable fiber that has been known to shatter rather dramatically into dust if not kept at the right temperature and moisture level. Many of the most beautiful beaded and embellished silk gowns are in desperate shape because of the fragile nature of the fabric. Often, because silk was sold by weight—and to allow the fabric to drape well—it was weighted with metals that over time have meant that the fiber has deteriorated. Hanging a heavily embellished garment can cause undue stress of the shoulder seams and rip the garment.

These garments and fabrics are sometimes hung up but more often stored in acid-free tissue paper in boxes and placed in climate-controlled rooms until they are displayed or used for research purposes to make sure there is no further degradation of the fibers. In some cases, they are never displayed for fear that they may completely fall apart. Lighting of displays is usually kept at a very low level so as not to disturb the textiles and harm them while on show for people to learn from and admire. Hats, purses, parasols, and shoes are all fitted with special supports to make sure they are not crushed further in the storage and display process.

Sometimes garments that have great historical value but are not in very good condition are received by museums. After a *condition report* is written, a plan is made to try to either restore the artifact or stabilize it so it does not decay any further. Painstaking hours are spent on single portions of garments to make sure they are saved for further study in the years to come. A single cuff may need the attention of a conservator for weeks or even months. The job of the conservator is often at odds with that of the curator, who is concerned with creating the displays and educating the public about the clothes in the collection. It is a sad day when a piece of clothing is too weak to display, especially when that item has exquisite detailing that should be seen by the museum-going public. There are thousands of historical garments stored away safely in museums around the world, many waiting to be studied.

Local museum collections will have items of interest to the history of the region, exemplifying what life was like throughout time in the community. Large urban museums will collect and house textiles and clothing from all over the world to give an idea of many different cultures and their ideas on dress and adornment.

The most famous museums with excellent costume collections include the Victoria and Albert Museum in London and the Costume Institute at the Metropolitan Museum of Art in New York. These two outstanding museums house excellent collections of all kinds of costumes from all over the world. They also have extensive study rooms with information on clothing and textile history. There are many other museums devoted to clothing artifacts, though, ranging from the purely civilian dress of the fashionable people to military uniforms.

The following is a list of collections with excellent resources that might be helpful to a student of clothing and history (websites and mailing addresses are included where available). This list by no means represents even a fraction of the many collections of costume, but it is meant to give the student of costume an idea of where to look for costume resources.

The Bata Shoe Museum
327 Bloor St. West
Toronto, ONT, Canada M5S 1W7
Phone: (416) 979-7799
www.batashoemuseum.ca

Bernberg Museum of Costume
Corner Duncombe Rd and Jan Smuts Ave
Forest Town, Johannesburg
Phone: (011) 646-0416
http://www.places.co.za/html/bernberg.html

Colonial Williamsburg
The Museums of Colonial Williamsburg
P.O. Box 1776
Williamsburg, VA 23187-1776
Phone: (757) 229-1000
http://www.history.org

Costume Museum of Canada
109 Pacific Ave
Winnipeg, MB, Canada R3B0M1
Phone: 204-999-0072
www.costumemuseum.com

Fashion and Textile Museum
83 Bermondsey Street
London SE1 3XF
http://www.ftmlondon.org/

Fashion Museum
Assembly Rooms
Bennett Street
Bath
Avon BA1 2QH
http://www.fashionmuseum.co.uk/

Fortress of Louisbourg, National Historic Site of Canada
259 Park Service Road
Louisbourg, NS, Canada B1C 2L2
Phone: (902) 733-2280
http://www.pc.gc.ca/

Gallery of Costume
Platt Hall
Rusholme
Manchester M14 5LL
http://www.manchestergalleries.org/our-other-venues/platt-hall-gallery-of-costume/

London Sewing Machine Museum
292-312 Balham High Road
Tooting Bec
London SW17 7AA
http://www.sewantique.com/

McCord Museum of Canadian History
690 Sherbrooke Street West
Montreal, QUE, Canada H3A 1E9
Phone: (514) 398-7100
http://www.mccord-museum.qc.ca/en/

The Metropolitan Museum of Art
1000 Fifth Avenue
New York, NY 10028-0198
Phone: (212) 535-7710
http://www.metmuseum.org/visitor/index.asp

Musee Carnavalet—Histoire de Paris
23 rue de Sévigné
75003 Paris
http://www.paris.fr/portail/Culture/Portal.lut?page_id=6468

Museo del Tessuto
Via Santa Chiara 24
59100 Prato (PO), Italia
Phone: +39 0574 611503
http://www.museodeltessuto.it

Museo Rubelli
Venice
Phone: +39 041-2417329
e-mail: museo@rubelli.com

Museo Stibbert
Via Stibbert 26
50134 Firenze
info@museostibbert.it

Museum of Greek Costume
7, Dimokritou Street
Kolonaki
Athens
http://www.athensinfoguide.com/wtsmuseums/greekcostume.htm

Pitti Palace Costume Collection
Florence
www.polomuseale.firenze.it

Royal Ceremonial Dress Collection
Kensington Palace
London W8 4PX
Phone: +44 (0)207 937 956
http://www.hrp.org.uk/

Royal Ontario Museum
100 Queen's Park
Toronto, ONT, Canada
M5S 2C6
Canada
www.rom.on.ca

The Shoe Museum
C&J Clark Ltd.
40 High Street
Somerset BA16 0YA

The Textile Museum
2320 S Street, NW
Washington, DC 20008-4088
Phone: (202) 667-0441
Fax: (202) 483-0994
http://www.textilemuseum.org/

Textile Museum of Canada
55 Centre Ave.
Toronto, ONT, Canada M5G 2H5
Phone: (416) 599-5321
info@textilemuseum.ca

Totnes Costume Museum
Bogan House
43 High Street
Totnes

SPECIALIZED COSTUME LIBRARIES

Centro Studi del Tessuto e del Costume di Palazzo Mocenigo, Venice: seven thousand volumes focusing on textile and costume history and textile collections from the sixteenth to twentieth centuries. http://www.museicivicivenezziani.it.

Metropolitan Museum of Art, New York, Antonio Ratti Textile Center and Reference Library: The reference library of the Textile Center contains approximately 3,400 books and journals related to the historical, technical, and cultural study of textiles. http://www.metmuseum.org/research.

Metropolitan Museum of Art, New York, Irene Lewisohn Costume Reference Library: One of the most important fashion libraries in the world, with 30,000 items related to clothing history. http://www.metmuseum.org/research.

Textile Museum, Arthur D. Jenkins Library of Textile Arts, Washington, D.C.: The materials preserved in the library's holdings, such as books, periodicals, and slides, cover every aspect related to textile and costume history, textile structures and techniques, and textile conservation. http://www.textilemuseum.org/library.htm.

COSTUME HISTORY SOCIETIES

There are a number of historical societies devoted to the study of costume history. In the United States, the Costume Society of America has a worldwide membership that represents interests in historical as well as historical theatrical costumes. This group meets every year for a national symposium that allows its members to share in the exciting developments in the areas of clothing history. Lectures and working sessions make the event highly worthwhile. The periodical *Dress* is a publication of the society. A similar organization in the United Kingdom is the British Costume Association, which also produces a journal, *Costume*, and has numerous events throughout the year for those interested in the study of clothing history.

About the Editor and Contributors

Jill Condra has taught clothing and textile history at the University of British Columbia, the University of Prince Edward Island, and the University of Manitoba. Her costume research has been largely based on using material history models to look at clothing in historical context, which has allowed her to do research at the most exciting costume collections around the world. Condra has also co-written a book on textiles called *Guide to Textiles for Interiors*, Third Edition. She is currently an independent scholar living in Minneapolis, MN, and Winnipeg, Canada.

Karrie Porter Brace is a specialist in museums and material culture, New World Native peoples, Mayan art, archaeology, and epigraphy at Arizona State University.

Suzanne Buchanan is the executive director of the Hingham Historical Society in Hingham, Massachusetts. She previously served as the chief curator at th Western Reserve Historical Society in Cleveland, Ohio, where she organized several exhibits of American costume ranging from the Revolutionary era to post–World War II. Ms. Buchanan has been a member of the Costume Society of America since 2004.

Isabella Campagnol Fabretti holds a graduate degree in art history and heritage conservation from the Ca' Foscari University in Venice with a specialization in the history of dress and textiles. She teaches the history of dress at the University of Udine, Italy, has written several essays about dress in the Napoleonic era and the history of Venetian textiles, and frequently lectures on these subjects in Italy, England, and the United States. She lives in Venice where she works as curator of the Rubelli Textile Collection.

Sara M. Harvey holds a master's degree in costume studies from New York University and currently teaches fashion design at the International Academy of Art and Technology in Nashville, Tennessee. She is also freelance costume designer and a novelist.

Mary Pluckhahn Masilamani is an independent scholar specializing in Asian textiles and costume history.

Aleasha McCallion is an independent scholar specializing in Korean textiles and paper art. She is also a fashion designer in Vancouver, British Columbia.

Jennifer Grayer Moore is an art historian with special interests in the history and iconography of dress. She resides in Manhattan, where she teaches art history and the history of fashion at the Art Institute of New York City.

Index

Luxury clothing: accessories, II:28; Italian, II:8, II:12; papal court, II:53; social status, I:113, II:19

Luxury fabric: Korea, II:224; mass production, II:251; silk, I:108, II:14, II:116, II:198

Luxury fiber: linen, I:198; silk, I:199, I:230

Luxury furnishings, Venice, II:8–11

Luxury goods: glass, II:8; Latin America, II:239; panther and lepoard skins, I:51–52; seventeenth century, II:97

Luxury laws. see Sumptuary laws

Luxury textiles: America early nineteenth century, III:39; blended Italian fabrics, II:117; cotton, II:106; regional specilization, II:251–52; Spain, II:117

Luxury trade, seventeenth century, II:101

Lycra, III:202–3, III:236

Lyons, I:200, II:118, II:251, III:20; silk industry, I:230, II:117

Macedonia, I:62, I:92

Machine-made lace, III:39

Machine-sewing, III:108

Mackintosh, III:44

Mackintosh, Charles, III:44

Macy's, III:23

Madder, I:29, I:202, II:113, II:114, II:115, II:118–19

Made-to-match suits, II:262

Made-to-order garments, II:252

Madison, Dolley, II:176, III:7

Madison, James, III:7

Madonna Louise Veronica Ciccone, III:198, III:202, III:204–5, III:207, III:224, III:237

Madras, II:100

Magazines, III:35, III:37, III:38

Magic, I:192, II:96

Maharajah, III:120

Maids dowries, II:52

Mail armor, I:207

Mainbocher, III:142

Maintenon, Madame de, II:83

Make Do and Mend, III:149

Makeup, I:209, II:76, II:142, II:147, III:35, III:63, III:158, III:186

Maki, Hiroshigi, III:221

Malcolm X, III:149, III:168

Male nudity, I:87, I:91–92

Male sex appeal, III:208–9

Male sexuality, II:42, II:262

Mal mal khas, II:218

Mambo pants, III:161

Manchester Company of London, II:110

Manchu, II:122, II:222

Mandarin collar, I:233

Mandille, II:57

Manet, Édouard, III:55, III:66

Manetho, I:20

Maniakion, I:123

Manila, II:98

Maniple, I:211, II:54

Man-made fabrics, forties, III:141

Mannerism, II:13, II:26, II:42–43

Manners, I:177

Manohar, II:213

Manor uniforms, I:222

Mantilla, III:32

Mantle: Andean colonial period, II:236; Aztec, II:235; Catholic vestments, II:53; Etruscan, I:99–101, I:101; Greek diagonal, I:82; Hellenistic Period, I:90; himation, I:87; men, I:84, I:111, I:205, II:39, II:42; Native Americans, II:175; shapes, I:100–101; Spiro temple mound, I:9; Venice commoners, II:51; women, I:82, I:91, I:113, II:25, II:255, III:49, III:62; woolen, I:98, I:100, I:111; Zapotec, II:236

Mantua, II:143, II:173, II:176, II:177, II:256

Manuel, Emperor, I:159

Manuel II Palaiologos, Emperor, I:140

Manufacture des Gobelins, III:20

Manufacturers, III:159

Manufacturing: Great Britain, II:246; Japanese procedures, III:19; punch-card looms, III:20

Manuscripts, I:197

Maphorion, I:126, I:148

Marcel, Etienne, I:217

Marcel Wave, III:130

Maria Louise, Empress of France, III:4, III:5

Maria style, III:60

Maria Theresa, Queen of France, II:83

Marie Antoinette, Queen of France, II:250, II:257 II:257–58

Marie-Louise, Queen of France, III:52

Marie of Champagne, I:170, I:177

Marie sleeve, III:46

Marimekko line, III:157

Marital status, II:224; Greek women, I:88; women, kosode sleeves, II:186

DaModena, Tomaso, II:45
Modern Girl, III:118
Modernity, III:118
Modesty: accessories, III:61; Byzantine style, I:120, I:148, I:151; China thirties, III:138; court styles, I:206; farthingale petticoats, II:152; indigenous women, II:238; men, I:231, I:233; nuns, Renaissance Italy, II:55–56; scarves, II:141; women, I:88, I:126, I:128, I:211, II:148–49, III:4, III:37, III:37
Modiste: American women, III:90; fashion merchants, II:252
Mod look, III:176–77
Modroni, II:47
Moen, II:168
Momoyama period, II:190, II:193
Mon, II:202–5
Monarchs, II:158
Monarchy, I:218; Austria, II:247; Charles I, King of England, II:86; eighteenth century, II:247; England, restoration, II:89; England, seventeenth century, II:129; France, II:249–50; France, seventeenth century, II:82, II:83; James I, King of England, II:85; Louis IX, as model, I:172; Louis XIV, II:84; medieval merchants, I:179; portraits, I:227; Roman, I:104; seventeenth century, II:81; taxation, I:213, I:215; Victoria I, Queen of England, III:4; women, English Civil War styles, II:141–42
Monasteries, I:134, I:139, I:188, I:193
Monasticism, I:147–48
Monastics, I:144, I:147–48
Monastic vocations, II:55–56
Mondrian, Piet, III:168
Mondrian dress, III:168
Money, fourteenth century France, I:215
Mongol Empire, II:222; fabrics, I:230; Persia, I:64, I:67
Mongols, I:67
Mongol women, II:217
Monks, I:147–48, I:187, I:188, I:193, I:194, I:211
Monmouth, Duke of, II:90–91
Monmouth cap, II:169
Monpe, Japan, III:150
Monroe, Marilyn, III:157
Montana, Claude, III:201
Montreal, II:175
Moon, I:192; crescent, I:66

Moors, II:112, II:117
Morals: flapper, III:114; India twenties, III:119
Mordants, II:112–13; Indian textiles, II:114; red and madder, II:118
Morning coat: men, III:56, III:71; men, eighteenth century, II:260
Morning dresses, Romantic Period, III:46
Morning gowns, men eighteenth century, II:262
Moro, Ludovico il, II:38, II:47
Morrill Lang-Grant Colleges Act, III:13
Morris, William, III:40, III:55, III:68, III:70
Morris and Co., III:68
Mortimer, Roger, I:216
Mortuary memorials, I:16
Mortuary monuments, I:18, I:21
Mortuary offerings, I:51–52
Mortuary ponds, I:12
Mosaics: Byzantine Early Period, I:128–29; floor, I:118; portraits, I:122
Moschino, Franco, III:197
Moss, Kate, III:225
Mossimo, III:234
Mother, I:47
Mother/daughter dresses, III:101
Motif: animal, I:65–66; cammino, II:15; China, Song dynasty, II:123; Classical, III:32; Dionysiac figures, I:128; dragon, II:123; embroidery seventeenth century, II:120; ethnographic, III:122; fleur-de-lis, III:33; griccia, II:15; Islamic geometric, I:66–67; Japan, decorative art, II:193; lace, Renaissance, II:17; Maya and European, II:234; nude goddess, I:80–81; paisley, III:18; patriotic, III:222; patterned velvets, II:15; pearl roundel, I:65–66; pineapple, I:230; pinecone, I:230; pomegranate, I:230, II:23; Qing court, II:124; senmuru, I:65–66; Seventeenth century, European imports, II:106; tapestries, I:227; Tree of Life, II:114, II:120; Uchikake, Genroku era, II:198; white, reserved, II:200; women, hair braiding, I:41
Mourning: black, II:18; Crinoline Period, III:62; Edwardian Period, III:99–100; seventeenth century, II:158; Victoria I, Queen of England, III:3; Victorian, III:82–85; World War I, III:111

mantua, seventeenth century, II:143; men, cote-hardie, I:232; men, tunics twelfth century, I:205; Minoan, I:78; Native Americans, II:174; pleated, Han Chinese, II:124; pocket dress, II:257; Renaissance Igirls, II:49; Renaissance women, II:13; *robe à l'anglaise,* II:257; saio, sixteenth century, II:41; seventeenth century, II:142; Spanish New World colonist, II:230–31; women: chains, I:208; seventeenth century, II:57; women, eighteenth century, II:255; women, seventeenth century, II:154

Skobister, Bessie, II:149

Skullcap, I:39, II:54, II:170

Slacks, III:200

Slash-and-puff sleeves, III:47

Slashed patterns: boys, sixteenth century, Italy, II:49; dress sleeves, sixteenth century, Italy, II:25; fabric cost, II:16; German, sixteenth century, II:69; men's doublet, sixteenth century, Italy, II:41

Slaves, I:69, II:246; Athens, I:73–74; Byzantine, I:136–37; children, I:69–70; colonial settlers, II:171; Frederick II, I:174; indigo production, II:176; North America, II:172; Rome, I:112; textile industry, III:22; textile production, I:107, II:178; U.S. nineteenth century, III:7–15

Slavic styles, I:143

Sleepers, III:136

Sleeveless overcoat, II:213

Sleeves: Amadis, II:159; bishop, III:47; boys, III:52; chemise, II:151; detachable, II:25, II:51; doublet, II:125; dresses, II:25, III:60; Empire dresses, III:32–33; England, seventeenth century, II:127; evening gown, III:61; French, III:161; furisode, II:186; girls, III:51; gowns, I:235, II:24, III:37, III:48; hanbok, II:223, II:224; jamas, II:211; koshimaki, II:230; kosode, II:186, II:196, II:201; late medieval fitted, I:219; long, I:35, I:78–79, I:92; men, I:111, I:205, I:206, I:232, II:39, II:42, II:129, II:130, II:260, II:263, III:43, III:44, III:57, III:58; pagoda, III:60; qaba embroidery, II:213; Renaissance, II:12, II:13, II:21, II:22, II:51; ribbons of childhood, II:156; sixteenth century,

men, II:69; slash-and-puff, III:47; tailoring, II:20; teddy boys, III:160; Uchikake, Genroku era, II:198; virago, II:141; V-neck dresses, I:35; women, I:22, I:209, I:237, II:72–76, II:73, II:140, II:141, II:142, II:143, II:171, II:256, III:55, III:74, III:75, III:78–79, III:95; women' sportswear, III:144

Slip dress, Cardine III:170

Slippers, I:68, I:127, II:29, II:147–48, II:213, II:219, III:39, III:44

Slits: men's coats, II:260; pocket dress, II:257

Sloane Rangers, III:199–200

Slump, III:129

Sluter, Claus, I:226

Smith, Paul, III:207

Smithson, James, III:9

Smithsonian Institute, III:9

Smock, II:151; colonial North American fashion, II:181; craftsmen, Renaissance Venice, II:51

Smocked dresses, girls, Bustle Period, III:81

Smocks: colonial workingmen, seventeenth century, II:171; embroidery, II:26; girls, III:52

Smoking jacket, III:57

Smyrna, II:112

Snake charmers, I:137–38

Snake Goddess, I:78

Snakes, II:174

Sneakers, III:222

Snefru, I:21

Snood, II:75, III:62

Snow, Carmel, III:154

Soap, II:20

Social categories (sumptuary law), I:219

Social causes, III:235

Social class. *see also* Aristocracy; Bourgeoisie; Middle class; Working class: accessories distinction, II:43–45; Argentina, III:117; bourgeoisie, I:218; camise, II:26; eighteenth century, II:248; fabric quality, I:67; figure quality, I:199; Italian color code, II:18; Japan, III:118; Louis IX, I:172–73; Middle Ages, I:239; Muromachi period, II:190; Renaissance Italy, II:11–12; Rome, I:104; servants, II:157; swaddling practices, II:48; twenties fashions, III:117; women, footwear, II:29; World War I, III:103